Studies in Public Choice

For further volumes:
http://www.springer.com/series/6550

Yilin Hou

State Government Budget Stabilization

Policy, Tools, and Impacts

Springer

Yilin Hou
University of Georgia
Athens, GA, USA

ISSN 0924-4700
ISBN 978-1-4614-6060-2 ISBN 978-1-4614-6061-9 (eBook)
DOI 10.1007/978-1-4614-6061-9
Springer New York Heidelberg Dordrecht London

Library of Congress Control Number: 2012954061

Printed on acid-free paper

Springer is part of Springer Science+Business Media (www.springer.com)

In memory of my parents, Shao-Yun and Shu-Lan C. Hou, who decades ago when we were in extreme difficulty said that I would be doing fine.

To my four elder brothers who protected and cared for me through many years of hardship.

Preface

This book project dates back to January 1998 when I had just started my doctoral studies at the Maxwell School of Syracuse University. The Government Performance Project (GPP), funded by the Pew Charitable Trusts, had then just been launched and I worked on the financial management section. Volumes of detailed survey responses from the state governments overwhelmed me, but soon I was beginning to absorb a lot of substance from this sea of rich materials on state practices in managing their revenue, expenditure, investment, pension, and debt, among others. Somehow a particular practice, the "rainy day fund," attracted my attention. GPP's survey had contained a question on the adoption and use of the rainy day fund, great insight from the project's Advisory Committee, from which I got the first spark of inspiration. I dug in, deeper and wider, for state legislation on this fund. In the next year or so, I was the heaviest user of the interlibrary loan service at Syracuse University Library for *Annual Budgets* and *(Comprehensive) Annual Financial Reports* of all 50 states. That extremely time consuming but worthwhile exercise sent me down the road … A 50-state 21-year data set was put together, with legislation of 39 states on the fund.

I decided to write a dissertation on the economics, law, and politics of the adoption, use, and effects of the rainy day fund. The literature was then thin, just starting to accumulate; I looked sideways to related literatures for ideas, insights, and methods. The 2001 recession provided a boost to this project; the research community began to pay more attention to this area; I was encouraged. In May 2002, I defended my dissertation that won a best dissertation awards from the Maxwell School and the Syracuse University. Since then I have been working in this narrow area, updating the data set every now and then, writing on different aspects of this topic. Over this period, I published over a dozen papers in different journals. Then the Great Recession struck. It is time for a summary of what I have done so far. Springer and the series editor Professor Randall Holcombe very quickly endorsed my book proposal and encouraged me to put together this volume.

Athens, GA, USA Yilin Hou

Acknowledgements

As with any research project, this book would have never been possible without the generosity, support, and care from many. The Maxwell School of Syracuse University was the home base and origin of this book. For 5 years and a half, the Maxwell Hall and the Eggers Hall were the center of my daily life; the institution provided everything I needed. In January 1998, Prof. Patricia Wallace Ingraham, principal investigator of the Government Performance Project and founding director of the Alan K. Campbell Institute at the Maxwell School, handpicked me into the project team; it was the project that nurtured this book. Pat has been a superb mentor ever since.

I was privileged to be close to a whole group of Maxwell professors who advised and mentored me and took me as a friend and colleague rather than a mere student. Prof. William Duncombe literally led me through the dissertation process; he was meticulous with details and aimed at perfection. Prof. John Yinger was a marvelous advisor, whose words, though few in number, were always to the very point of academic sublimity. Prof. Bernard Jump's advice on budgeting and accounting issues was always delivered as support and assurance. Prof. Stuart Bretschneider remained one of my first sources in solving technical problems. Many other professors at the Maxwell School also helped. It is impossible to name all of them but I should at least mention a few: Jeffrey Straussman and Philip Joyce on the budgeting side and Dave Richardson, Douglas Hotz-Eakin, Chihua (Duke) Kao, Dan Black, Jerry Kelly, Jan Ondrich, and Stacy Dickert-Colin on economic aspects and details of methodological techniques. William C. Banks offered insight from the legal and constitutional perspective.

In the decadelong exploration, I owe a lot to fellow researchers and colleagues in many institutions, some very senior, who had been working on related topics. These include James Alm, Donald Bruce, Gary Cornia, Edward Gramlich, Brian Knight, Arik Levinson, Rick Mattoon, Ray Nelson, Russell Sobel, and Gary Wagner. Dr. Gramlich, then a governor on the Federal Research Board, even wrote me a letter to show support and provide advice. I also owe a lot to my collaborators and friends who filled in holes that I would not have been able to cover. These include Gene

Brewer, William Duncombe, Steven Lee, Donald Moynihan, and Wen Wang among many others. My research assistants and doctoral students at the University of Georgia provided excellent assistance through the years: Whitney Afonso, Emily Craft, Sungmin Park, James Kilpatrick, Jongmin Shon, Daniel Smith, and Ping Zhang among others. I owe more than I can express to numerous state officials in the Comptroller's and Budget Offices, who spent time answering my numerous questions, through email, fax, and phone call. Many of them sent me boxes of documents that were otherwise not available. It is worth the space to list them here, in the attached table for easy checking.

My journey of scholarly pursuit was not a lonely one. My wife Zhihui (Sophie) D. and my son Sixuan (David) made it together with me. We came to the United States in 1997 for a richer intellectual life. We have each been working hard, as one. Their company and love is everything to me.

Table 1 List of state officials who provided valuable help in data collection and verification

State	Name and position of officials
Alabama	Marie Hamilton, Financial Reporting Section, Office of the Comptroller
Alaska	Kim Garnero, Controller's Office (later Director of Finance, Department of Administration)
Arizona	Douglas Yeskey, Senior Statewide Accounting Manager
	Lawrence Celano, Statewide Accountant II
Arkansas	Joseph LaFace, Research Administrator
	George Lepper, CPA, Accounting Department; both in Department of Finance and Administration
California	William J. Steffenhagen, Division of Accounting and Reporting
	Robert Scott, Fiscal Analyst, Division of Accounting and Reporting, Budgetary/Legal Section; both at State Controller's Office
Colorado	Henry Sobanet, Deputy Director, Office of State Planning and Budgeting
	Alan Boisvert, CPA/CISA, Director of Reporting and Analysis Section, Controller's Office
Connecticut	Robert Gribbon, Budget and Financial Analysis Division
	Robert Krueger, Assistant Director for Accounting Services, Comptroller's Office
Delaware	Becki Surguy, FMS Specialist, CPA/CGFM, Compiler of CAFR, Division of Accounting, Department of Finance
Florida	Molly C. Merry, Financial Administrator, Bureau of Accounting, Comptroller's Office
	Alan Johansen, Staff Director, Senate Finance and Taxation Committee
Georgia	Dawn Striblin, Executive Secretary, Auditor's Office
Hawaii	Glenn Miyashiro
Idaho	Sherrill Geddes, Reporting and Review
	Darla Rankin, CPA, Bureau Chief; both at State Controller's Office
Illinois	Matt Ciotti, Manager, SAMS Information Warehouse, Comptroller's Office
Indiana	Karen Swango, Office of State Auditor
	Michele Fleming, Project Assistant to Auditor
Iowa	Calvin McKelvogue, Department of Revenue and Finance

(continued)

Table 1 (continued)

State	Name and position of officials
Kansas	Elaine Frisbie, Division of the Budget
Kentucky	Ed Ross, Controller
Louisiana	F. Howard Karlton, Director, Office of Statewide Reporting and Accounting, Division of Administration
Maine	Terry Brann, Deputy State Controller
Maryland	William Donald Schaefer, Comptroller
Massachusetts	Martin J. Benison, Comptroller
Michigan	Laura Mester, Acting Director of Budget Office
Minnesota	Harley Will
	David McKeen
Mississippi	Sandra Lohrich
	Diane Langham, Director of Financial Reporting Bureau, Department of Finance and Administration
Missouri	Shawn McCauley, Office of Accounting
Montana	Accounting Division
Nebraska	Paul Carlson, Accounting Division Administrator
	Bruce Snyder, Financial Systems Audit Coordinator, DAS Accounting Division
	Mike Calvert, Legislative Fiscal Office
Nevada	Brenda Laird
New Hampshire	Harold McArdle
New Jersey	James Kelly
	Sandra L. Smith; both at State Treasurer's Office
New Mexico	Michael Spanier, Deputy Director, State Budget Division, Department of Finance and Administration
	Anthony I. Armijo, State Controller
New York	Gary Armstrong
	Matthew Dzierga; both at State Comptroller's Office
North Carolina	John Barfiled, CPA, Financial Reporting Manager
	Carmen Dixon, Office of State Controller
North Dakota	Eileen Holwegner
	Chuck Lang, Director of Accounting
Ohio	Loretta Herron
	Andrea Joffe; both at Office of Budget and Management
Oklahoma	Mark Meadors, Comptroller
Oregon	Jeanne Bock, CPA, State Controller's Division
Pennsylvania	Don Edmiston, Director, Bureau of Financial Management and Comptroller of Operations, Governor's Office of the Budget
	Arthur Deemer
Rhode Island	Lawrence Franklin, Controller
	Guy Girard, Supervisor of Financial Reporting
South Carolina	Donald Lovett, Deputy Comptroller General
South Dakota	Vernon Larson, Auditor
	Gary Drewes, Deputy Auditor
	Lloyd D. Johnson, Accounting Manager

(continued)

Table 1 (continued)

State	Name and position of officials
Tennessee	Clyde Philips
	Margaret Wallace, CPA, General Fund Coordinator
Texas	Larry Lazicki, Executive Assistant, Fiscal Management Division
	James LeBas, Revenue Estimating Division; both at Office of Texas Comptroller of Public Accounts
Utah	Lynn Vellinga, Assistant Comptroller then Assistant Director of Division of Finance
	Dan Olsen, Division of Finance
Vermont	Eric Nadler, Director of GAAP Management
Virginia	William E. Echelberger, Jr.
	William Landsidle, Comptroller
	John M. Bennett, Staff Director, Senate Finance Committee
Washington	Wendy Jarrett
West Virginia	Chris Sforza, Financial Accounting and Reporting Section, Department of Administration
	Becky Hayes
	Todd Childers, CPA, Director of Accounting, State Auditor's Office
	Roger Smith, Director, State Budget Office
Wisconsin	Marilyn Klement, GAAP reporting
Wyoming	Jeanne Hartman
	LuAnn Chaffin
	Don Richards, Legislative Service Office

Contents

Part III Implications for Budgeting and Financial Management

Abbreviations

BBR	Balanced budget requirements
BSF	Budget stabilization fund
CAFR	Comprehensive annual financial report
CBO	Congressional budget office
CCFC	Counter-cyclical fiscal capacity
CCFP	Counter-cyclical fiscal policy
GAAP	Generally accepted accounting principles
GAO	United States general accounting office
GASB	Government accounting standards board
GFB	General fund balance
GFE	General fund expenditure
GFOA	Government finance officers association
GFS	General fund surplus
GNE	General expenditure
NASBO	National association of state budget officers
NCSL	National council of state legislatures
NGA	National governors association
OSE	Own-source expenditure
TEL	Tax and expenditure limitations
UUB	Unreserved undesignated balance of the general fund

Chapter 1
Introduction and Overview

Abstract This is the introduction and overview chapter of the book. Section 1.1 starts with the choice of the book's topic – why the book focuses on the budget stabilization role of government and on the subnational level, state governments in the USA, and then it specifies two groups of readers of the book, researchers and practitioners. Section 1.2 places the budget stabilization role of subnational governments under the public choice perspective to set the stage for the book. It starts with the "norm of budget balance" as illustration, and then it links boom-year savings to the public choice theory. Section 1.3 offers an overview of the 12 chapters and an appendix chapter (altogether 13 chapters); it also mentions the contribution of the book as well as its limitations.

1.1 Introduction to the Book

1.1.1 What Is the Book About?

This book studies the stabilization of government budgets. It examines how government can better weather revenue fluctuations due from economic cycles in order to smooth the expenditure side, program outlays for public service provision. This research is inspired by the core question of how the government sector can well play its due and necessary role in the smooth and stable provision of public services, as related to the broader issues of governance and development. This pursuit of scholarship is solidly based in the public administration and policy tradition, with an interdisciplinary approach toward economics, law, and politics.

Among different levels of government, this book focuses on the subnational level, state governments in the United States. The choice of this level for analyses is made for two important reasons, both related to the federalist structure of the country. As in a federalist country, American state governments operate on their own constitutions within the federal constitutional framework; they run most of their policies by

Y. Hou, *State Government Budget Stabilization: Policy, Tools, and Impacts*, Studies in Public Choice 8, DOI 10.1007/978-1-4614-6061-9_1,

interpreting the federal policies in their own contexts and implement these policies according to the will and needs of citizens in their jurisdiction. On another hand, all local governments in a state are, by a long-standing, widely accepted court ruling, "creations of the state" that are subject to state laws and rules. Thus, the state governments straddle between the central and local governments, playing a unique and substantive role in carrying out the key functions of government. The uniqueness of the states is derived from the middle-ground status of state governments; the substantiveness of state governments is derived from their revenue portfolio that is capable of generating amounts of tax dollars next only to the federal government, and states thus can run programs that cover most key areas of public service, from transportation, welfare, education to public safety, and law enforcement. Therefore, it makes perfect sense for this book to focus on the subnational level, the states.

Local governments are in fact more important than states are in providing the key, day-to-day public services; any study of public service provision is incomplete without adequate coverage of local governments. However, local revenue portfolio differs from that of the state in many important ways, and local revenue sources are subject to state laws; local officials are at only arm's length from their voters and taxpayers, which factors heavily into the financial operation and political calculation at the local level. Therefore, treatment of the local level is best to be the topic of a separate book. In this book, I only touch upon the landscape of budget stabilization at the local level in the course of discussing the state level, leaving detailed examination of the local level for another book.

To study budget stabilization, the book explores the mechanisms of countercyclical fiscal policy (CCFP) and related policy instruments. In particular, I meticulously examine the budget stabilization fund (BSF), along with the general fund surplus (GFS), as a fiscal and budgetary institution for outlay stabilization. In doing so, the analysis will dissect the statutory features of BSF legislation state by state, the mechanisms of the political process in enabling BSF as an institution, the fiscal outcomes of implementing the stabilization policy, as well as the implications on budgeting and a few other aspects.

1.1.2 Whom Is the Book for?

This book is written for two groups of general as well as targeted audience. The first group includes scholars in public administration, public policy, and related areas who are interested in similar topics, especially those who are pursuing or will conduct research on these topics. The second and a very important group includes practitioners – elected as well as appointed officials as policy makers and implementers, in particular those in subnational (states in the USA) governments. Within this group are governors, law makers, commissioners, department heads, program managers, and field officers in areas of planning, revenue, budgeting, and specific programs. These are an outstanding group of civil servants, usually with strong motivation, solid training, and often many years of experience who work at the frontline of public service provision, with intuitive understanding, knowledge, and accumulated expertise about how program outlays have been volatile and should be smoothed across economic cycles. Any policy suggestions from academia must be placed under the scrutiny of these field experts for examination and testing.

1.2 Budget Stabilization Under the Public Choice Perspective

The intellectual approach I take for this book is to place the role of budget stabilization by subnational governments under the public choice perspective. The concept and practice of subnational budget stabilization across the economic cycle is possible only by bridging both sides of the fiscal account, revenue and expenditure (Buchanan 1975), which is different from a purely "economic" approach of exclusive studies of taxation or revenue volatility, also different from a narrowly defined political science approach of solely studying the political game in budgetary decision-making or that by public administration scholars of exclusively focusing on budgetary processes. Let me illustrate the connection between budget stabilization and public choice with a brief historical review of the "norm of budget balance" as revealed in the surpluses and deficits of the US federal government.

1.2.1 The Norm of Budget Balance

Budgeting scholars and economists have traced the "norm of budget balance" to mid-Victorian era England (Buchanan and Wagner 1977; Savage 1988; Webber 1980; Webber and Wildavsky 1986): "Living within one's means" was a universal virtue for individuals and households; "making the ends meet" was the bottom line for survival by farms and small enterprises of the early Industrial Revolution era when credit was not easy to establish and bankruptcy was frequent. When the structures and mechanisms for public budgeting were being formulated around the turn of the nineteenth century in Britain, France, and Germany, it was probably taken for granted that since the practice of continually balancing one's finances (income versus outlay) was so important for survival and creditworthiness, it should also apply to governments. This may have been the genesis of the norm of budget balance for the public sector. Scholars have since noted that this household-government analogy is probably "faulty" (Hansen 1941), to some extent "folklore" (Burkhead 1954), and fundamentally a "political symbol" (Savage 1988). A political reason for assuming this norm by the legislatures in the industrializing countries in Western Europe might have been an implicit desire to prevent, and if possible to eradicate, the rampant war debts that kings used to lavishly incur in the past.

Methods for budget making were largely available in the formation stage of public budgeting. The technique of "account recording" was already available (Webber 1980). In the fourteenth or fifteenth century, commerce in the city states of northern Italy had developed the fundamental equation of accounting: "Assets equal liabilities plus owners' equity." Manipulating this equation for the government sector derives "assets minus liabilities equal fund balance" (Finkler 2005, 315–6). This equation made accurate bookkeeping possible and applicable; it was also a foundation for the development of governmental accounting, the "language of public budgeting" (ibid). Another important technical advance was "fund consolidation," which further paved the way for the invention of public budgeting. Consolidation was to synthesize all revenue sources and expenditure items to obtain one single aggregate for purposes of budgeting (financial planning) for the next fiscal period (year).

Coupling the idea of balance with the practice of budgeting leads to "budget balance," a normative principle linked with the enlightenment philosophy. French economist Jean-Baptiste Say (1767–1832) defined the budget as "a balance between the needs and the resources of the State."[1] A later French law also implicitly included the balance idea in its definition of the budget as "a document which forecasts and authorizes the annual receipts and expenditures of the State."[2] By the mid-nineteenth century, the core of the balanced budget ideology had been formulated (Webber 1980), with the norm of balance firmly and widely established as a set of precepts.

C. F. Bastable (1892/1922) even argued that the budget should be balanced each financial year except during emergencies (Bastable 1922, 669). Authors following them (like Gastom Jeze [1910, 1922]) simply took the budgetary principles and the implicit norm of balance as value judgment, retained them, and restated them as requisites of sound budgetary practice, so did Wilner Sundelson in his (1935) study of budgetary principles. To Sundelson, these precepts were "features of governmental activity and policy which all collective societies have in common" (239).

Burkhead (1954) offers one of the earliest comprehensive studies of the balanced budget concept. It reviews the ideas of classical (and neoclassical) economists on deficits and debts and on the Keynesian doctrine by the time of his writing. Burkhead succinctly pointed out that neither economists nor public policy scholars had treated this issue with conceptual clarity and that the issue was linked to notions about the role of government vis-à-vis the economy. Wildavsky (1988) elaborates on the "norms of budgetary behavior," by which he bundled the norm of balance with the principles of annularity and comprehensiveness. He specifies that the norm of balance "establishes equilibrium between spending and taxing," assuming "accepted limits on taxes and spending." Annularity assumes "predictability for a year," and comprehensiveness assumes "departmental control of spending" (397–402).

1.2.1.1 Budgetary and Economic Logic in the Norm

Thus defined, the norm of budget balance carries obvious marks from the agrarian, individualistic society with the following elements: restraint in spending, light taxation, maintenance of a surplus whenever possible, minimal borrowing, and quick

[1] In *Tribunat* 1800, quoted from Stourm 1917, p. 5.

[2] Article 5 of the *Decree on Regulations* of May 31, 1862, quoted from Stourm 1917, 2.

retirement of debt that has incurred in emergencies (Webber 1980, 172). In the norm embeds a bipartite budgetary and economic logic. The budgetary part is of the annual structure of the budget: When government is small and its spending is limited, there is no need for much taxation. In order to exercise light taxation, restraint in spending is the prerequisite. Still, the aggregate taxation (revenue) should be larger than total spending so that surplus is possible. The norm does not prescribe about the size of annual surpluses. By classical economics – the economic thought prevalent while the norm was assumed for public budgeting – government should be small in size and limited in its functions. Thus, the annual surplus is ideally small; large surpluses would have extracted too much from the more productive private sector.

The economic logic of the norm extends beyond budgetary annularity to the economic cycle (or incidental wars): When an emergency (recession or war) occurs, borrowing is necessary because the tax rates shall remain relatively constant (at least not raised too much) to avoid extreme behavioral distortion by producers and consumers in an effort to evade high marginal tax rates; constant tax rates also help maintain and protect productivity. However, even in cases of emergency, borrowing should be minimal. Given restraint in daily operational spending and the norm of balance is universally accepted, minimization of debt is possible. In classical economics, government debt should be minimal because it takes away resources that could have been more productively used in the private sector. Thus, the balanced budget norm implicitly yet unmistakably implies that budget balance is not expected for every year but to be materialized across the whole economic cycles or the war-peace cycles.

The last element of the norm, quick retirement of debt from emergencies, may not fit the economic reality. In fact it goes against two basic economic principles – efficiency and equity. For economic efficiency, tax rates are best to be constant, at least in relative terms. Raising taxes for quick retirement of debt may cause too much distortion in the behavior of economic agents. For intergenerational equity, the retirement of recession or war debts should extend over a rather long period, probably even over several economic cycles, because at least a whole generation of the population would benefit from winning a war or from mitigating the adverse effects of a deep recession. Imposing all costs of debt retirement on a few years is unfair for the tax-productive group in that period and causes much efficiency loss. These several elements of the norm of budget balance form a coherent whole and should be maintained as such. Destruction to any part of it will result in malfunction of the norm; if the destruction lasts over time, the harm will turn the mechanism abnormal.

As society evolves from the agrarian to the manufacturing and then to the service or information societies, the application of the norm must be examined from, as German scholar Fritz Neumar pointed out about the budgetary principles, "…a logical development of…the political system of the country as well as the current fiscal theories."[3] Sundelson (1935) also observed that the great value of the [norm of balance] and budgetary principles in fact was "as a framework for *descriptive studies* of the budget" because "an author taking a definite stand regarding *his primary*

[3] Quoted from Sundelson 1935, 238.

interests can adhere to his viewpoint in a consistent and logical manner by handling *only those principles* which are *relevant* to his approach" (239–40; emphasis added). This selectivity has eluded many observers.

1.2.1.2 The Norm's Annual Component: Deficits

Fluctuations in annual budgetary implementation are natural as long as surpluses cancel out the deficits through cycles of bust-boom of the economic or the war-peace alternation. Indeed this had been the general pattern from the founding of the United States to the mid-twentieth century despite the absence of the norm of budget balance from all the important legal documents of the nation and the lack of coordination between revenues and expenditures before governments in the United States adopted the executive budget at the turn of the twentieth century.[4] The heyday of the norm of budget balance lasted from 1789 to 1930, in a partial sense through 1960. In those 170 years all major wars brought deficits of over 50% of total annual outlays. Wars were usually preceded and then succeeded by continuous years of surpluses. In other words, although wars always incurred the largest deficits, the pattern of annual budgetary surplus would resume as soon as a war was over.

The other major cause of deficits was recessions and financial panics, which were far more frequent in the nineteenth century than in the twentieth century. Recessions and panics would cause huge damage to the economy and thereby to government revenues. Severe as the recessions were, surpluses would return as soon as the economy climbed out of the trough. The exception in this regard was the Great Depression – before the economy fully recovered, the nation went into World War II.

As implied in the norm of balance, surplus in each and every year is not possible. Instances of intermittent surpluses and deficits are not at all surprising. Trends of change are identifiable in how the norm of budget balance had applied from 1789 through 1960. The first change was in the reduction of the number of surplus years from the earlier to the later segments of that period, which indicates that the norm was particularly strong at the beginning and then gradually started to diminish in force. The decline of the norm had started much earlier, most likely related to changes in socioeconomic factors. The second change is most strikingly seen in the reduction over time of the magnitude of the fluctuations, surpluses, as well as deficits, as a ratio of the annual outlay. Smaller surpluses may be interpreted as technical advances in financial administration; reduction in deficits during recessions may be an indication of improvement in the overall economy. Worth our attention are the much smaller deficit ratios in recession years (except during the Great Depression) than in the earlier decades, which reflects on the fact that in those early decades, even the federal government did not practice countercyclical fiscal policy. Government in those years simply did not play the stabilization function; it mainly rode the tide of the economy, high or low.

[4] An excellent account of the US deficit history from 1789 to the early 1980s is provided in Anderson 1986. For detailed data, see the *Historical Statistics of the United States*, vol. 2, 1104.

1.2.1.3 The Norm's Cyclical Component: Debts

National debts are directly related to annual deficits. If annual surpluses are practiced as the norm, budget implementation results in savings which can be used to retire debts. If deficits occur only intermittently and surpluses return soon after wars or recessions, the budget still balances out over a relatively not-too-long period, adding no new debts. But if annual deficits become a persistent structural problem, the resulting chronic deficits will increase debts. To examine how well "quick debt retirement" was practiced, the most direct and intuitive method is to check whether the total nominal amounts of outstanding debt went up or down through time. Decreases of the outstanding debt mean surpluses had been used to retire existing debts; otherwise, debt would have remained flat or increased.

Historical record shows a pattern generally in line with, but somewhat different from, the quick debt retirement part of the norm. The new nation financed its Revolutionary War with I.O.Us; but by 1810, retirement with annual surpluses had almost halved the total debt. The war of 1812 incurred new debts; again the policy of quick retirement cut it by over two-thirds by year 1830. That round of debt retirement was made possible, apart from the huge annual budgetary surpluses during that period, also through the sale of public domain (Anderson 1986). The policy of debt deterrence was for a time carried to the extreme by 1835; then the Mexican War debt was retired within 5 years by 43%. The recession of 1857 did not change the landscape; but the Civil War caused "the most radical war-related national debt" (Anderson 1986, 12). In the late 1860s, annual debts averaged 60-fold of its prewar level. The practice of debt retirement in peacetime was applied during the next three decades so that the level of outstanding debt went down by about 20% every 10 years; by 1893 almost two-thirds of the Civil War debt had been retired. The remaining amount, however, stayed at a platform 20-fold higher than before the Civil War, never going down again.

The next dozen years saw a series of disturbances – the 1893 recession, the 1898 Spanish-American War, the 1904 recession, the 1907 bank rush, the 1908 recession, and the 1912 recession – but national debt did not rise much in level: The 1915 level ($1.19 billion) was only 24% higher than in 1893. Involvement in WWI raised debt level which was again followed by quick retirement: By 1930 total debt had been reduced by one-third. The long string of annual deficits throughout the Great Depression and WWII years pushed national debt up to the quarter trillion zone. Since then, the nominal amount never fell below that neighborhood.

The above account shows that as a fiscal practice, quick debt retirement was at its peak in the mid-nineteenth century; it applied through the post-Civil War and WWI eras till the onset of the Great Depression. Examining debt level as a ratio of the gross domestic product (GDP) draws a picture similar to, but rosier than, the above account because the economy in the nineteenth and early twentieth centuries was growing at an accelerating speed. In rough terms, decreases of debt up till 1930 were a result of quick retirement and economic growth. Since 1946, reductions in debt-GDP ratio occurred mainly from economic growth (plus super-inflation since the late 1960s) rather than debt retirement – it was the so-called grow out of debt model. This account tells us that as a nation we used to issue and retire debt against wars and recessions. During the Great Depression, a major policy change occurred toward government playing a pro-active role in stabilizing the economy, in conjunction with the rise of Keynesianism in economic thought. After WWII the fast pace of economic growth led to the adoption of a new debt model.

The question for now is given that our economic growth at the turn of the twenty-first century is no longer as fast as before and that recessions remain a major woe to economic stability, should we at the technical level reclaim countercyclical use of debt, which at a more theoretical level is to reconsider the norm of balance, at least some element from the norm?

1.2.2 Boom-Year Savings Under Public Choice Perspective

1.2.2.1 Tax-Smoothing Theory and Public Choice Perspective

Debt retirement after the Civil War and WWI was gradual rather than "quick," which conforms to the efficiency and equity principles. The tax-smoothing model of optimal taxation (Barro 1979; Lucas and Stoley 1983) well explains the heyday of the norm, the pattern of federal deficits and debts from 1789 to 1930. By this theory, tax rates are better kept relatively constant to ensure certainty so that individuals and businesses can plan their finances in advance and to minimize the possible distortionary effects of taxation on economic agents. The constant tax rates coupled with economic fluctuations result in surpluses in expansion years; the surpluses can accumulate in boom years in order to serve as a buffer to smooth out deficits that occur in recessions. These financial reserves are countercyclical savings.

The public choice perspective has been applied to various aspects of economics and public finance (Wintrobe 1997). Downs (1957) argues for applying economic models to the analysis of policy-making processes. Buchanan and Tullock (1962) use individual rational choices to explain political decision-making. Along this line of argument, Ostrom and Ostrom (1971) argue that individuals create representative organizations that reflect collective action and provide public service in an effort to maximize their utilities and that these representative organizations should construct a constitutional system to enable the organizations to determine "an optimal mix of different public goods and services" (211, emphasis added). Rose-Ackerman (1981) asserts that federal legislation reflects the varied preferences of voters. Holcombe (1998) places tax policy under the public choice perspective: These decisions are made in a political environment and incur political costs. From these we can in fact discern some connection between public choice explanations of economic policy making by politicians, considerations of professional financial managers, and the household norm of budget balancing that we have discussed above.

1.2.2.2 Government Savings and Public Choice

Once we establish the necessary role of modern government in mitigating the adverse effects of recessions (this will be discussed in more detail in Chapter 2) and the inherent link between revenue and expenditure, the rationale of boom-year savings from the norm of budget balance regains rigor. If the government wants to be serious with a fiscal policy that goes against the economic cycle, then government must possess the financial means one way or another in order to implement the policy. Thus, saving surpluses in boom years comes to the forefront, derived naturally from the norm of budget balance. The norm seems to be simple household common sense; but it reflects a basic demand, a preference from the taxpayers and voters. The mechanism to accumulate savings is also plain to see through; therein lies the link from a private individual choice to public choice. Financial managers in government see the need for smooth financial operations whether the economy is in boom or in bust, and policy makers must make sure that the key function of government be played, above and beyond their political motive for votes and (re-)election. The bottom line is to maintain standards of living via stabilizing government budget if not the macroeconomy.

1.3 Overview of the Book

1.3.1 Chapter Plan of the Book

This book contains 12 chapters plus one appendix chapter, arranged into four parts. Part I with two chapters provides the raw materials for the book. Chapter 2 offers the theoretical basis of the book: It traces the evolution of government functions and the economic justifications for government; then it narrows down from the role of economic stabilization by the central government to the role of budget stabilization by subnational governments with countercyclical fiscal policy defined. Chapter 3 provides details of the two major policy tools, general fund surplus and the budget stabilization fund.

Part II contains four chapters, two on how state governments save in boom years and two on the effects of the savings during bust years. Chapter 4 is an empirical study of how the two major policy tools interact: Once BSF is introduced, how it supplements state savings and how much it substitutes GFS. Chapter 5 examines in detail how the structural features of BSF affect the level of boom-year savings, in the presence of balanced budget requirements. Chapter 6 tests the effects of boom-year savings on three types of state outlays – general expenditure, general fund expenditure, and own-source expenditure, over several economic cycles. Chapter 7 develops countercyclical fiscal policy into countercyclical fiscal capacity (CCFC), links CCFC to governance capacity, and then tests its effect on mitigating budget cuts, tax hikes, and net revenue changes during recessions. Both Chapters 6 and 7 offer evidence on how and how much CCFP can help states stabilize their program expenditure during a downturn.

Part III extends from the impacts of CCFP to its implications for budgeting and financial management. This part consists of three chapters and one appendix chapter. Chapter 8 attempts to tackle budget theory, advocating for a change from the annual perspective to a multiyear perspective in preparing and implementing budgets. Chapter 9 discusses the potential of how BSF and GFS may have, or have not, affected revenue forecasting. Chapter 10 makes an extra step of taking debt use as another countercyclical fiscal tool, with simulation results to show how such use of debt may help states to play the stabilization role in a downturn, though it seems to be a bold deviation from current practices and intergenerational equity. The appendix chapter is a supplement to Chapter 10. It discusses the other side of debt – pay-as-you-go (cash) financing of capital projects in boom years. The idea is that used in tandem, debt and pay-go can facilitate budget stabilization across economic cycles.

Part IV offers retrospect and prospect on subnational level budget stabilization, with two chapters. Chapter 11 examines another fiscal policy tool – intergovernmental grants – and advocates for its countercyclical use. The chapter proposes a fiscal policy framework with federal grants for infrastructure and public service, as well as tax relief for employment retention. With the federal government involved to coordinate federal-state policies and public-private investment, this chapter goes beyond budget to economic stabilization. Chapter 12 concludes the whole book. It first examines the fiscal landscape before and during the Great Recession and how countercyclical savings helped from years 2008 to 2010. Then it looks into the future: What problems remain? How to further improve current policy and practices? What needs to be further explored in CCFP? The chapter ends with a realistic note that boom-year savings are not a panacea; fiscal discipline matters.

1.3.2 Contribution and Limitations of the Book

This book contributes both to the theory and the practice of public finance and public budgeting. At the theoretical level, the book clearly defines the role of subnational governments in the macroeconomy: It probably is not economic stabilization, but it is mainly and definitely budget stabilization for smooth provision of public services. The book further defines such policy as countercyclical and links it to governance. The book also extends countercyclical fiscal policy to the use of debt and intergovernmental transfers. With regard to public budgeting, the book links budget stabilization to the length of budget window and advocates extending the planning span of budgets. With empirical evidence and estimates on the effects of savings, the book carries more implications for further refinement of budget theories.

On the policy front, the book provides empirical evidence on the utility and magnitude of boom-year savings. Most of the chapters contain policy suggestions or implications that are worth the attention of practitioners. Even though these suggestions may look still detached from practice, many of them can turn into useful tools with polish and refinement by experts in the field.

The usual caveats apply. Needless to say, the book still has many limitations, some from data and some from empirical methods. Because of these, several issues that may seem important to some readers have not been covered; some aspects of the countercyclical fiscal policy that should have been addressed in order to make CCFP more practicable are not yet touched upon. These, as room for improvement, are left for the next edition of the book when the author has conducted more thorough and more comprehensive research.

References

Anderson GM (1986) The US federal deficit and national debt: a political and economic history. In: Buchanan JM, Rowley CK, Tollison RD (eds) Deficits. Basil Blackwell, New York, pp 9–46

Barro R (1979) On the determination of public debt. J Polit Econ 87:940–971

Bastable CF (1922) Public finance. Macmillan, London

Buchanan JM (1975) Public finance and public choice. Natl Tax J XXVIII(4):383–394

Buchanan JM, Tullock G (1962) The calculus of consent: the logical foundations of constitutional democracy. University of Michigan Press, Ann Arbor

Buchanan JM, Wagner RE (1977) Democracy in deficit – the political legacy of Lord Keynes. Academic, New York

Burkhead J (1954) The balanced budget. Q J Econ 68(2):191–216

Downs A (1957) An economic theory of democracy. Harper, New York

Finkler SA (2005) Financial management for public, health, and not-for-profit organizations, 2nd edn. Pearson-Prentice Hall, Upper Saddle River

Hansen A (1941) Fiscal policy and business cycles. W.W. Norton, New York

Holcombe RG (1998) Tax policy from a public choice perspective. Natl Tax J 51(2):359–371

Jeze G (1910) Traite de science des finances – Le Budget, Giard, Paris

Jeze G (1922) Théorie Générale du budget. Vol. II of the 6th edn of The Cours de science des finances et de législation financière française, Giard, Paris

Lucas R, Stoley N (1983) Optimal fiscal and monetary policy in an economy without capital. J Monet Econ 12:55–93

Ostrom V, Ostrom E (1971) Public choice: a different approach to the study of public administration. Public Adm Rev 31(2):203–216

Rose-Ackerman S (1981) Does federalism matter? Political choice in a federal republic. J Polit Econ 89(1):152–165

Savage JD (1988) Balanced budgets and American politics. Cornell University Press, Ithaca

Sourm E (1917) The budget (translated by Thaddeus Plazinsky from the 7th edition of the French, 1913). New York: D. Appleton and Company for the Institute of Government Research

Sundelson JW (1935) Budgetary principles. Polit Sci Q 50(2):236–263

Webber C (1980) Development of ideas about balanced budgets. In: Wildavsky A (ed) How to limit government spending. University of California Press, Berkeley

Webber C, Wildavsky A (1986) A history of taxation and expenditure in the western world. Simon and Schuster, New York

Wildavsky A (1988) The new politics of the budgetary process. Foresman Scott, Glenview, revised edn

Wintrobe R (1997) Modern bureaucratic theory. In: Mueller D (ed) Perspectives in public choice: a handbook. Cambridge University Press, New York

Part I
From Economic Stabilization to Budget Stabilization: Theory and Tools

Introduction

This part consists of two chapters, discussing the theory of budget stabilization in Chapter 2 and the tools for budget stabilization in Chapter 3, respectively. The theory chapter starts with an introduction to the concept of the economic cycle and how Mankind has been coping with economic fluctuations; then it traces the evolution of the stabilization function of government: How it was started and theorized as a necessary addition to the allocation and distribution functions and why fiscal policy is necessary. Section 2.2 discusses economic stabilization at the central level. This role carries with it some inherent problems, in particular three types of lag in identifying recession, in taking policy action, and in obtaining the designed effect of the policy. What is the core of the debate about the efficacy of the stabilization function? Why has such policy long been practiced despite the absence of consensus? Section 2.3 elaborates on why the stabilization function that was assumed to be exercised solely by the central government was extended to the subnational level and how US state governments experimented with their fiscal practices. The chapter concludes that the stabilization function at the subnational level is best taken as budget stabilization for smooth provision of public services across the economic cycle.

Chapter 3 deliberates on two major policy tools for budget stabilization at the subnational level. They are general fund surplus (GFS) and the budget stabilization fund (BSF). This chapter dwells on these two tools with regard to their definition, working mechanisms, data sources, and changing patterns over their evolution in the past 50 years. The chapter starts with general fund surplus as the informal policy tool then treats budget stabilization funds as the formal policy tool. The chapter pays more attention to BSF, providing details on their enabling legislation, structural features, and diffusion across US states over six decades. Early research of subnational budget stabilization did not provide concise definitions of concepts used or paid due attention to the enabling legislation of BSFs; the couplet of the two aspects partly contributed to confusion and difficulty in data mining. This chapter clearly defines GFS and BSF and offers detailed analysis of state BSF legislations and reliable data sources using a unique data source and collection method. BSF structural features are classified into purposes, funding sources, balance caps, and use approval procedures. This chapter also analyzes the trends of GFS and BSF to reveal some unforeseen findings, thereby laying a solid foundation for empirical work in the rest of the book.

Chapter 2
From Economic Stabilization to Budget Stabilization

Abstract This chapter starts with an introduction to the concept of the economic cycle and how Mankind has been coping with economic fluctuations; then it traces the evolution of the stabilization function of government: How this function was started and theorized as a necessary addition to the allocation and distribution functions and why fiscal policy is always necessary besides monetary policy. Section 2.2 discusses economic stabilization at the central level. This role carries with it some inherent problems, in particular three types of lag – those in identifying recessions, in taking policy actions, and in obtaining the designed effects of the policies. What is the core of the debate about the efficacy of the stabilization function and why such policy has long been practiced despite the absence of consensus? Section 2.3 elaborates on why the stabilization function that had long been assumed to be exercised solely by the central government was extended to the subnational level and how state governments in the USA experimented with their fiscal practices. The chapter concludes that the stabilization function at the subnational level is best taken as budget stabilization for smooth provision of public services across the economic cycle.

2.1 The Stabilization Function of Government: An Overview

Boom-bust cycles are a natural phenomenon that is inherent in the economy. Despite decades of intensive academic and policy studies, economic cycles still "stubbornly" defy human mastery to remain unavoidable, even incomprehensible. The Great Recession of 2007–2009 played a joke with the overoptimistic assumption that was raised just a few years before that the era of recessions was over. The Great Recession reminds the policy and research communities again that the inherent, not-yet-mastered forces of the market and the economy are still "at large," defying easy control, and that we must pay due and adequate attention to them. It was revealed after the onset of the Great Recession that economic forecasts conducted with the most sophisticated models, and the most advanced computing power turned out to be guesstimates; a major recession can still render the economy as volatile as ever.

Y. Hou, *State Government Budget Stabilization: Policy, Tools, and Impacts*, Studies in Public Choice 8, DOI 10.1007/978-1-4614-6061-9_2,

Recessions, however, can be taken on the positive side as signals and occasions for correction of errors accumulated in the expansionary phase of the economic cycle; the corrective action is reallocation of resources in the macroeconomy, most of which can and should be done through the market mechanism in the most efficient fashion. But reallocation may be accompanied by drastic economic decline during downturns that necessarily causes tremendous disruptions to existing productivity as well as the normal standards of living. Amelioration of such disruption is often beyond the concern and the capacity of the private sector; it falls at least partly, if not squarely, on the public sector as the function of macroeconomic stabilization.

2.1.1 Economic Cycle

According to the *Webster's Collegiate Dictionary*, a cycle is (a) "an interval of time during which a sequence of recurring succession of events is completed"; and (b) "a course of events that recur regularly and usually lead back to the starting point." Regular cycles are predictable ones; they are observable in our daily lives, days, and years being typical examples. Irregular cycles are unpredictable, thus imposing uncertainty onto human lives. Examples of irregular cycles include agricultural harvests that are unusually rich or poor due from climate conditions in any particular year and performance of the macroeconomy that is either in a boom or a recession. In this book we focus on the latter example. Irregular economic cycles with high degrees of uncertainly cause disruptions to productivity, public services, and our daily lives. Fluctuations of the economy are first and foremost related to businesses, and the private sector provides most of the jobs and income to the majority of the general public. Therefore, these cycles are also referred to as the "business cycle" in the academic literature.

Each economic cycle is divided into two broadly termed phases, "expansion" and "contraction." An expansion starts when the economy has hit the bottom during a recession, called the "trough"; at that point, key indicators like output and employment stop decline and begin to rise. Expansion will continue till the economy has reached its highest point, called the "peak"; then key indicators show signs of decline. Output will shrink and unemployment tips up, starting the contraction phase. Typically, expansions are longer than contractions. The exact dates of the turning points between the two phases are not known until the economy has developed further along its course. The National Bureau of Economic Research (NBER) has a Business Cycle Dating Committee, a panel of distinguished macroeconomists, who track the key indicators on a monthly basis and determine ex post the dates of transition between the two alternating phases.

The study of economic cycles has a history almost as long as the market economy in the Western world, because periodic shocks to the economy – recessions – were a repeated frustration and perplexity to business owners and executives, elected officials and scholars, which pressed for explanations, answers, and solutions. In fact Mankind has been dealing with the cycle of rich and poor harvest years since the beginning of agriculture. The rich versus poor harvest years are the cycles of the nature reflected in the output of agricultural activity. Out of centuries' experience, some commonsense insight accumulated. Long-standing is the teaching to "save grains in case of famine." Lessons like this are recorded in our history. In *The Bible, Old Testament, Genesis*, Chapter 41, we have:

> The King had a dream that he could not understand; so he summoned his wise advisors for interpretations. Among those was Joseph who foresaw a famine. Joseph got approval from the King to purchase and store grain in seven years of good harvests in a row. Then seven years of famine followed. The stored food enabled Egypt to feed its people, with some surplus to help refugees.

Similar records are also seen in ancient history of other civilizations. In the Zhou Dynasty of ancient China, each year's harvest was divided into four equal parts, with three parts for current year consumption and one part for savings; thus, saving one part for 3 years would have accumulated enough grain to last for one more year. Then taking 30 years as a long fiscal cycle, the nation would have accumulated enough savings to last for another 10 years.[1] In an ancient Chinese history book (*The Book of Rituals* or *Li Ji*), we see the following:

> For a nation, it is inadequate without enough savings to last for nine years; it is emergency without enough to last for six years; and the nation would no longer be a nation without enough to last for three years.[2]

As Mankind entered the era of Industrial Revolution in the mid-eighteenth century, dramatic improvement of productivity and continuous, substantial increase of the overall economy both enlarged the cyclical fluctuations of the economy and made such fluctuations more acutely felt, with increasingly more damage to productivity and human lives. Thereby, the need to better handle such economic shocks had become increasingly urgent.

2.1.2 *Evolution of Theory*

In his 1985 article on the "Fiscal Science," Richard Musgrave traces the evolution of economic theory on stabilization to the mercantilists. Sir James Steuart in his (1767) *An Inquiry into the Principles of Political Economy* said: Stagnant money "lent to government is thrown into a new channel of circulation, thereby to augment the prominent income of the country.[3]" By Jean Baptiste Say's (1821) Law: Since commodities exchange against commodities, supply would create its own demand.

---

[1] This is quoted from Du and Fang (1992, 371). The original in Chinese is: 周朝把“每年的收成分成四份, 用其三而储其一; 每年余一, 三年余三, 即三年储备可供一年之用; 以三十年为一大财政年, 则有十年之蓄。”

[2] The original in Chinese is: 《礼记-王制篇》载, “国无九年之蓄, 曰不足; 无六年之蓄, 曰急; 无三年之蓄, 曰国非其国也。”

[3] Vol. II, 642, 644, quoted from Musgrave 1985, 45.

Thomas Robert Malthus in his (1824) *Principles of Political Economy* analyzed the causes of recession to a chain of actions from diminishing demand to unemployment to market depression. He offered budget policy as a possible solution for deficient consumer demand through redistribution of income (via taxation). These were the early Keynesians. Musgrave concludes that economic theory till the 1930s distinguished mainly two kinds of effects from budget policy, alternative use of resources, and distribution of income that he had termed as the "allocation function" and the "distribution function" of government in his (1959) *Theory of Public Finance*. Indeed, the dominant economic philosophy in America prior to the 1930s had long been the Jeffersonian ideal of the least possible interference by government with the private economy (Hansen 1941, 110). In the 1930s, the work of John Maynard Keynes introduced the later dubbed "Keynesian Revolution" that treated aggregate demand as a major determinant of the level of employment. With this development, the stabilization function was added to the other two functions of budget policy (Musgrave 1985, 44).

The introduction of Keynesianism led to the emergence of the theory and practice of "countercyclical fiscal policy" (CCFP). Keynes' breakthrough was his emphasis on using fiscal policies to stimulate aggregate demand during recessions. In the 1930s, American fiscal policy "moved into the center of macro economics" (Musgrave 1985, 44). The unprecedented devastating effects of the Great Depression on the national economy pushed scholars to thoroughly reexamine economic policies, both monetary and fiscal, by the federal, state, and local governments. Scholars were shocked to find that all levels of government till then had been following the waves of the economic cycle, spending more during booms and cutting back during recessions, especially during the Great Depression. The reason was, at least partly, due from the noninterference tradition carried over from the Jeffersonian philosophy and the binding requirement to balance the budget annually at each and all levels of government. Table 2.1 cites examples from Hansen and Perloff's (1944) study which found that the federal sales taxes in 1933 were in fact heavier than in 1931 and that when the federal government increased public expenditure during the depth of the Great Depression, states and localities reduced their expenditure, thus mitigating the effects of the federal expansionary policy.

In a 1932 paper, Simeon E. Leland of the University of Chicago studied how the public sector could better meet the challenges imposed by financial crises. He found fault with the fiscal year, arguing that the annual budget cycles did not consider the cyclical fluctuations of the economy. He therefore called for financial programs longer than the fiscal year to constitute a wiser fiscal policy (Leland 1932). His proposal was discussed in the following year by a University of Chicago roundtable (of which Leland was a key member) as a method the federal government could use to balance the budget over the economic cycle. Results of the roundtable were three points. An overall idea was to take budget balancing as consecutive long-term operations that are designed to strike equilibrium between revenues and expenditures not by the fiscal year but over a number of years, a full economic cycle. During the bust years, deficits will incur and debts thus increase as a result of government efforts to stimulate the aggregate demand; then during the boom years, surpluses

Table 2.1 Federal, state, and local fiscal policy indices 1928–1939 (Figures are in millions of nominal dollars)

	Net income-increasing expenditures		Expenditures for new public construction		Taxes on sales	
FY	Federal	State and local	Federal	State and local	Federal	State and local
1928	−77	810	188	2,104	1,054	NA
1929	−232	928	188	2,104	1,065	NA
1930	388	1,221	307	2,469	1,060	NA
1931	2,419	1,291	422	2,156	839	538
1932	1,797	676	460	1,334	739	560
1933	1,809	−705	647	707	961	550
1934	3,460	−1,165	1,380	794	1,404	806
1935	3,568	−657	1,234	616	1,573	964
1936	4,374	−450	2,335	881	1,794	1,229
1937	1,114	−244	2,043	845	2,104	1,406
1938	2,225	−321	2,139	1,089	1,935	1,508
1939	3,581	209			1,905	1,530

Source: Hansen and Perloff (1944)

will be budgeted from current revenues for faster debt retirement than at the normal rate. In this fashion, though the budgets are still prepared and implemented annually, the perspective has shifted into the window of a full cycle, so as to better handle revenue fluctuations from the economic cycle.

This was a daring policy recommendation against the background of the dominance of the balanced budget norm in those years, especially the fact that in 1932 Franklin D. Roosevelt campaigned on a balanced budget platform and Roosevelt attacked Edgar Hoover for having not been able to balance the federal budget. It was several years before Keynes published his *General Theory of Money, Interest, and Employment*; but the stimulative fiscal policy was quickly introduced and implemented after Roosevelt won the election, to stabilize the economy. The policy instruments for this tremendous task were monetary policy and fiscal policy. In 1941, Alvin Hansen of Harvard University further expanded the idea of the Chicago economists. Hansen observed that to promote security for unemployed workers and the stability of the economy during the Great Depression, the federal government at first relied primarily on monetary policy, but the huge number of the unemployed compelled enormous expenditures. Fiscal policy, more by accident than by design, came onto the front stage, because monetary policy had shown limitations, were inadequate, and therefore must be reinforced with fiscal policy. Hansen further pointed out that this countercyclical use of fiscal policy should include a spending component as well as a tax component, both to be countercyclically adjusted and administered. Milton Friedman in his (1948) *American Economic Review* paper on economic stability proposed a framework with both monetary and fiscal policies and tools. In the framework, he called for balancing two sides, efficiency of the economy for long-run growth and short-run stability to reduce fluctuations. The evolution of theories culminated in Richard Musgrave's (1959) *Theory of Public*

Finance, where he formally expresses economic stabilization as one of the three major functions or economic justifications for modern government. Musgrave defines stabilization as key performance indicators of the macroeconomy such as high employment, price stability, sound foreign accounts, and reasonable economic growth. The stabilization role has conventionally been presumed to be reserved for the central government (Musgrave 1959; Oates 1972). It is believed that fiscal policy at the subnational level is procyclical: When a recession hits, subnational governments would reduce expenditures or increase taxes, while in boom years tax cuts and expenditure increases by these governments would be expected.

2.2 Economic Stabilization by Central Government

To well play the stabilization role following the above theory, government is supposed to implement both monetary and fiscal policies against the expansionary and contractionary phases of the economic cycle. Monetary policy is at the sole control of central government. The policy tools, like prime interest rate, reserve requirement, and discount rate, are designed to run against the cycle. There has rarely been any doubt about the countercyclical practice of these tools, because the primary goal of monetary policy is economic stability. When monetary policy is not used against the cycle, problems begin to ferment. Irving Fisher (1911) examined the 1837–1841 and 1873–1879 recessions; he found a strong link between over-borrowing during the boom and recessions that followed. A later edition of this book (1933) applied this theory of financial crisis to the 1929–1933 Great Depression and only proved it to be true. Monetary policy is not within the scope of this book; I focus on fiscal policy.

2.2.1 Fiscal Policy for Economic Stability

In contrast to monetary policy in its goal exclusivity, fiscal policy simultaneously pursues tripartite goals – to control government size (allocation), to strive for equity (distribution), and to constrain cyclical fluctuations of the economy (stabilization). Goal multiplicity in fact places stabilization often in conflict with the other two goals, leading to serious compromises in its countercyclical practice and policy outcome. Since emergence of fiscal policy in the 1930s as a countercyclical policy (Keynesianism), most central governments all over the world have in most cases been applying this policy in every recession. The basic principle behind its application is common sense that Mankind has practiced for ages: Save while harvests are bountiful for use in years of famine. In contemporary context, it is to apply the main tools of fiscal policy – taxation, public expenditure, and debt – against the boom-bust cycles of the macroeconomy: Save surplus tax revenues and retire debt during booms in order to increase public expenditure during busts. However, the cyclical orientation of fiscal policy, to be procyclical or countercyclical, was for a long time not clear; part of the reason lies in its goal multiplicity.

The working mechanisms of fiscal policy instruments are of two kinds. The first are automatic stabilizers, those that are designed into the expenditure and tax systems and do not need any policy action for them to be put to use; the policy tools are triggered by indicators of the economy. An example is the progressive marginal rates of the individual income tax: In boom years people earn more money and are subject to higher marginal tax rates (for higher income brackets); during recessions their income fall and are subject to lower marginal rates. Another example is unemployment insurance that is effective when workers are unemployed and automatically become eligible for this benefit. The second mechanism is discretionary; such fiscal policies are made for specific occasions and events. Examples include temporary tax reductions that come with a legislative action and other expenditure programs that need legislative approval.

2.2.2 Problems with Discretionary Policies

Problems often occur when fiscal policies are placed at the discretion of policymakers. Scholars have identified technical problems as three types of lags (Friedman 1948, 255–6; Blinder 2006). The first is the lag between the need for government action and recognition of the need. The lag arises because politicians need economists for analysis of the economy; economists need data to conduct the analysis whereas data are post ante, always behind the reality. On the other hand, policymaking relies heavily on forecasting, which is constantly a "failing" business: Because there always exists a lag between data and reality, results are often not reliable. The magnitude of lag depends on the discretionary policy proposal; the lag can be very long or very short. But such lags are very small or almost nonexistent for automatic stabilizers.

The second type is the lag between recognition of the need for action and taking the action, which exists even for automatic stabilizers, because financial administration takes time whether it is collecting taxes or processing and mailing transfer payments. However, appropriate construction and administration of tax and transfer systems, in particular with advanced information technology that is now readily available, can potentially reduce this lag to a negligible extent. For discretionary actions, the length of the lag depends on the action to be taken: In cases where it is necessary to change expenditure policy, the lag can be the longest; even elaborate advance planning will not be able to eliminate the lag. If the policy involves capital construction, it necessarily takes time to get projects under way without causing much efficiency loss. The third type of lag is that between the action and the policy showing designed effects, which will be present in both automatic and discretionary actions.[4]

Besides, there are political problems with discretionary policies, mostly related to the second type of lag. These problems occur due to conflict between the White

[4] As far as I know, Friedman (1948) first identified these three types of lag. Blinder (2006) calls the first and third types "inside lags" and the second "outside lags."

House and the Congress, especially when the executive and the legislative branches of the federal government are controlled by different political parties. These problems also occur within the Congress, shown as conflict between the majority party and the minority party. Heavy influence of interest groups and struggle between different states for federal resources also may give rise to conflicts. This is why there has been long lead time between recognition of the need for action and taking policy actions. (However, there are exceptions. Seidman (2003) cites examples of very short lags, in 1975 and 2001, when emergencies prompted quick action by both the President and the Congress.)

To be effective in stabilizing a downturn economy, the total size of the countercyclical fiscal policy, including stimulative public expenditure, debt issuance, and tax reductions, must be large in amount. Effective economic stabilization thus requires the federal and state governments to coordinate their fiscal policies. When the federal government increases expenditure, the policy outcome will be reinforced if states follow suit by increasing their own outlays to supplement federal spending; the outcome will be less effective if states simply maintain their usual spending level, without supplements to federal outlay; the worst is when states reduce their own spending. In the last scenario, the outcome of federal policy is seriously compromised. Effective stabilization also calls for government to offer fiscal incentives for businesses to increase capital investment and retain their workforce.

2.2.3 Debate on Stabilization Policy

Because of the many problems with discretionary fiscal policy discussed above, there has been heated debate among scholars about the efficacy of such policies. Despite the fact almost all central governments resort to fiscal policy during each recession, the debate has been far from being settled. Founder of countercyclical fiscal policy J. M. Keynes and the forerunner of this policy in the USA Paul Samuelson both emphasized the multiplier effect of government expenditure in downturns; but later empirical studies found the multiplier effect is "transitory." Alan Blinder admits that "[t]he macro economy has the natural-rate property"; "output returns to potential"; and "[t]he path of potential output is unaffected by either monetary or fiscal policy" (2006, 28). Indeed many causes can be identified that lead to variation in revenue flows (Stonecash 1994), including actions of politicians, new taxes, and raising and cutting existing taxes; changes in the economy and recession are just part of the basket of potential reasons. Therefore, despite the long-standing support among Keynesian economists for economic stabilization, other economists cast a skeptical eye about the utility of stabilization policy.

Gregory Mankiw (1992) summarizes the opposing views in three connected points. First, the best option is probably a passive policy instead of an active one. Second, if the consensus is to do something, then the optimal route is to be committed to some pre-set, fixed policy rule rather than granting policymakers' discretion over monetary and fiscal policy. Indeed theoretical and empirical research by Finn

Kydland and Edward Prescott (1977) and John Taylor (1982) reveal substantive advantage of rules over discretion. Third, even if we can stabilize the economy with ideally designed and implemented policy sets, the benefits would not be large if we believe in the natural rate hypothesis, by which the actions of stabilization policy merely level off the intensity of cyclical fluctuations around the natural rate but do not change the average level of output and employment. By the real business cycle theory, cyclical fluctuations are the "optimal response of the economy to changing technology"; therefore "policymakers should not stabilize the economy, even if it were possible" (Mankiw 1992, 486).

A direct answer to such doubts is straightforward: Drastic fluctuations in the budgets of state governments have in history caused and will again and again cause huge interruption to public life. Revenue shortfalls due from economic cycles have repeatedly shown that the subnational sector is prey to economic fluctuations. Public expenditures should not be a subject to cyclical fluctuations as private investment is.[5] Stabilization of state budgets is therefore a big public good, which is worth the effort. As shown in subsection 2.1.2, for decades scholars and practitioners have been calling for countercyclical fiscal policy. The tide has been rising with recessions and ebbing with expansions – the lesson is still not thoroughly learned.

Regardless of the academic debate among economists, demand is high during every recession for government to take stabilization actions. It would be politically incorrect and ethically unacceptable if government does not do something to at least temporarily ameliorate the sufferings of the unemployed during the depth of recessions. The fact that central governments worldwide launched stimulus packages to mitigate the Great Recession helps reconfirm that fiscal policy faces a practical, worldly expectation, if not pressure, to be applied against the economic cycle. The damage of no action would be devastating to productivity and the unemployed.

2.3 Stabilization at Subnational Level

The procyclical fiscal behavior of the states has long been noticed, as Hansen (1941) pointed out about the procyclicality of state fiscal actions during the Great Depression (see Table 2.1). Local governments are even more procyclical. Rafuse (1965), the Advisory Commission on Intergovernmental Relations (ACIR 1978), and Fisher (1984) found further evidence of the cyclical patterns of the state-local sector from 1957 to 1977 and from 1978 to 1984, respectively, by examining the quarterly change rates of revenue, expenditure, and budget surpluses. Their findings are summarized in Table 2.2, which shows budget surplus of the state-local sector was a direct function of the economy: Surpluses accumulate during expansions and disappear during contractions. Such patterns of procyclical fiscal behavioral, however, are not surprising given their operating environment: States (and localities) operate

[5] Musgrave 1978, 31.

Table 2.2 State-local fiscal behavior 1957 III to 1982 IV

Peak	Trough	Receipts growth (%)	Expenditure growth (%)	Surplus change (billion $)
Panel A: Behavior during recessions				
1957 III	1958 I	1.7	2.9	–0.55
1960 I	1960 IV	1.9	2.1	–0.10
1969 III	1970 IV	2.8	3.2	–0.46
1973 IV	1975 I	2.6	3.3	–1.32
1980 I	1980 II	0.5	1.9	–4.70
1981 III	1982 IV	1.3	1.8	–1.66
Panel B: Behavior during expansions				
1960 I	1958 I	2.4	1.5	0.34
1969 III	1960 IV	2.5	2.4	0.08
1973 IV	1970 IV	2.9	2.5	0.80
1980 I	1975 I	2.5	2.1	6.15
1981 III	1980 II	1.8	1.3	3.06
1984 IV	1982 IV	2.1	1.8	4.95

Data source: 1957–1977 data, ACIR 1979, Report A-70; 1978–1984 data, Fisher 1984, 107

under legally binding balanced budget requirements, (now) face revenue and expenditure limitations, and are restrained by statutory debt limits.

2.3.1 *Stabilization Theory Extended to Subnational Level*

In the mid-1940s, after countercyclical fiscal policy (CCFP) had taken shape and been implemented by the federal government to take the country out of the Great Depression, Alvin Hansen and Harvey Perloff (1944) extended the argument for such a policy orientation to the subnational level, the state governments in the United States. They suggested that a rational countercyclical fiscal policy was urgently needed not only at the federal level but also at all levels, and the policies at national and subnational levels should be coordinated (41). In this groundbreaking book, Hansen and Perloff offer details of their "rational" or ideal countercyclical fiscal policy on tax rates, level of public expenditure, borrowing and debt: In years of recession, tax rates should be reduced, and public expenditure should be high by drawing on accumulated reserves and incurring public debt. Fiscal policy in general shall be directed toward increasing consumer purchasing power and stimulating investment and business activity. For this purpose, tax rates during economic booms should be high in order to drain off excess consumer purchasing power and to accumulate reserves for revenue shortfalls in the future; public expenditure in contrast should be kept low, at a level just adequate to maintain essential social services. Borrowing for further expansion in such periods should be eliminated, and accelerated repayment of public debt should be pursued if the boom is strong (48–49).

Intuitively the countercyclical features of such a fiscal policy make sense, but in practice they are difficult to implement in the real world of popular voting and budgetary politics, especially during economic prosperity. Major obstacles may come from three sides. To begin with, states are limited by their constitutions or statutes from accumulating high levels of surpluses. Even in the absence of legal restraints, individual and corporate taxpayers tend to exert spending pressure on elected officials during booms to expand public expenditures and/or reduce tax rates; and elected officials either share the general optimism or simply follow the voters' will to facilitate their own reelections (even if these elected officials may understand the validity of the rational fiscal policy). Finally, the goals of economic development lead to inter-state competition for businesses (investment) which induces, or even dictates, reduction of tax rates. Thus, in the federalist framework of the United States a subnational government can resort to one or more of the following three means in a recession to implement against-the-cycle fiscal policy, each with its pros and cons. First, since the federal government has monetary policy and controls more and wider taxing power, federal grants are a valuable financial source. However, obtaining such grants is often unreliable. As experience goes, federal grants may not come as early or at the amount states may need and expect. Besides, where a grant is based on a matching ratio, poor states are hit hard. When a state is in fiscal distress, it often has to cut its assistance to local governments.

The capital market is another means of addressing recession pressures, since increasing public debt for capital projects in downturns is technically sound. However, recession years are the time when states often have to adopt drastic fiscal measures which adversely affect their credit rating and thus erode their borrowing capacity on the market. Besides, strict debt limitations as prescribed in state constitutions or statutes do not grant states indefinite room for incurring debts. Then, the only means that is consistently reliable, independent of outside control is own-source reserves. The availability of reserves depends on two internal factors. First, the legal framework – statutory balanced budget requirements on a (bi)annual basis offer little room for flexibility in this context. Second is the human factor – chief elected officials must possess not only the managerial foresight for the necessity of reserves but also the political courage and skills to resist and manipulate spending pressures during prosperity. Once accumulated, reserves must be guarded against any possible raids in boom years. The best means for counteracting these two internal factors is an institutionalized device that provides statutory protection of the reserves.

The July 1949 "Budget Theory Symposium" held at Princeton, New Jersey, dealt with the legal framework. Conferees to the Public Administration Clearing House (PACH) succinctly pointed out that "there is no magic" about the 1-year period of the annual budget; that the most important issue is "stabilization of tax expectance [for businesses]"; and that "longer projections and more frequent reviews by the legislative body are both desirable….[6]" This statement partially

[6] Symposium on budget theory. Public Administration Review, 1950, 1(10), 20–31.

softens the theoretical foundation of the annual budget. The theory, however, stayed at a stalemate. Musgrave (1959) cautioned that the stabilization function is to be played exclusively by the central government because lower levels do not fit: Subnational governments do not have monetary policy; their revenue sources are limited and taxes cannot be structured progressively; further, capital and labor as factors of production are fully mobile.

Explorations kept going. Rafuse (1965) checked the patterns of change in state and local annual surpluses in the form of general fund balance from the 1930s to the late 1950s; he found these surpluses followed a cyclical pattern of accumulating in boom years and declining in bust years and became "more and more stabilizing with each succeeding [business] cycle" (118). A report by the United States Advisory Commission on Intergovernmental Relations (ACIR) confirms this policy change: "...during each economic downswing since World War II, state and local fiscal behavior was 'correct' [meaning 'counter-cyclical'] because [spending more from reserves] added to aggregate demand [during downturns]" (1978, 6). Bahl (1984) also provides evidence that US state and local governments do implement some practices that go against the economic cycle: They put aside some balances in their general fund even under the balanced budget requirement and spend these reserves once a recession hits.

Another round of systematic theoretical exploration came in 1987 when Edward Gramlich published his seminal paper on the subject. Citing macroeconomic evidence, Gramlich argues that (a) "demand shifts in the whole country are not highly correlated; (b) labor may not be highly mobile; (c) regional import and export propensities may not be as high as was previously assumed; (d) domestic debt of the national government is no longer different from external debt of subnational governments; (e) the open economy critique and inter-generational critique against stabilizing fiscal policy at the national level seems less relevant at subnational levels;" and (f) "states have persistent business cycles independent of the national cycle" (Gramlich 1987 3–27). Therefore, Gramlich concludes that the conventional wisdom in this regard may have been inaccurate – states should not only pursue countercyclical fiscal policies but have in fact adopted such practices to stabilize their budgets, and that we can reasonably assume that subnational fiscal policy can exert at least short-term influence.

Analyzing the cyclical response of state budgets over the economic cycle, Gramlich (1991) distinguishes three types of state fiscal policies: neutral, perverse, and stable. The first type discourages subnational governments from conducting the countercyclical policy, and advocates automatic fluctuation of taxes and budget surpluses with changes in income. The term "neutral" implies no countercyclical action and no changes to the tax structures over the economic cycle, so revenues move procyclically; but state expenditures grow at a constant rate through the economic cycle. The budget would balance over the whole cycle but not year by year. If following a perverse-type policy, governments would initiate discretionary tax increases and/or expenditure reductions during recessions, and cut taxes and increase spending in boom years. This is perverse policy – balancing the budget year by year amplifies the fluctuation from the economic cycle. This tripartite theory traces back to Hansen and Perloff's (1944) book but carries its own merit. Gramlich advocates a fiscal policy for stability: Subnational governments should try to smooth the economic cycle by using countercyclical fiscal policy – raising taxes and/or cutting spending during expansion to accumulate reserves, then lowering taxes and/or increasing spending during recession by releasing (decumulating) reserves. The latter part resembles the so-called active fiscal policy at the national level. Such a policy aims at accumulating more reserves in booms so as to be able to release more during a recession than the neutrality policy can afford. The budget would then be balanced over the economic cycle. What Gramlich means here by balancing the budget is total revenues equal total expenditures over the economic cycle. This is different from the statutory balanced budget requirements (BBR) in the states. BBR focuses on deficit prevention but leaves open the option for states to run surpluses, which is the practice adopted by many states. This remained true even after the tax revolt movements in the late 1970s and early 1980s.

Gramlich's proposal was an intensive version of subnational countercyclical fiscal policy, involving accumulating reserves and tax rate changes. No states have adopted this version of the policy. The reason is easy to see. While saving reserves in one way or another is common, tax rate changes, especially permanent ones, are much more difficult and thereby less common because tax increases are politically unpopular. A weaker version of his proposal with only countercyclical reserves but no tax rate changes is what many states have practiced.

2.3.2 *Stabilization Practices by State Governments*

In the real world of government administration, New York was the first state to respond, in 1946, to the previous theoretical progress that culminated in the 1944 Hansen and Perloff proposal. This was the first "budget stabilization fund" (BSF) at the state level – the New York State "Tax Stabilization Reserve Fund." The purpose of the fund was for stabilizing own-source "revenues of the state from taxes, fees and other sources required by law," with the funding source being annual fiscal-year end cash surpluses.[7] In the official language of the state, the fund was "a safeguard against possible future declines in revenues.[8]"

The concept and adoption of the budget stabilization fund spread very slowly. In 1959 Florida legislated its "working capital fund" to "avoid deficits due to minor fluctuations in revenue or spending," with savings from annual excess resources.[9] Another 13 years passed before Tennessee adopted its "reserve for revenue

[7] For details, see *New York State Consolidated Laws, Chapter 56: State Finance Law, Article VI: Funds of the State.* New York State, Albany, NY; Section 92.

[8] *Annual Report of the Comptroller for the Fiscal Year Ending March 31, 1946.* State of New York, Albany, NY, 1946; 5.

[9] For details, see *Florida Statutes, Title XIV: Taxation and Finance, Chapter 215: Financial Matters: General Provisions.* State of Florida: Tallahassee, FL.; Section 215.32.

fluctuations" to "meet unexpected shortfalls of revenue or expenditure requirements in excess of budgeted appropriation levels," with monies from annual general fund appropriations.[10] In another 4 years, California and Georgia followed suit by establishing their own BSFs. These first state BSFs were designed following a weaker version of the Hansen and Perloff model, that is, to save the annual surpluses in prosperity but not to raise tax rates in boom and then temporarily lower the rates in a recession. In fact, it has been almost universal that state BSFs are weaker versions of the proposals by theorists.

As a state with a large share of the manufacturing industries, Michigan's economy and government finances suffered huge fluctuations in the 1974–1975 and earlier recessions. The severe economic and budgetary difficulties forced the state to seek a permanent solution. Such efforts led to the creation in 1977 of the Michigan "countercyclical budget and economic stabilization fund,[11]" which, in comparison with its earlier counterparts in other states, has two new features. First, it places an economic element in the purpose of the fund – to assist in stabilizing not only governmental revenue during periods of recession but also employment when the rate of unemployment is high. Second, the source and use approval of the fund are by a pre-set formula – the percentage above the 2% annual growth rate benchmark determines the amount to transfer into the fund in the next fiscal year, and the percentage of negative annual growth rate determines the amount to be used from the fund in the current fiscal year. The Michigan legislation became a model for many other states. It was "copied" in Ohio, Indiana, and Washington, and it influenced the BSF legislation in many more states. It is not an exaggeration to say that widespread adoption of BSFs among the states started with the 1977 Michigan model legislation accompanied by other social economic factors. Though these first BSFs were lonely swans among the 50 states, the practice of countercyclical fiscal policy had spread out through a wise use of general fund surpluses accumulated from boom years; thus, the perverse policies of the 1930s were gradually evolving into the more rational fiscal policies since World War II.

2.3.3 Summary: Budget Stabilization

Thus, we can conclude that even though debates among economic theorists have not achieved consensus on the efficacy or ultimate utility of macroeconomic stabilization, governments do need to make strong and committed efforts in order to stabilize government budget, that is, to smooth public service provision across the economic cycle, because this is the demand from the society, individuals, households as well

---

[10] For details, see *Tennessee Code Annotated.* State of Tennessee: Nashville, TN; 9-4-211.

[11] For details, see *Act 76 of 1977 (repealed),* and *Act 431 of 1984*; also *Michigan Compiled Laws, Chapter 18: Department of Management and Budget.* State of Michigan: Lansing, MI; Section 351–359.

as businesses. Therefore, countercyclical fiscal policy are demanded, justified, and has been shown as useful. In a more realistic sense, the stabilization function is best interpreted as macroeconomic stabilization for central governments; at the subnational level it is budget stabilization for smoother public services through the economic cycle.

However, a rational policy and proper policy tools are not a panacea to cure all ills from governmental revenue shortfalls. The countercyclical policy and relevant tools are but the means, which must go through the human hands of implementation to be effective, that in turn lies ultimately in the domain of politics. Specifically, a wise fiscal policy may be brushed aside; appropriate policy instruments can run distorted; and fiscal reserves that are adequate by the most sophisticated formula might as well be used off the right target. Therefore, the solution returns to the very basics of fiscal restraint and budgetary discipline. It would be a misconception that a rational policy can solve the problem once and for all.

Countercyclical fiscal policy among the states, as with many other practices that were initiated at the subnational level and later transplanted into the federal government, has drawn the attention of the federal government. Although the federal government with monetary policy in its hands does not need a distinct budget stabilization fund,[12] the General Accounting Office (GAO) in a special report to the United States Senate Committee on the Budget recommends that "should the Congress decide to move to a reserve-funding model for emergencies, state practices [to provide a cushion for budget uncertainty] provide some insight in designing such a process.[13]" In history the federal government played some role in providing countercyclical fiscal help to the states; whether that should be resumed in the future may also come onto the agenda of the national leaders at some time.

References

Advisory Commission on Intergovernmental Relations (ACIR) (1979) State-local finances in recession and inflation, Report-70. Washington, DC

Bahl RW (1984) Financing state and local governments in the 1980s. Oxford University Press, New York

Blinder A (2006) The case against the case against discretionary fiscal policy. In: Kopche RW, Tootell G, Triest R (eds) The macroeconomics of fiscal policy. The MIT Press, Cambridge, MA

Du WY, Fang ZY (1992) A general history of Chinese political system – the Ming Dynasty. People's Press, Beijing

Fisher I (1911) The purchasing power of money. MacMillan, New York

Fisher I (1933) The debt deflation theory of great depressions. Econometrica 1(4):337–357

Fisher RC (1984) Statement before the intergovernmental relations and human resources subcommittee of the committee on government operations. In: U.S. Congress (1985) Federal and state

[12] *States' Use of Surplus Funds.* Congressional Budget Office: Washington, D.C., November 1998.

[13] *Budgeting for Emergencies – State Practices and Federal Implications.* GAO/AIMD 99–250. The United States General Accounting Office: Washington, D.C., 1999; 1–4.

roles in economic stabilization. United States House of Representatives, 99th Congress, 1st Session, report 99–460, pp 101–107
Friedman M (1948) A monetary and fiscal framework for economic stability. Am Econ Rev 38(3):245–264
Gramlich EM (1987) Subnational fiscal policy. In: Quigley JM (ed) Perspectives on local public finance and public policy, vol 3. JAI Press, Greenwich, pp 3–27
Gramlich EM (1991) The 1991 state and local fiscal crises. Brookings papers on Economic Activity (2): 249–287
Hansen AH (1941) Fiscal policy and business cycles. W.W. Norton, New York
Hansen AH, Perloff HS (1944) State and local finance in the national economy. W.W. Norton, New York
Kydland FE, Prescott EC (1977) Rules rather than discretion: the inconsistency of optimal plans. J Polit Econ 85(3):473–491
Leland SE (1932) How governments can best meet the financial crisis? Conference paper, Convention of the International City Managers' Association, Cincinnati, 24 Oct1932
Mankiw NG (1992) Macroeconomics. Worth, New York
Musgrave RA (1959) Theory of public finance. McGraw-Hill, New York
Musgrave RA (1985) A brief history of fiscal doctrine. In: Auerbach A, Feldstein M (eds) Handbook of public economics, vol 1. North Holland, New York, pp 1–60
Oates WE (1972) Fiscal federalism. Harcourt Brace Jovanovich, New York
Rafuse RW (1965) Cyclical behavior of state-local finances. In: Musgrave RA (ed) Essays in fiscal federalism. The Brookings Institution, Washington, DC, p 118
Seidman LS (2003) Automatic fiscal policies to combat recessions. M.E. Sharp, New York
Stonecash JM (1994) The revenue problem: revenue fluctuations and forecasting, New York State, 1950–1990. In: Khan A, Hildreth WB (eds) Case studies in public budgeting and financial management. Kendall/Hunt, Dubuque, pp 153–163
Symposium on budget theory (1950) Public Administration Review 1(10): 20–31
Taylor JB (1982) The Swedish investment funds system as a stabilization policy rule. Brook Pap Econ Act 1:57–99
The United States Advisory Commission on Intergovernmental Relations (ACIR) (1978) Counter cyclical aid and economic stabilization. GPO, Washington, DC
The United States General Accounting Office (GAO) (1999) Budgeting for emergencies: state practices and federal implications. GAO/AIMD, Washington, DC, pp 99–250

Chapter 3
Subnational Government Tools for Budget Stabilization

Abstract The two major policy tools for budget stabilization at the subnational level are general fund surplus (GFS) and budget stabilization funds (BSF); this chapter elaborates on these two tools with regard to their definitions, working mechanisms, data sources, and changing patterns over their evolution in the past half century. The chapter starts with general fund surplus as the informal policy tool, then treats budget stabilization funds as the formal policy tool. The chapter pays more attention to BSF, providing details on their enabling legislation, structural features, and diffusion across US states over time. Early research of subnational budget stabilization did not provide concise definitions of concepts used nor paid due attention to the enabling legislations of BSFs; the couplet of the two aspects partly contributed to confusion and difficulty in data mining. This chapter clearly defines GFS and BSF and offers detailed analyses of state BSF legislations and reliable data sources using a unique data source and collection method. BSF structural features are classified into purposes, funding sources, balance caps, and use-approval procedures. This chapter also analyzes the trends of GFS and BSF balances from 1979 to 1999, thereby laying a solid foundation for empirical work in the rest of the book.

3.1 Introduction

Once a countercyclical fiscal policy (CCFP) is shown to be rational with theoretical soundness both at the national and the subnational levels as well as practical use at both levels, the natural next step is to examine what policy instruments are available and what have been used. State governments have faced the task of choosing policy instruments that are technically sound, administratively convenient, and politically operable in order to accumulate fiscal reserves necessary for handling revenue

---

Subsection 3.3.3 and Section 3.4 draw from data and analysis in Hou Y (2004) Budget stabilization fund: structural features of the enabling legislation and balance level. *Public Budgeting and Finance* 24(3): 38–64, published by John Wiley & Sons Ltd.

Y. Hou, *State Government Budget Stabilization: Policy, Tools, and Impacts*, Studies in Public Choice 8, DOI 10.1007/978-1-4614-6061-9_3,

shortfalls in a downturn. The two most frequently mentioned and used CCFP tools are general fund surplus (GFS) and the budget stabilization fund (BSF), though conceptually there can be many more possible instruments (some are variations of BSF and GFS in different forms). For example, to practitioners, all forms of reserves including various contingency funds should be counted in the BSF category – those that are fine for one-time use and will be returned as soon as the economy recovers. In fact, the Government Finance Officers' Association (GFOA 1999) lists contingency funds as the same as BSF. Till the late 1990s, most studies used loosely defined concepts of budget stabilization funds and general fund "balances." Data sources are mostly from the Census or the *Fiscal Survey of States* series assembled and published by the National Association of State Budget Officers (NASBO). This chapter is to redefine these two key concepts, to present a data source that is based on governmental accounting rules and a unique way of collecting data under these strict definitions, and to analyze the trends of development of these two tools over two decades (1979–1999) as have been employed by American state governments in smoothing state budgets through recessions.

3.2 Informal Tool: General Fund Surplus

3.2.1 Defining General Fund Surplus

As studied by Rafuse (1965), surpluses in the general fund have long been a fiscal tool. Such surpluses, however, are not the same as the generic "general fund balance" (assets minus liabilities) which appears as the total in the fund balance section of government annual financial statements. This total general fund balance (GFB) serves several purposes: "as a hedge against forecasting errors; as reserves against one-time expenses (like natural disaster, court-mandated spending or liability payments); and as working funds to meet cash flow requirements" (NASBO, various years); thus, general fund balances include (when details are included and offered in the financial statement as separate lines) "reservations" and "designations." The former are amounts kept for purposes that the legislature or the court has specified; the latter are amounts the executive branch has intensions for. This book uses the *unreserved undesignated balance* (UUB) of the general fund to refer to general fund surplus, the portion of the balance that is neither reserved under existing laws for other purposes nor designated for specific purposes by current administration. This narrowly defined general fund surplus refers specifically and unambiguously to the part of general fund balance that is free of obligations and usable for appropriation without any restrictions.

There has long been misunderstanding, even confusion, about government savings among the general public, even researchers. "Governmental savings" is an encompassing concept; it can and should be decomposed into four blocks that build from the lowest to the highest level. We can use a four-layer cake (four enclosed circles) as analogy for illustration, as shown in Fig. 3.1. The four layers are more

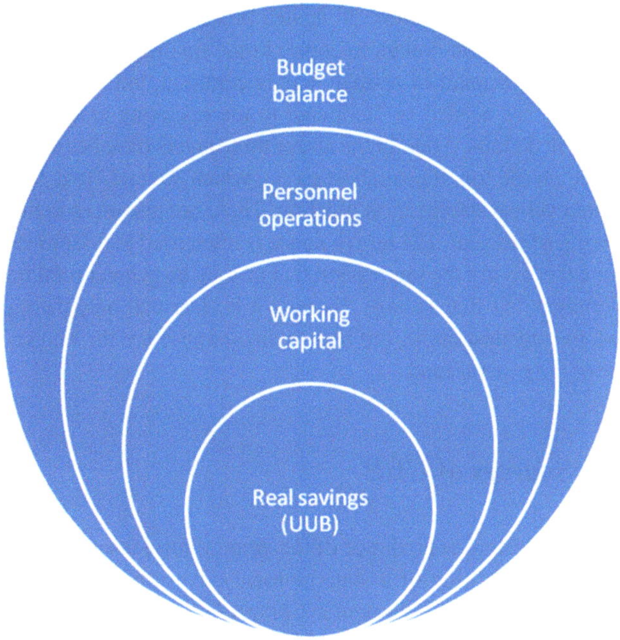

Fig. 3.1 Enclosed circles (four-layer cake) analogy of government general fund balance

exactly four embedded circles; they are derived from varying perspectives via different managerial, administrative, and political mechanisms, each serving different purposes and uses. All of the four circles are not available for use as countercyclical reserves; thus, they are not real savings. Misunderstanding occurs about government savings because the four layers are confused as the same thing.

The bottom layer, the largest inclusive circle, is "budget balance," as defined in Hou (2006). Since balanced budget requirements hold tight on financial operations, this balance can be taken as a "hard budget constraint" that governments must satisfy throughout the boom-bust cycle. The "balance" is not zero (revenue = expenditure) but positive year-end balance. The budget balancing requirement disallows deficits; actual operations will not end a fiscal year in exact zeros; thus, a positive balance is the result, which, however, is not necessarily savings. Because the aggregate "general fund balance" is a basket of resources for multiple purposes, it was often targets of attack by voters, as in the case of Proposition 13 in California and the case in some other states (Gold 1983), and by politicians. Results from previous studies show that when recessions hit, general fund balances are always the first to be depleted (Sobel and Holcombe 1996, 33).

The lower-middle layer, the second largest circle, is "personnel operation" that demands some redundant resources because fringe benefits and other liabilities lie anywhere, and by employment laws, personnel are not all subject to fire when government revenue falls. Such redundancy is to keep the government door open; it is not real savings either. The upper-middle layer, the third largest circle, is "working capital" that is needed for the continuous operation of service provision. After all, service programs must not stop to wait for tax dollars to come. In the financial reports of governmental entities, such working capital of a small size is common, but this part is not savings either because they are needed as "lubricant to the operating machine" even when a government falls in deficits. After all the above three layers have been built up, real savings are possible on the top, the smallest circle, which we call "real savings" that can serve the countercyclical stabilization function. These are resources to fill in gaps in tax collections during a bust year. The term balance is often used to refer to the aggregate of this four-layer cake, giving the impression that as long as general fund balance is positive, the government has real savings. By now it is clear that only the top of so-called total balances, the smallest circle, are real savings. These are the unreserved undesignated balance of the general fund.

3.2.2 Data Sources of UUB

This unreserved undesignated balance of the general fund is a more objective observation of the fiscal condition of a state or local government. The "standard" data sources of UUB are each government's *Comprehensive Annual Financial Report* (CAFR) that is compiled for each fiscal year in accordance to the "generally accepted accounting principles" (GAAP) and audited by an independent agency. As long as states compile and publish CAFRs, the consistency of data is guaranteed through accounting and auditing technicalities and principles. For years before states began to publish CAFRs, consistency can be achieved by picking the unreserved undesignated balance or the appropriable balance whether it was on budgetary basis or modified accrual basis of accounting. Since states did not start publishing CAFRs in the same year, this is a difficult but necessary choice. Potential problems occur that the balances are not from the same basis of accounting. However, as long as the bottom line is the unreserved undesignated balance, we have drawn something comparable. Throughout the book, the term GFS refers exclusively to UUB.

3.2.3 Changing Patterns of General Fund Surplus

The level of general fund surplus has long been taken as an important indicator of the fiscal health of state governments and used as countercyclical reserves; this use has remained as an important function even after budget stabilization funds have been widely adopted. The historical (1979–1999) average level of general fund surplus (UUB) of the 50 states expressed as a ratio of their general fund expenditure is provided in Table 3.1. In those years, 11 states had a mean of negative UUB (their aggregate GFB might be positive though); another 17 states kept a mean level between 0 and 4%; 16 states maintained in the high (7–12%) and very high (12–18%) ranges. Summary statistics of these ratios are shown in Table 3.2: The overall average level of general fund surplus as a ratio of general fund expenditure was

Table 3.1 Historical (1979–1999) mean level of state general fund surpluses expressed as UUB/general fund expenditure ratios

Status	Percent range (%)	Number of states
In deficit	–21–0	11
Very low	0–1.99	8
Low	2–3.99	9
Medium	4–6.99	6
High	7–11.99	12
Very high	12–17.99	4

Table 3.2 Summary statistics of general fund surplus UUB ratio 1979–1999

Panel A: all 50 states				
50 states	Average (%)	Median (%)	High (%)	Low (%)
Mean	3.42	3.28	17.25	–9.07
Median	3.46	2.85	13.62	–3.13
Low	–20.59	–18.48	0.00	–146.44
High	17.95	15.23	65.73	6.78
Panel B: excluding Alaska				
49 states	Average (%)	Median (%)	High (%)	Low (%)
Mean	3.91	3.42	16.26	–6.27
Median	3.47	2.96	13.35	–2.49
Low	–15.82	–18.48	0.00	–27.13
High	17.95	15.23	53.22	6.78

3.4%. With the extreme outlier (huge deficits and wide ups and downs) of Alaska taken out, the balance is not changed much.

By grouping states into the eight Census geographic regions and calculating their historical averages, we get some patterns (two versions for the Far West region: one with Alaska, one without). The 21 sample years can be divided into three periods: 1979–1983 are the second half of a full cycle, mainly the double dip recession of the early 1980s; 1984–1992 are a full cycle, with expansion of the late 1980s and the 1990–1991 recession; and 1993–1999 are the expansionary phase of a full cycle. Calculating the averages of these regions again, we find that, first, the eight regions fall roughly into a Western group and an Eastern group. Results are shown in Table 3.3. The Western group includes the Southwest, Plains, Rocky Mountains, and Far West regions; the eastern group includes the Southeast, Mideast, Great Lakes, and New England regions. The Western group surpasses the Eastern in the average, the median, and the highest levels of general fund surpluses. Second, the variance between the high and the low levels is larger for the West than the East (except the Mideast which is higher than the Plains), suggesting that general fund surpluses may have been used more in recession years in the Western than in the Eastern states. Third, all regions except the Mideast show a decline of the average level from Period 1 to Period 3, which I will discuss in Section 3.3.

Table 3.3 Historical (1979–1999) average level of general fund surplus by census regions and by periods

	Historical average					In three periods		
	Average (%)	Median (%)	High (%)	Low (%)	Variance (%)	1979–1983 (%)	1984–1992 (%)	1993–1999 (%)
Far West	1.62	3.49	20.78	−21.33	42.11	8.00	6.35	−9.04
Southwest	7.94	6.90	21.35	−2.50	23.85	15.64	3.60	8.01
Plains	7.91	7.71	16.91	2.30	14.62	9.72	5.58	9.61
Rocky	7.41	5.86	19.05	2.85	16.20	13.41	4.73	6.56
Far West (no AK)	6.06	5.38	19.66	0.35	19.30	8.16	6.80	3.60
Southeast	3.19	3.17	5.98	0.37	5.62	4.21	2.33	3.57
Mideast	0.38	−0.28	8.30	−7.09	15.39	−0.95	−1.91	4.28
Great Lakes	−0.21	0.21	6.82	−6.98	13.80	0.40	0.55	−1.63
New England	−0.34	−0.82	4.50	−6.44	10.94	0.26	−0.16	−1.00

What factors may have significantly affected the level of general fund surpluses over the years? In our pursuit for possible answers, fiscal tradition pops up first. Tradition is a messy term, covering many not easily observable or isolatable factors, but we can somehow discern their display. For example, as shown in Table 3.3, four regions (Plains, Rocky Mountains, Far West excluding Alaska, and Southeast) never had negative average levels, however high or low their highest surpluses were. This may have been a tradition of protective fiscal conservatism in practice.[1] At the individual state level, 11 states never had negative GFS and 8 states never had their GFS above 3.99%. For example, Hawaii always maintained very high surpluses; its lowest level was near 7%. Alabama's highest level was only 2.4%, but its lowest was 0.31% – a typical conservative state both politically and fiscally. At the other extreme, the states of New York and Illinois had their UUB in the red in 19 of the 21 years (IL 81–99, NY 80–98). The general fund of Alaska had never been in the black since its Constitutional Reserve Fund had the first balance in 1992; even its general fund deficit in 1982–1986 had little to do with its economy – the growth rate of its gross state product (GSP) was near 5% and 11%, respectively, in 1984 and 1985. Nothing could have explained these except their fiscal tradition which is invariably rooted in the legal and political institutions of the states. An extreme case is Arkansas which did not carry (at least not report) surpluses or incurred deficits as reflected by UUB. Its ultimate tool against unexpected revenue shortfall seemed to be expenditure cuts,[2] a typical state that "rides the curve of the business cycle," deferring fiscal restraint (Pollock and Suyderhoud 1986).

3.3 Formal Tool: Budget Stabilization Fund

General fund surplus is part of the operating fund of a government, which is why we call it an "informal policy tool." It easily becomes a target of spending pressure in boom years. For this reason, practitioners have long sought for a more formal tool of the countercyclical fiscal policy, which is ideally separated from the daily financial operations in order to overcome the shortcomings of the informal tool. This formal tool is the budget stabilization fund (BSF). This section discusses in detail the definition, origin, and evolution of this fund as well as its diffusion among the states.

3.3.1 Origin and Evolution

The budget stabilization fund (BSF), popularly called the "rainy day fund" (RDF), is a fiscal device used by subnational governments to store extra revenues during economic booms for use in economic downturns in order to supplement inadequate

---

[1] This author interviewed seven state budget directors and budget analysts in the spring of 2001 during NASBO's annual conference in Scottsdale, Arizona. State officials held this opinion.

[2] Author's correspondence in 2001 with an Arkansas budget officer.

resources for meeting outlay demands. Since the early 1980s, this countercyclical device has attracted increasingly more academic attention.

The concept and practice of countercyclical reserves date back to Biblical times. In the American government system, the BSF also enjoys a relatively long history, dating back to the second half of the nineteenth century. With ineffective controls and too frequent transfers, many cities then had difficulty keeping departmental spending within budgeted levels, so the cities created contingency funds for emergencies. Early contingency funds were very small as a percentage of the budget or in absolute amounts. Rules regarding the use of the funds were developed involving consensus between the executive and the legislative branches.

The earliest use of the name "rainy day fund" was by New York City in the 1930s. The NYC rainy day fund had inadequate restrictions on approval procedures and an insufficient mandate on replenishment; its balance was very "modest" by the early 1960s. "When NYC borrowed for operating expenses, it also decided to make use of its rainy day fund."[3] The fund soon went into disuse and was forgotten. The lesson is apparent: A BSF cannot exist long without restrictive approval procedures. A consensus mechanism between the executive and the legislative branches is a necessary feature. At the state level, "New York was the first to adopt a formal BSF 1946, as a safeguard against possible future declines in revenues" (New York Legislation 1946).

3.3.2 *Defining Budget Stabilization Fund*

As a formal policy instrument, a budget stabilization fund is defined as a fund that is equipped with three overarching features. First and foremost, a BSF has an enabling legislation as its legal basis; thereby the fund possesses binding force on the key players in the budgeting process who exert heavy influence on state finance and in each state's budgeting process. The enabling legislation prescribes the structural features of the fund and protects the fund balance against attacks from political pork barreling or overspending in boom years. In contrast, maintaining a sizable level of surplus in the general fund or in contingency funds may or may not need an enabling legislation.

Second, the budget stabilization fund as a countercyclical reserve fund goes across fiscal years (budget cycles) and operates over the whole economic cycle, which is ideally displayed in fund deposits during boom years for accumulation of savings and withdrawals in lean years for use against revenue shortfalls. By this feature, it is clear that a working capital fund or general fund reserve designed to operate within fiscal years (budget cycles) is not a real budget stabilization fund. In contrast to general fund surplus that is often under spending pressure, a properly structured BSF is a good vehicle for savings during boom years for use in recession (Michigan Legislation 1977; US Congress 1985; Sobel and Holcombe 1996).

---

[3] See U.S. Congress (1985). This is a comment by Mr. Ted Weiss who in the early 1980s was chairman of the House Subcommittee on Intergovernmental Relations and Human Resources. Mr. Weiss was on the New York City Council in the early 1960s.

Finally, the budget stabilization fund is a government-wide reserve for general purposes, not just for use by any particular department or for a single purpose; its primary target is budgetary stabilization in times of revenue shortfalls. According to a report by the General Accounting Office (GAO 1999), state governments in the USA maintain reserves that fall into three categories: (a) government-wide reserves for general purposes, (b) government-wide reserves for specific purposes, and (c) agency-specific reserves for specific purposes. Budget stabilization funds explored in this book are government-wide reserve for general purposes. Any reserves for single or special purposes or for use only by specified government agencies are not in this category. This is why Alabama's "Education Trust Fund for Proration Prevention" is not counted as a BSF in this study.[4] Contingency funds as currently in use by many governments are across-fiscal-year (across budget cycle) reserves, and they can be government wide or agency specific, but on the whole, these funds are reserves for specific purposes, for example, natural disasters, litigation settlements, self-insurance, and so on. Thus, contingency funds are not the same as BSFs and are distinguished from BSFs in this study.

With the above discussion, we can see two distinct definitions of BSF; one is strict and the other is loose. The strict definition is:

> A budget stabilization fund is money set aside while good economic conditions prevail and then drawn down during poor economic times to lessen the extent to which state governments will have to reduce expenditures or raise taxes to cope with a recession. (US Congress 1985, 11; NASBO 1985, 6; Sobel and Holcombe 1996, 31)

The loose definition goes: Money set aside … against the chances of "reducing service levels or raising taxes and fees because of temporary revenue shortfalls or unpredicted one-time expenditures" (GFOA 1999, 17). The loose definition is in fact broad enough to include contingency funds that are different in use procedures from BSFs. This book endorses the strict definition, which distinguishes this study from previous ones.[5]

In accord to the strict definition, 39 of the 50 states had established their own stabilization funds and deposited their first balances into the fund by the end of fiscal year 1999; in the 2000s, a few other states followed suit. As of 2008, 47 states

---

[4] The Alabama Education Trust Fund for Proration Prevention is treated as a BSF in the *Fiscal Survey of States* series compiled by NASBO and in documents published by the National Conference of State Legislature (NCSL), for example Eckl (1993). A common feature of these publications by professional organizations is their reliance on self-report by the states.

[5] For example, Eckl (1993) counts 45 states as having a BSF; NASBO (1999) also counts 45, and Sobel & Holcombe counts 44 (1996, 30). New Mexico and Wisconsin did establish budget stabilization funds in 1978 and 1985 respectively, but they never put any money in the funds. Kansas did set up a BSF in 1992 using $70 million of a "disproportionate share of money through the Title XIX Medicaid Program", but the fund went into disuse soon after the money was drawn up. In this sense, it was never a real BSF. Colorado, Kansas, New Mexico and Wisconsin keep a within-fiscal-year general fund reserve which will not be able to serve the full role of BSFs. Arkansas adopts a unique "no reserve no surplus" policy because the state intends to deal with recessions solely with expenditure cuts. Louisiana and Hawaii had their first balances only in 1999 and 2000. We are not able to test their effects for the recent recessions, so these two are excluded from this study.

had a stabilization fund, at least in name. Those without a fund or with no deposits made into their fund compose only a small minority.

3.3.3 Structural Features of BSF Enabling Legislation

In this subsection I conduct a textual analysis of state laws that enable the stabilization fund in each state. The BSF enabling legislation of six states appears in their state constitutions; they are Alaska, Delaware, Oklahoma, South Carolina, Texas, and Virginia. The rest are in their statutes. I examine the detailed legal language, as prescribed in state statutes or constitutions, regarding the operation of state BSF; then I classify these descriptions into analytical units that I call "structural features." In summary form, these structural features fall into four categories: (1) purposes of the fund; (2) funding sources; (3) maximum balances allowed, that is, caps on balance levels; and (4) approval procedures for cash withdrawal from the fund. These features are crucial to players in state finances as the rules (flexible though) for operating these reserve funds, and the features are essential for us to obtain a clear and thorough understanding of the BSF. It is these features that separate BSF from any other countercyclical fiscal tools that do not necessitate an enabling legislation to operate.

3.3.3.1 Purposes of Budget Stabilization Funds

We can identify four common purposes that a state may create a BSF for. These are revenue shortfall, emergency, cash flow, and any use. The first three are the most common; the last one is a very special, inclusive authorization for its use. Among the first three, the first two overlap – while the word emergency can mean almost any urgent situation that calls for immediate action, for example, natural disasters, revenue shortfall is a special case of emergency. Cash flow is closely related to daily operations. These four range from very specific to very broad; state varies from single to multiple purpose BSFs. Among all four purposes, use of BSF against revenue shortfall is the original and primary one. The wide diffusion of BSF indicates the recognition by policy makers and the public of problems prevalent in the budgetary system. The case of legislators changing their perception about public budgeting is best illustrated by the Washington State Revised Code; a paragraph from the code reads: "The current budgetary system of Washington lacks stability. It encourages crisis budgeting and results in cutbacks during lean years and overspending during surplus years."[6]

[6] Revised Code of Washington, Title 43: State Government – Executive, Chapter 43.135 State Expenditure Limitations (formerly: Tax Revenue Limitations), 43.135.045 Emergency reserve fund. This legislation was adopted in 1981.

State BSF legislations spread over six decades, from the pioneer New York (1946) to the most recent newcomer Illinois (2001). Over this long diffusion process, legislators and government officials deepened their understanding as well as appreciation of BSF and its relationship to the economic cycle; "rainy day fund" as the popular name of BSF also began to attract the attention of the general public. Thereby it is natural to see changes made to state finance laws that reflect this increasing acceptance of this new policy and policy tool. Given the diversity among states with their economy, politics, demographics, and tradition, among others, it is not surprising that states vary a lot on the purposes each state's BSF legislation prescribes. For example, the Michigan law lists stabilization of employment and the Nebraska law lists property tax relief though these are unique exceptions. Two states do not specify the purpose of their BSF; four states list "any" or multiple purposes.

Of the common purposes, dominant is reservation for revenue shortfalls. State BSF legislation makes this purpose very explicit. The New York law puts it as, "[it is] for the stabilization of the revenues of the state derived from the taxes, fees, and other sources required by law to be paid into the general fund of the state treasury."[7] The Pennsylvania statute says, "[it is] to minimize future revenue shortfalls and deficits; to provide greater continuity and predictability in the funding of vital government services; and to minimize the need to increase taxes to balance the budget."[8] The option of using BSF to fund operating deficits is related to, though different than, the primary purpose. Delaware can use its BSF "… to fund any unanticipated deficit in any given fiscal year";[9] Florida can use its fund "to avoid deficit due to minor fluctuations in revenue or spending,"[10] while South Carolina can use its fund "only for purpose of covering operating deficits of state government."[11] In fact these languages can be taken as similar to, if not the same as, those above regarding revenue shortfalls. On the other hand, such wording also suggests that lawmakers may have taken BSF as budgetary buffer for missteps in financial management or technical errors in revenue forecasting. For instance, BSF can be used in North Dakota when "general fund revenue is two and a half percent below *estimate*" (emphasis added) and in Virginia "when general fund revenues appropriated exceed revised general fund revenue *forecast* by over 2% of the revenue in the last fiscal year" (emphasis added). From these two examples, we can infer recognition or vision by lawmakers of at least two scenarios where stabilization of the budget calls for fiscal reserves, one from economic cycle impact – national recessions or regional downturns – and the other from administrative missteps that lead to imbalances between revenue and outlay.

[7] New York State Consolidated Laws, Chapter 56 State Finance Law, Article VI: Funds of the State, Section 92.

[8] Pennsylvania Consolidated Statutes, Title 72, Section 3741.201-05.

[9] Delaware Constitution, Article VIII, Section 6(d).

[10] Florida Statutes, Title XIV: Taxation and Finance, Chapter 215 Financial Matters: General Provisions, Section 215.32.

[11] South Carolina Constitution, Article III, Section 36 (B); South Carolina Code of Laws, Section 11-11-310.

The cash flow purpose of BSF is seen in both the first and the second BSF laws: New York's (1946) Tax Stabilization Reserve Fund can be used as "temporary loan to the general fund as working capital" and "Working Capital Fund" was the original name of Florida's (1959) BSF which can be used "as revolving funds for short-term transfers" when it is not used to fill in for revenue shortfalls.[12] These two earliest laws were a model for states that created BSF more recently, like Iowa (1992) and West Virginia (1994). So far, about 10 states co-list revenue shortfall and working capital as purposes for their BSF. These two purposes, however, are distinctively different. BSF temporarily used as working capital must be returned to the fund, whereas use for revenue shortfall during recessions does not necessarily require repayment of the fund in many states.

The rationales for this dual purpose practice are not difficult to discern. In a technical sense, dual usage of the BSF funds means higher efficiency, which adds to the legitimacy of countercyclical reserves in face of political pressure against boom-year savings and thus lends more protective force to the fund. Thus, as a trend, more states may co-list cash flow as a purpose for their BSF. In a more significant sense, this dual purpose grants BSF one of the conventional roles of general fund surplus so that the interaction between the two may crowd out the functions and reduce the amount of GFS in states that have adopted BSF. I will examine the interaction between GFS and BSF in Chapter 4.

A further extension of the functions of the BSF is for emergencies or natural disasters as the third purpose of BSF, which can be taken as evidence that the BSF also serves the conventional roles of general fund surpluses. Of the nine states that prescribe this role for their BSF, seven adopted this fund in the 1980s and 1990s, which probably is linked to the tax revolts of the late 1970s Proposition 13 and the early 1980s Proposition 2½. Listing another purpose adds to the legitimacy of the savings, as I mentioned above for the cash flow purpose. Examples of this purpose include the Massachusetts Stabilization Fund that can be used "for any event which threatens the health, safety, or welfare of the people of the Commonwealth or any of its political subdivisions"[13] and the Idaho BSF that can cover "expenses incurred as the result of a major disaster declared by the Governor."[14]

For "any purpose" is by far the broadest, very special case seen in the BSF legislation of four states. The Alaska Constitutional Budget Reserve Fund "may be [used] for *any public purpose* if the amount available for appropriation for a fiscal year is less than the amount appropriated for the previous fiscal year" (emphasis added).[15] Among the four states, Alaska probably can afford to spend its reserve fund for any purposes, because the extraordinary natural resources in the state

---

[12] Florida created a separate budget stabilization fund in 1965; later, the two funds were combined.

[13] General Laws of Massachusetts, Part I: Administration of the Government, Title III: Laws Relating to State Offices, Chapter 29: State Finance, Section 2H.

[14] Idaho Statutes, Title 57: Public Funds in General, Chapter 8: Fund consolidation Act, Section 14.

[15] Alaska Constitution, Article IX, Section 17.

provide for a huge BSF, which is an exception among the states. The Washington Emergency Reserve Fund "may be appropriated *for any purpose* if it is approved by two-thirds of each house and by a vote of the people at the next general election" (emphasis added). As illustrated in the paragraph cited at the start of this section, the State of Washington holds insightful appreciation of the role of BSF in reforming its budgetary system. As Washington employs a most volatile tax structure with no personal income tax but with heavy reliance on the sales tax, we can make three inferences out of the state's wording on the purpose of its BSF. First, by the time of creating the BSF, lawmakers of the state had keenly felt the pain from the volatility of the state's revenue portfolio, so they purposely left the door of usage wide open so that in times of need the legislature can make the fullest use of the limited reserves. Second, this wide-open door on BSF purpose was the result of political compromise between a considerate (compromising) legislature and a powerful governor at the time of drafting the legislation. Finally, the "any purpose" language was a device to evade public outcry against government savings at that particular time (1981).

The BSF in two states can in fact be open for any purpose: The State of Maine BSF legislation lists multiple purposes; the Missouri law puts the state's BSF "for use in meeting program funding requirements of the state."[16] No doubt the intended primary purpose of the BSF in these four states is the same as in other states, but the legal language as cited above opens the door to many purposes other than revenue shortfall. The consequence of this open purpose will be seen in testing the effects of the structural features on the levels of BSF balance. In general, restrictive uses of BSF are expected to push up balance levels, whereas liberal uses divert balance levels in the opposite direction.

3.3.3.2 Funding Sources of BSF

State BSFs are funded from four sources: (1) by a predetermined formula from the general fund, (2) from special revenues, (3) transfer from the general fund when surpluses occur, and (4) appropriations from the general fund. This is in the order from less political control and more economic impact to more political control and less economic impact. Simultaneous use of more than one source is common.

The design purpose of formula funding is to minimize political interference such that policy makers in the executive branch or the legislative branch have their say only in creating the formula, and in drafting and passing the law. After that point, these officials lose much of their discretionary control over funding the BSF, with automatic transfer of money into the fund once the economic indicators reach the predetermined point. In 1977, Michigan, the "model BSF legislation state" (U.S. Congress 1985), was the first to adopt this source: "The percentage of annual growth

---

[16] Missouri Revised Statutes, Chapter 33: State Financial Administration, Section 33.285 BSF created.

rate over two percent shall be multiplied by total state general fund revenue of current fiscal year to determine the amount to be transferred to the fund from state general fund in next fiscal year."[17] In 1982, Indiana followed suit: "Monies (calculated from a formula) are deposited automatically into the fund if growth rate in adjusted personal income exceeds 2%."[18] In the 1990s, Arizona and Virginia adopted this practice, only making their formulas more specific, easier to implement, and less subject to any variance from personal interpretation. The Arizona formula introduces the "trend" concept and partly combines the formula with the appropriation process: "When annual growth rate exceeds the trend rate, the excess growth rate times total general fund revenue determines the amount to be appropriated into fund."[19] (However, the law does not specify how the trend is calculated.) This is an interesting development: Though the amount is determined by formula, the action is dependent upon legislative approval, which indicates involvement that is more political. The Virginia formula also uses the "trend" concept though it is an implicit one – the average annual increase of the six immediate preceding years.[20] Besides, Virginia adds appropriation as another source: "Additional appropriations may be made at any time" if the cap is not exceeded, which shows a development in the opposite direction from that of Arizona. Instead of struggling for more control of the appropriation process, the Virginia Legislature endorses fiscal conservatism in the favorable sense – in case the formula cannot provide adequate funding for the BSF, the legislature will be ready to make it up.

Funding BSF from special revenues is restricted to only very few states, usually as an additional source. These states either have rich natural resources or resort to one-time revenues to jump-start their BSF. The former case includes Alaska that has more than enough natural resources to fund its BSF with severance tax receipts from oil and gas exports and Texas which also uses the oil and gas tax but only as a supplement (75% of any oil and gas production taxes above the amount received in the benchmark year, FY 1987). The latter case includes Nebraska that employed a temporary (9 months) sales tax collection for the initial funding, and then shifted to the general fund for recurring deposits, and Hawaii, at the creation of its BSF in 1999, provided 40 percent of its expected tobacco settlement receipts as a supplement to regular appropriations.[21] Of the two types of cases, natural resources are a lasting

[17] Michigan Compiled Laws, Chapter 18: Department of Management and Budget, Section 351–359.

[18] Indiana Code 4-10-18.

[19] Arizona Revised Statutes, 35–144, 2B.

[20] "The General Assembly shall make deposits to the Fund equal at least fifty percent of the product of the certified tax revenues collected in the most recently ended fiscal year times the difference between the annual percentage increase in the certified tax revenues collected for the most recently ended fiscal year and the average annual percentage increase in the certified tax revenues collected in the six fiscal years immediately preceding the most recently ended fiscal year." Virginia Constitution, Article X, Section 8: Limit of Tax and Revenue, paragraph 2.

[21] Hawaii Revised Statutes, Section 328 L-3.

funding, whereas one-shot revenues are not dependable. In Section 3.4 of this chapter, empirical tests will generate evidence.

The third source – "from the general fund when surpluses are available" – is much more political than the first two. "General fund surplus" is truly an indicator of a state's fiscal health, but it results as much from political manipulation as from overall economic strength and proper financial management. Even when total available revenues exceed the normal expenditure needs and state finance officers exercise professional and conservative financial management, annual budget execution does not necessarily end in surplus if either the governor or the legislature, or both, goes out of their way to spend more in order to win popular support. Among such states, New York and California are two typical examples of running general fund deficits (on the unreserved undesignated balance) during the record-long economic expansion in the 1990s. Therefore, general fund surplus may not be as reliable as a funding source for stabilization funds as it is assumed to be. Nevertheless, 30 states have chosen to place the funding of their BSF in the hands of their elected policy makers, which must have its deep root in state political dynamics, political accountability, and representative oversight on financial management first and foremost among other factors.

As political as "from general fund surpluses," or even more so, is "funding with appropriations from the general fund", because this funding source relies on three prerequisites. First, the state economy is strong; second, the governor is willing to recommend transfers into the BSF; and finally, the legislature happens to be in a supporting mood for the transfer as recommended by the governor. Co-occurrence of the three may not be rare, but it is not as frequent as we would like it to happen either. Fortunately, among the 14 states that use this source, only six list it as the sole money channel. The other eight states resort to more than one source. Obviously, how to fund a BSF has been, and will remain to be, a political phenomenon in most states, just as the choice of the funding source has been more a political process than pure financial management. As empirical evidence will show in Section 3.4, less political sources are more favorable to keeping more savings.

3.3.3.3 Maximum Amount Allowed: Caps on BSF Balance Levels

We can identify some economic and political reasons for setting caps on BSF funds; the two types of reasons are interrelated and intertwined. The economic reason is efficiency – resources should stay where they can be put to the highest utility, which is not the public sector. The political reason is to prevent waste and to control abuse of power by bureaucrats, a typical example being the most recent round of tax revolt movement that started in 1978 with Proposition 13. With these as the background, it is then not difficult to understand why state legislatures have chosen to prescribe a maximum amount allowed, or caps on balance levels, for their stabilization funds. In many BSF laws, such caps are a percentage of the general fund expenditure, some as a percentage of general fund revenue or a percentage of appropriations in the previous fiscal year.

For convenience of discussion, I convert these caps all in a rough measure into general fund expenditure in the current fiscal year. I assume this is acceptable because although revenues are usually larger than expenditures, the expenditure in the current fiscal year is closer in amount to the revenue in the previous fiscal year. Also for convenience of discussion, I classify the caps in an increasing order, from low to high balances, into four ranges with the balance level expressed as a percentage of general fund expenditures of each state: (a) Cap I (low cap): 2 up to 4%; (b) Cap II (medium cap): 4 up to 7%; (c) Cap III (high cap): 7 up to 12%; and (d) Cap IV: no limit to BSF balance. Besides, the BSF laws of six states provide for a minimum amount of the BSF balance. This provision presents an obvious floor effect during economic recovery following a recession, when the BSF balance jumps to the floor level within 1 or 2 years instead of the typical slow accumulation over years that is common among states that do not have this provision. This provision is not a cap; it stands by itself.

As far as I know, there have not been positive criteria on what balance levels are the most proper or preferred; what I can find is a normative "5%" rule of thumb that practitioners and professional organizations constantly refer to as the so-called standard, which was provided by a Wall Street executive in the late 1970s and mid-1980s.[22] Professional organizations such as the National Association of State Budget Officers (NASBO), the National Conference of State Legislatures (NCSL), and the Government Finance Officers Association (GFOA) have since continued to recommend this standard.[23] Recent academic research like Joyce (2001), however, has placed this standard in doubt, and some empirical studies of individual states have proven 5% to be inadequate in times of need (e.g., Pollock and Suyderhoud 1986; Sobel and Holcombe 1996; Navin and Navin 1997). An exception may be scenarios where stabilization funds are used to fill in holes due from forecasting errors, not revenue shortfall from recessions. For example, a case study of California's revenue forecast errors shows the 5% rule is usable and accepts it (Vasche and Williams 1987). Nevertheless, the 5% rule has so far been the most commonly adopted range among the states – 21 of the states with BSF use this range. It is taken in this section as benchmark – the medium cap. Above the benchmark, ten states adopt the high cap; below it, four use the low cap. And four states do not set a cap on their balance (Alaska, Wyoming, Nebraska, and California). When a cap is set on the balance of a BSF, especially a medium cap, there tends to be a cap effect. A typical feature of the cap effect is that the BSF balance stays roughly at one flat level, while general fund surplus keeps rising during economic expansions.

[22] In an interview, Robert H. Muller, then assistant vice president of the Standard & Poor's Corporation, described a certain percentage of general fund unobligated balances as a ratio to expenditures as "a key financial number, one of the first things you ask for," and said that he considered 5% is "a good solid number for a state surplus, unless you have a cyclical economy" (National Governor's Association 1978, 12). Then in a presentation at NCSL's Fiscal Chairmen's Seminar on Jan. 6, 1984 in Denver, Mr. Muller, then Vice President of Morgan Guaranty Trust, used again the 5% as a guideline (Gold and Eckl 1984).

[23] See NASBO, *Fiscal Survey of States*, Washington, D.C., 1975–1999; NCSL (1998); and GFOA (1999, 17).

3.3.3.4 Procedures for Use Approval

Procedures to obtain approval for withdrawal from a BSF are written to protect fund balances from being used during economic booms; without such provisions, a BSF cannot be countercyclical. Three procedures are identified in state BSF laws. In the order from less to more restricted access by the executive branch, they are the following: (1) by executive discretion, (2) by predetermined formula, and (3) by appropriation.

Using BSF by executive discretion grants the easiest access to the fund. Nine states allow executive action without legislative involvement at the time of use. For example, in Florida and Georgia, the governor can decide to transfer money out of the fund; in Vermont, "transfer is to be made by the Commissioner of Finance and Management to the extent necessary,"[24] and in Mississippi and Minnesota, the Treasurer or Commissioner of Finance merely needs to notify the Legislative Budget Office or Legislative Advisory Commission when transfers occur.[25] In Connecticut, once the Comptroller determines the amount of deficit, the transfer is automatic.[26] In three (Indiana, Michigan, and Arizona) of the four states that employ a formula as the funding source for their BSF, use of the fund is automatic through transfers by either the State Treasurer or the Finance Director, based on the formula.

Appropriation by legislative action is the most restrictive approval procedure, which precludes executive discretion and better secures BSF balance. The fact that three quarters of the BSF states adopted this procedure indicates that the use of BSF is under strict legislative control. Interestingly, Virginia uses a formula as the funding source, but to withdraw money from the fund, legislative approval is necessary. This easy-in, restrictive-out approach may help better protect their fiscal reserves. However, the formula and the appropriation mechanisms may not be as distinct or definitive as they seem on the paper. In practice, officials in the executive branch and the legislators have at their disposal more than one way to circumvent legal restrictions on moving money into and out of the fund, though the existence of a formula sets a default that adds to the complexity of political manipulation. We may reasonably assume at the same time that political manipulation would be more difficult with the BSF law as part of the state constitution instead of its statute. Among the four states that set a formula as a funding source, only Virginia's BSF is in its constitution.

The name of each state's stabilization fund, its year of creation/adoption, and the year of the first balance each state places deposits into its BSF are provided in Table 3.4. Details on the structural features of each state's BSF enabling legislation as well as its source are provided in General Appendix A at the end of this book.

---

[24] Vermont Statutes, Title 32: Taxation and Finance, Chapter 5: Budget, Section 308.

[25] Mississippi Code, Section 27-103-203: Working Cash-Stabilization Reserve Fund established; use of funds; notice of transfers. And Minnesota Statutes 1999, 16A.152: Budget Reserve and Cash Flow Account.

[26] Connecticut Statute, Section 4-30a.

Table 3.4 State budget stabilization fund names and year of creation

State	Fund name	Creation	First bal
New York	Tax Stabilization Reserve Fund	1946	1946
Florida	Working Capital Fund	1959	1965
New Mexico	General Fund Operating Reserve	1966	1967
Tennessee	Reserve for Revenue Fluctuations	1972	1972
California	Special Fund for Economic Uncertainties	1976	1977
Georgia	Revenue Shortfall Reserve	1976	1976
Delaware	Budget Reserve Account	1977	1979
Michigan	Countercyclical Budget and Economic Stabilization Fund	1977	1978
New Mexico	General Fund Tax Stabilization Reserve	1978	
South Carolina	General Reserve Fund	1978	1978
Connecticut	Budget Reserve Fund	1979	1981
Ohio	Budget Stabilization Fund	1981	1985
Washington	Emergency Reserve Fund	1981	1989
Colorado	Required Fund Balance (non-accumulating)	1982	1982
Indiana	Countercyclical Revenue and Economic Stabilization Fund	1982	1985
Mississippi	Working Cash-Stabilization Reserve Fund	1982	1983
Wyoming	Budget Reserve Account	1982	1983
Kentucky	Budget Reserve Trust Fund Account	1983	1987
Nebraska	Cash Reserve Fund	1983	1984
Minnesota	Cash Flow Account	1984	1984
Idaho	Budget Stabilization Fund	1984	1984
Maine	Maine Rainy Day Fund	1985	1985
Maryland	Revenue Stabilization Fund	1985	1987
Massachusetts	Commonwealth Stabilization Fund	1985	1987
Oklahoma	Constitutional Reserve Fund	1985	1988
Pennsylvania	Tax Stabilization Reserve Fund	1985	1986
Rhode Island	Budget Reserve and Cash Stabilization Account	1985	1985
Wisconsin	Budget Stabilization Fund	1985	1985
South Carolina	Capital Reserve Fund	1986	1986
Utah	Budget Reserve Account	1986	1987
New Hampshire	Revenue Stabilization Reserve Account	1987	1987
North Dakota	Budget Stabilization Fund	1987	1990
Vermont	General Fund Budget Stabilization Reserve	1987	1987
Texas	Economic Stabilization Fund	1988	1990
Alaska	Constitutional Budget Reserve Fund	1990	1992
Louisiana	Revenue Stabilization and Mineral Trust Fund	1990	1999
New Jersey	Surplus Revenue Fund	1990	1993
Arizona	Budget Stabilization Fund	1991	1994
Nevada	Fund to Stabilize Operation of State Government	1991	1994
North Carolina	Savings Reserve Account	1991	1991
South Dakota	Budget Reserve Fund	1991	1992
Florida	Budget Stabilization Fund	1992	1995
Iowa	Cash Reserve Fund	1992	1994
Iowa	Economic Emergency Fund	1992	1993
Missouri	Budget Stabilization Fund	1992	1992

(continued)

Table 3.4 (continued)

State	Fund name	Creation	First bal
Virginia	Revenue Stabilization Fund	1992	1993
Kansas	General Fund Ending Balance	1993	1994
West Virginia	Revenue Shortfall Reserve Fund	1994	1995
Minnesota	Budget Reserve Account	1996	1996
Hawaii	Emergency and Budget Reserve Fund	1999	2000
Illinois	Budget Stabilization Fund	2001	2002
Arkansas	Rainy Day Fund	2002	
Oregon	Rainy Day Fund	2007	2007
Alabama	General Fund Rainy Day Account	2008	
Wisconsin	Required General Fund Balance	?	1993
Montana	No		

3.3.4 Patterns of BSF Adoption and Diffusion

Although budget stabilization funds have had some history in this country, their adoption by the states has been slow and mostly recent. New York was the first state to adopt it, in 1946. But the use of the fund was loose, with little money going in and few people cared about it. (Even today, NY's BSF balance is very insignificant in amount.) Among other possible causes for the diffusion of BSF, recessions have kept reminding states of the utility of the stabilization fund as a useful policy tool, especially in the context of voter revolts against tax increases. At least it seems there has been some correlation between recession and state adoptions (Gold 1983; Gold and Eckl 1984). By chronological order, the 1957–1958 recession brought in Florida (1959). Following the 1973–1975 recession, Georgia and California joined the BSF club in 1976, Michigan and Delaware joined in 1977, and South Carolina in 1978, increasing the number of states with a BSF to 14. The 1980–1982 double dip recessions brought in many more so that the number reached 24 by the end of 1985 and 30 states by the end of 1989. The 1990–1991 recession further diffused BSF to make the number to 39 states by 1995. A close browse of Appendix A can reveal the close correlation between recessions and BSF adoption. Among other causes of BSF adoption beyond the recession effects, the tax revolt movement of the late 1970s and early 1980s that led to widespread adoption of tax and expenditure limitations was one leading cause. A further explanation is no doubt the peer effect from neighboring states that have adopted a BSF.

Adoption and implementation of CCFP by the states have been welcomed and encouraged by legislators, the market, and professional organizations. In 1985, the United States Congress concluded that "the states believe there is a role for [state] government in countering recession, irrespective of Federal action." Three design issues are prominent: First, state reserve funds have to be large enough to buffer revenue shocks in a recession. There is no uniform level of the reserve proper to all states. The level varies by each state's cyclical economic fluctuation. Second, states need a policy of maintaining reserves of a given size to avoid year-to-year debates about the proper size. Third, the accumulation and release of reserves should be gradual.[27]

In 1990, research by the Government Finance Officers' Association (GFOA) argues that establishing a fund balance policy and the BSF can alleviate sudden short revenue shocks or deficits (Allen 1990). GFOA advocates the adoption of countercyclical fiscal policies and lists it as a best practice (GFOA 1999). Credit rating agencies claim that "maintaining an operating reserve is the most effective practice that can enhance an issuer's credit rating" and lists it as the first of 12 best practices that have "significant rating value" (Fitch 2000). Thus, CCFP at the subnational level in the United States has been widely accepted and adopted.

3.3.5 State BSF Data Sources and Balance Levels

When seeking state BSF data, our first concern is how BSF balances are reported in official documents like the *Budget* or the *Comprehensive Annual Financial Report* (CAFR). Consistent and uniform (ideally standardized) reporting of BSF balances is crucial for auditing and policy evaluation. This so far has not been a reality. Five states do not report BSF balance in their CAFRs. California puts BSF balance in its *General Fund Cash Basis Report* and Texas in *Annual Cash Report*; for Idaho, North Dakota, and Washington, the sources vary. Two states classify BSF as a trust fund instead of as part of the general fund. In Alaska, it is a "constitutional reserve fund"; in Louisiana, it is an expendable trust fund. These are reported in the relevant sections of their CAFRs. In four states, BSF is a special revenue fund. Connecticut takes it as a special revenue fund, but their CAFRs (1995–1999) report the balances in the notes to the general fund statement.

Most states that have a BSF take them as a "sub-fund" or "an account" within the general fund. Among these, 15 states directly report the balances in the "Combined Balance Sheet – All Fund Types," and 12 report the balances in notes to the statements, mostly in the note to "reserve funds." There are two exceptions. Nevada places their BSF balances in the "Statistical Section" of the CAFR. North Carolina places theirs in the "Letter of Transmittal," under "savings reserve."

To strive for robust results, this study makes extra efforts in data collection, adopting a *survey-initiated, document-based, multi-check* process for BSF data. This method distinguishes the current study from previous ones that rely mostly on existing survey results. Detailed steps are in Box 3.1. These were used in the initial data collection in years 1998–2000.

The data set that I have compiled for this study uses the BSF "unreserved undesignated cash balance" by the end of fiscal years instead of "total equity" of the BSF, because when revenue shortfalls occur, it is the unreserved undesignated cash balance available that can be used to make up the revenue shortages. Loans from the

[27] *Federal and State Roles in Economic Stabilization.* United States House of Representatives, 99th Congress, 1st Session, report 99–460, December 31, 1985, 3 and 14.

Box 3.1 The Survey-Initiated, Document-Based, Multi-Check Data Collection Steps

Step One: Initial Sources of Data

(a) Government Performance Project (GPP) State Surveys 1998 and 2000: Balances for FY 1994–1999 from survey responses
(b) NASBO *Fiscal Survey of States* series 1977–2000 (BSF balances 1983–1999)
(c) State BSF legislations from state constitutions/statutes

Step Two: Checks and Verification

(a) Check against state CAFRs or other official reports of corresponding fiscal years, and *Fiscal Survey of States* of corresponding years. If the balances are the same, jump to Step Three; if different, go to b.

(b) Verify with GPP's state contacts (usually in the Budget Office) about source of data, reliability of NASBO data, and reason for the discrepancy.

Step Three: Main Source of Data

(a) Write to the Comptroller's Office of each state, requesting the following: (1) BSF balances 1979–1999 (where applicable), (2) general fund unreserved undesignated balances 1979–1999, and (3) copies of relevant reports or relevant pages of the reports for verification purposes.[28]

(b) Three Checks

- Check their 1994–1999 balances against the verified 1994–1999 figures obtained through Steps One and Two.
- Check against state CAFRs (for GAAP Years) and *Annual Financial Reports* (for non-CAFR years) through interlibrary loans of such documents
- State BSF legislations from state constitutions/statutes.

(c) Verification for Explanation

- Frequent correspondence/call with contacts in State Comptroller's Office.

(d) Use this protocol for subsequent years

[28] Tools used are (a) three waves of e-mail letters, for most states; (b) two extra waves of faxes, for non-responding states; and (c) frequent phone calls with Comptrollers' Offices.

BSF to the general fund are not useable before they are returned to the fund. The difference between the cash balance and total equity can be huge.

There are differences between the balances reported in the CAFRs and those in Comptroller's reports due to the differences in the basis of accounting. This is what the Government Accounting Standards Board (GASB) calls a "perspective difference" by timing. There is a difference in the structure of the general fund and the Budget Reserve Fund based on the accounting method used for the two reports. On a legal or budgetary basis (modified cash accounting), the budgeted reserve balance is made up of two components. One is the amount reserved for transfer to the Budget Reserve Fund from that fiscal year's surplus, which has not yet been moved. Therefore, it is still considered part of the general fund for reporting purposes. The other is the amount that is already in the Budget Reserve Fund from prior years, which is reported separately from the general fund. On a GAAP basis, BSFs are not considered a separate fund, but rather part of the general fund for reporting purposes. This is primarily because these funds can only be used for general fund purposes (i.e., to eliminate a deficit in the general fund). Therefore, both the amount reserved to be transferred (on a legal basis) and the balance of the BSFs from prior years are both considered part of the general fund under GAAP and reported as such.[29] NASBO's *Fiscal Survey of States* series rely solely on survey responses from the states for BSF data. My data set corrects the errors in the NASBO set.

3.3.6 Changing Patterns of BSF Balance

The average historical (up to 1999) level of each state's BSF balance against their general fund expenditure was low: 4 states below 1%, 8 states 1–2%, 18 states 2–3.9%, 7 states 4–6.9%, and only 2 states at 7–12% (Alaska being an outlier). The average of the historical averages among the states is 5.04%, median 2.47%. With the outlier of Alaska taken out, the average lowers to a mere 3.05%, at the middle of the low cap range, the median to 2.42%. Funds that are set up at different time periods present different average levels, although the difference is not significantly large: Those set up more recently maintain higher average levels: 2.92% for those set up between 1946 and 1979 (7 states), 3.14% for those set up between 1980 and 1989 (20 states), and 3.22% for those set up between 1990 and 1995 (11 states, excluding the outlier of Alaska; with Alaska, the average is 9.83%).

The average of averages reveals some variation between different regions. The Rocky Mountain and Great Lakes states kept the highest balances (in the medium cap range); five other regions are in the low cap range, while New England states kept the lowest level of balance, even below the low cap range (Table 3.5, panel a).

[29] Author's correspondence in year 2000 with a Connecticut budget official.

Table 3.5 Historical (1979–1999) mean level of state BSF and general fund surplus

Panel A: savings level by census regions

	Rocky 3	Lakes 3	Plains 6	Far West 3
BSF mean	5.42%	4.77%	3.69%	3.61%
GSP variance	9.74%	13.38%	11.43%	8.58%
	Southwest 3	Mideast 5	Southeast 9	New England 6
BSF mean	3.12%	2.48%	2.37%	1.98%
GSP variance	9.84%	8.17%	9.53%	11.50%

(Alaska as an extreme outlier is excluded from the Far West region. The *numbers* after region names indicate the number of states that have BSF)

Panel B: savings level against GSP and location

	BSF mean (%)	GFS mean (%)	BSF+GFS (%)	GSP variance (%)	Location (%)
Rocky (3)	5.42	7.41	*12.83*	9.74	*West*
Plains (6)	3.69	7.91	*11.60*	11.43	*West*
Southwest (3)	3.12	7.94	*11.06*	9.84	*West*
Far West (3)	3.61	6.06	*9.67*	8.58	*West*
Southeast (9)	2.37	3.19	*5.56*	9.53	*East*
Lakes (3)	4.77	–0.21	*4.56*	13.38	*East*
Mideast (5)	2.48	0.38	*2.86*	8.17	*East*
New England (6)	1.98	–0.34	*1.64*	11.50	*East*

Panel C: 50-state average savings level in three periods

All 50 States	1979–1983 (%)	1984–1992 (%)	1993–1999 (%)
GF surplus	5.89	2.71	2.56
BSF	1.96	3.20	5.60
BSF+GFS	7.85	5.91	8.16

Panel D: 50-state average savings level in 1979 and 1998/1999

	1979 (%)	1998 (%)	1999 (%)
GFS	9.91	4.20	2.62
BSF	2.66	8.24	7.32

Considering the variance of their regional gross state product variance (maximum-minimum levels of growth rates), larger variance necessitates higher average level of reserves; states in the Rocky Mountain and Great Lakes regions adopted safer fiscal policies. Mideast states seem to have a reason for their low balance level; New England states, however, fall much behind others with high GSP variance but the lowest BSF. This *East–west Divide* becomes much clearer when we combine BSF balances with general fund surpluses – since both are countercyclical fiscal tools – and compare the sum against the variance between the highest and lowest rates of the regions' gross state product: Higher reserves score better[30] (Table 3.5, panel b).

While we can assume that in general there does not exist economic differences between BSF, GFS, and other forms of reserves – because total cash position at times of a budget shortfall is the issue (Allan 1990, 4; Sobel and Holcombe 1996, 30) – it is important to remember that since budgeting is always closely related to politics, the real test for the above assumption is whether elected officials, and taxpayers collectively, can "administratively and politically" exercise adequate fiscal self-restraint on a routine basis in times of expansion (CBO 1998, 15–16), that is, to protect fiscal reserves against current spending pressure for use in a subsequent downturn. Dividing the 21 years of 1979–1999 into three periods and obtaining the average of 50-state averages in those years, respectively, we do find a decreasing trend for general fund surplus which is in the opposite direction of the trend for the average BSF balances: When GF surpluses and BSF balances are put together, the second period is low, with little difference between the first and third periods. It is interesting to notice, however, that the 50-state averages of GFS and BSF balances in 1979 and 1998 (1999) display a reverse pattern of contrast – at the end of the 1970s, general fund surpluses were dominant in total reserves; the situation reverses to BSF dominance in the late 1990s, that is, after near 40 states had established BSFs, much of general fund surpluses had turned in BSF balances (Table 3.5, panels c and d). Historical balances (1978–2010) of each state's BSF and GFS are provided in Appendixes B and C, respectively, at the end of this book.

3.4 BSF Structural Features and Balance Levels

Subnational countercyclical fiscal policy is a complex issue.[31] To tackle it necessitates systematic methods and approaches to properly handle each aspect of it. Based on discussion in the above sections, this section makes use of data collected in an effort to reveal the trend and patterns of BSF balance in the presence and the changing patterns of general fund surplus.

The literature is slowly building up on the effects of the budget stabilization fund on fiscal stress in lean years (Sobel and Holcombe 1996; Douglas and Gaddie 2002; Hou 2003). Empirical evidence from these earlier studies shows that BSF accumulated in boom years are an effective means to boost bust-year revenues; more boom-year savings grant states higher countercyclical fiscal capacity that translates into actual performance which is highly ideal in periods of economic downturn (Hou

[30] Though we do not know the exact relation between variance of GSP and total reserves, we do know by intuition that a higher GSP variance indicates a more volatile economy, which hence needs more reserves.

[31] This section draws heavily from data and analysis earlier published in Hou (2004).

et al. 2003). So it is strategically right and necessary for state governments to maintain a sizable BSF balance for protection against revenue shortfalls.

In this small literature, two papers stand out; both use some BSF structural features, but their dependent variable is fiscal stress, not the BSF balance level. The first paper (Sobel and Holcombe 1996) uses variables like "saving requirement," "cap on BSF," "cap percentage," and "withdrawal requirement" to test the effects of these variables on reducing or increasing state fiscal stress during the 1989–1992 recessionary period. The second paper (Douglas and Gaddie 2002) revisits the same data and uses the same model, but two other features. Besides these two studies, there have been virtually no empirical tests of what structural features of BSF legislation contribute to higher BSF balance levels. In this section I attempt to fill in this niche. The focus is on state governments in the USA; local governments are not included. This is because local governments are bound by state finance laws. In the case of New Jersey, the state does not allow local governments to set up countercyclical funds. Therefore, to start with the state level is a reasonable choice.

Under the definition of BSF discussed in Section 3.3 of this chapter, this section explores the causal relations between the structural features of BSF as prescribed in their enabling legislation and the actual BSF balance levels. Specifically, in this section I attempt to answer two major questions. First, which structural features of state BSF enabling legislation tend to push up BSF balances, which do not or tend to pull down the balance levels, and in what conditions of state finances? Historically general fund surpluses have served as a reserve against revenue shocks, which still makes intuitive sense now. Then the next research question is the relationship between the levels of unreserved undesignated balance (UUB, or GFS as defined in Section 3.2) of state general fund and that of BSF. If a state keeps a high level of UUB, does it also maintain a high level of BSF at the same time? Related to these two primary questions, this section also examines the role of balanced budget requirements (BBR) and state party politics in maintaining BSF balances. The empirical test that follows is based on the detailed analysis of the structural features of state BSFs that have been presented in Section 3.3 of this chapter. Next I will fist introduce data and methodology; then I will discuss results of empirical analyses, which is followed by policy recommendations on what state governments can do to increase their BSF balance level as a means to raise their countercyclical fiscal capacity.

3.4.1 Data and Methodology

The empirical test uses a panel data set. The sample period, from fiscal years 1979 through 1999, is chosen for strong reasons. The last two decade of the twentieth century was the period that saw the fastest expansion of BSF among the states. By my strict definition of the budget stabilization fund, 39 states had a real BSF with balances deposited into the fund by year 2000. Among these, 31 deposited their first balance after 1978, confirming a period of fast policy diffusion. Those two decades cover three national recessions, which provides an ideal window to test the political will and administrative capability of the states to save during boom years, against the socioeconomic as well as political context for the diffusion of stabilization funds.

Year dummies are created to capture the aggregate across-sectional effects at the national level; state dummies are used to absorb time-invariant state-specific effects and to avoid missing variable bias. The dependent variable is BSF balance at the end of fiscal year as a percent of the actual general fund expenditure (GFE) in each state. Data are the cash or the unreserved balances from the *Comprehensive Annual Financial Reports* of each state.

A key control variable is general fund surplus (GFS or UUB) which is also expressed as a percent of actual GFE. Knight and Levinson (1999) find that adoption of BSF increases state total savings dollar for dollar; however, evidence from Wagner (1999) does not support the savings increase proposition. Since both are saving devices, it is natural that BSF and UUB tend to rise and fall in tandem: In boom years, both increase with the strong economy; in bust years, both are drawn down. However, the positive correlation between the two devices does not mean that high BSF balance prerequires high UUB balance, because a state may choose to maintain high levels of BSF, but not high UUB, and another state may choose the opposite combination. Even the same state may change policies over time, from high BSF balances to high UUB or vice versa. My statistical analyses in previous subsections have shown the patterns of change of BSF versus those of UUB. For example, before Wyoming deposited its first BSF balance in 1983, its UUB remained between 20 and 52% of its GFE. In the next 5 years, its UUB declined to less than 10% while its BSF stayed high between 16 and 31%. During the following recession period, BSF was drawn down from FY 1989 to FY 1993, while UUB rose to about the same level as BSF till after 1994 when UUB surpassed BSF.

Other control variables include balanced budget requirements (BBR). Since every state is under some kind of legal requirement to balance its budget,[32] and the specific requirements vary significantly in form and stringency from state to state, balanced budget requirements are believed to exert much influence on state finances. This section uses the four BBR dummies published in *The Book of the States* series by the National Governors' Association. This series came out every 2 years (in this sample period), but policy changes are all recorded so that a time series thus constructed is reliable. These dummies include the following: (1) Governor must submit a balanced budget, (2) legislature must pass a balanced budget, (3) governor must sign a balanced budget, and (4) state may carry over deficits into the next fiscal year. Some studies adopt a composite measure of BBR, like the 0–10 index of stringency created by staff of the Advisory Commission on Intergovernmental Relations (ACIR 1987). I believe that the dummies have an inherent advantage: We know the exact effect of each variable, which is something an index cannot provide. Time-series data of these four dummy variables display that state policies on balanced

[32] Vermont is widely said to be a state with no such requirements, which is not true. Its "governor is statutorily required to submit recommendation to alleviate deficits from previous fiscal years in the budget request" (ACIR 1987).

budgets did change over the time period of this study, implying that controlling for these policies could be important.[33]

I use five variables to control for state politics which has been an essential part in studies of finance; exclusion of them could lead to omitted variable bias.[34] A dummy is created for political party confrontation between the governor and the majority of state legislature; this binary is designed to identify any effects due from the cooperation or friction between the executive and the legislative branches on savings or spending policies. Here I assume that political confrontation between the two makes increasing savings more exercisable, because confrontation checks against public spending – the legislature may obstruct executive spending initiatives and the governor may in turn veto or somehow block at least some political pork barreling. On the other hand, if both sides realize that they cannot ignore the political strength of the other, either of them may be open to compromises that result in more public savings. Thus, the sign of this variable is expected to be positive.[35]

To capture the political party effect, two binaries are created for the majority of the House being Democrat and the majority of the Senate being Democrat. Here the underlying assumption is that the two major parties uphold different fiscal policies out of ideologies differences. However, as Rivlin (1987) points out, lawmakers tend to "be pragmatists willing to work out non-ideological compromises across party lines." In a more realistic world, as Bretschneider et al. (1989) showcase, it is the dominance of the House or the Senate, or both, by one party that can overwhelm political obstruction by the other party, so the dominant party adopts policies of its choice. Using the Bretschneider et al. (1989) method, I calculate two ratios – dominance of the House by one party and dominance of the Senate by one party. The ratios are calculated from the number of seats in each of the two chambers of the state legislature – the number of seats held by one party is divided by the number of seats occupied by the other party, and then the calculation is repeated, reversing the

[33] More states require balanced starts of the fiscal year. In 1979, only 23 states required their Governors to submit a balanced budget; after the 1980 and 1982 recessions, this number rose to 43, and further to 45 in 1992. In 1979, only 21 states required their legislatures to pass a balanced budget. After the recession, this number rose to 39 in 1983. Back in 1979, Governors in 29 states were required to sign into law a balanced budget, but in 1999 the number of states increased to 37. The change, however, is not just toward stringency. Consideration was given to the smooth operation of the government and stable provision of public services, instead of cutting expenditures or increasing taxes. The number of states that allow carry-over of deficits from one budgetary cycle into the next increased, from 11 in 1979 to 21 in the early 1980s, after the recessions. When the economy became strong, this number declined to nine in 1987. After the 1991 recession, it rose to 14, only to come down again to nine in 1999, after the continued boom in the 1990s. The different requirements and changes in them may have exerted influence on state spending, especially during downturns.

[34] Some related studies include Poterba (1994), Alt and Lowry (1994, 2000).

[35] Rivlin (1987) touches upon the same topic in discussing the federal case: The divided power between the two branches creates a hurdle to the making and implementation of fiscal policies. The hurdle is low when the two branches agree; the hurdle turns medium or even high when the two branches disagree.

order of the two parties. Suppose in the House of a state, Democrats hold one-third of the seats (50 out of 150) and Republicans hold the other two-thirds (100 out of 150). The first step is to divide fifty by one hundred to arrive at a ratio of point five (0.5), and the second step is to divide one hundred by fifty to arrive at a ratio of two (2). Only ratios larger than one are considered dominance, those smaller than one are deleted. In the example, ratio two (2) is kept and 0.5 is discarded. The Nebraska case of unicameral legislature is given a ratio of 1, that is, no dominance is present. Summary statistics are provided in Table 3.6.

I exclude the state of Alaska from the data set, which is standard practice in studies of the states. An extra reason for this exclusion is that the Alaska Constitutional Budget Reserve Fund is even larger than the state's general fund, and this fund is too large to be of comparison with the BSF in any other states. The complete model runs:

$$\begin{aligned} \mathrm{BSF}_{\mathrm{it}} &= \beta_1 \mathrm{Source}_{\mathrm{it}} + \beta_2 \mathrm{Cap}_{\mathrm{it}} + \beta_3 \mathrm{Approval}_{\mathrm{it}} + \beta_4 \mathrm{Purpose}_{\mathrm{it}} \\ &\quad + \lambda_1 \mathrm{UUB}_{\mathrm{it}} + \lambda_2 \mathrm{BBR}_{\mathrm{it}} + \lambda_3 \mathrm{PP}_{\mathrm{it}} + \alpha_{\mathrm{i}} + \gamma_{\mathrm{t}} + \varepsilon_{\mathrm{it}} \end{aligned}$$

where the dependent variable BSF is the balance level; source is the funding of BSF; cap refers to the BSF level caps; approval is the procedures for use approval and purpose the use that BSF is put to; UUB refers to the level of general fund surplus, BBR the four binaries of state balanced budget requirements, and PP the political party variables; α is the state dummy, γ the year dummy, and ε the error term.

3.4.2 Empirical Methodology

My first step in the empirical analyses is to use the ordinary least squares (OLS) estimator and run BSF balance level against the structural features and the control variables for the whole sample period. The annual balance of BSF as a percent of general fund expenditure and the annual UUB balance, also as a percent of general fund expenditure, are serially correlated. One of the best methods to overcome this problem is to convert the variables into first-difference change of the rates instead of using the level. That, however, is not the purpose here because this section is to test the effects of the structural features on the level. The year-by-year change in the rate does not mean much to us. Therefore, my second step is to employ the Prais-Winsten (1954) estimator to correct for first-degree autocorrelation in the OLS model,[36] and then contrast estimates thereof with results from the ordinary least squares (OLS) model. In this section, results from the OLS model and the Prais-Winsten model are similar, indicating that the results are reliable.

[36] For detailed explanation of the model, see Prais and Winsten (1954).

Table 3.6 Summary statistics for tests in Section 3.4

Variable	Mean	Standard deviation	Minimum	Maximum
BSF balance	0.031	0.035	0	0.311
GFS/UUB balance	0.030	0.084	–0.271	0.325
Purpose of use				
For revenue shortage	0.880	0.325	0	1
For cash flow	0.231	0.422	0	1
For emergencies	0.161	0.368	0	1
For any purpose	0.065	0.246	0	1
Source of BSF			0	1
By formula	0.093	0.291	0	1
From general fund surplus	0.727	0.446	0	1
By appropriation	0.359	0.480	0	1
From special revenue	0.019	0.137	0	1
Maximum balance allowable				
Cap I: 2 up to 4%	0.118	0.322	0	1
Cap II: 4 up to 7%	0.512	0.500	0	1
Cap III: 7 up to 12%	0.268	0.443	0	1
Cap IV: No limit to balance level	0.102	0.304	0	1
Minimum requirement	0.140	0.348	0	1
Procedure for use approval				
By executive discretion	0.292	0.455	0	1
By appropriation	0.546	0.498	0	1
By formula	0.068	0.253	0	1
Balanced budget requirements				
Governor submit balanced budget	0.831	0.375	0	1
Legislature pass balanced budget	0.717	0.451	0	1
Governor sign balanced budget	0.620	0.486	0	1
May carry over deficits	0.241	0.428	0	1
Party politics				
Governor-legislature confrontation	0.486	0.500	0	1
House majority being Democrat	0.641	0.480	0	1
Senate majority being Democrat	0.583	0.494	0	1
House dominance ratio	2.273	2.182	1	23.2
Senate dominance ratio	2.218	1.987	1	21.5

Notes
1. The total number of observations is 526
2. Sources of BSF and UUB balance levels are *(Comprehensive) Annual Financial Report* of the states, different years, collected by author, calculated as percent of general fund expenditure from *Fiscal Survey of States* by the National Association of State Budget Officers
3. Source of BSF structural features are state BSF laws. For details of the sources, see notes in the paper and General Appendix 1

Then regressions with fixed effects are run only with each group of the structural features, setting one variable in each group as the default, to obtain more exact estimates of the relative effects of each of these features. For purposes of use, the default is "for cash flow" because this usage guarantees repayment to the fund while other uses do not. For funding sources, it is "by special revenue." For maximum balance allowable, "cap I: 2 up to 4%" is the default; it is assumed that the low cap leads to lower balance levels than higher caps. Among the three use-approval procedures, "use by executive discretion" serves as the default because, without strict restriction, this method of approval grants the easiest access to the fund and may lead to lower balance levels.

To obtain more reliable results about the behavioral pattern of the stabilization fund and its balance level during economic downturns and upturns, I divide the data into four subsets according to the growth rate of gross state product (GSP) in the previous year. This is because GSP growth is calculated by calendar year whereas state finance figures are by state fiscal year; there exists a 6-month lag for most of the states, so that last year's GSP is a strong indicator of state economic condition and thereby state financial health. That is, when a state's economy is down, its revenue is expected to fall short of expectation and that is the time for use of BSF; whereas a strong economy would enable a state to stock up its BSF instead of drawing it down.

The first subset includes observations where the previous year's GSP growth is negative (< 0%). In these years, states are not only unable to deposit extra money into their BSF but also draw from the funds to fill in holes in current spending. Therefore, for this subset, the funding source variables and balance cap variables are dropped. The second subset contains observations where last year's GSP growth is from 0 up to 2% as a marginal case of state economy. For this subset, I drop the BSF source variables but keep the balance cap variables, which forms a contrast with the first subset. The third subset collects observations where a state had relatively high growth last year (GSP rate 2 up to 4%). In many, though not necessarily all, cases this growth range permits deposits into BSF. None of the structural feature variables are dropped for the regression; this subset is the reference group covering all variables in the model. The fourth subset are observations with strong GSP growth rates (>4%) when deposits into BSF are normal while withdrawals are rare; so approval procedure variables are dropped for contrast to lower growth rates. I run regressions of these four subsets with defaults in each group of the structural features; then run regressions with fixed effects again only with each group, omitting the default, to arrive at the relative effects of the features under different economic conditions.

I also tried dividing the sample period into recession and expansion phases of the economic cycle, the former being 1979–1983 and 1989–1993 and the latter being 1984–1988 and 1994–1999 at the national level. For the two recessionary periods, the BSF source and cap variables are dropped assuming that in lean years states are drawing down instead of depositing money into the fund. For the two expansion periods, variables for use approval are dropped under the assumption that in these years states are stocking up instead of using the reserves. But the results are not reliable since states may have gone through different regional downturns.

3.4.3 Results and Discussion

This subsection reports and discusses empirical results. Table 3.7 provides results for the whole sample period, column 1 for the OLS model and column 2 for the Prais-Winsten model. When the model was run with 49 states (including states that do not have a real BSF but excluding Alaska; results not reported), signs and magnitudes of coefficients are very similar. The discussion here focuses on the 38-state sample, following the order of the variables list in the table. The OLS model has higher explanatory power than the PW model but unsatisfactory Durbin-Watson statistics, which is corrected in the PW model; otherwise, the two models are similar with their signs and statistical significance for most variables.

The key control, UUB level is as expected positively correlated with BSF balance, the point estimate being statistically significant at the 1% level in the OLS model but not significant in the PW model. The point estimate is very small (both variables are ratios against GFE): One percentage point increase of UUB sees about six-hundredths percentage point growth in BSF level, which indicates that when a state's economy is strong, both BSF and UUB levels rise. The two go parallel in direction but are not at all close in their pace of change. The small points of estimate for BSF imply that the increase of BSF is by no means at the same speed as UUB: The balances of BSF increase at a much slower rate than UUB. It may need quite a few years for BSF to accumulate to the 5% benchmark level. More detailed exploration into the relationship between BSF and GFS will be done in Chapter 4.

All four BSF purpose variables pose a negative sign. Except use for cash flow, the coefficients for the other three purposes are statistically significant. That is, whatever a state lists as the purpose of its BSF, presence of the feature may lead to lower BSF balance. However, use of BSF for revenue shortfall is normal and the reduction of balances is not unexpected. The largest reduction (–0.063) occurs when the purpose of BSF is set for "any purpose," which is what we need to avoid in policy design. Use of BSF for emergency does cut the balance level but by a very small margin.

Among the BSF source variables, three – funding by formula, from general fund surplus, and by appropriation – are not statistically significant and their points of estimate are very small, though funding by formula is relatively large. The fact that these three major sources (used by most states) do not produce significant results implies that the funding sources themselves may not be the only factors that exert an influence on the balance level. Some other, "invisible" forces are playing an active role in determining the balance level. Funding from special revenue shows negative coefficients in both models and is statistically significant in the OLS model, suggesting that adoption of this funding source on average reduces the BSF balance and the margin is large (–0.036) relative to the magnitudes of other funding sources.

All four balance cap variables, as expected, have generated positive and statistically significant coefficients. Interesting but not unexpected is that higher caps lead to high BSF balances; overall, the higher the cap is set, the larger the coefficient goes. This bears obvious implications in how to design a BSF that may bring about

Table 3.7 Effects of fund structural features on BSF level 1979–1999. Dependent variable is BSF balance level as percent of general fund expenditure

Column	(1)		(2)	
Model	OLS		Prais-Winsten	
Independent variables	Coef	t-stat	Coef	t-stat
GFS/UUB balance level	***0.057	3.04	0.019	1.01
Purpose of use				
Use for revenue shortage	***–0.061	–9.41	***–0.037	–2.81
Use for cash flow	–0.005	–1.10	–0.010	–1.10
Use for emergencies	*–0.008	–1.80	–0.011	–1.15
Use for any purpose	***–0.063	–6.45	*–0.036	–1.84
Source of BSF				
Funding by formula	0.011	1.13	0.016	0.82
Funding from general fund surplus	0.003	0.58	0.003	0.27
Funding by appropriation	–0.003	–0.59	0.003	0.32
Funding from special revenue	***–0.036	–3.31	–0.030	–1.35
Maximum balance allowable				
Cap I: 2 up to 4%	***0.109	3.71	**0.074	1.95
Cap II: 4 up to 7%	***0.108	3.66	**0.073	1.98
Cap III: 7 up to 12%	***0.110	3.76	**0.079	2.12
Cap IV: No limit to balance level	***0.118	3.97	***0.097	2.47
Minimum requirement of balance	0.002	0.39	–0.000	–0.03
Procedure for use approval				
Use by executive discretion	–0.006	–0.88	0.004	0.29
Use by appropriation	0.002	0.37	0.005	0.38
Use by predetermined formula	0.015	1.25	0.021	0.78
Balanced budget requirements				
Governor must submit a balanced budget	–0.003	–0.71	0.003	0.59
Legislature must pass a balanced budget	***0.020	4.32	***0.017	2.81
Governor must sign a balanced budget	–0.005	–1.50	–0.001	–0.21
May carry over deficits	***0.011	3.23	0.005	1.27
Party politics				
Governor-legislature confrontation	**0.006	2.29	0.001	0.32
House majority is Democrat	**–0.008	–2.23	**–0.008	–2.15
Senate majority is Democrat	–0.002	–0.66	–0.003	–0.72
House dominance ratio	–0.001	–0.71	0.002	1.40
Senate dominance ratio	0.001	0.44	–0.001	–0.98
Prob>F	0.00		0.00	
DW Statistic	0.50		1.92	
R^2	0.45		0.20	
Adjusted R^2	0.40		0.12	
Sample size	526		526	

Significance levels: *10%; **5%; and ***1%

high BSF balances. The minimum requirement variable does not produce significant results. One possible reason is that setting a minimum requirement is a relatively new feature in BSF laws and it has not yet played a major role in determining the BSF balance in the sample years; another explanation is those states that adopt this requirement do not have a BSF according to the strict definition; in this sense, the result is not surprising.

With regard to the use-approval procedure variables, though none of the three produce statistically significant coefficients, the fact that use by appropriation and by formula are positive and use by executive discretion is negative may be a clue when checking the pattern in different economic conditions. A possible indication is that executive discretion reduces BSF balance, whereas use by formula may increase it. I will revisit this point in discussing results from Tables 3.9 and 3.10.

Of the four BBR variables, that the legislature passes a balanced budget posts a positive sign at 1% significant level in both models: A state with this rule may have its BSF level higher by about 2% age points, ceteris paribus. This requirement may have worked in two directions to hit this target. In one way, by balancing the budget, the legislature reduces the possibility of drawing down the BSF to fill in revenue holes. In the other, balancing the current budget may have meant controlling current year expenditure within available means and thus the state is able to set aside deposits into the BSF. Allowing carryover of deficits into the next budget cycle also raises the BSF balance. This is an expected result, because tolerating deficits in the current fiscal year and being less stringent on the statutory balanced budget rule means the state does not need to spend all its current BSF balance to wipe out the deficits. The practice of allowing deficits makes more sense if we imagine a scenario where the fiscal situation experiences little improvement in the year following a recession and therefore the need for BSF continues.

Among the state politics variables, political party confrontation between the governor and the legislature may increase the balance level, that is, such a political scenario serves as a guard for the BSF – the confrontation makes it more difficult for either side to take money away from BSF. A better interpretation can be that unless the fiscal situation turns out to be really urgent, it would not be easy for the two major players of the appropriation process to come to agreement. Linking the coefficients of this variable to those for the "use of BSF by appropriation" renders this interpretation more reasonable. Democrats, when they are the majority in the House, tend to spend money from, or deposit less money into, the BSF so that BSF balance falls by 0.8 percentage points.

3.4.3.1 Relative Effects of the Features

Now look at the relative effects of the structural features by running regressions with each group of these features separately, dropping the defaults. The results are in Table 3.8. In the use purposes group (Panel A), statistically significant coefficients for "revenue shortage" and "any purpose" indicate that relative to the default variable,

Table 3.8 Effects of structural features, 1979–1999, with defaults. Dependent variable is BSF balance level as percent of general fund expenditure

Independent variables	Coef	t-stat
Panel A: purpose of use, default="for cash flow"		
Use for revenue shortage	**–0.023	–1.90
Use for emergencies	–0.007	–0.76
Use for any purpose	**–0.036	–2.00
Prob>F	0.00	
DW statistic	1.92	
R^2	0.12	
Panel B: sources of BSF, default="from special revenue"		
Funding by formula	**0.034	2.10
Funding from general fund surplus	0.011	0.93
Funding by appropriation	0.011	1.20
Prob>F	0.00	
DW statistic	1.94	
R^2	0.12	
Panel C: maximum balance allowable, default="Cap I"		
Cap II: 4 up to 7%	0.010	0.93
Cap III: 7 up to 12%	0.019	1.60
Cap IV: No limit to balance level	**0.033	2.10
Prob>F	0.00	
DW statistic	1.96	
R^2	0.12	
Panel D: procedure for use approval, default="executive discretion"		
Use by appropriation	0.008	1.11
Use by predetermined formula	***0.039	2.50
Prob>F	0.00	
DW statistic	1.93	
R^2	0.12	

Significance levels: *10%; **5%; and ***1%

both uses reduce BSF balances, the latter carrying a larger effect than the former. In the BSF sources group (Panel B), all three estimates are positive, though only "by formula" is statistically significant, with the largest coefficient. The results are a clue that "from special revenue" as used by states in this data set may not be a reliable source to fund BSF. For the cap variables (Panel C), though only "cap IV" is statistically significant, all three are positive and the coefficients rise with the cap level, indicating the possibility that higher caps lead to higher balance levels. For use-approval procedures (Panel D), "use by formula" obviously better keeps the BSF balance than by "executive discretion" and "use by appropriation" shows a positive sign though it is not statistically significant.

Table 3.9 Subsets of data by level of previous year growth rate of gross state product (GSP)

Group	Column	(1)		(2)		(3)		(4)	
	Select if GSP_{t-1}	< 0%		0 up to 2%		2 up to 4%		4 up to 6%	
	Independent variables	Coef	t-stat	Coef	t-stat	Coef	t-stat	Coef	t-stat
Group	UUB balance level	0.052	0.42	**0.101	2.49	*0.045	1.90	0.023	0.45
A	*Purpose of use*, default = "for cash flow"								
	Use for revenue shortage	***–0.153	–1.67	***–0.036	–3.96	–0.012	–1.49	0.009	0.60
	Use for emergencies	–0.016	–0.70	–0.002	–0.20	*–0.009	–1.89	–0.010	–0.63
	Use for any purpose	***–0.173	–3.33	***–0.045	–3.90	***–0.028	–2.67	***–0.051	–3.12
B	*Source of BSF*, default = "from special revenue"								
	Funding by formula					–0.002	–0.22	**0.101	2.31
	Funding from general fund surplus					0.004	0.75	**0.084	2.24
	Funding by appropriation					0.007	1.45	***0.120	3.28
C	*Maximum balance allowable*, default = "Cap I: 2 up to 4%"								
	Cap II: 4 up to 7%			–0.007	–0.73	0.010	1.59	0.012	0.71
	Cap III: 7 up to 12%			–0.014	–1.30	0.004	0.45	***0.084	3.82
	Cap IV: No limit to balance level			–0.024	–1.57	–0.010	–1.30	0.028	0.85
	Minimum requirement of balance			–0.003	–0.37	***–0.018	–2.98	***0.033	2.65
D	*Procedure for use approval*, default = "by executive discretion"								
	Use by appropriation	–0.005	–0.27	**0.007	1.22	0.004	1.05		
	Use by predetermined formula	–0.222	–0.59	***0.046	3.91	***0.056	3.94		
	Balanced budget requirements								
	Governor submit a balanced budget	0.044	1.34	–0.004	–0.53	***0.016	3.04	0.006	0.46
	Legislature pass a balanced budget	0.007	0.29	***0.022	3.35	***0.014	2.71	0.000	–0.01
	Governor sign a balanced budget	0.028	1.30	–0.004	–0.65	***–0.016	–3.66	0.002	0.19
	May carry over deficits	0.024	0.94	0.003	0.52	–0.004	–0.90	–0.007	–0.82

(continued)

Table 3.9 (continued)

Group	Column	(1)		(2)		(3)		(4)	
	Select if GSP_{t-1}	< 0%		0 up to 2%		2 up to 4%		4 up to 6%	
Group	Independent variables	Coef	t-stat	Coef	t-stat	Coef	t-stat	Coef	t-stat
	Party politics								
	House majority is Democrat	–0.018	–0.82	–0.011	–1.56	0.003	0.61	0.008	1.12
	Senate majority is Democrat	–0.006	–0.26	–0.004	–0.59	**0.008	1.93	–0.005	–0.70
	House dominance ratio	0.001	0.19	–0.002	–0.83	–0.002	–1.28	*–0.0044	–1.73
	Senate dominance ratio	0.001	0.08	0.002	0.53	–0.001	–0.30	0.000	0.06
	Prob>F	0.00		0.00		0.00		0.00	
	R-squared	0.79		0.84		0.66		0.90	
	Adj R-squared	0.57		0.74		0.54		0.80	
	Number of observations	52		95		155		133	

3.4.3.2 Patterns in Boom and Lean Years

The patterns of BSF balance in different phases of state economy are better revealed from regressions with the four subsamples of the data. These results are presented in Table 3.9, which provide a clear comparison with results from Table 3.7. While three purpose of the fund (Group A) present a negative sign relative to "use for cash flow", "use for revenue shortfall" is negative at statistically significant levels only when the economy is poor (GSP growth<0) or weak (GSP 0–2%). The negative sign when GSP is fair (2–4%) may indicate that this purpose is applicable not only for the real lean years but also possible in good years, which is not surprising if we recall that state laws allow quite different, and wide, uses under the heading of "revenue shortfall", technical errors of revenue estimation being one example. And the sign turns positive when the economy is strong (GSP growth 4–6%), though not significant. "Use for emergency" is not protruding, in comparison to "revenue shortage" and "any purpose," when the economy is poor or weak, but it becomes so when GSP is fair. By far the most consistent result and largest coefficient is use of BSF for any purpose – whatever the economy is, this usage reduces BSF balance by the largest margin.

The three funding sources (Group B) do not produce statistically significant results when the state economy is fair (column 3). The point estimates become statistically significant when GSP growth is strong (column 4): Funding by either formula, general fund surplus or appropriation all lead to higher balances than by special revenue.

The balance cap variables (Group C) are negative and not significant when GSP growth is weak, all turn positive and two also significant with a strong economy. In general, higher caps lead to higher BSF balances. When economic growth is strong, "high cap" increases the BSF level by the largest margin at a percent significant level. The BSF "minimum balance requirement" is negative with fair GSP growth, but it turns positive at strong GSP rates, suggesting that this requirement may be effective only when economy is strong.

Point estimates for use-approval procedures (Group D) are not significant in the lean year model (column 1). With weak or fair economic growth, both "use by appropriation" and "use by formula" can better maintain BSF than "by executive discretion" – the easiest way to withdraw money from the fund. In contrast, "use by formula" can best safeguard the reserves. The UUB-BSF correlation is not significant with negative GSP growth. When GSP growth is marginal and fair, UUB goes in the same direction as BSF, and at higher GSP growth rates, the result is not significant anymore. Results about the BBRs show no obviously consistent patterns.

3.4.3.3 Relative Effects of the Features in Lean Versus Boom Years

Finally running regressions by matching the group of the structural features with GSP growth rates reveals more on the relative effects of the features in lean years versus boom years; the results are shown in Table 3.10. Panel A is on the BSF purposes, with "for cash flow" as the default. All three purposes show a lower balance with a poor or weak economy (columns 1 and 2), "for any purpose" carrying a larger

Table 3.10 Effects of structural features with defaults, by groups and by GSP stages

Panel	Column	(1)		(2)		(3)		(4)	
	Select if GSP_{t-1}	< 0%		0 up to 2%		2 up to 4%		4 up to 6%	
	Independent variables	Coef	t-stat	Coef	t-stat	Coef	t-stat	Coef	t-stat
A	*Purpose of use*, default = "for cash flow"								
	For revenue shortage	***−0.136	−6.99	**−0.069	−2.08	0.004	0.41	0.003	0.20
	For emergencies	−0.011	−0.72	−0.002	−0.04	**−0.014	−2.43	***−0.122	−4.51
	For any purpose	***−0.146	−4.20	***−0.081	−2.46	−0.012	−0.98	***−0.095	−5.01
	Prob > F	0.00		0.03		0.00		0.00	
	R-squared	0.73		0.49		0.36		0.87	
	Comparison: default = "for revenue shortage"								
	For cash flow	0.076	1.56	−0.007	−1.11	−0.006	−1.25	−0.003	−0.20
	For emergencies	***−0.240	−5.07	−0.014	−1.38	**−0.011	−2.14	***−0.116	−4.30
	For any purpose	***−0.133	−3.44	**−0.021	−2.05	*−0.013	−1.72	***−0.095	−5.01
	Prob > F	0.00		0.00		0.00		0.00	
	R-squared	0.88		0.59		0.59		0.87	
B	*Source of BSF*, default = "by special revenue"								
	By formula					***0.072	2.61	0.030	1.52
	From general fund surplus					***0.066	2.89	***0.109	6.49
	By appropriation					*−0.032	−1.74	*0.040	1.63
	Prob > F					0.00		0.00	
	R-squared					0.74		0.87	
C	*Maximum balance allowable*, default = "Cap I: 2 up to 4%"								
	Cap II: 4 up to 7%			0.010	1.52	0.003	0.20	0.020	1.25
	Cap III: 7 up to 12%			***0.023	2.89	***0.055	2.77	***0.079	5.01
	Cap IV: no limit to balance level			0.018	1.58	**0.037	2.01	***0.110	6.13
	Prob > F			0.00		0.00		0.00	
	R-squared			0.60		0.76		0.87	

D	*Procedure for use approval*, default = "by executive discretion"							
	By appropriation	***0.133	2.73	**0.011	2.00	**0.037	2.02	
	By formula	0.057	1.06	***0.046	4.31	***0.080	4.60	
	Prob > F	0.00		0.00		0.00		
	R-Squared	0.88		0.65		0.76		
	Comparison: default = "by formula"							
	By executive discretion	–0.007	–0.13	0.007	0.33			
	By appropriation	***0.233	4.92	**0.034	2.08			
	Prob > F	0.00		0.00				
	R-squared	0.88		0.58				
	Number of observations	52		95		155		133

coefficient than "for revenue shortage". This corresponds to and confirms the results from the full model in lean and boom years (Table 3.9). When the economy is fair or strong (columns 3 and 4), "for revenue shortage" is not negative any more though not statistically significant, and "for emergency" erodes the BSF balance, which makes intuitive sense in that during boom years, major uses of BSF are likely for natural disasters as opposed to revenue shortage. "For any purpose" remains negative and significant in boom years, confirming the lessons from previous models. Then I change the default for this group from "for cash flow" to "for revenues shortage"; the change bears two findings that confirm results from the "cash flow default" model. First, "for any purpose" cuts BSF balance deeper than "for revenue shortage" under all economic conditions; second, "for emergency" also cuts BSF deeper, particularly when the economy is poor or strong. While the latter makes sense, the former may sound a warning: The –0.24 estimate may be due to either inadequate reserve for natural disasters or other disguised reasons not politically correct to make explicit (we will find a clue soon). Estimates for "cash flow" are not significant.

Panel B is on BSF funding sources. Years of fair economic growth (Column 3) show "by formula" as a strong BSF balance pusher and "from general fund surplus" follows closely behind; "by appropriation" comes even worse than "by special revenue." With a strong economy the picture changes: General fund surplus presents the largest estimate and "by appropriation" turns positive. These results make intuitive sense: Boom years generate the luxury of more abundant general fund surpluses and as a result the legislature is more willing to allocate funds for reserve funds.

Panel C is of the cap variables. Though the 4–7% cap generates positive (but not significant) results relative to the low-cap default, the 7–12% cap poses the largest positive coefficients in weak and fair economies; and setting no limit to the balance level further pushes up the reserve level in strong growth years. The message is that a high(er) cap is the best way to restore BSF balance as soon as the economy is rising and to maintain high reserves during boom years.

Panel D is of use-approval procedures. The two regressions here provide a possible answer to the question posed during the discussion of use purposes. With "executive discretion" as default, "by appropriation" shows a positive and significant point estimate that is much larger than the one for "by formula" (0.133 versus 0.057, Column 1). Changing the default to "by formula," "by discretion" is negative, as expected; but "by appropriation" poses again a large coefficient. The message is now clear: Even when the economy is poor and the predetermined formula ensures that BSF is used for its designed purposes, the "by appropriation" procedure may be a block to the timely use of BSF. A plausible explanation is the time lag from identifying the problem to policy formulation and then implementation. It may not be that the legislature is not cooperating with the executive branch; it is simply the process and procedure.[37] Therefore, executive officials may have used "emergencies" as an excuse (Panel A,

[37] There is at least anecdotal evidence to this finding. In my spring 2001 interview of state budget directors and officers (see note 3), some state officials complained to me that when the executive branch urgently needs money from BSF, the appropriation often takes far too long to be "practically effective."

Column 1, comparison group). This "advantage" of "by appropriation" over "by formula" remains true in years of weak economy (Column 2, point estimate 0.034), when some states still need to use BSF to give the economy a boost.

3.4.4 Policy Recommendations

State BSF laws contain huge variation; the four groups of structural features are preliminary abstractions of them in an effort to understand and obtain estimates the effects of these features on BSF balance levels. This chapter has addressed only some aspects of the research question; the rest are reserved for future studies. From the above results four tentative policy recommendations emerge, one on each of the structural feature groups. These four suggestions are offered here for consideration by state governments in designing their BSF legislation or revising their existing BSF laws if they target higher BSF balances.

On the purpose of a state BSF, it is *best to be exclusively reserved for revenue shortfall and budget stabilization. Broad uses should be avoided.* States have assigned different, and often multiple, purposes for their BSF; the most appropriate single purpose is to reserve BSF for revenue shortfalls, so that BSF is maintained and stocked up in boom years for budget stabilization in downturns. Allowing BSF to be used for "any" purpose is not good policy or even no policy. For shelter from tax revolts, a few states combined their working capital fund and budget stabilization fund. If the combination brings more cash into BSF and makes the fund more politically operable, it is good strategy.

On the funding sources for BSF, *by formula seems to be a more preferable option* while special revenue, in particular one-time deals as a source may go astray. Funding a BSF by formula is worth considering because a preset formula potentially minimizes political interference from elected officials which is common when BSF relies on general fund surplus or appropriation as its source. This is because surplus is not necessarily the sure outcome of budget execution even in boom years and (at least some) legislators may favor more current spending for winning reelection than targeting longer-term stabilization of state expenditures.

On the amounts of BSF balance allowable, *setting the cap at the high range (7–12%) helps most increase the BSF balance level.* Over half of the states in this sample (24 out of 38) by year 2000 were following the old rule-of-thumb 5% in setting their cap at the 2–7% range. If these states are serious about maintaining an effective countercyclical fiscal tool, they need to reconsider their current cap on the BSF balance. No doubt, popular support is indispensable – if the populace perceives the BSF as idle money that wastes their tax dollars, the high cap will lack support from the grassroots level. On the other hand, support from both parties in the House and the Senate is crucial as well. Therefore, setting a high cap is technically desirable, but politically demanding. To put it into practice takes courage, wisdom, and skills.

On the use-approval procedures, *use by formula seems to work the best for maintaining BSF balances while serving the design purpose of BSF for budget stabilization during downturns.* The predetermined formula precludes most political manipulation: When the state economy or revenue is down to the preset benchmark, the signal triggers automatic use of BSF, which minimizes the lags in the recognition of downturn, in policy making after a recession. In contrast is use by appropriation which involves executive-legislative cooperation – executive officials first identify the need for using BSF balances and initiate it to the legislature which then deliberates the proposal for adoption. This process can eliminate many of the possible discretionary uses by the executive branch. However, there exists the possibility of considerable delay in the recognition of a recession and in policy making as well as adoption. How to synchronize appropriation of BSF use with practical urgency for the reserves remains an issue for further exploration.

References

Advisory Commission on Intergovernmental Relations (ACIR) (1978) Counter-cyclical aid and economic stabilization, Report A-69. Washington, DC

Advisory Commission on Intergovernmental Relations (ACIR) (1987) Fiscal discipline in the federal system: experience of the states. Washington, DC

Allan IJ (1990) Unreserved fund balance and local government finance. Research Bulletin, Research and Analysis on Current Issues. GFOA, Chicago

Alt JE, Lowry RC (1994) Divided government, fiscal institutions, and budget deficits: evidence from the states. Am Polit Sci Rev 88(4):811–828

Alt JE, Lowry RC (2000) A dynamic model of state budget outcomes under divided partisan government. J Polit 62(4):1035–1069

Bretschneider SI, Gorr WL, Grizzle G, Klay E (1989) Political and organizational influences on the accuracy of forecasting state government revenues. Int J Forecast 5:307–319

U.S. Congress (1985) Federal and state roles in economic stabilization. United States House of Representatives, 99th Congress, 1st Session, report 99–460. Washington, DC

Congressional Budget Office (CBO) (1998) States' use of surplus funds. Washington, DC

Douglas JW, Gaddie RK (2002) State rainy day funds and fiscal crises: rainy day funds and the 1990–1990 recession revisited. Public Budg Finance 22(1):19–30

Eckl C (1993) Rainy day funds. NCSL Legisbrief, vol 1, no 9, March. Denver

Fitch IBCA (2000) Impact of management practices on municipal credit. Special Report in its Public Finance Newsletter, 4 May 2000. http://www.fitchibca.com. Accessed June 2000

Gold SD (1983) Preparing for the next recession: rainy day funds and other tools for the states. Legislative Finance Paper No. 41. National conference of State Legislatures, Denver

Gold SD, Eckl C (1984) State fiscal condition in 1984. NCSL Legislative Finance Paper 42, Denver

Government Finance Officers Association (GFOA) (1999) Develop policy on stabilization funds. In: Recommended Budget Practices 17, a framework for improved state and local government budgeting, Section 4.1, Chicago

Hou Y (2003) What stabilizes state general fund spending during downturns: budget stabilization fund, general fund unreserved undesignated balance, or both?". Public Budg Finance 23(3):64–91

Hou Y (2004) Budget stabilization fund: structural features of the enabling legislation and balance level. Public Budg Finance 24(3):38–64

Hou Y (2006) Budgeting for fiscal stability over the business cycle. Public Adm Rev 66(5):730–741

Hou Y, Moynihan D, Ingraham PW (2003) Capacity, management and performance: exploring the links. Am Rev Public Adm 33(3):295–315

Joyce PG (2001) What's so magical about five percent? A nationwide look at factors that influence the optimal size of state rainy day funds. Public Budg Finance 21(2):62–87

Knight B, Levinson A (1999) Rainy day funds and state government savings. Natl Tax J 52(3):459–472

Michigan Legislation (1977) Michigan Compiled Laws, Chapter 18: Department of Management and Budget, Section 351–359

National Association of State Budget Officers (NASBO) (1977-presnet) Fiscal Survey of States series since 1977. Washington, DC

National Conference of State Legislators (NCSL) (1998) State tax and expenditure limits, Denver

National Governor's Association (1977-2010). Book of the states series, Lexington

Navin JC, Navin LJ (1997) The optimal size of counter-cyclical budget stabilization funds: a case study of Ohio. Public Budg Finance 17(2):114–127

New York Legislation (1946) New York State Consolidated Laws, Chapter 56 State Finance Law, Article VI: Funds of the State, Section 92

Pollock R, Suyderhoud JP (1986) The role of rainy day funds in achieving fiscal stability. Natl Tax J 43(4):485–497

Poterba JM (1994) State responses to fiscal crises: the effects of budgetary institutions and politics. J Polit Econ 102(4):799–821

Prais SJ, Winsten CB (1954) Trend estimators and serial correlation. Cowles Commission discussion paper no. 383, Chicago

Rafuse RW (1965) Cyclical behavior of state-local finances. In: Musgrave RA (ed) Essays in fiscal federalism. The Brookings Institution, Washington, DC, pp 63–121

Rivlin AM (1987) Economics and the political process. Am Econ Rev 77(1):1–10

Sobel RS, Holcombe RG (1996) The impact of state rainy day funds in easing state fiscal crises during the 1990–1991 recession. Public Budg Finance 16(3):28–48

United States General Accounting Office (1999) Budgeting for emergencies – state practices and federal implications. Washington, DC

Vasche JD, Williams B (1987) Optimal governmental budgeting contingency reserve funds. Public Budg Finance 7(1):66–82

Wagner GA (1999) Essays on the political economy of state government saving and the role of budget stabilization funds. Ph.D. dissertation, University of West Virginia, Morgantown

Part II
Boom-Year Savings and Effects in Bust Years

Introduction

This part contains four chapters that test the effects of boom-year savings in bust years. The four chapters each deal with one different aspect of this broad policy issue. Chapter 4 takes general fund surplus and budget stabilization fund as cofunctional policy instruments and looks into their interaction during supplementation, assuming substitution effects in supplementation process. The new instrument, BSF, interacts with the old, GFS, causing supplementation and substitution effects. This chapter conducts empirical analyses and finds evidence that despite partial substitution (15 %), supplementation dominates (85 %) the interaction between the two policy instruments, that the reinforcing effect from the new instrument may trickle off over time, and that a reinforcing instrument can be effective over a certain span of policy duration.

Chapter 5 explores how the saving behavior of state governments is affected by the adoption of budget stabilization funds and by the balanced budget requirements (BBR). BSF and BBR were adopted for different reasons; both could have influenced state saving behavior with their unique design features. This chapter examines the effects of BSF and BBR over three economic cycles; I find evidence that adopting a BSF can raise state savings by 2.5 percentage points and that some BBR rules may also boost the savings level.

Chapter 6 examines the distribution of the effects of boom-year savings across three expenditure types over the economic cycle – general, own-source, and general fund expenditures of the states during downturns and upturns. The results show a "division of work" between BSF and GFS: Though the use of BSF concentrates on own-source spending, BSF are used to boost general expenditure more than general fund expenditure in downturns but to increase general fund expenditure more than general expenditure in upturns. The effects of GFS are significant only on general fund expenditure in upturns. This finding suggests that states may have some unstated or implicit "strategy" on when and where to use the two types of savings. The specifics of the strategy need to be further explored.

Chapter 7 extends countercyclical fiscal policy to government capacity in the area of financial management. Assuming a basic challenge for state governments is to maintain budgetary stability and program predictability in economic downturns, states can best meet this challenge by developing what "countercyclical fiscal capacity" – creation and use of financial tools – that help states maintain countercyclical spending and program stability during revenue shortfalls. The chapter tests the effects of fiscal reserves on mitigating spending cuts and tax increases during the recessions in 1991 and 2001. Evidence confirms the efficacy of countercyclical fiscal capacity and argues for greater investments in this aspect of government capacity.

Chapter 4
Patterns of State Savings with Budget Stabilization Funds and General Fund Surplus

Abstract In pursuing a policy goal, government often reinforces one instrument with another. These policy tools are called "cofunctional instruments" for supplementation. But substitution effects may emerge in the supplementation process. This chapter examines such effects between BSF and GFS as two major instruments of the budget stabilization policy at the subnational level. American states used to keep savings as general fund surplus (conventionally but incorrectly referred to as general fund balance) and have over the past few decades added budget stabilization funds to store reserves during boom years. The new instrument interacts with the old, causing supplementation and substitution effects. This chapter conducts empirical analyses and contributes to the academic literature and policy practice with evidence over three recent economic cycles. The tests control for features and adoption of the budget stabilization fund, state economy, budgetary institutions, state politics, and time trend. Results from the empirical tests show that despite partial substitution (15%), supplementation dominates (85%) the interaction between the two policy instruments. The reinforcing effect from the new instrument, however, may trickle off over time. The chapter concludes that a reinforcing instrument can be effective over a certain span of policy duration.

4.1 Introduction

In order to achieve a policy goal, government and its entities often need to employ more than one instrument. The need for multiple instruments is due from many reasons; for example, certain instruments better fit some regions of the jurisdiction,

---

This chapter draws heavily from data and analysis in Hou Y, Brewer G (2010) Substitution and supplementation between co-functional policy instruments – evidence from state budget stabilization practices. Public Adm Rev 70(6): 915–25, published by Wiley-Blackwell.

Y. Hou, *State Government Budget Stabilization: Policy, Tools, and Impacts*, Studies in Public Choice 8, DOI 10.1007/978-1-4614-6061-9_4,

some groups of the society, or some of the (national or state) economy but not the others. Another reason that is often seen and fits the subject of this book is that after one instrument has been in use for some time, it becomes subject to resistance born out of the implementation process and thus gradually loses its "teeth." This said instrument may stay in use, but before it becomes completely blunt, it becomes necessary, even essential, to design and implement a second instrument with the purpose of reinforcing, and perhaps reviving, the first instrument. We call these two instruments "cofunctional instruments," with the second instrument designed and employed for supplementation. In due course, a substitution effect may emerge. That is, when the first and the second instruments are deployed together, the total effect from the two instruments may not be the sum of the separate effects of the two, because there may be some "discount" – the new instrument subsumes part of the role of the original instrument and substitutes part of its effect. This type of supplementation and substitution is common in policy processes, but despite the large literature on technical details of policy implementation (Pressman and Wildavsky 1973; Bardach 1977) and on the concepts of failure, learning, and redirection in implementation (May 1992; Bennett and Howlett 1992), the phenomenon of supplementation and substitution has not been adequately documented and explained. This chapter attempts to fill in this niche by examining such effects in the emerging and increasingly important policy area of state governments over a quarter century (1978–2003): Does the adoption and use of the budget stabilization fund substitute or supplement the role of the general fund surplus in mitigating revenue shortfalls during an economic downturn?

This chapter is organized as follows. In Section 4.2, I briefly review the development of the economic stabilization function of government in general and the countercyclical fiscal policy and policy instruments at the subnational level. In Section 4.3, I discuss the possibility of substitution and supplementation of the two policy instruments. I begin Section 4.4 with a statistical analysis of the trends of state savings over the sample period and then deliberate on empirical methodology and model specifications. In Section 4.5, I present and discuss the empirical results and results from sensitivity tests. I conclude the chapter by summarizing the implications of this study for state budget stabilization practices and the broader topic of the interaction effects between cofunctional policy instruments.

4.2 State Policy Instruments for Budget Stabilization

As I have discussed in Chapter 3, economic stabilization in public finance theory, as advocated by John Maynard Keynes (1936) and Richard Musgrave (1959), is one important function of government. Though controversy remains over its use and effects, central governments all over the world now seem to believe the stabilization function is necessary and politically convenient to pursue, especially when signs of deep recession emerge. The policy for the stabilization function is "countercyclical," which means essentially that government uses monetary and fiscal tools to stimulate economic growth during recessions. Countercyclical fiscal policy is usually the exclusive domain of central governments.

In the USA, state and local governments generally did not follow this policy orientation of the federal government. Theoretical analysis demonstrates that states and localities should not (Oates 1972). But the bitter experience from the Great Depression was translated into a policy: Though states are more limited than the federal government in stabilizing the overall economy, they can at least try to stabilize their budgets to provide smooth, predictable service levels. I have discussed this last point in Chapter 2. Since the mid-1930s, it has been a long-standing practice of state governments to maintain sizable "general fund balance" (GFB) – surpluses that are used not merely as working capital for managerial convenience but more importantly for budget stabilization. The surpluses are fiscal reserves for revenue shortfalls and emergencies. The general fund surplus as a rule accumulates in boom years and draws down in lean years. Thus, boom-year surpluses began to serve as countercyclical savings against revenue shortfalls from recessions (Refuse 1965; Fisher 1984) and made countercyclical fiscal policy accessible to subnational policy makers.

The accumulation of general fund surplus as a policy instrument relies much more heavily on prosperity of the economy (the revenue side) than on budgetary policy (the expenditure side) (Firestone 1960), which means that general fund surplus is not an adequate instrument to implement the countercyclical budget stabilization policy at the state level, for at least two reasons. The first reason is political – spending pressure from politicians who seek reelection and taxpayers who seek utmost immediate current benefits. Such pressure is particularly strong in boom years: When tax revenues exceed current outlay needs, taxpayers demand either higher levels or quality of services or tax reductions, or both. Politicians tend to follow voters' demands. The second reason is institutional – all states are subject to one or more forms of balanced budget requirements. These binding requirements must be implemented without regard to the ups and downs of the economy. Balanced budget requirements straddle over the business cycle: Its foot on the recession years kicks away deficits; the other foot, on the boom-year side, bounces off big surpluses. Such mechanisms of these requirements are insensitive to not only deficits but also big surpluses. The anti-deficit leg of such requirements has been widely known, but their anti-surplus leg has evaded most academic attention. It is this second leg of the requirements in conjunction with political spending pressure under electoral politics that has made it almost impossible for states to accumulate as much general fund surplus in boom years as they need to offset revenue shortfalls in lean years.

As I have said in Chapter 3, the budget stabilization fund was adopted to overcome the two aforementioned hurdles to implementing a countercyclical budget stabilization policy. The budget stabilization fund as a second, reinforcing instrument of CCFP is often established with enabling legislation which fends off spending pressure during economic expansion. The fund stores extra revenues from booms and protects the savings for exclusive use during economic downturns. The money cannot be used for other purposes (Hou 2003). Budget stabilization funds also circumvent the anti-surplus articles of balanced budget requirements by placing the savings outside the jurisdiction of balanced budget requirements. This working mechanism successfully overcomes the political and institutional hurdles states face in trying to implement a countercyclical fiscal policy. Meanwhile, their general fund surplus remains intact as a conventional instrument of state budget stabilization policy. From the mid-1940s to the 1970s, the overall economy was strong with robust growth rates; every state was in a construction and expansion mode with little lasting concern for downturns (Oates 1972). The tide changed in the mid-1970s: Two consecutive oil shocks and stagflation altered the states' mind-set. The 1978 "Proposition 13" in California triggered a nationwide wave of tax revolts that cut deep into state coffers. Then, the double-dip recession of the early 1980s led to widespread adoption of the budget stabilization fund among the states as an additional policy instrument to stabilize their budgets. Prodded by multiple factors, states began to take the budget stabilization policy and the new CCFP instrument more seriously than ever before.

4.3 Supplementation and Substitution Between Policy Instruments

The state-level countercyclical budget stabilization policy with GFS and BSF as policy instruments provides a golden opportunity to observe the policy implementation process and test the interaction effects between these two cofunctional policy instruments. Because the budget stabilization fund is designed to protect savings, its adoption reinforces the countercyclical feature of the policy by increasing the amount of savings. Thus, a supplementation effect is expected. However, the trigger for the design and adoption of the second instrument, the stabilization fund, was the inadequacy of the first instrument: The general fund surplus was vulnerable to spending pressure and limitations from balanced budget requirements. In this sense, introducing the second instrument was a state's choice – the more vulnerable a state's general fund surplus, the stronger the incentive for the state to adopt the stabilization fund. The two instruments are therefore endogenous: States that have vulnerable general fund surpluses may be more inclined toward adopting the stabilization fund; furthermore, these states may find it worthwhile, for better policy outcome, to shift at least part of their year-end surpluses into the stabilization fund, which produces a substitution effect. Increases in the stabilization fund are accompanied by decreases in the general fund surplus. In other words, the effect of the stabilization fund on total savings may be inflated because it includes part of the effect from the general fund surplus that has been moved into the legally protected savings haven. This is the interaction between the two instruments, where we expect to observe both the supplementation effect and the substitution effect.

Thus, it is natural to ask: Does adopting the budget stabilization fund as a second saving device increase state net savings dollar for dollar? Or does the stabilization fund add some new net savings but at the same time substitute for some of the original general fund surplus as a mechanism to reduce spending pressure and circumvent the balanced budget requirements? Put another way, do states shift some original general fund surpluses into the stabilization fund to ward off spending pressure and to avoid balanced budget requirements? To provide an answer, we examine state saving levels before and after state adoption of the stabilization fund. A basic assumption is that general fund surpluses and budget stabilization funds are the two major instruments for states to reserve fiscal resources from boom years for use in lean years. There have not been many studies in this specific policy area. Some studies of individual retirement savings have examined the issue of substitution between alternative saving devices. For example, Poterba et al. (1995) examine the interaction between 401(k) and other personal saving devices; Englehardt (2002) looks into the relation between spending distributions and pension accumulation.

There have been only two previous studies on state government saving practices that have been done with great care but generated very different results. Knight and Levinson (1999) analyze data from 47 states in the 1980s and 1990s and find that states with the stabilization fund have higher total savings than states without the fund; states with the fund also have higher savings after adoption of BSF than before. These are expected results confirming the supplementation effect of the second policy instrument. They conclude that deposits into the budget stabilization fund increased total savings dollar for dollar, meaning that there was no substitution between the two instruments. In fact, the authors report coefficients of 1.14 from the fixed-effects model and 1.37 from the OLS model. That is, the second instrument not only does not trigger any substitution from the first instrument but it also multiplies the original effect of the first instrument.

Wagner (2003) uses his own survey data for 42 states from 1974 to 1997. He separates his observations into two groups – states that have stationary (18 states) and nonstationary (10 states) total savings and stabilization funds; his tests on these two subsets generate coefficients of 0.44 for stationary states and 0.49 for nonstationary states. That is, the supplementation effect is small while the substitution effect is very large. The budget stabilization fund is verbatim substitutable with general fund surplus.

These two studies expose an important issue that begs further exploration from the perspective of policy design. If adopting a new saving device increases savings more than the amount deposited into the new device, as Knight and Levinson found, we are doubly blessed and policy design becomes much easier. But we intuitively know that this does not comport with reality. If there is substitution, as Wagner found, we need to know the extent. Substitution of the original instrument by the second one is understandable and acceptable to a certain degree. However, if substitution is substantial, policy makers may need to reevaluate the problem and explore alternative policy instruments.

This chapter expands on previous research and contributes to the literature in several ways. First, because widespread adoption of budget stabilization funds occurred after the 1980–1982 recessions and state general fund surpluses underwent drastic changes in the 1980s due to the tax and expenditure limitations movement, the sample period of this study is FY 1978 through FY 2003, covering three recent business cycles. Second, unlike the previous two studies, this study excludes only one state (Alaska) so that my results may be more representative and generalizable. Third, to provide more evidence on possible differences across adoption years, this study also tests differential effects from three adoption periods and effects of budget stabilization funds in two full business cycles. And finally, to render more convincing results, this study controls for institutional causes of substitution, design features of the stabilization fund, and budgetary institutions.

4.4 Data, Methodology, and Model Specification

4.4.1 State Savings: A Statistical Analysis

To match the diffusion of BSF among the states that occurred mainly from the early 1980s to the early 2000s, the sample period of the data set for this chapter spans three business cycles: the partial pre-1982 cycle and two full cycles, 1983–1992 and 1993–2001. For easy comparison with the two previous studies on this topic (Knight and Levinson 1999 and Wagner 2003), GFS and BSF data are taken from the *Fiscal Survey of States* series (*FSS*) published by the National Association of State Budget Officers (NASBO). The *FSS* series reports BSF only since 1984. For BSF from 1978 to 1983, I use state audited financial reports as data source. Some previous research notice two problems with the *FSS* data: One is non-reporting of general fund deficits and the other is double counting of BSF (Hou 2005). There is nothing I can do about the first problem except using a different data source, which is not an option here. To solve the second problem, I checked each data entry by state and year and cleaned up all double counting of BSF in the series that I have identified as problematic; thus, my data are reliable to the utmost extent I can control.

To illustrate my data and the sample period, let me start with some summary statistics. The term "state savings" refers to the sum of the general fund surplus (GFS) and budget stabilization fund (BSF), the two major instruments of the budget stabilization policy. State average per capita savings from 1978 to 2003 (in year-2000 dollars) present a wide range: Alaska is an extreme outlier among high-saving states, with its total savings about 20 times the 50-state average of $150 and about eight times of Wyoming, the next highest state. Delaware, Hawaii, and North Dakota have savings above $200 per person, and another nine states between $100 and $200. Among states with low savings, Arkansas and Vermont have less than $10 per person. And seven other states have savings below $50. The 49-state (excluding Alaska) average per capita savings before the 1980 recession reached a peak in 1979 at $128; it went down to $40 after the early 1980s recessions, rebounded to $109 in 1989, and was drawn down to $44 at the end of 1991. After the long expansion of the 1990s, savings peaked in 2000 at $163 before the year-2001 downturn.

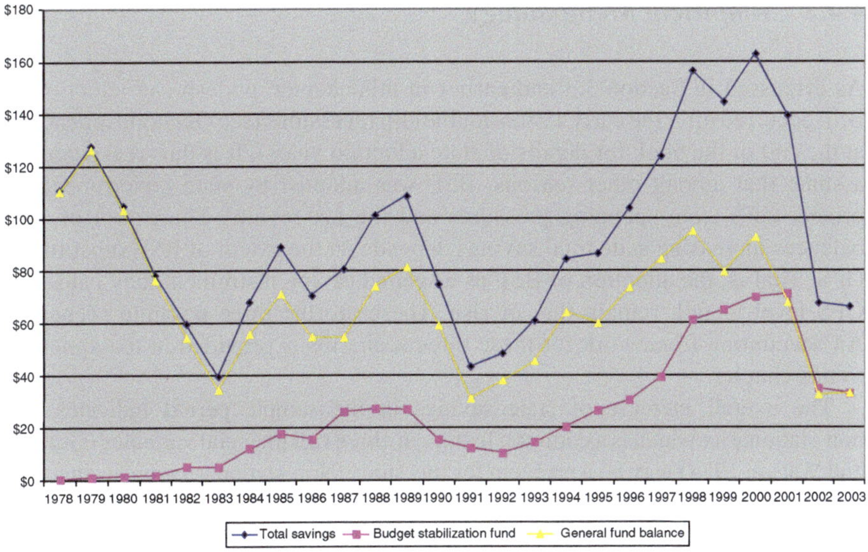

Fig. 4.1 State average per capita real savings

The average shows an over-time increase of 27.5% from the first to the third economic cycle ($163 over $128), indicating substantial increase of net savings, as shown in Fig. 4.1.

To test supplementation and substitution effects, I need to decompose total savings into the two saving instruments: BSF was below $1 in 1978 and was only about $5 in 1983, inadequate to be a major factor in combating the recessions of the early 1980s. Then BSF increased to over $27 by 1990; it played a role in mitigating the 1990–1991 recession – states drew down their BSF balance by 39% in 1990–1992. With more states adopting this instrument, the average BSF rose to over $71 by the end of FY 2001, and BSF became an important device in stabilizing state budgets during the 2001 recession. As a percentage of total savings, BSF rose from only 1% in 1979 to 25% by 1989 and further to 43% in 2000.

With the increase of BSF, the GFS level did go down, discounting some of the increases in total savings. With the pre-1980 peak at 127 dollars, GFS fell to 82 dollars before the start of FY 1990, the decrease being more than the absolute increases in BSF. GFS returned to 93 dollars in 2000, at only 73% of the 1979 peak level. This decrease was less than the BSF increase. With more states adopting BSF, the average total saving level went up by 27.5% despite the reduction of GFS. The fall of GFS and the rise of BSF are apparently sensitive to time. Thus, it makes perfect sense not only to check the effects of BSF during the whole sample period but the effects during the few different economic cycles in the sample period. I will create several variables of the economic cycles in the sample to capture such variation.

4.4.2 Empirical Methodology

As discussed in Section 3.3 and earlier in this chapter, widespread adoption of BSF occurred after the early 1980s double-dip recessions (see General Appendix 1 at the end of the book for details of state adoption years). It is thus reasonable to assume that among other reasons, BSF was adopted by state governments to protect GFS from spending pressures and the tax revolts. The extent of BSF balances increasing state total savings depends on the extent of BSF substituting GFS. That is, the adoption of BSF as a second saving instrument may cause the GFS level to fall, remain flat, or rise. These are the three possible scenarios. An accounting framework for these three scenarios is provided in the appendix to this chapter.

The overall increase of state savings in the sample period indicates that non-stationarity which is a common feature in almost all financial variables (Granger and Watson 1984) may be a problem for this study. Non-stationarity means that data points tend to rise over the sample period with no inclination to return to the mean value, thus causing distortion to results of estimation and to the error term, making them unreliable. Non-stationarity comes in two types, trend non-stationarity and difference non-stationarity. In this chapter, I take several steps to handle these problems. First, all monetary figures are transformed into year-2000 per capita dollars. To treat potential trend non-stationarity in state savings, a time trend variable is created with year 1978 as the start (1) and each following year as one number higher. As for difference non-stationarity, because the total BSF balance is capped in most states at a certain percentage point (2, 5, or 7) of their general fund revenue or expenditure (see Section 3.3 for details) and the BSF balance fluctuates a lot from year to year (even in boom years), difference non-stationarity does not seem to be a major concern for this study.

Another potential technical problem is serial correlation of the first or higher order in the disturbance which is common with most panel data sets. I conduct the Durbin-Watson test, the Durbin's alternative test, and the Breusch-Godfrey test; I find first-order but no higher-order serial correlation. For treatment, I use the Prais-Winsten model with state- and year-fixed effects for correction. As shown in the empirical results, the problem is corrected to a satisfactory level.

While it is a convention to exclude both Alaska and Hawaii as in state studies' offshore states, I exclude only Alaska because it is an outlier in terms of its extremely large BSF balance (as explained in the previous subsection) and huge general fund "loans" from BSF. In fact, the source of its BSF is unique and the operation of its general fund has been different from other states since the creation of BSF. Thus, the exclusion of Alaska is reasonable and necessary. I choose to retain Hawaii because I believe this state presents no extremism in its saving behavior. Its distance from the continent or being offshore does not make the case for its exclusion from the whole. The data include all the 48 other states because they are not outliers and wider inclusion makes the sample more representative for generalizability of the results.

4.4.3 Model Specifications

The dependent variable, S_{it}, is per capita total savings which is the sum of per capita BSF and GFS. This construct will generate coefficients that will reveal the effects of BSF adoption on total savings. The empirical model is specified as the following form:

$$S_{it} = \alpha + \delta_1 BSF_{it} + \delta_2 B_{it} + \beta_1{}'X_{it} + \beta_2{}'Z_{it} + \lambda_i + \gamma_t + \mu_{it}.$$

where λ = state effects *and* i = 1 to 49, and γ = year effects and t = 1 to 26. The key variable in the model is *BSF*, real per capita BSF balance level. Because total savings in the sample period show a trend of net increase (except during recession years when it is drawn down), the expected sign for coefficients of δ_1 is positive. A coefficient of 1 indicates dollar-for-dollar increase of total savings by BSF – supplementation effect with no substitution. A coefficient smaller than 1 indicates substitution of GFS by BSF; the difference between 1 and the coefficient $(1-\delta_1)$ is the extent of substitution. A coefficient of larger than 1 would point to multiplication of GFS by BSF; that is, one more dollar of BSF not only increases total savings by 1 dollar but also raises GFS by the difference between the coefficient and 1, which is the scenario where a state increases not only its BSF but also GFS at the same time; the causal relation, however, is not clear.

As shown in Fig. 4.1, BSF balances trend up in my sample period as in that of the two previous studies lies. One possible cause for the striking difference between the findings of those two studies lies in their different sample periods. In order to find a more convincing explanation, I incorporate eight more key variables with BSF to capture the potential "sample period" effects in three separate specifications: three indicators for the different adoption periods of BSF, three indicators for the three groups that were adopted in different periods, and two indicators for effects of BSF during the two full economic cycles. To create the first three, I divide the 46 states that have BSF into three adoption-period groups: Ten states that adopted BSF prior to 1982 (inclusive) are in the first group (Alaska excluded). Twenty-seven states that adopted BSF between 1983 and 1992 (inclusive) are in the second group. Nine states that adopted BSF after 1993 (inclusive) are in the third group. An indicator of 1 is created for these states with BSF from the year of BSF adoption to the end of their period group (1982, 1992, and 2001, respectively); these indicators then are multiplied by the per capita BSF balance to create three interaction terms to use in regression. The three interaction terms will capture the effects of BSF on total savings in years of the first business cycle immediately after their creation. More specifically, the "BSF adoption 1978–1982" variable captures the effects of those BSF created before 1982 in the half cycle from 1978 to 1982; "BSF adoption 1983–1992" catches the impact of those created between 1983 and 1992 in the 1983–1992 cycle; "BSF adoption 1993–2001" identifies effects of those created between 1993 and 2001 in the 1993–2001 cycle, respectively.

So far, none of the states that have adopted a BSF has repealed this fund. To capture the cumulative effects of the funds in each BSF adoption group throughout the sample period since their adoption, three more binary variables are created: one for each of the three groups. The "group" binaries differ from the "adoption" binaries in that the group binaries are designed to capture the distinct effects of each group on total savings throughout the sample years, whereas the adoption binaries capture the effects only in the few years immediately after adoption. These group indicators are also interacted with real per capita BSF balance; these group-BSF interaction terms will test whether funds adopted in different periods show lasting differences in their effects on total savings. Further, to capture the mean cumulative effects of all BSF funds during the two complete economic cycles in the sample period, this study created two extra indicators. The first full cycle went from trough in the fourth quarter of 1982 (FY 1983) to peak in the third quarter in 1990. For this, I have all BSF that were set up before and during this period. Those created before are coded as "1" for all years in this cycle; those created during the cycle are coded "1" only after their creation. The second full cycle went from trough in the first quarter in 1991 (FY 1991) to peak in March of 2001 (FY 2001). Coding was done in the same manner as for the first full cycle. Interacting these two indicators with BSF level will reveal the effects of BSF balance during the two full economic cycles.

The design features of each state's budget stabilization fund as specified in their enabling legislation are important control variables for this study. The Knight and Levinson (1999) study includes two deposit rules, three rules on the maximum balance level, and two withdrawal rules; the Wagner (2003) study includes three deposit rules and three withdrawal rules. I control for four deposit rules, three rules on the maximum balance level, and four withdrawal rules; these are in the B_{it} matrix. The deposit rules are, by the order of increasing stringency, deposit from general fund surplus whenever surplus is available, deposit by legislative appropriation, deposit by a preset formula, and deposit as a requirement. The withdrawal rules are, also by the order of increasing stringency, by executive discretion, by a preset formula, by legislative appropriation, and for revenue shortfall only. The three caps on balance level are 2%, 4–7%, and over 7% of the general fund expenditure. Data source of the design features is Hou's (2004) comprehensive study of state BSF legislation (also see Section 3.3). These binary variables are interacted with BSF balance. Estimated coefficients on these features will tell how much each design feature, coupled with presence of BSF balance, will increase or decrease total savings.

Besides, I control for socioeconomic factors, budgetary institutions, and state politics in the X matrix. Socioeconomics includes five factors: state population (in millions) captures effects of state size on savings, state general fund expenditure (per capita, in thousands) captures the effect of government size on the need for savings, personal income (per capita, in thousands) captures the marginal propensity to save, poverty rate catches effects of state social programs on the need for savings, and finally annual average unemployment rate captures the business cycle effect on savings. I expect higher personal income to present higher propensity to save, higher poverty rate to pull up the need for more savings, and higher unemployment to reduce savings. In contrast, bigger states and bigger governments are expected to be prone to high spending.

The four state budgetary institutions that I believe may contribute to the effects of BSF on savings are tax limitations, expenditure limitations, biennial budget cycles, and strict balanced budget requirements. Twenty-eight states now have a tax and expenditure limit clause either in their statute or constitution; three-quarters of these were adopted in the late 1970s and early 1980s in the wake of the tax-revolt movements initiated by Proposition 13 in California. The literature on the consequences of Proposition 13 (and its counterparts in other states) on state finance generally agrees that taxpayers were angered by the high levels of general fund balance accumulated in the 1970s; they initiated the revolts to restrict state taxing and spending power, which caused drastic decline of state general fund balance; consequently, state officials (elected as well as appointed) sought ways to manage their shambled finances. Therefore, I have reason to argue that states might have opted to adopt BSF as a second instrument of the budget stabilization policy to protect savings from citizen pressure (Gold 1984; Knight and Levinson 1999). In general, I expect revenue and expenditure limitations to present a positive sign. Data for these two variables are taken from Mullins and Wallin (2004). Biennial budgets are a historical remnant from periods of part-time legislators; it has maintained some of its advantages as well as disadvantages in terms of financial operations. Of the 50 states, 21 still practice biennial cycles. I expect the biennial nature may require higher saving levels than do annual budgets. Though states are all under some legal requirement to balance their budgets, the requirements vary significantly in form and stringency. Among the requirements reported in *The Book of the States* series, the most stringent, according to Bohn and Inman (1996), is that the state may not carry over deficits into the next fiscal year. The expected sign is negative because the strict rule not only presses down the possibility of annual deficits but it also works against high-saving levels.

The state politics variables are gubernatorial election year, democratic majority in state legislature (this dummy is set as "0" for Nebraska's nonpartisan unicameral legislature), and divided government. In most states, the governor plays a key role in making fiscal policy, in the budgeting process in particular, and budget implementation, but the political business cycle literature (Nordhaus 1975) has produced evidence that election years almost always see big spending increases. Thus, the expected sign for election year is negative. Choice of the Democratic legislature is based on the assumption that the two major political parties adopt different ideologies and that Democrats are prone to spending on social welfare. So, the expected sign is negative. In contrast, divided party between governor and legislative majority may create tension in passing spending bills and would result in more year-end savings. Descriptions of these variables and data sources are in Table 4.1; summary statistics of level variables (nonbinary) are in Table 4.2.

Table 4.1 Variables, description, and data sources. Sample years = 1978–2003; sample size is 1,271 with Alaska excluded

Variable	Description	Source
Socioeconomics		
Population	State population in millions	Census
State expenditure	Real per capita general fund expenditure in thousands	NASBO
Personal income	Real per capita personal income in thousands	BEA
Poverty rate	Poverty rate	Census
Unemployment rate	Annual average unemployment rate of each state	BEA
Budgetary institutions		
Revenue limitation		Mullins and Wallin 2004
Expenditure limitation		Mullins and Wallin 2004
Biennial budget cycle		NASBO
Strict balanced budget requirement	No deficit is allowed to carry over into next year	NASBO
State politics		
Gubernatorial election year		*Book of the States*
Democratic legislative majority		
Divided government		
Key variables		*Fiscal Survey of States*
State total savings	Sum of per capital real BSF balance and GFB balance	
BSF balance (rbsf)	Real per capita BSF balance (rbsf)	
BSF adoption 1978–1982	BSF adoption 1978–1982 * rbsf (78–82 only)	
BSF adoption 1983–1992	BSF adoption 1983–1992 * rbsf (83–92 only)	
BSF adoption 1993–2001	BSF adoption 1993–2001 * rbsf (93–01 only)	
BSF 1978–1982 group	BSF 1978–1982 * rbsf (all years since adoption)	
BSF 1983–1992 group	BSF 1983–1982 * rbsf (all years since adoption)	
BSF 1993–2001 group	BSF 1993–2001 * rbsf (all years since adoption)	
BSF 1983–1990 cycle	BSF dummy * rbsf: 1983–1990 cycle	
BSF 1992–2001 cycle	BSF dummy * rbsf: 1992–2001 cycle	
Trend	1978 = 1; 2003 = 26	
Features of BSF legislation		Hou 2004
Deposit by appropriation	Deposit by appropriation * rbsf	

(continued)

Table 4.1 (continued)

Variable	Description	Source
Deposit by formula	Deposit by preset formula * rbsf	
Deposit with surplus	Deposit if general fund has surplus * rbsf	
Deposit as required	Deposit as a required balance * rbsf	
Low cap (2%)	Low cap (2%) * rbsf	
Medium cap (4–7%)	Medium cap (4–7%) * rbsf	
High cap (>7%)	High cap (>7%) * rbsf	
Withdraw by discretion	Withdraw of fund by executive discretion * rbsf	
Withdraw by formula	Withdraw by preset formula * rbsf	
Withdraw by appropriation	Withdraw by appropriation * rbsf	
Withdraw for shortfall	Withdraw only in case of revenue shortfall * rbsf	

Table 4.2 Summary statistics of major variables

Variable	Mean	Std. Dev.	Min	Max
State total savings	92.58	117.25	–369.78	974.93
Budget stabilization fund balance	24.98	47.55	0	461.17
General fund balance	67.55	102.16	–369.78	798.02
Population (,000,000)	5.16	5.51	0.43	35.50
State expenditure (,000)	1.37	0.50	0.50	3.40
Personal income (,000)	24.26	4.45	14.79	41.45
Poverty rate	13.01	4.03	2.90	27.20
Unemployment rate	5.93	2.05	2.20	18.00

Note: Financial figures have been converted into per capita year-2000 dollars

4.5 Empirical Results and Discussion

Table 4.3 presents the empirical results. The Prais-Winsten model generates satisfactory transformed Durbin-Watson statistics. Results of the F-test show the models to be reliable, and the explanatory powers of the specifications are reasonable. The coefficients of all key variables are positive as expected and are statistically significant at 1% level. Column 1 shows the mean effect: On average if a state has a BSF in place in the sample period and keeps balance in the fund, this state has a total savings level higher by 85 cents for each dollar of BSF than a state without BSF; a state that adopted BSF during the sample period raised its total savings by 85 cents in contrast to pre-adoption of the fund. The net effect of BSF on total savings is smaller than unity; substitution of GFS by BSF is a fact. While BSF do increase total savings substantially, the increase is smaller than a dollar-for-dollar scale. On a second thought, it is only natural that the net effect of BSF on total savings is less than 1 because BSF is created to shelter savings from popular spending

Table 4.3 Prais-Winsten AR(1) regression estimates. Dependent variable is per capita real total savings; sample years = 1978–2003; sample size is 1,271 with Alaska excluded

	Column 1		Column 2		Column 3		Column 4		Column 5	
	Coef.	Std. Err.	Coef.	Std. Err.	Coef.	Std. Err.	Coef.	Std. Err.	Coef.	Std. Err.
Socioeconomics										
Population	0.000	0.000	0.000	0.000	0.000	0.000	0.000	0.000	0.000	0.000
State expenditure	***–50.295	15.312	***–45.251	16.186	***–49.822	15.329	***–47.819	15.675	***–56.277	15.459
Personal income	***12.461	3.071	***17.334	3.274	***12.422	3.072	***13.970	3.142	***12.070	3.134
Poverty rate	0.566	1.117	1.012	1.163	0.603	1.119	0.998	1.146	0.804	1.120
Unemployment rate	***–10.550	2.511	***–11.410	2.651	***–10.369	2.519	***–11.540	2.573	***–10.560	2.554
Budgetary institutions										
Revenue limitation	17.532	14.265	19.065	15.179	17.052	14.270	17.052	14.581	16.590	14.495
Expenditure limitation	12.717	12.872	12.609	13.691	12.752	12.894	11.105	13.160	11.878	13.003
Biennial budget cycle	19.712	14.142	13.416	14.929	* 22.788	14.162	18.026	14.476	22.457	14.285
Strict balanced budget requirement	–7.938	8.261	–4.059	8.676	–7.609	8.273	–6.358	8.465	–7.985	8.303
State politics										
Gubernatorial election year	*–6.434	3.805	*–6.445	3.932	*–6.703	3.808	*–6.844	3.907	*–6.503	3.789
Democratic legislative majority	*–13.787	8.329	–9.143	8.760	*–13.651	8.348	–11.902	8.527	–13.377	8.365
Divided government	*8.139	4.860	**10.600	5.091	*8.294	4.866	**9.642	4.981	*7.822	4.875
Key variables										
BSF balance (rbsf)	***0.854	0.060								
BSF adoption 1978–1982			***0.852	0.327						
BSF adoption 1983–1992			***0.978	0.120						
BSF adoption 1993–2001			**0.634	0.297						

BSF 1978–1982 group					***0.949	0.141				
BSF 1983–1992 group					***0.839	0.068				
BSF 1993–2001 group					***0.832	0.205				
BSF in 1983–1990 cycle							***0.845	0.107		
BSF in 1992–2001 cycle							***0.721	0.081		
Trend	***–6.031	1.115	***–6.379	1.197	***–6.018	1.115	***–5.307	1.143	***–5.864	1.140
Features of BSF legislation										
Deposit by appropriation									0.149	0.180
Deposit by formula									0.239	0.590
Deposit with surplus									***0.691	0.212
Deposit as required									**0.560	0.274
Low cap (2%)									0.153	0.450
Medium cap (4–7%)									**0.420	0.181
High cap (>7%)									0.360	0.259
Withdraw by discretion									0.042	0.301
Withdraw by formula									0.019	0.745
Withdraw by appropriation									0.016	0.341
Withdraw for shortfall									–0.023	0.207
DW statistic transformed	1.79		1.78		1.79		1.76		1.78	
F-test of model	***10.09		***7.46		***9.86		***8.91		***8.94	
Adjusted R-squared	0.38		0.31		0.38		0.35		0.37	

Significance levels: *10%; **5%; and ***1%.

pressure. By design, policy makers would have shifted some GFS into BSF for legal protection. On the other hand, the substitution of (1–0.85 =) 15 cents per dollar of BSF is by no means very large.

The next three columns provide evidence on decomposition of the funds that were created in different periods and their performance in different business cycles. When I break the funds into three groups by time order of their adoption and look at their effect during the period of their adoption (column 2), the point estimates do tell a story of varying impacts. Those funds created before 1982 raised total savings by 85 cents for each dollar of BSF in the 1978 to 1982 period. Funds created between 1983 and 1992 did better: Each dollar of BSF raised savings by almost 98 cents in the 1983 to 1992 period. The funds created between 1993 and 2001 faired the least: Each dollar of BSF raised total savings by only 63 cents.

Another way of looking at the stabilization funds that are adopted in the three different periods is to examine their effects throughout the sample period. In other words, though the 1983–1992 group fared the best and the 1993–2001 group the worst in the first few years of their creation, their average policy outcome over all the sample years may be different from that of the first few years. These results are in column 3. The pre-1982 group on average raised state savings by 95 cents for each dollar of BSF in comparison with the other two fund groups and states that did not have a BSF. The 1983–1992 group raised savings by 84 cents for each dollar of BSF in contrast to the other two fund groups and states that did not have a BSF; funds in the 1993–2001 group raised savings by 83 cents all things being equal. These three coefficients do reveal an increasing rate of substitution from the earliest adoptions to the latest adoptions. It is thus probably reasonable to infer that the earliest funds were created more for increasing savings, while the later-created funds were more to shelter savings than increasing them.

Finally, I look at the collective, average policy outcome of all the funds in the two complete economic cycles in the sample period (column 4), one from the end of the 1982 recession to the end of the 1980s boom and the other from FY 1992 to 2001. In the first full cycle, states that had a BSF had their savings higher by 85 cents for every dollar of BSF than states that did not or not yet have BSF. In the second full cycle, each dollar of BSF raised the respective state's savings by 72 cents. The observation of "increasing substitution" first obtained in column 3 is confirmed here. Thus, I have reason to speculate that as time goes on, the saving effect of BSF may be subject to more substitution. In fact, the time trend variable does capture the decreasing trend over time in state total savings, which is in conformity with the results from the "three groups" specification (column 3) and the "two full cycles" specification (column 4).

Effects of the BSF design features are shown in column 5. Among all the 11 features examined, three generate statistically significant results. The requirement that a deposit must be made into BSF if the general fund is in surplus increases savings by almost 70 cents for each dollar of BSF. The provision for a required balance in BSF increases savings by 56 cents for each dollar of BSF. And the medium cap on BSF balance also raises total savings, but by only 42 cents for each dollar of BSF. Other features are not significantly different from zero.

Among the socioeconomic factors, coefficients of population size and poverty rate are not significantly different from zero. The other three factors do generate reliable results. A state with larger expenditures keeps less saving; for each thousand-dollar increase in per capita general fund expenditures, the state's total savings drop between 45 and 56 dollars. Rich states tend to save more: For each thousand-dollar increase in per capita personal income, the state's savings may be higher between 12 and 17 dollars. The business cycle casts an obvious impact on savings: For each percentage point increase in the annual average unemployment rate, a state's savings will drop between 10.5 and 11.5 dollars. The budgetary institutions do not show statistically significant results, except the biennial budget in one case. Among the political variables, a gubernatorial election year will cost on average around 6.5 dollars per capita from savings, while divided government may push up the savings between 7.8 and 10.6 dollars. The results on these two variables are consistent throughout all five specifications. Results on democratic legislative majority are significant in two specifications – when it is significant, it shows the expected negative sign with the magnitude being about 13.5 dollars.

4.5.1 Sensitivity Tests

To test whether the above results are sensitive to changes in model specification, I conducted the augmented Dickey-Fuller (ADF) test (Fuller 1976) of the dependent variable, per capital total savings, and the key variable, per capita BSF balance. From the tests I found 15 states that have stationary saving levels. I reran the model with these 15 states, as a contrast to results in column 1 of Table 4.3. The results from the 15 stationary states are very similar to those in the all-state panel: There are no sign flips and almost all major variables remain statistically significant at high levels. The BSF coefficient is 0.97; that is, budget stabilization fund substantially increases total savings, with minimal substitution. From the ADF test, six states have stationary BSF balance levels, five of them coinciding with the 15 states with stationary savings. I also reran the model on these six states and again obtained similar results, with key variables keeping their original sign and high significant levels. The BSF coefficient is 0.75 – the substitution rate is a little higher, but the net effect of BSF on total savings remains substantial.

4.6 Conclusion

In this chapter, I have treated BSF and GFS as two cofunctional instruments of the countercyclical budget stabilization policy and explored the interaction between them through an empirical examination of the supplementation and substitution effects. Building on previous research, I estimated the net changes in state government savings after adopting the budget stabilization fund as a second saving device to reinforce an existing device, general fund surplus. Using a more complete data set than two previous studies, and controlling for more factors that influence state savings as well as the design features of the new policy tool, I have found that over three recent economic cycles, once an average state has adopted the new instrument (the budget stabilization fund), the state's total savings seem to increase substantially. Each dollar in the stabilization fund increases state total savings by 85 cents. This study has not found a single case of the key coefficient being larger than 1; thus, there is no evidence suggesting that adoption of a stabilization fund can increase the level of general fund surplus. Substitution of the general fund surplus by the stabilization fund averages only 15 cents per dollar of the stabilization fund. That is, the stabilization fund as a second major saving device has been very effective in increasing the overall level of state savings.

By placing state budget stabilization funds into three groups by their year of adoption, I have revealed some intergroup differences. The average effect of early (before 1982) and late (after 1993) adopters was higher for the whole sample period than for the few years immediately after adoption. The performance of those adopted between 1983 and 1992, in contrast, was the opposite: Their average effect was lower for the whole sample period than for the few years after adoption. Testing the cumulative effects of all funds in the two full business cycles separately shows that these effects are about the same as the average (0.85) during the 1983–1992 period, but this effect dropped in the 1992–2001 period by about 15% (from 0.85 to 0.72). Overall, these results show that the budget stabilization fund is an effective saving device. Though some substitution is observed, the amount is not very large. We can conclude that, as a policy tool, such funds should be more widely used (*ceteris paribus*). Sensitivity tests confirmed the results as solid and reliable.

As generalization of the empirical results in this chapter, I think the following inference can be made: A newly added policy instrument does tend to reinforce existing instruments. The second instrument can supplement the effect of the first instrument by up to 85%. In doing so, substitution of policy effects from the first instrument by the second is possible, but probably not very large (in the 15% range). After introducing the second instrument, the aggregate effects of the cofunctional instruments may dwindle over time. That is, the second instrument gradually subsumes or replaces the first instrument, at least in terms of effect. Thus, we can tentatively conclude that a reinforcing instrument for an existing policy tool can be highly effective over a certain (early) time span. As a caveat, multiplicity between cofunctional instruments is another complex issue. This study has not found any evidence of such effects in state budget stabilization practices, which does not rule out its existence. A full investigation of multiplicity effects will require further studies.

Appendix: An Accounting Framework for Analyzing BSF-GFB Interactions

Let S stand for total per capita savings, G for per capita GFS, and B for per capita BSF. Before a state adopts BSF, its total per capita savings is

$$S = G, \tag{4.1}$$

Each dollar increase in GFS is one-dollar increase in total savings. After adoption of BSF, S' being the new savings, Eq. 4.1 becomes

$$S' = B + G, \qquad B > 0 \tag{4.2}$$

Holding G constant as it is in (or as long as G does not change from) Eq. 4.1, S' is larger than S. Then, subtracting Eq. 4.1 from Eq. 4.2 yields the difference between S' and S, which is B, net increase in total savings:

$$S' - S = (B + G) - G = B, \qquad S' > S \tag{4.3}$$

Under this scenario, by adopting BSF a state increases its total savings, S, by B; the net increase is exactly B. One more dollar in BSF equals one-dollar net increase in total savings. But we should not expect the real world to be as clear-cut as Eq. 4.3 demonstrates. The National Association of State Budget Officers (NASBO) reports in its *Fiscal Survey of States* series (*FSS*) that 47 states have BSF by the end of fiscal year 2003. A recent study of BSF legislation shows vast heterogeneity in the structural features of BSF (Hou 2004); heterogeneity also exists in the size of BSF and GFS among the states. These are some of the reasons for us to believe that GFS and BSF interact very differently in the states, which leads to changes to GFS after adoption of BSF. A one-dollar increase in BSF does not necessarily result in one-dollar increase in total savings. Let G' stand for the changed G after adopting BSF:

$$S' = B + \Delta G, \quad \Delta G = G' - G, \quad G' > \text{or} < G \tag{4.4}$$

Changes to GFS from the interaction of the two saving devices can be classified into three categories. In category one, G does not change (or does not change much) after BSF is created; that is, $G' \approx G$, so $S' - S \approx B$. This is the case with Eq. 4.3, which indicates net dollar-for-dollar increase of savings by adopting BSF, as argued for in Knight and Levinson (1999). The second category shows a possible displacement (substitution) effect of GFS by BSF, $G' < G$, where BSF adoption reduces GFS; in other words, "the revenue deposited into [BSF] may only represent funds that would otherwise have been saved in [GFS]" (Knight and Levinson 1999, 459).

Let d stand for displacement. It is an index between 0 and 1, representing the part of GFS remaining after displacement, 1 for no displacement and 0 for complete displacement. A case of complete displacement of GFS ($d=0$) will be one as in

Eq. 4.1 with *B* displacing *G*. It is a mere change of name, GFS into BSF, with no net increase in total savings. From a practical point of view, this is almost unlikely because GFS serves some functions that BSF cannot (like working capital, see Section 3.2). Thus, we can exclude cases of complete displacement ($d=0$) from our discussion. A case of no displacement will be one as in Eq. 4.3, which is already clear. With only part of the original GFS displaced into BSF (partial displacement, $0<d<1$), Eq. 4.2 becomes

$$S' = B + G * d, \quad 0 < d < 1, \text{ and } (G * d)(= (\Delta G)) \text{ is negative;} \tag{4.5}$$

Displacement can be substantial (*d* close to 0) or minor (*d* close to 1). As long as BSF is larger than the displaced amount, $B>G*(1-d)$, where BSF is composed of some original GFS and some new savings, then there is net increase in total savings, $S'>S$. If BSF is smaller than the displaced amount of GFS, $B<G*(1-d)$, in which case BSF does not represent new savings and it is even less than the decrease in GFS, then there is net decrease in total savings, $S'<S$. This scenario was likely the case in the late 1970s and early 1980s.

The third category presents not only no substitution but multiplication of GFS after adopting BSF. That is, once *B* is introduced, $G'>G$: GFS increases at the same time when BSF brings in new savings. BSF seemingly presents a multiplier effect. Such a scenario was highly possible during boom years, the late 1990s record-long prosperity being an example. Let *m* be the multiplier, an index starting from 1 where there is no multiplication. The multiplication effect can be substantial (*m* much larger than 1) or minor (marginally larger than 1). Multiplication occurs when a state adopts a strong version of the countercyclical fiscal policy (Hansen 1941; Gramlich 1987). Let S″ now stand for total savings in the multiplication case:

$$S'' = B + G * m, \quad m > 1, \text{ and } (G * m)(= (\Delta G)) \text{ is positive;} \tag{4.6}$$

Whether it is substantial or minor multiplication, the net increase in total savings (S″–S) is BSF plus the increased part of GFS; it is

$$(S'' - S) = B + G * (m - 1), \tag{4.7}$$

Then Eq. 4.2 becomes

$$S'' = B + G * m, \qquad S'' > S' \tag{4.8}$$

The behavioral pattern of state total savings is not so much related to the amount of BSF per se as to the change of GFS after the adoption of BSF – whether GFS remains unchanged; if it changes, whether the change is decrease or increase; and if GFS decreases, whether the displaced amount is larger than BSF. Such changes in the amount of GFS determine whether the total savings will see net increase or decrease.

References

Bardach E (1977) The implementation game: what happens after a bill becomes a law. MIT Press, Cambridge, MA

Bennett CJ, Howlett M (1992) The lessons of learning: reconciling theories of policy learning and policy change. Policy Sci 25:275–294

Bohn H, Inman RP (1996) Balanced-budget rules and public deficits: evidence from the U.S. states. Paper at Carnegie-Rochester conference series on Public Policy

Braathen NA (2005) Environmental agreements used in combination with other policy instruments. In: Croci E (ed) The handbook of environmental voluntary agreements: design, implementation and evaluation issues. Springer, Dordrecht, pp 335–364

Englehardt GV (2002) Pre-retirement lump-sum pension distributions and retirement income security: evidence from the health and retirement study. Natl Tax J 55(4):665–685

Firestone JM (1960) Federal receipts and expenditures during business cycles 1879–1958. Princeton University Press, Princeton

Fisher RC (1984) Statement before the intergovernmental relations and human resources subcommittee of the committee on government operations. Washington, DC

Fuller WA (1976) Introduction to statistical time series. Wiley, New York

Gold SD (1984) Contingency measures and fiscal limitations: the real world significance of some recent state budget renovations. Natl Tax J 37(3):421–432

Gramlich EM (1987) Subnational fiscal policy. In: Quigley JM (ed) Perspectives on local public finance and public policy, vol 3. JAI Press, Greenwich, pp 3–27

Granger CWJ, Watson MW (1984) Time series and spectral methods in econometrics. In: Griliches Z, Intriligator MD (eds) Handbook of econometrics, vol 2. Elsevier Science, Amsterdam, Ch. 17

Hansen, AH (1941) Fiscal policy and business cycles. W.W. Norton & Company, Inc., New York

Hou Y (2003) Budget stabilization fund. In: Rabin J (ed) Encyclopedia of public administration and public policy. Marcel Dekker Press, New York

Hou Y (2004) Budget stabilization fund: structural features of the enabling legislation and balance level. Public Budg Finance 24(3):38–64

Hou Y (2005) Fiscal reserves and state own-source expenditure in downturns. Public Finance Rev 33(1):117–144

Keynes JM (1936) The general theory of employment, interest and money. Harcourt, Brace

Knight B, Levinson A (1999) Rainy day funds and state government savings. Natl Tax J 52(3):459–472

May PJ (1992) Policy learning and failure. J Public Policy 12(4):331–354

Mullins D, Wallin BA (2004) Tax and expenditure limitations: introduction and overview. Public Budg Finance 24(4):2–15

Musgrave RA (1959) The theory of public finance. McGraw-Hill, New York

National Association of State Budget Officers (NASBO) (1977–2004) Fiscal survey of States, series. Washington, DC

Nordhaus WD (1975) The political business cycle. Rev Econ Stud 42(2):169–190

Oates WE (1972) Fiscal federalism. Harcourt Brace Jovanovich, New York

Poterba JM, Venti SF, Wise DA (1995) Do 401(k) contributions crowd out other personal saving? J Public Econ 58(1):1–32

Pressman JL, Wildavsky A (1973) Implementation. University of California Press, Berkeley

Rafuse RW (1965) Cyclical behavior of state-local finances. In: Musgrave RA (ed) Essays in fiscal federalism. The Brookings Institution, Washington, DC, pp 63–121

Wagner GA (2003) Are state budget stabilization funds only the illusion of savings? Evidence from stationary panel data. Q Rev Econ Finance 43(2):213–238

Chapter 5
Budget Stabilization Fund in Interaction with Balanced Budget Requirements

Abstract In this chapter, I examine how the budget stabilization fund (BSF) interacts with balanced budget requirements (BBR); that is, in what way and to what extent the saving behavior of state governments is affected by the adoption of the stabilization fund in a BBR environment. While BBR are a long-standing institution, BSF is new. Though these two budgetary institutions were adopted for different reasons, both could have exerted substantive influences on state saving behavior, depending on the unique design features of the two in each state. This chapter empirically tests the effects of BSF and BBR on state savings covering three economic cycles. The 25-year (1979–2003) panel data also include information on state economy, social services, politics, and economic cycles. The results show that the adoption of a BSF can raise state savings level by 2.5% points; however, the effects depend crucially on the design of BSF, and that BBR rules requiring state own-source revenue to match budgeted expenditures and requiring the legislature to pass a balanced budget may also boost the savings level.

5.1 Introduction

In Chapter 4, I elaborated on the interaction between BSF and GFS as two major instruments of the countercyclical budget stabilization policy that came into use one after the other. In this chapter, I examine the interaction between BSF and balanced budget requirements (BBR) as two budgetary institutions, BBR being a set of long-standing operating rules in government budgeting and BSF a new institution.

This chapter is adapted from Hou Y, Duncombe W (2008) State saving behavior: effects of two fiscal and budgetary institutions. Public Budg Finance 28(3): 48–67, published by John Wiley & Sons Ltd.

Y. Hou, *State Government Budget Stabilization: Policy, Tools, and Impacts*, Studies in Public Choice 8, DOI 10.1007/978-1-4614-6061-9_5,

As I have discussed in previous chapters, maintaining a sizable general fund balance (GFB) has long been a practice of most state governments for several purposes (Rafuse 1965; NASBO series).[1] But as my analysis shows in Section 3.3, the total GFB of a state is not necessarily all for countercyclical uses; among the four layers of GFB, general fund surplus (GFS) is exclusively reserved for countercyclical use. Research has found that the size of a state's GFS is primarily related to fluctuations in revenues rather than spending (Firestone 1960) and that GFS tends to accumulate in boom years and is drawn down in lean years (Rafuse 1965; Fisher 1984). In this sense, GFS serves as buffer for state governments to mitigate the adverse effects of revenue shortfalls during recessions (Refuse 1965; Fisher 1984).

However, there always exist hurdles to save in boom years. One hurdle is political pressure during expansions either to increase spending or cut taxes, which makes it very difficult for states to save as much as they need to stabilize budgets in lean years. The other hurdle is BBR which is the focus of this chapter. BBR originated from the *norm of balance* that dates back to the 1830s–1840s (see Section 1.2.1) and later evolved into state policies on financial administration and management (Hou and Smith 2006). BBR are commonly categorized into four levels of restrictiveness: (1) governor required to submit balanced budget, (2) legislature required to pass balanced budget, (3) governor required to sign a balanced budget, and (4) no deficit carryover into the next budget cycle allowed. Recently, a new, more elaborate framework for classifying BBR has been proposed (Hou and Smith 2006), which identifies nine BBR articles along a political-technical continuum. This framework carries the potential of more explanatory power. BBR rules do not consider the ups and downs of state finances across the economic cycle. Though these rules often prohibit deficits and may even require positive fund balances despite drastic revenue shortfalls and service demand increases during a downturn (Hou 2006, 731), they also prevent the accumulation of surpluses in boom years. In this sense, they are somewhat "impractical" (Schick 1998). Thus, states with strict balanced budget requirements may have a particularly difficult time stabilizing budgets during recessions.

To address the above-mentioned political conundrum and BBR bondage on savings, budget stabilization funds have become widespread in recent decades as a second major vehicle for savings beside GFS. Established with enabling legislation, BSF is a device to store surpluses during economic booms and to legally protect these resources against spending pressure for use exclusively during economic downturns. The legal protection and prohibitive use articles help BSF circumvent BBR, provide statutory protection against misuse of savings, and/or increase the total amount of savings (BSF and GFS) available for emergencies. Then a key issue is whether implementing a BSF in a state has reduced the size of its GFS; that is, does BSF supplement or merely substitute for GFS funds? In Chapter 4, I have addressed this question and provided my answer.

[1] For the purposes of this study, a general fund balance (GFB) is defined as the difference between current assets and current liabilities on the general fund statement of net assets. We are using pre-GASB 34 accounting standards and financial information.

In this chapter, I focus on a similar research question – whether adopting a BSF increases the level of state savings; put another way, how has BSF interacted with existing BBR? I expand on previous research in three important ways. First, I use a sample period (1979–2003) that is long enough to capture a more recent recession and three full business cycles. The 2001 recession should provide an important test for many state governments of whether states using a BSF fared differently. Second, my BSF and GFS data for this study are not from surveys of state officials; they are actual figures that I have collected from audited, officially published annual financial statements. As I will elaborate in the section on data and measures, data thus collected are free of biases and of subjective opinion of state officials. Third, this chapter examines the interaction between other institutional factors and the political environment on the impact of BSF on savings. A particular focus is on how BSF interact with other institutional constraints, such as BBR, to affect state saving behavior.

The chapter is organized as follows. In Section 5.2, I will model the determinants of state saving behavior and the potential role of a BSF. Section 5.3 presents the data sources, measures, and empirical methodology used in the tests. Empirical results are presented in Section 5.4 with analysis of the effects of BSF with other institutional constraints and political variables. I will conclude with a brief summary of the findings and the potential political implications for state fiscal policy.

5.2 Modeling State Saving Behavior

Under the assumption for budget stabilization policy, the basic reason that states need to and do save surplus revenues in boom years is to dampen the differential effect of economic cycles on revenues and expenditures. Studies on revenue volatility show that state revenues tend to be more volatile than demand for public services are (Dye and McGuire 1992), which leads to large, cyclical revenue-expenditure gaps between current revenue and current outlay during recessions. These gaps would become deficits if they are not eliminated within the budget cycle. Such structural deficits are not allowed under strict balanced budget rules.

There are four means that states can employ to cope with these revenue gaps (Bohn and Inman 1996; Poterba 1994): (1) raising taxes, (2) cutting spending, (3) using temporary fiscal adjustments (one-shots), or (4) drawing on savings that have been accumulated during economic expansions. We know that tax increases are politically difficult to make; so are spending cuts, especially during downturns when more people need basic public services. We also know that one-shot strategies to cope with revenue shortfalls are temporary with small one-time revenues. Then the use of savings to cover cyclical revenue gaps may be the most reliable means (if not the only means). Let us assume for the moment similar fiscal institutions and political environment across states, the target savings level (S*) would be determined by the size of the typical revenue-expenditure gap. States with highly volatile revenue systems and significant demands on social service spending would all else equal need to save more than other states in order to avoid deficits (Joyce 2001).

Revenue volatility is affected by the underlying structure of the state tax system (*R*) and the volatility of the underlying tax bases (*B*). Heavy use of personal and corporate income and severance taxes will probably be associated with more volatile revenue systems than revenues received by states that are more dependent on general sales (and gross receipt taxes) and user fees and charges (Fox and Campbell 1984; White 1983). States with more generous social service programs (*SS*) and a larger share of low-income households (*LI*) should also experience higher deficits. Target level of savings (S*) can be modeled as a function of revenue volatility (σ_R) and expenditure volatility (σ_E). Thus, the savings equation is as follows:

$$S^* = f\left(\sigma_R(R, B), \sigma_E(SS, LI)\right)$$

But states differ in terms of their fiscal institutions and political environment; the assumption of cross-state similarity does not hold. Therefore, the actual saving level (*S*) that a state selects often diverges from the target level because the consequences of deficits differ across states due to variant operating environment. If they can accurately predict the probability of gaps/deficits of a certain magnitude, states could have set aside savings during expansions in order to cover the gaps/deficits with a certain probability of occurring. However, officials in states with the same underlying fiscal volatility and target saving levels might select different saving levels (S) due to different assessments of the political costs of running deficits in a recession and/or of accumulating savings in an expansion.

The difference between *S** and *S* could depend on the political environment (*P*) and the fiscal institutions (*F*) in the state. We might expect that states with one party dominating both the executive and the legislative branches will be able to reduce deficits more easily than states with divided governments. The chosen solution of Republicans and Democrats may be different (Alt and Lowry 2000; Matsusaka 1995), but the political costs of coping with a deficit are likely to be lower than trying to reach compromise between parties (Poterba 1994). These political risks of dealing with a deficit need to be balanced against the political costs to maintain a large surplus, because surpluses can be a target for permanent fiscal changes such as tax cuts or new government programs. Some scholars have argued that the 1978 tax revolts in California and later in some other states were driven in part by voters angry over high levels of general fund balances (Gold 1995; Elder 1992). State responses to the large surpluses of the late 1990s included permanent tax cuts and spending increases in many states.

Some heavy constraints that could have affected the difference between the target and selected saving levels (*S-S**) are from fiscal and budgetary institutions that are embedded in state laws. These institutions include balanced budget requirements, tax and expenditure limitations (TEL), line-item vetoes, and debt limits (Bohn and Inman 1996; Poterba 1995). Of particular importance to us in this chapter are BBR, because they dictate how and when states will have to deal with fiscal deficits. BBR generally affect the general fund only and can go from relatively weak requirements (the governor only has to propose a balanced budget) to quite strict requirements (state cannot carry over a deficit to the next fiscal year). The stricter the balanced budget requirements, the more onerous the effects of a deficit on budgetary decisions (Bohn and Inman 1996) and the more likely a state will increase its savings in good years to avoid these effects. Tax and expenditures limitations (TEL) that restrict growth in state revenues and expenditures can reduce state government flexibility in eliminating a deficit, which might also encourage higher levels of savings. Thus, we modify our model of state saving behavior as follows:

$$S = g\,(S^{*}, P, F) = f\left(\sigma_R(R, B), \sigma_E(SS, LI), P, F\right)$$

In both the savings equation and the above modified model, I have taken state savings as one lump-sum amount of reserves; but as I discussed in Chapter 4, this is not the case. GFS and BSF are separate instruments that states use to accumulate savings; balances in the two instruments are not perfect substitutes. GFS is typically at the discretion of the governor (with or without approval by the legislature; a portion of the unreserved balance of the general fund can be *designated*, by the legislature, for future uses). In contrast, BSF balances are legally reserved exclusively for revenue shortfalls in a downturn (Hou 2004; see Section 3.3). While regulations on BSF vary in their stringency, state governments clearly face more restrictions in using the BSF than the unreserved general fund balance. State officials may be hesitant to run large general fund surpluses during economic expansions, because the surpluses are easy targets for tax cuts and spending programs. BSF could be more invisible to the public and more insulated than GFS from diversion into nonemergency purposes. If the target saving level (S^{*}) is significantly higher than the selected saving level (S) and the political costs of using the BSF are fairly low, we might expect that implementation of a BSF could expand state savings by almost the full amount of the BSF. If on the other hand, the difference between S^{*} and S is relatively small, we should expect little change in S when a BSF is implemented.

Besides, BSF also interacts with the political environment and other institutional constraints on state savings. For example, the political consequences of an unanticipated deficit could be more serious in states that have a history of divided government. BSF could be viewed as an effective tool for increasing state savings to avoid deficits, given that both tax increases and spending cuts are politically difficult to implement; but we know the former is more so than the latter. Therefore, states dominated by the Democratic Party may be more apt to use BSF to protect state programs during downturns than Republican-dominated states (Alt and Lowery 2000). The deficits associated with a fiscal crisis could provide an opportune moment for Republicans to cut programs. Regarding institutional variables, states with strict balanced budget requirements and tax and expenditure limitations may be more likely to have a BSF and to use it to increase savings. However, the political fallout in tax revolt states of large fund balances might limit the use of GFS as a savings device. Thus, the final model of state saving behavior incorporates interactions between the use of BSF and political as well as institutional factors:

$$S = f\left(\sigma_R(R, B), \sigma_E(SS, LI)\; P, F, (1 + BSF) \times (P, F)\right)$$

5.3 Data and Empirical Methodology

I assemble a panel data of all 50 states over 25 years that cover three economic cycles (1979–2003). The empirical model expands on previous research in this area (Knight and Levinson 1999; Wagner 2003) in several ways. Details of data sources, measures, and empirical methods are discussed in the following pages.

5.3.1 Data Sources and Measures

State savings (*S*) is defined as the sum of the balances of BSF and the unreserved undesignated balance (UUB) of the general fund or general fund surplus (GFS) as defined in Section 3.2. UUB refers to the part of general fund balance that is available after excluding legal reservations and administrative designations; it is the amount that is available for reappropriation for the next fiscal year (Ruppel 2005). In contrast, total general fund balance, as used in previous studies, is not free of reservations and designations; they are not necessarily real savings and may even include BSF in some cases (for details, see Section 3.2.1).[2] While it is possible that state officials could use the name of a few other funds to hold and protect savings from political intervention, Bohn and Inman (1996) did not find significant use of other funds to cover or hide deficits. Moreover, most state balanced budget requirements apply only to the general fund (NASBO 1992), which is confirmed by recent research (Hou and Smith 2010). The relative scale of savings is measured with the ratio of total fund balances (BSF+UUB) over general fund expenditures (GFE), which is a common measure used in government financial analysis (NASBO 1977; GFOA 1999); "relative savings" is our dependent variable. The sources for BSF and UUB are the *Comprehensive Annual Financial Report* (CAFR) series of each state. These sources are assumed to be accurate, because CAFR are compiled in accordance with the generally accepted accounting principles (GAAP) and audited each year by internal auditors as well as external, independent accounting firms. The source of general fund expenditure is the *Fiscal Survey of States* series that is compiled and published twice a year by the National Association of State Budget Officers (NASBO).

I use an indicator for the presence of BSF. This binary variable captures the differential effects between states that have adopted the fund and those that have not. Because over 30 states adopted BSF after the early-1980 double-dip recessions – within the sample years of this chapter – this binary variable will also capture, for states that created this fund in the sample years, the differences between years before and after the adoption of the fund. The BSF adoption years are shown in Section 3.3

[2] This is because some states maintain their BSF under, and report it as part of, their general fund balance, which leads to a double-counting problem. A cursory examination of the CAFR can reveal this problem. The *Fiscal Survey of States* by NASBO also indicates this in the notes.

and General Appendix A. However, adopting BSF is one thing; increase of savings is another, because a state with a BSF may choose not to deposit any money into the fund, as was the case with New Mexico and Wisconsin, or deposit very little as did New York. As shown in several studies (Douglas and Gaddie 2002; Wagner 2003), it is the features of BSF rather than its adoption that actually explains the BSF balance level. Therefore, I incorporate into the model specific design features of BSF including purposes for use, sources of funding, caps on balance level, and use approval procedures (see Section 3.3 and General Appendix A for details). An alternative is to develop an index from these features rather than using these individual features. Though an ordinal index has the advantage of being "simple" and "straightforward," the index may hide the direct effects of some significant features. Thus, we chose to use the features themselves.

To capture effects of balanced budget requirements on state savings, I include nine indicators in the model for the (Hou-Smith 2006) BBR system to capture the effects of BBR. Many tax and expenditure limitations were passed in the 1970s and 1980s; these new constraints could affect state savings directly.[3] As noted previously, some analysts of the TEL legislation have argued that taxpayer anger over high levels of general fund balance accumulated in the 1970s was one catalyst for these movements. TEL restricted state taxing and spending power, which caused drastic decline in state fund balances. Consequently, states with TEL may be more apt to adopt BSF as a device to protect savings from citizen pressure and to use the BSF to expand state savings.[4] Data for tax and expenditure limitations are taken from Mullins and Wallin (2004) – so far the most detailed study of this topic – and double-checked against the *State Budget Processes* series assembled and published by NASBO.[5]

Most states used to follow a biennial budget cycle when state lawmakers were part-time; now more than half of the 50 states have shifted from the biennial cycle to the annual budget cycle. Still about 20 states are using biennial budgets. Some studies argue that a longer-term budget perspective associated with biennial budgeting is beneficial for maintaining fund balances (Forrester 1991). For this reason, the biennial budget binary is included; data are from the *Book of the States* series. Another budgetary institution we would like to control for is gubernatorial veto power as proxy for governor's authority in the budgetary process. Unfortunately, data are not readily available for all of our sample years; NASBO has reported this variable for only a few years. I have to go without it.

Economic measures are included in the model to capture the underlying volatility of state economy and the relative income of residents, which could affect saving

[3] Twenty-eight states now have some type of tax and expenditure limitation either in their statute or constitution; three-quarters of these were adopted in the late 1970s and early 1980s in the wake of the tax revolt movements initiated by Proposition 13 in California.

[4] Knight and Levinson mention this, by citing Gold (1984), as a potential cause for the spread of BSF (1999, 469).

[5] See *State Budget Processes*, 1985, 1988, 1992, 1995, 1998, and 2002 editions, compiled and published by the National Association of State Budget Officers (NASBO).

rates of the states and the potential use of social services by residents. Income is measured with per capita personal income (in thousands) adjusted for inflation. Volatility measures would have been ideal for the major tax bases; but consistent measures are not available for a time series of this length. Instead, I use a measure of real income volatility over the previous 10 years.[6] This is a coefficient of dispersion measured as the standard error of estimate from a 10-year linear trend that fits on real per capita personal income divided by the state average for this measure. The volatility of state tax revenues is affected by the tax structure, particularly unstable taxes such as personal and corporate income taxes and severance taxes. Since revenue stability and its effects on state budgets is a factor in setting tax policy, the existing revenue structure and saving rates may be determined simultaneously. To go around this issue, I use indicator variables instead for whether a state uses the personal income tax, corporate income tax, and general sales tax. Besides, severance tax is also used to add extra explanatory power for those few states that export a lot of natural resources. States rarely make decisions to implement or remove a major tax; these decisions are unlikely to be related to annual savings rates.

Other control variables include the following. Poverty rate measures the underlying demand for social services; data are from the Current Population Survey of the US Census Bureau. Unemployment rate provides a measure of the business cycle; the growth rate of real gross state product accounts for any effect of economic momentum on the level of savings. State population and real total state personal income, both in millions, are used to capture effects from varying state sizes.

I borrow from research on the impacts of state politics on fiscal outcomes (Alt and Lowery 1994, 2000; Bohn and Inman 1996; Poterba 1994) on measures of state political environment. I use indicators of whether the governor is a Democrat, whether both houses of the legislature are controlled by the Democrats, and whether the legislature is controlled by the party different from that of the governor. Governor's party affiliation is included because the governor in most states plays a key role in making fiscal policy, particularly in the budgeting process. I also control for gubernatorial election year, assuming that if any year coincides with gubernatorial (re-) election, the saving level will go down because electoral pressure inclines toward more current year spending. The sample for the analysis includes 49 states over 25 years. Alaska is excluded from the panel as an extreme outlier, because this state depends heavily on severance taxes in terms of its revenue structure and it keeps an extremely high-savings rate. A list of variables and their data sources are offered in Table 5.1; summary statistics of all variables are provided in Table 5.2.

5.3.2 *Empirical Methodology*

I take several steps to remove potential omitted variable biases in the regression. First, as said in Section 5.3.1, I have included a number of control variables to

[6] This volatility measure was developed by William Duncombe.

Table 5.1 List of variables: definitions and data sources

Key variables	Data sources
Budget stabilization fund balance	*Comprehensive Annual Financial Report* series, each state
Unreserved undesignated balance of general fund	*Comprehensive Annual Financial Report* series, each state
State general fund expenditure	*Fiscal Survey of States* series by NASBO
Socioeconomics	
Real per capita personal income in thousands	Bureau of Economic Analysis
Growth rate of real state gross product	Bureau of Economic Analysis
State income stability (10-year average dispersion of coefficient)	Census
State annual average unemployment rate	Bureau of Economic Analysis
Population in millions	Bureau of Economic Analysis
Poverty rate	Bureau of Economic Analysis
Budget stabilization fund	
Adoption of budget stabilization fund	Hou 2003
Design features of budget stabilization fund	Hou 2004
Other budgetary institutions	
Balanced budget requirements	Hou and Smith 2006
Limitation on revenue	Mullins and Wallin 2004
Limitation on expenditure	Mullins and Wallin 2004
Biennial budget cycle	*Book of the States* series
State tax structure	
Personal income tax	Tax foundation facts and figures
Corporate income tax	Tax foundation facts and figures
General sales tax	Tax foundation facts and figures
Severance tax	Tax foundation facts and figures
State politics	
Governor is Democrat	*Book of the States* series
Majority of legislature is Democrat	*Book of the States* series
Divided government	*Book of the States* series
Year of gubernatorial election	*Book of the States* series

account for differences in the socioeconomics and political environments and tax policies; these included a broader range of controls than past research has done on fiscal institutions. Second, to control for time-invariant omitted variables, including state-specific factors (e.g., historical precedent and political culture) related to the adoption of BSF and BBR, I include state-fixed effects in the models. Given that BSF are created in different years across states, I include year-fixed effects to control for differences in the national economy or national budget, which may have affected state savings rates.

A thorny issue in testing institutions is the choice between fixed effects and random effects estimators. When the institutions do not change over time, the fixed-effects estimator will generate unreliable error terms, which calls for use of the random effects estimator. However, in the case of this study, BSF and BBR both

Table 5.2 Summary statistics

Variable	Mean	Std dev.	Min	Max
Total savings as % of general fund expenditure	0.058	0.099	−0.271	0.536
Adoption of budget stabilization fund	0.567	0.496	0	1
Design features of budget stabilization fund				
Source of BSF is required balance	0.056	0.229	0	1
Source of BSF is by formula	0.053	0.224	0	1
Source of BSF is general fund surplus	0.404	0.491	0	1
Source of BSF is from general fund by appropriations	0.200	0.400	0	1
Source of BSF is special revenue	0.011	0.106	0	1
BSF balance cap: 2 up to 4%	0.064	0.244	0	1
BSF balance cap: 4 up to 7%	0.289	0.453	0	1
BSF balance cap: 7 up to 12%	0.148	0.355	0	1
No limit on BSF balance	0.054	0.226	0	1
Minimum balance of BSF is required	0.080	0.271	0	1
Use of BSF is by appropriation	0.313	0.464	0	1
Use of BSF is by executive discretion	0.155	0.362	0	1
Use of BSF is by predetermined formula	0.036	0.186	0	1
Purpose of BSF is for revenue shortage	0.490	0.500	0	1
Purpose of BSF is for cash flow	0.122	0.328	0	1
Purpose of BSF is for emergencies	0.092	0.289	0	1
Balanced budget requirements				
Governor submit balanced budget	0.762	0.426	0	1
Own-source revenue match expenditures	0.166	0.372	0	1
Own-source rev and debt meet expenditures	0.697	0.460	0	1
Legislature pass balanced budget	0.647	0.478	0	1
Limit on debt for deficit reduction	0.443	0.497	0	1
Governor sign balanced budget	0.025	0.157	0	1
With controls on supplementary appropriations	0.320	0.467	0	1
Within FY controls in place to avoid deficits	0.561	0.496	0	1
No deficit carryover	0.134	0.341	0	1
Other budgetary institutions				
Limitation on revenue	0.260	0.439	0	1
Limitation on expenditure	0.360	0.480	0	1
Biennial budget cycle	0.407	0.492	0	1
State tax structure				
Personal income tax	0.878	0.328	0	1
Corporate income tax	0.898	0.303	0	1
General sales tax	0.918	0.274	0	1
Severance tax	0.122	0.328	0	1
Socioeconomics				
Real per capita personal income in thousands	24.388	4.456	14.787	41.446
Growth rate of real state gross product	0.03	0.03	−0.09	0.15
State income stability	2.46	1.46	0.44	10.52
State annual average unemployment rate	5.95	2.07	2.20	18.00
Population in millions	5.19	5.54	0.45	35.50
Poverty rate	13.07	4.04	2.90	27.20
State politics				
Governor is Democrat	0.512	0.500	0	1
Majority of legislature is Democrat	0.504	0.500	0	1
Divided government	0.473	0.499	0	1
Year of gubernatorial election	0.259	0.438	0	1

present some, though minor, variation over the sample period. Therefore, we decide to use the fixed-effects models as the base line and then use the random effects models as sensitivity tests for consistency.

I have also addressed a couple of potential problems, which if not treated may bias the reported standard errors. To correct for possible serial correlation across error terms, I have included a time trend variable in the model and estimated the model using the Prais-Winsten panel-corrected standard-error (PCSE) method for first-order serial correlation. I have also corrected for possible heteroscedasticity problems using robust standard errors, which correct for clustering at the state level.

5.4 Empirical Results and Discussion

Regression results are shown in Tables 5.3 and 5.4. The basic Prais-Winsten (1954) model generates satisfactory transformed Durbin-Watson statistics (these basic model results are not reported), suggesting that serial correlation has been adequately corrected. In all specifications, the explanatory powers of the models are reasonable, based on the results of the F-test (basic Prais-Winsten). Table 5.3 presents models using composite measures of BSF or BBR. Column 1 includes the composite measures of both; column 2 includes a composite for BSF and detailed characteristics of the BBR, while the reverse is presented in column 3 (detailed BSF features and composite BBR). Table 5.4 shows results on specific features of both BSF and BBR. Among the BSF design features, "special revenue" is omitted as default for the source variables; "2 up to 4%" is omitted as default for the balance cap variables; "by executive discretion" is omitted for the use approval procedure indicators; and "emergency" is omitted as default for purpose of use indicators. Among the nine indicators for balanced budget requirements, "governor submitting a balanced budget" is omitted as default. All other budgetary institutions, socioeconomics, tax structure, and state politics are present in all specifications. Regression results appear to be robust, as the signs and magnitudes of the coefficients and levels of statistical significance are not sensitive to the change in model specification.

5.4.1 *Effects of BSF Adoption and Design Features*

Results in columns 1 and 2 of Table 5.3 show that when a measure of BSF adoption is included in the model, the increase in savings is estimated to be between 1.8% and 2.1% of general fund spending. The result indicates that a state with a budget stabilization fund keeps a higher saving level than a state without the fund and that a state's saving level tends to go higher after adopting the fund than before the adoption. Given the average saving level of 5.8% of general fund expenditure (see Table 5.2), adopting the budget stabilization fund may raise the saving level between 31 and 36%.

Table 5.3 Empirical results. *Dependent variable* = total savings (BSF + UUB) as percent of general fund expenditure, 1979–2003

Independent variables	Coef.	Std error	Coef.	Std error	Coef.	Std error
Budget stabilization fund (BSF)						
Adoption of BSF and in use	**0.018	0.009	**0.021	0.010	–0.002	0.024
Source of BSF is required balance					***–0.071	0.027
Source of BSF is by formula					0.001	0.052
Source of BSF is general fund surplus					–0.045	0.029
Source of BSF is from general fund by appropriations					**–0.054	0.025
BSF balance cap: 4 up to 7%					**0.052	0.025
BSF balance cap: 7 up to 12%					***0.090	0.034
No limit on BSF balance					**0.089	0.042
Minimum balance of BSF is required					0.008	0.024
Use of BSF is by appropriation					0.026	0.021
Use of BSF is by predetermined formula					–0.054	0.068
Purpose of BSF is for revenue shortage					–0.006	0.025
Purpose of BSF is for cash flow					0.033	0.022
Balanced budget requirements						
Dummy for presence of severe BBR constraint	**0.032	0.015			**0.030	0.014
Own-source revenue match expenditures			0.014	0.020		
Own-source rev and debt meet expenditures			–0.013	0.020		
Legislature pass balanced budget			0.020	0.014		
Limit on debt for deficit reduction			**0.042	0.018		
Governor sign balanced budget			0.066	0.043		
With controls on supplementary appropriations			–0.022	0.017		
Within FY controls in place to avoid deficits			*0.022	0.013		
No deficit carryover			*0.030	0.019		
Other budgetary institutions						
Limitation on revenue	–0.009	0.013	–0.017	0.014	–0.017	0.013
Limitation on expenditure	**0.028	0.012	**0.025	0.011	**0.027	0.012
Biennial budget cycle	**0.025	0.011	**0.028	0.013	*0.021	0.011

(continued)

Table 5.3 (continued)

Independent variables	Coef.	Std error	Coef.	Std error	Coef.	Std error
Socioeconomics						
Real per capita personal income in thousands, lag	**0.005*	0.003	***0.009*	0.004	0.004	0.003
Growth rate of real state gross product, lag	***0.165*	0.072	**0.159*	0.095	****0.181*	0.073
State annual average unemployment rate, lag	–0.003	0.002	–0.003	0.002	–0.004	0.002
State income stability	****0.010*	0.003	**0.011*	0.006	****0.011*	0.003
Population in millions	****–0.005*	0.002	****–0.008*	0.002	****–0.006*	0.002
Poverty rate	–0.001	0.001	–0.001	0.001	–0.001	0.001
State tax structure						
Personal income tax	–0.017	0.053	–0.037	0.052	0.022	0.056
Corporate income tax	–0.003	0.057	0.042	0.054	–0.043	0.061
General sales tax	0.031	0.028	0.014	0.039	0.036	0.027
Severance tax	****0.080*	0.023	****0.099*	0.034	****0.093*	0.023
State politics						
Governor is Democrat	0.009	0.005	0.008	0.006	**0.010*	0.005
Majority of legislature is Democrat	–0.008	0.008	–0.007	0.007	–0.011	0.008
Divided government	0.002	0.005	0.000	0.005	0.002	0.005
Year of gubernatorial election	0.001	0.004	0.001	0.003	0.001	0.004
R-squared		0.33		0.37		0.36
Transformed Durbin-Watson statistic		1.88		1.87		1.86
Prob>chi2		0.00		0.00		0.00

Notes
a. Significance level: * at 10%; ** at 5%; *** at 1%
b. Alaska is excluded as an extreme outlier; sample size is 1,225
c. Prais-Winsten model is used to correct for serial autocorrelation

The inclusion of the specific design features of the BSF takes away statistical significance from the BSF indicator variable (Table 5.3, column 3 and Table 5.4, column 2). The cap of the BSF balance has a significant impact on the state savings rate. A BSF balance cap of 4–7% is associated with an increase in the savings rate of approximately 5% points relative to a lower balance cap. When the balance cap is over 7%, the increase in the savings rate is around 9% points. With regard to funding sources, we find that if the source of a BSF is a "required balance" of the general fund or from the general fund by appropriations, the total-saving level goes down (relative to special revenue as the source). This result suggests that if the general fund is the principal funding source of BSF, there is a substitution effect between BSF and GFS (see Chapter 4). With regard to purpose of use provisions, requiring the BSF to be used for cash flow purposes may necessitate higher balances, although these results are not statistically significant at conventional levels.

Table 5.4 Empirical results continued. *Dependent variable* = total savings (BSF + UUB) as percent of general fund expenditure, 1979–2003

Independent variables	Coef.	Std error	Coef.	Std error	Coef.	Std error
Budget stabilization fund (BSF)						
Adoption of BSF and in use			0.007	0.016		
Source of BSF is required balance	–0.072	0.046	–0.072	0.046	****–0.073*	0.027
Source of BSF is by formula	0.010	0.040	0.009	0.039	0.013	0.052
Source of BSF is general fund surplus	–0.041	0.028	**–0.044*	0.027	–0.041	0.027
Source of BSF is from general fund by appropriations	***–0.053*	0.023	***–0.055*	0.023	***–0.053*	0.024
BSF balance cap: 4 up to 7%	****0.052*	0.019	***0.049*	0.021	***0.049*	0.024
BSF balance cap: 7 up to 12%	****0.092*	0.037	***0.089*	0.037	****0.088*	0.034
No limit on BSF balance	0.073	0.063	0.072	0.063	0.070	0.046
Minimum balance of BSF is required	0.015	0.019	0.016	0.018	0.015	0.025
Use of BSF is by appropriation	**0.031*	0.019	0.030	0.019	0.030	0.021
Use of BSF is by predetermined formula	–0.051	0.056	–0.053	0.056	–0.053	0.066
Purpose of BSF is for revenue shortage	–0.014	0.026	–0.015	0.027	–0.015	0.024
Purpose of BSF is for cash flow	0.033	0.023	0.032	0.024	0.032	0.022
Balanced budget requirements						
Own-source revenue match expenditures	0.022	0.020	0.022	0.020	0.021	0.018
Own-source rev and debt meet expenditures	–0.006	0.020	–0.006	0.020	–0.006	0.017
Legislature pass balanced budget	0.018	0.015	0.018	0.015	0.018	0.013
Limit on debt for deficit reduction	***0.042*	0.018	***0.041*	0.018	***0.041*	0.018
Governor sign balanced budget	0.061	0.049	0.061	0.049	0.062	0.046
With controls on supplementary appropriations	**–0.029*	0.018	**–0.029*	0.018	**–0.030*	0.016
Within FY controls in place to avoid deficits	0.014	0.013	0.014	0.013	0.014	0.011
No deficit carryover	**0.036*	0.019	**0.037*	0.020	**0.036*	0.021
Interaction of BSF adoption and BBR constraint					0.002	0.007

(continued)

Table 5.4 (continued)

Independent variables	Coef.	Std error	Coef.	Std error	Coef.	Std error
Other budgetary institutions						
Limitation on revenue	−0.023	0.015	−0.023	0.014	*−0.022	0.013
Limitation on expenditure	**0.025	0.012	**0.025	0.012	**0.026	0.012
Biennial budget cycle	*0.024	0.013	*0.024	0.013	**0.024	0.011
Socioeconomics						
Real per capita personal income in thousands, lag	**0.009	0.004	*0.010	0.004	***0.010	0.003
Growth rate of real state gross product, lag	*0.174	0.095	*0.173	0.095	**0.174	0.074
State annual average unemployment rate, lag	−0.003	0.002	−0.003	0.002	−0.003	0.002
State income stability	*0.012	0.006	*0.012	0.006	***0.012	0.003
Population in millions	***−0.008	0.002	***−0.008	0.002	***−0.008	0.002
Poverty rate	−0.001	0.001	−0.001	0.001	−0.001	0.001
State tax structure						
Personal income tax	−0.004	0.059	−0.005	0.059	−0.007	0.056
Corporate income tax	0.010	0.062	0.011	0.062	0.012	0.060
General sales tax	0.019	0.039	0.019	0.039	0.019	0.028
Severance tax	***0.115	0.037	***0.115	0.037	***0.115	0.023
State politics						
Governor is Democrat	0.009	0.006	0.009	0.006	*0.009	0.005
Majority of legislature is Democrat	*−0.010	0.006	*−0.010	0.006	−0.010	0.008
Divided government	0.000	0.005	−0.001	0.005	−0.001	0.005
Year of gubernatorial election	0.001	0.003	0.001	0.003	0.001	0.004
R-squared		0.40		0.40		0.40
Transformed Durbin-Watson statistic		1.85		1.85		1.85
Prob>chi2		0.00		0.00		0.00

Notes
a. Significance level: * at 10%; ** at 5%; *** at 1%
b. Alaska is excluded as an extreme outlier; sample size is 1,225
c. Prais-Winsten model is used to correct for serial autocorrelation

5.4.2 *Effects of Balanced Budget Requirements*

Results in columns 1 and 3 of Table 5.3 shows that a relatively restrictive BBR is associated with a statistically significant increase in savings level of approximately 3% points. Among the balanced budget requirements, two articles consistently show positive, statistically significant coefficients – "limit on the use of debt for deficit reduction" and "no deficit carryover to the next fiscal year." Both measures limit the shifting of budget deficits onto future years and are associated with an increase in the savings rate of 3–4.2% points (Table 5.3, column 2 and Table 5.4, all columns). Restrictions on deficit carryover have been found to help with budget balancing in previous studies. "Within fiscal year controls to avoid deficits" shows positive and significant result in one model (Table 5.3, column 2), but this result is sensitive to changes in model specification. "Controls on supplementary appropriations" consistently presents a negative effect on savings (Table 5.4, all columns).

The results show that other budgetary institutions can also influence state savings levels. State expenditure limitations and biennial budgets are both associated with statistically significant increases in the savings rate of approximately 2.5% points. Surprisingly, tax limitations are associated with a decrease in the savings rate, although this result is not statistically significant at conventional levels in all models. Our findings for BBR, TELs, and biennial budgets suggest that budgetary institutions can exert a substantive effect on state savings rates, even when they were created for other purposes. I also examined how the interaction of BSF with the existence of other fiscal institutions affects state savings rates. An example is the interaction of BSF and the composite measures of BBR presented in Table 5.4 (column 3) which is not close to being statistically significant. I did not find significant interaction effects between the adoption of a BSF and the existence of a TEL or biennial budget (not reported).

5.4.3 *Effects of Socioeconomic Factors, Tax Structure, and Politics*

The point estimates of the social and economic variables fit expectations; most coefficients are estimated with precision. State saving levels follow the economic cycle: They increase during periods of economic growth (growth rate in gross state product) and decline during periods of recession when unemployment rates rise (not statistically significant). Higher income states and those with a more stable economic base (as represented by income stability) also have higher savings rates. I find evidence that the level of state savings declines with increases of population size. It is possible that smaller states are more vulnerable to economic shocks since their economies may be less diverse and these states increase their savings to compensate. While not statistically significant, savings rates are negatively related to poverty, which suggests that savings rates decline with an increased demand for social services.

I fail to find a strong relationship between the tax structure and saving levels, except for severance taxes. Use of the severance tax (primarily by Texas, Louisiana, and Wyoming) is associated with an increase between 8% and 11.5% points in the savings rate. Unexpectedly, state sales taxes are positively related to savings rates, although the coefficient is not estimated with precision. The coefficients on the personal and corporate income taxes are inconsistent and statistically insignificant. Interacting BSF adoption with these taxes did not generate statistically significant results either (results not reported). These results suggest that states are not adjusting their savings rate targets to reflect the volatility of their tax portfolios with the exception of states with a significant severance tax.

Among the political variables used, only two generated results are statistically significant. The governor being a Democrat is associated with higher savings rates (Table 5.3, column 3), which is the opposite of the expected relationship. Democratic legislatures, on the other hand, are associated with lower savings rates (Table 5.4, columns 1 and 2). Both results, however, are sensitive to change in model specifications. While I hypothesized that divided governments will have more difficulty maintaining savings, the result is mixed and not significant. I also do not find any statistically significant interaction between BSF and any of the political variables (not reported). It is possible that the lack of statistical significance reflects little within state variation in the political variables.

5.5 Conclusion and Policy Implications

This chapter builds on and extends previous research on state saving behavior. Here I have explored the effects of adopting the budget stabilization fund on saving levels in the context of each state's balance budget requirements. In particular, I have examined the use of different design features of the BSF-enabling legislation as well as nine rules of state balanced budget requirements. The chapter finds that over a period of three economic cycles, once a state adopts a budget stabilization fund and deposits money into the fund, the total-savings level may go up by about 2% points of its general fund expenditure. Checking the effects of the BSF design features, I find that maintaining a medium- or high-range cap on the BSF balance has the largest positive effect on saving levels, but requiring the use of the general fund balance or appropriations as the source for BSF reduces savings. I find that other fiscal institutions can affect the savings rate of a state, even though they were not designed for this purpose. A stringent balance budget requirement is associated with an increase of 3% points in the savings rate. Of particular importance are BBR provisions that restrict the shifting of deficits into future fiscal years through the use of debt or deficit carryovers. State expenditure limitations and biennial budgets are also associated with increases in state savings.

From the perspective of budgetary policy and fiscal policy, we can make several inferences from findings on BSF effects in interaction with BBR. Since maintaining a sizeable savings level is sound fiscal policy that will contribute to smoother operation of state governments and more stable provision of services over the economic cycle, we would naturally expect that state policy makers seriously consider three points. First, states should consider adopting a budget stabilization fund if they have not done so already, because empirical evidence in this chapter shows again that a stabilization fund increases state savings. Second, the specific design of the BSF matters. States should consider adopting BSF provisions more conducive to high-saving levels, particularly raising caps on the allowable balance level to 7% of general fund expenditure or higher. Third, it is important that when states evaluate changes to other fiscal institutions, they consider the impact of the changes on the level of savings.

Needless to say, there remains considerable room for further investigation. An important area for future research is to investigate how BSF interacts with other fiscal institutions and fiscal policies to affect savings and budget stability.

References

Alt JE, Lowry RC (1994) Divided government and budget deficits: evidence from the states. Am Polit Sci Rev 88:811–828
Alt JE, Lowry RC (2000) A dynamic model of state budget outcomes under divided partisan government. J Polit 62(4):1035–1069
Bohn H, Inman RP (1996) Balanced-budget rules and public deficits: evidence from the U.S. states. Paper read at Carnegie-Rochester conference series on public policy. NBER Working Paper No. 5533, Rochester, NY
Douglas JW, Gaddie RK (2002) State rainy day funds and fiscal crises: rainy day funds and the 1990–1990 recession revisited. Public Budg Finance 22(1):19–30
Dye RF, McGuire TJ (1992) Sorting out state expenditure pressures. Natl Tax J 45(3):315–329
Elder HW (1992) Exploring the tax revolt: an analysis of the effects of tax and expenditure limitations. Public Finance Q 20:47–63
Firestone JM (1960) Federal receipts and expenditures during business cycles 1879–1958, NBER studies in business cycles series. Princeton University Press, Princeton
Fisher RC (1984) Statement before the intergovernmental relations and human resources subcommittee of the committee on government operations. In: U.S. Congress (1985), Federal and state roles in economic stabilization. United States House of Representatives, 99th Congress, 1st Session, report 99–460, Washington, D.C, pp 101–107
Forrester JP (1991) Multi-year forecasting and municipal budgeting. Public Budg Finance 11(2):47–61
Fox WF, Campbell C (1984) Stability of the state sales tax income elasticity. Natl Tax J 37(2):201–212
Gold SD (1984) Contingency measures and fiscal limitations: the real world significance of some recent state budget renovations. Natl Tax J 37(3):421–432
Gold SG (ed) (1995) The fiscal crisis of the states – lessons for the future. Georgetown University Press, Washington, DC
Government Finance Officers Association (1999). Develop policy on stabilization funds17, 26. In: Recommended budget practices. GFOA, Chicago
Hou Y (2003) What stabilizes state general fund spending during downturns: budget stabilization fund, general fund unreserved undesignated balance, or both? Public Budg Finance 23(3):64–91
Hou Y (2004) Budget stabilization fund: structural features of the enabling legislation and balance level. Public Budg Finance 24(3):38–64
Hou Y (2006) Budgeting for fiscal stability over the business cycle. Public Adm Rev 66(5):730–742
Hou Y, Smith DL (2006) A framework for understanding state balanced budget requirement systems: re-examining distinctive features and an operational definition. Public Budg Finance 26(3):22–45
Hou Y, Smith DL (2010) Do state balanced budget requirements matter? – testing two explanatory frameworks. Public Choice 145(1):57–79

Joyce P (2001) What's so magical about five percent? Public Budg Finance 21(2):62–87
Knight B, Levinson A (1999) Rainy day funds and state government savings. Natl Tax J 52(3):459–472
Matsusaka J (1995) Fiscal effects of direct legislation: evidence from the last 30 years. J Polit Econ 103(3):587–623
Mullins DR, Wallin BA (2004) Tax and expenditure limitations: introduction and overview. Public Budg Finance 24(4):2–15
National Association of State Budget Officers (NASBO 1977–2004) Fiscal survey of states series. NASBO, Washington, DC
National Association of State Budget Officers (NASBO) State budget processes. 1985, 1988, 1992, 1995, 1998 and 2002 editions. Washington, DC
National Association of State Budget Officers (NASBO) (1992) State balanced budget requirements: provisions and practice. NASBO, Washington, DC
Poterba JM (1994) State responses to fiscal crises: the effects of budgetary institutions and politics. J Polit Econ 102(4):799–821
Poterba JM (1995) Balanced budget rules and fiscal policy: evidence from the states. Natl Tax J 48(3):329–336
Prais SJ, Winsten CB (1954) Trend estimators and serial correlation. Cowles Commission discussion paper no. 383, Chicago
Rafuse RW (1965) Cyclical behavior of state-local finances. In: Musgrave RA (ed) Essays in fiscal federalism. The Brookings Institution, Washington, DC, pp 63–121
Ruppel W (2005) GAAP for governments. Wiley, New York
Schick A (1998) A contemporary approach to public expenditure management. The World Bank Institute, Washington, DC
Wagner GA (2003) Are state budget stabilization funds only the illusion of savings? Evidence from stationary panel data. Q Rev Econ Finance 43(2):213–238
White FC (1983) Trade-off in growth and stability in state taxes. Natl Tax J 36(1):103–114

Chapter 6
Effects of Boom-Year Savings Across Three Types of State Expenditures

Abstract This chapter examines the distribution of the effects of countercyclical savings across three types of state expenditure over the economic cycle. As I have discussed in Chapter 3, boom-year savings refer to budget stabilization funds (BSF) and general fund surpluses (GFS). I use panel data of 49 states from 1979 to 1999 to test the effects of BSF and GFS on general, own-source, and general fund expenditures of the states during downturns and upturns. I find a "division of work" between the two saving devices: Though the use of BSF concentrates on own-source spending, BSF are used to boost general expenditure more than general fund expenditure in downturns but to increase general fund expenditure more than general expenditure in upturns. The effects of GFS are significant only on general fund expenditure in upturns. This finding suggests that states may have some unstated or implicit "strategy" on when (downturn or upturn) and where (which the three types of expenditures) to use the two kinds of savings.

6.1 Introduction

This chapter empirically tests the effects of countercyclical fiscal policy (CCFP) at the state level. Since the mid-1980s, about a dozen papers have examined this topic from various angles focusing on individual expenditure types, mostly on general fund expenditure (Hou 2003; Pollock and Suyderhood 1986; Sobel and Holcombe 1996a; Wagner 1999), one on own-source expenditure (Hou 2005), but so far no

This chapter is adapted and expanded from Hou Y (2006) Distribution of the effects of savings across expenditure types: evidence from the states. Munic Finance J 26(4): 1–28, published by the Civic Research Institute, New York; and Hou Y (2005) Fiscal reserves and state own-source expenditure in downturns. Public Finance Rev 33(1): 117–144, published by the Sage

Y. Hou, *State Government Budget Stabilization: Policy, Tools, and Impacts*, Studies in Public Choice 8, DOI 10.1007/978-1-4614-6061-9_6,

study has been seen that encompasses more than one expenditure type. This chapter fills in the niche by testing the effects of CCFP devices across three major expenditure types over a period of two economic cycles. Specifically, this chapter tests three propositions: First, the effects of countercyclical savings on public expenditure distribute unevenly across types of state program outlays; second, the effects of the two saving devices differ; and third, the effects vary in downturns from upturns of the economic cycle.

As I have discussed in previous chapters, countercyclical savings refer to money laid aside in boom years for use exclusively in lean years. Devices for saving of this purpose are mainly budget stabilization funds (BSF) and, to a lesser extent, general fund surplus (GFS). The two devices are for the whole government entity instead of being limited to some departments and are (at least assumed to be) for general purposes. In this sense, BSF and GFS are the two major countercyclical fiscal tools at the control of subnational governments. This chapter is restricted to testing the effects of these two devices.

The chapter is organized as follows. Section 6.2 defines the three types of expenditures to examine. Section 6.3 develops propositions to test. Section 6.4 covers methodology and data issues. Section 6.5 presents and discusses the empirical results as well as validity tests. Section 6.6 conducts further, more detailed analyses on state own-source expenditure using two data sources of BSF and GFS. The final section concludes.

6.2 Three Types of Expenditures to Examine

To test the distribution of the effects of boom-year savings, I examine three expenditure types of state governments. The three types are (1) general fund expenditure (GFE), (2) own-source expenditure (OSE), and (3) general expenditure (GNE). The general fund is one of five governmental fund types,[1] holding all money that does not belong in any of the other four fund types. In most states, it is the single largest pool of money, accounting for the daily operations of the government. As the fund that is used for the routine, ordinary activities of government (Finkler 2005), general fund expenditure (GFE) "accounts for all activities of the government unless there is a compelling reason to account for the activities in another fund" (Ruppel 2004, 53). Using GFE as a dependent variable will enable us to estimate the effects of savings on state routine activities or operational expenditures. Data source of GFE is the *Fiscal Survey of States* series by the National Association of State Budget Officers (NASBO). This is so far the most authoritative source for state general fund expenditure.

[1] These five types of governmental funds are (a) general fund, (b) special revenue funds, (c) capital projects funds, (d) debt service funds, and (e) permanent funds. See Chapter 3 of *GAAP for Governments 2004,* by Warren Ruppel, John Wiley & Sons, Inc. 2004.

Own-source expenditure (OSE) is the portion of each state's total outlay that is solely from its own revenue sources – taxes and user fees. Own-source expenditure is of our interest for obvious reasons. Tax revenues, the largest source of own-source inflow, are procyclical: It follows economic growth, high during expansion years and low during recession. In contrast, service demand is countercyclical: Taxpayers rely more on the government in lean years than in boom years. During downturns, the federal government often increases aids and grants to states to boost the economy, some of which require matching funds; thus, the use of state own-source revenue in lean years may have to be "strategic." Therefore, state OSE is of particular importance to a study of the effects of countercyclical fiscal policies. OSE data are taken from the Census *State Government Finance* series, obtained by deducting all federal grants from state general expenditure.

General expenditure (GNE) includes all state expenditures except those of insurance trust, liquor stores, and utility.[2] As such, it is a comprehensive indicator of state spending through economic cycles because insurance trust outlays are mostly outside state control, and expenditures incurred by liquor stores and utilities are only a tiny fraction of state total outlay. GNE data are also from the Census *State Government Finance* series. Of the three expenditure types, GNE is the largest, OSE on average is in the middle, and GFE is the smallest. These three types overlap in coverage; thus, they may not seem to be very "intuitive." However, their importance in the study of state budgetary policy warrants detailed examination.

Each of the three presents a wide variation in their size among the 50 states. The ratios of own-source expenditure (OSE) and general fund expenditure (GFE) as a percent of general expenditure (GNE) can be calculated with GNE as benchmark: GFE_{it}/GNE_{it} and OSE_{it}/GNE_{it}. Summing up the ratios of all sample years and then dividing the sum by the number of sample years yields the average of each state's general fund ratio and own-source ratio (T=21, 1979–1999). Then summing up the average ratios of each state and dividing the sum by the number of states (50) generates the panel averages of the two ratios: 0.49 for GFE and 0.73 for OSE. The average GFE ratio is more dispersed, with its minimum being 0.28, maximum 0.76, and standard deviation 0.10. The average OSE ratio is more centered, with its minimum being 0.63, maximum 0.83, and standard deviation of 0.04.

6.3 Propositions

On the revenue side, both of the saving devices (BSF and GFS) are located under the general fund in state budgets and financial reports. GFS, as this name indicates, is part of the general fund. BSF poses some confusion in understanding: The name "budget stabilization fund" suggests that it is a separate "fund," but under current governmental fund-accounting system, BSF are created under, and its balances kept

[2] This definition is by the Census. See the *State Government Finance* series.

in, the general fund. This placement or concentration of the savings in the general fund often leads to a natural, but unwarranted, belief that the effects of savings "should" be the largest on general fund expenditure. This belief, however, may not pass empirical tests for three reasons. First, GFS and BSF are two separate saving devices with different nature. As discussed in Chapter 3, GFS can be used as discretionary money for almost any purpose. In contrast, BSF are subject to the rule of its enabling legislation – its balance in most cases can be used only to mitigate the adverse consequences of revenue shortfall. GFS can be used throughout the economic cycle. For example, extra money as working capital is needed both in boom and in lean years, whereas the use of BSF is mostly seen in downturns. The two devices also differ in their sizes: BSF is subject to a size limit as prescribed in its enabling legislation. GFS often does not have to face this restriction: When the economy is continually strong and the government has met current spending demands, including stocking BSF to its cap level, extra revenue resides in the general fund as surpluses (see Chapter 3 for details).

Second, the above differences between the two saving devices might have rendered state governments "strategic" in their use of the two kinds of savings across the three major expenditure types, and their strategy might also differ in downturn years from upturn years. When the needy occasion arises, savings would be spent only on items that require state own resources, not on any item that can be covered with non-own-source dollars. Therefore, the effects of savings are expected to be the largest on own-source expenditure. Because both general fund expenditure and general expenditure include money from the non-own sources, the effects of savings on GFE and GNE would understandably be smaller than on OSE. However, because the use of BSF is legally more restricted than GFS, a state's GFS may be used first and foremost as general fund expenditure after the state sets up BSF. Finally, BSF balances are always spent only as own-source revenues, and BSF effect on own-source expenditure is also expected to be the most obvious. But own-source expenditure is often required as matching money for winning more federal grants, especially during a recession. Once a state has won grants, it spends these federal dollars as general expenditure for non-daily operational purposes, not into general fund expenditure to cover daily operational expenses. In other words, this use of BSF may produce a chain effect on general expenditure – increases of own-source expenditure can win back more grants to push up general expenditure. This chain effect, however, may not be present in upturn years when the federal government cuts back grants on social programs. This chapter sets up tests to examine these propositions.

6.4 Methodology and Data

The sample period runs from 1979 to 1999, covering two complete economic cycles. Different from some past studies (Knight and Levinson 1999; Sobel and Holcombe 1996a) that use aggregates of the BSF and GFS with the assumption that the two devices carry the same properties, I take BSF and GFS as two separate fiscal tools under strict definitions with different structural features (see Chapter 3). The data source for both BSF and GFS is the *Comprehensive Annual Financial Reports* (CAFR) of the states. For those years when the states had not started compiling and publishing such reports (CAFR), the data source is the *Annual Financial Reports*. For those years when a state has started publishing CAFR in accordance with the generally accepted accounting principles, consistency of data is guaranteed through accounting and auditing standards. For those years when the non-GAAP *Annual Financial Reports* were the only data source, I pick the "unreserved undesignated" or "appropriable balances" or "unencumbered balance available to finance appropriation" whether these reports were compiled on the budgetary, cash, or modified accrual basis of accounting. Potential problems occur that the balances are not from the same basis of accounting. However, since the bottom line is the unreserved undesignated balances, I have drawn something comparable.

Unlike other studies of the states that follow the convention of excluding both Alaska and Hawaii, I retain Hawaii because this state presents no extremism in its BSF and GFS features. Its distance from the continent does not make the case for its exclusion. Alaska is excluded because it is an outlier in terms of its extremely large BSF balance and huge general fund "loans" from the BSF. In fact, the source of its BSF is unique, and the operation of its general fund has been different from other states since the creation of its BSF – its BSF-GFE ratio is way above all of the other states. Another point about data is I use 1-year-lag values of BSF and GFB in order to capture the effects of accumulated savings from the last fiscal year on the current fiscal year.

6.4.1 Dependent Variables

To detect the effects of counter-cyclical savings on expenditures over the economic cycle, I first examine how far state actual expenditures deviate from their underlying trends and then how much the two kinds of savings can minimize the variance from the trends. The use of deviation-from-trend as the dependent variables makes the research questions operable because it is convenient and straightforward to estimate how much BSF and GFS can minimize the deviation of actual expenditures from their trends.

Following the practice of previous studies (Pollock and Suyderhold 1986; Sobel and Holcombe 1996a), I assume that state expenditures (data points) move randomly around a trend line and that the trend picks up the whole range of variances of actual expenditures (E) from their trends (E*), depicting the pattern and identifying the gaps between the two. I use ordinary least squares (OLS) regression to calculate a trend line for each expenditure type. Specifications of the OLS model are

$$E_{it}{}^{*} = \alpha_i + \beta_i T_t,$$

where $E_{it}{}^{*}$ is the predicted value of expenditure for state i in year t, α_i is the constant for state i, β_i is the linear trend parameter for state i, and T_t is value of the year in year *t*. Then, I calculate the variances of actual expenditures in each year from the trends. The variances divided by the trends are "gaps" of the three expenditures from their trends:

$$\text{Expenditure gap} = (\text{actual exp} - \text{trend exp}) / \text{trend exp}.$$

The term "gap" is usually used to refer to inadequacy from a target. In this chapter, the gap thus calculated can be higher or lower than the trend. They are the three dependent variables. The gaps fluctuate around the trends: They are positive gaps when $E > E^*$ and negative when $E < E^*$. Here a technical issue is worthy of attention. A trend obtained via simple regression, especially when the time series is not very long, may produce residuals that are mainly positive at the beginning and end of the sample period and mainly negative in the middle. If that is true, technically the variable is problematic. Plotting the gaps of all states, I found that is true in a few states but not true in most others states – the gaps cross the trend line several times in each case. Thus, I can use this method for the calculation. Among the three dependent variables, general expenditure gap (GNE Gap) is the most centered with the smallest standard deviation, own-source expenditure gap (OSE Gap) is the second most centered, and general fund expenditure gap (GFE Gap) is by far the most dispersed.

The next step is to explore the relationship between the expenditure gaps and the economic cycle. To obtain the cyclical properties of these gaps, I regress them against the first-difference growth rates of gross state product (GSP) in the current year and the past 5–8 years, roughly the length of an economic cycle. The model specification is

$$\text{Gap}_{\text{it}} = \alpha_{\text{i}} + \text{v}_{\text{t}} + \beta_0 \Delta \text{GSP}_{\text{i,t}} + \beta_1 \Delta \text{GSP}_{\text{i,t-1}} + \ldots + \beta_3 \Delta \text{GSP}_{\text{i,t-8}} + \varepsilon_{\iota\tau}.$$

The Prais-Winsten (1954) model of transformed regression estimator is used to correct for first-order serially correlated residuals. The model is run with fixed effects to identify whether exclusion of aggregate variation at the national level produces any obvious difference in the results. The results, as shown in Table 6.1, reveal that the three gaps all tend to be procyclical[3] – when economic growth is positive, state actual expenditures rise above trend lines; when growth is negative, actual expenditures fall below the trends.

Although the three gap measures are all procyclical, the magnitude of procyclicality of the three differs from each other. GFE gaps are the most procyclical, followed by OSE gaps, and GNE gaps are the least procyclical. Take the second

[3] In the table, the negative sign on the current-year GSP does not count because there exists an inherent lag between state finance data that go from July 1st to June 30th and Census data that go by the calendar year.

Table 6.1 Cyclicality of expenditure gaps to gross state product

	Prais-Winsten two-step with year-fixed effects					
Model	GNE gap		GFE gap		OSE gap	
Dependent variable	Coef	t-stat	Coef	t-stat	Coef	t-stat
Panel A: 5-year lags						
Current GSP	−0.0857	−1.30	−0.2364	−2.19	−0.1037	−1.18
GSP t-1	0.0025	0.04	0.1659	1.57	0.0090	0.10
GSP t-2	0.1877	2.98	0.3756	3.68	0.2786	3.24
GSP t-3	0.2826	4.66	0.4783	4.86	0.4341	5.24
GSP t-4	0.2511	4.26	0.4037	4.22	0.3232	4.03
GSP t-5	0.2286	3.98	0.1360	1.44	0.2710	3.52
Observations	784		784		784	
Prob>F	0.0000		0.0000		0.0000	
R^2	0.2673		0.1878		0.1909	
Adjusted R^2	0.1965		0.1093		0.1127	
DW statistic (original)	0.7641		0.8732		0.6161	
DW statistic (transformed)	1.7658		1.5912		1.7824	
Panel B: 8-year lags						
Current GSP	−0.0120	−0.16	−0.1288	−1.08	−0.0609	−0.06
GSP t-1	0.1142	1.53	0.3287	2.76	0.1088	1.10
GSP t-2	0.3255	4.49	0.5511	4.74	0.4481	4.65
GSP t-3	*0.3478*	4.81	*0.6922*	5.99	*0.5023*	5.23
GSP t-4	0.2117	3.02	0.4591	4.12	0.1978	2.12
GSP t-5	*0.2961*	4.36	0.1714	1.58	*0.2997*	3.32
GSP t-6	0.2486	3.75	*0.4193*	3.96	0.2765	3.13
GSP t-7	0.2287	3.46	0.2790	2.65	0.2962	3.37
GSP t-8	0.1658	2.55	0.2332	2.20	0.2426	2.83
Observations	637		637		637	
Prob>F	0.0000		0.0000		0.0000	
R^2	0.3075		0.2587		0.2114	
Adjusted R^2	0.2232		0.1685		0.1155	
DW statistic (original)	0.8115		1.0000		0.6968	
DW statistic (transformed)	1.7670		1.5782		1.7448	

lag year, for example, the coefficients for gaps of GFE, OSE, and GNE are 0.38, 0.28, and 0.19 in the 5-year lag model (Panel A) and 0.55, 0.45, and 0.33 in the 8-year lag model, respectively (Panel B) (this order of decreasing magnitude holds true also in the third lag year). This finding may bear real consequences on the stabilizing effects of BSF and GFS on these three expenditures. The obvious procyclicality of general fund expenditure confirms my proposition that daily operations expenses tend to be cut when the economy is down.

6.4.2 Model Specification

Tests are done with the panel data fixed-effects model, specified as

$$GAP_{it} = \lambda_1 \mathrm{BSF}_{\mathrm{it-1}} + \lambda_2 \mathrm{GFS}_{\mathrm{it-1}} + \beta_k{}' X_{kit} + \alpha_{\mathrm{i}} + \gamma_{\mathrm{t}} + \mu_{it}$$

The actual BSF balance at the end of each fiscal year is expressed as a percent of current general fund expenditure. A BSF dummy is designated for years after a state has established the fund and the first balance recorded. It picks up the effects of states that have adopted BSF but kept zero balances; the expected sign of the dummy is negative. General fund surpluses (defined as unreserved undesignated balance or UUB) on the modified accrual basis of accounting are expressed also as a percentage of general fund expenditure. States began adopting GAAP in different years, and fund balances conforming to GAAP are very different from those based on the budgetary basis of accounting. One of the major differences is that under GAAP guidelines, states are required to report amounts of legal reservations and various designations, which cannot be appropriated in the next fiscal year and are also deducted from current year's unreserved undesignated balance, whereas on the budgetary basis of accounting, such reservations and designations may not be deducted from current year's balance. In simple language, unreserved undesignated balances are smaller than general fund balances on the budgetary basis. For years before states published the CAFR, however, general fund balances on the budgetary basis are the only choice. To correct distortion from mixing the two accounting practices, a dummy (of 1) for the modified accrual basis distinguishes the effects of the budgetary from the GAAP balance figures. The expected sign for this dummy is also negative. Because both BSF and GFS are calculated as percentages of actual GFE, a general fund ratio is created to indicate the varying ratios of GFE against GNE. Values of the three controls are also lagged for 1 year because we are targeting the effects of savings on current expenditures.

The *X* matrix stands for state characteristics covered by four groups of controls. The first group includes four socioeconomic factors. Personal income and population change are to reflect demand for public services when the economy is strong; welfare spending and unemployment rate are to reflect demand for social services when the economy is on the downside. In both cases, higher demand for services increases state expenditure. Since spending is a function of the services that state governments provide, total spending is assumed to be positively related to population size. Personal income as another measure of economic activity is to be negatively related to spending both in recession and in boom years. As one of the biggest expenditure items of state governments in recession years, welfare outlay is expected to be countercyclical. The ratio of welfare outlay against general expenditure increases during a recession and decreases in a boom. The expected sign is positive. State unemployment as a percent of the national average, a measure of state economic health, implies negative relationship with expenditure.

It is to identify the effects of changes in employment on state spending, with positive expected signs.

The second group is balanced budget requirements (BBR). Though every state is bound by some legal requirement to balance its budget, the requirements vary significantly in form and stringency. I use binary variables to present four such requirements as reported in *The Book of the States* series (National Governors' Association): (1) Governor must submit a balanced budget, (2) legislature must pass a balanced budget, (3) governor must sign a balanced budget, and (4) state may carry over deficits into the next fiscal year. Time-series data of these four dummies display that state policies on balanced budgets did change over the sample period.

A third group is state economic structure, the time-varying composition of which contributes to changing levels of tax revenue, thereby accounting for some fluctuations in expenditures over the economic cycle. To pick up these effects, I include eight sectors of the economy measured as percents in total gross state product. They are (1) manufacturing of durable goods; (2) manufacturing of nondurable goods; (3) mining; (4) agriculture, forestry, and fishing; (5) construction; (6) finance, insurance, and real estate; (7) electronic equipment and industries; and (8) the government sector. The data are from the US Bureau of Economic Analysis.

The final group has five controls for state politics. Political party confrontation (dummy) between the governor and legislative majority is to control for the effect of cooperation or fraction between the executive and the legislative branches on state spending. The assumption is that cooperation makes it more exercisable to increase public spending, while confrontation goes against increasing spending – the legislature may obstruct executive-spending initiatives and gubernatorial veto may overthrow pork barreling. In another scenario, both sides may be willing to make compromises that result in more spending. Thus, the sign of this variable may go either way. Majority of the House and majority of the Senate being Democrat are two dummies to capture the party effect. The assumption is that the two parties hold different fiscal policies. The literature in general agrees that the Democrats are more inclined toward increasing public welfare and social services (Wildavsky 1988, 265). On the other hand, lawmakers as "pragmatists" are "willing to work out nonideological compromises across party lines" (Rivlin 1987, 2–3). Thus, it may be the dominance of the House or Senate by one party that kicks out political obstruction by the other party so that the dominant party can adopt public policies of their choice. I use two ratios, invented by Bretschneider et al. (1989) for these two variables. The ratios are calculated from the number of seats in each of the two chambers of state legislature. The definition and descriptive statistics of all the control variables are listed in Table 6.2.

State and year dummies are used in order to capture the effects of time-invariant (state-fixed) and across-sectional (national level, year-fixed) factors. Estimation is made first with an OLS model. However, to test the effects of BSF and GFS over the economic cycle, it is important to control for sample selection, that is, to separate the sample years into those of downturn and upturn years, respectively, because on top of national recessions, states experience regional downturns and booms of their own that occur in different years.

Table 6.2 Descriptive statistics of variables used (Alaska excluded, n = 1029)

Variable	Mean	Std Dev	Minimum	Maximum
Dependent variables				
General expenditure gap	0.0026	0.0717	−0.2434	0.3010
General fund expenditure gap	0.0032	0.1065	−0.3026	1.2690
Own-source expenditure gap	−0.0129	0.0755	−0.2053	0.4291
BSF and GFS				
BSF balance as percent of general fund expenditure	0.0157	0.0292	0.0000	0.3111
GFS as percent of general fund expenditure	0.0387	0.0898	−0.2713	0.5322
Modified accrual basis of accounting, dummy	0.5905	0.4920	0.0000	1.0000
BSF presence, dummy	0.5122	0.5001	0.0000	1.0000
General fund expenditure-general expenditure ratio	0.4896	0.1134	0.2220	1.0763
Related socioeconomic factors				
Population change from year to year	0.0108	0.0233	−0.0907	0.1966
Increase rate of real per capita personal income	0.0197	0.0232	−0.1300	0.1740
Own-source welfare spending as a % of general expenditure	0.0731	0.0367	−0.1583	0.2092
State unemployment rate as % of national unemployment rate	0.9494	0.2474	0.3971	2.0000
Balanced budget requirements dummies				
Governor must submit a balanced budget	0.7920	0.4061	0.0000	1.0000
Legislature must pass a balanced budget	0.6987	0.4590	0.0000	1.0000
Governor must sign a balanced budget	0.5996	0.4902	0.0000	1.0000
May carry over deficits	0.2585	0.4380	0.0000	1.0000
Sector contribution to GSP				
Share of durable goods manufacturing	0.1062	0.0527	0.0049	0.2919
Share of nondurable goods manufacturing	0.0795	0.0408	0.0149	0.2425
Share of mining	0.0314	0.0642	0.0001	0.4642
Share of agriculture, forestry, and fishing	0.0286	0.0289	0.0038	0.2014
Share of construction industry	0.0450	0.0104	0.0265	0.1023
Share of finance, insurance, and real estate	0.1581	0.0450	0.0898	0.4116
Share of electronics industry	0.0253	0.0202	0.0001	0.1682
Share of government sector	0.1353	0.0305	0.0782	0.2637
State party politics				
Governor-legislature party confrontation, dummy	0.4811	0.4999	0.0000	1.0000
House majority is Democrat, dummy	0.6521	0.4765	0.0000	1.0000
Senate majority is Democrat, dummy	0.6132	0.4873	0.0000	1.0000
House dominance by one party	2.6792	3.0398	1.0000	29.0000
Senate dominance by one party	3.0319	4.6386	1.0000	39.0000

6.4.3 Heckman Sample Selection Model

I use the Heckman (1979) model for sample year selection, separating downturn from boom years. It is a two-stage model: The first stage calculates an inverse mills ratio, which is sample selection, and the second stage generates estimates.

For example, to estimate effects of savings in recession years, the first stage examines the likelihood (mills ratio) of a state's spending going below the trend line when the expenditure gap is negative (below-trend years). The second stage then estimates the effects of BSF and GFS on state expenditures during an economic downturn. To examine the effects on the expenditure gaps in boom years, the benchmark will be set differently so that sample years selected from the first stage will be different from those for lean years.

Variables used in the first stage are some major factors that help explain state revenues: gross state product (GSP), economic structure, and tax portfolio. To avoid endogeneity, regional average GSP growth rate is used as a proxy for state GSP. Economic structure variables are the same eight economic sectors. Tax portfolio consists of dummies for personal income tax, corporate income tax, and general sales tax. Controls are used for balanced budget requirements, socioeconomic factors, and state politics. All variables except BBR and tax dummies are lagged for 1 year. Variables used in the second stage are the same as in the OLS model.

To make sure that the comparison of coefficients between equations makes sense, I have used methods for consistency of estimates from the three regressions: (a) Both BSF and GFB are expressed as a ratio of the general fund expenditure, (b) a general fund expenditure ratio (against general expenditure) is a control variable used in all three regressions, and (c) own-source welfare spending is also a ratio against general expenditure. From a more practical consideration, these three methods for consistency carry over into the Heckman sample-selection model.

6.5 Results and Discussion

Results from the OLS model with fixed effects are shown in Table 6.3. Coefficients of the two key variables present expected signs in regressions on all three expenditure gaps. The positive signs of BSF indicate that BSF balances push state expenditures up toward the positive side. Coefficients of the BSF dummy are negative, indicating that if a state has set up a BSF but keeps no money in it, the zero BSF balance pulls expenditures down toward the negative. In other words, with absence of savings (BSF) in times of need, a state cannot narrow its expenditure gaps. This is evidence that BSF balances exert countercyclical effects on all three types of expenditures.

Positive signs of GFS mean that in general the presence of GFS also pushes expenditures toward the positive side. The dummy for modified accrual basis of accounting also displays negative coefficients, confirming the negative relation between the accounting basis and level of state expenditures. However, the coefficients of GFE ratio flip signs for the three dependent variables. On GFE gap, it is positive, that is, the higher the ratio, the more the GFE gap inclines toward the positive. This makes sense in that both BSF and GFS are calculated as a percentage of the actual annual GFE, so that the higher this ratio, the higher the BSF and GFS balances are, ceteris paribus, relative to the GFE. On the gaps of GNE and OSE, this

Table 6.3 OLS model with fixed effects expenditure gaps

Column	(1)		(2)		(3)	
Dependent variable	GNE Gap		OSE Gap		GFE Gap	
Independent variables	Coef	T-Stat	Coef	T-Stat	Coef	T-Stat
(Intercept)	−0.05	−0.51	−0.22	−1.79	−0.32	−1.60
BSF balance as % of actual GFE (t-1)	*0.58*	6.81	*1.03*	10.71	*0.36*	2.33
Dummy: presence of BSF (t-1)	0.00	−0.43	−0.03	−4.09	−0.01	−0.70
GFS as % of actual GFE (t-1)	*0.00*	0.07	*0.04*	1.31	*0.13*	2.63
Dummy: GFS on MAB of accounting (t-1)	0.00	−0.64	−0.01	−0.98	−0.02	−1.43
General fund expenditure ratio (t-1)	−0.04	−1.28	−0.02	−0.40	*0.30*	4.71
Related socioeconomic factors						
Population change	0.01	0.17	−0.05	−0.57	0.17	1.14
Own-source welfare spending ratio	0.31	3.27	0.73	6.76	0.02	0.11
Per capita personal income growth rate	−0.68	−6.07	−0.91	−7.12	−1.01	−4.94
State unemployment rate ratio	0.02	1.24	0.03	1.70	−0.01	−0.29
Balanced budget requirement dummies						
Governor must submit a balanced budget	0.01	1.47	0.01	1.06	0.02	1.88
Legislature must pass a balanced budget	0.01	1.68	0.00	−0.39	−0.03	−2.66
Governor must sign a balanced budget	−0.02	−2.12	−0.01	−1.40	0.02	1.18
May carry over deficits	0.01	2.33	0.02	2.72	−0.02	−1.64
Sector contribution to GSP						
Durable goods manufacturing	−0.15	−0.75	−0.08	−0.37	0.21	0.56
Nondurable goods manufacturing	−0.57	−2.25	−1.17	−4.05	−0.24	−0.51
Mining	−0.13	−0.80	0.55	3.00	0.42	1.43
Agriculture, forestry, and fishing	0.28	1.01	0.64	2.00	0.15	0.30
Construction	1.67	5.05	2.47	6.56	2.78	4.56
Finance, insurance, and real estate	−0.10	−0.56	−0.24	−1.24	0.06	0.19
Electronics and equipment	0.10	0.53	0.12	0.55	0.14	0.39
Government	−0.06	−0.20	−0.38	−1.10	−0.20	−0.35
Party politics						
Dummy: governor-legislature confrontation	0.01	2.17	0.01	1.46	0.02	2.62
Dummy: House majority is Democrat	0.00	0.16	0.00	−0.60	−0.02	−1.92
Dummy: Senate majority is Democrat	0.00	0.62	0.01	0.76	0.01	1.11
House dominance ratio	0.00	3.08	0.00	1.84	0.00	2.18
Senate dominance ratio	0.00	0.01	0.00	−1.44	0.00	−2.57
F value	11.81		9.09		4.43	
R^2	0.54		0.48		0.31	
Adjusted R^2	0.50		0.43		0.24	
Observations	1,023		1,023		1,023	

GFE ratio displays negative signs. This leads to an important finding: On the surface, the flip of signs is mere indication of the different sizes of the three expenditures, GNE being the largest, OSE the second largest, and GFE the smallest. In fact, the flip of signs points to the location – which one of the three expenditures – where more of savings are spent.

The magnitude of effects on the three dependent variables shows a large variation. The effects of BSF on own-source expenditure are the largest, followed by general expenditure; BSF effects on general fund expenditure are the smallest: One percentage point increase of the BSF balance pushes up the OSE gap by about one percentage points (1.03), the GNE gap by 0.58 percentage points, but the GFE gap by only 0.36 percentage points. The percent-for-percent effect of BSF on OSE gap is relatively easy to explain – once BSF funds are laid aside for later countercyclical use, the saved money is to be spent only on items requiring state own resources. Therefore, the effects are the largest on own-source expenditure. Since both general fund expenditure and general expenditure include portions of money from non-own sources, the effects of BSF are understandably smaller on them than on own-source expenditure.

The distance between the coefficients for GNE gap (0.58, Column 1) and GFE gap (0.36, Column 3) is the focus of this study, but it takes effort to interpret. Since general expenditure (GNE) is the largest of the three types and general fund expenditure (GFE) is the smallest, the magnitude of BSF effects may be expected to be larger on GFE gap than on GNE gap, but the above results present an opposite image. This inverted size of the effects seems to make no sense, but this apparent absurdity strikes the point that BSF are spent more on general expenditure items than on general fund expenditure items. The flip of signs of the GFE-ratio variable on the three expenditures provides extra evidence on this point. The higher the GFE ratio, the larger the overlap is between general expenditure and general fund expenditure, such that items that used to be covered under general expenditure now come under general fund expenditure. It is this increasing coverage of the general fund expenditure against general expenditure that generates larger effects on general fund expenditure, ceteris paribus. For each percentage point increase of the GFE ratio, the GFE gap is pushed up by 0.30%age points.

This finding is important in that it would have been often assumed that since BSF balances are created and kept within the general fund, its effects should have been most obvious on general fund expenditure, but it turns out to be otherwise – BSF balances are kept in the general fund but they are spent more on non-general fund items. This is not difficult to understand if we take a step back: General fund items are more routine, daily operational costs that are relatively stable. When recessions hit, such costs are among the first items to be frozen or cut. This point is confirmed by the fact that GFE is the most procyclical of the three expenditure types (Table 6.1) and the fact that the GFE gap is the most dispersed of the three expenditure gaps. In comparison, expenditure on items in the other two outlay types may increase. Checking the actual expenditure figures by item in the general fund and special revenue funds of New York state from 1989 to 1992, I found supporting evidence. From 1990 to 1992, many items covered by general fund expenditure underwent reductions over the previous year, whereas many more items in the special revenue funds had increases.

The general fund surplus (GFS) coefficient is statistically significant only on the general fund expenditure (GFE) gap among the three regressions and also is the largest among the three GFS coefficients: Each percentage point increase of GFS can push up GFE gap by 0.13 percentage points. This unique feature is provocative: Why is general fund surplus significant only with GFE gap? My interpretation is that general fund surplus is spent more on general fund items than on items covered under the other two expenditure types. This is an important point: If this is proved to be true and reliable, then this test is providing evidence that BSF and GFS are not only with different cyclical properties, but they are also kept and used for different purposes. BSF balances are reserved more for general expenditure items than for general fund expenditure items, whereas GFS are kept more for items under the general fund expenditure than under the general expenditure. Evidence comes next.

6.5.1 Downturn and Upturn Years

Applying the Heckman sample-selection model distinguishes upturn years (when actual expenditures go above the trends) from downturn years (when expenditures fall below the trends). Since the expenditure gaps are procyclical, testing the effects of BSF and GFS in downturns and upturns separately reveals the effects of the two saving devices during not only national but also regional and state economic cycles. Results show that BSF exerts not only fairly large countercyclical effects during downturn years, as expected, but also obvious positive effects on state spending in non-downturn years. Results are shown in Table 6.4.

In downturn years, BSF coefficients are positive and statistically significant on all three expenditures (Columns 1–3), indicating that BSF do exert positive impacts on state spending during years when state economies are sluggish. The coefficients do vary among the three expenditure types. Specifically, during a downturn, each percentage point increase of BSF can minimize negative gaps of general expenditure (GNE) by 0.65 percentage points and own-source expenditure (OSE) by 0.60%age points but only 0.25 percentage points of the general fund expenditure (GFE) gap.

This difference in the magnitude of the countercyclical effects of BSF confirms findings from the OLS model: In lean years, BSF is spent more on general expenditure than on general fund expenditure. This is why the BSF coefficient on GFE gap is the smallest. BSF balances are spent only as own sources, but own-source expenditures often may be matching money for winning more federal grants, which, once won over, go into general expenditure on non-daily items instead of going into the general fund to cover daily operational expenses. In other words, own-source expenditure pushes up general expenditure in lean years. This is why the BSF coefficient on GNE gap is even larger than that for own-source expenditure gap.

In upturn years, however, BSF coefficients remain positive and significant (Columns 4–6). That is, even when the economy is not in a downturn and the actual

Table 6.4 Results from the Heckman sample-selection model

Column	(1)		(2)		(3)		(4)		(5)		(6)	
Phase of business cycle	Downturn years (negative exp gap)						Upturn years (positive exp gap)					
Dependent variable	GNE gap		OSE gap		GFE gap		GNE gap		OSE gap		GFE gap	
Independent variables	Coef.	z-stat	Coef.	z-stat	Coef.	z-stat	Coef.	z-stat	Coef.	z-stat	Coef.	z-stat
BSF balance as % of actual GFE (t-1)	*0.65*	*7.23*	*0.60*	*4.84*	*0.25*	*2.55*	*0.13*	*1.76*	*0.49*	*5.10*	*0.24*	*1.80*
Dummy: presence of BSF (t-1)	–0.02	–3.29	–0.02	–4.07	–0.01	–2.08	0.00	0.60	–0.01	–0.97	–0.01	–0.72
UUB as % of actual GFE (t-1)	*–0.03*	*–1.42*	*0.02*	*0.83*	*–0.02*	*–0.52*	*0.01*	*0.34*	*0.03*	*0.80*	*0.14*	*2.78*
Dummy: GFS on MAB of accounting (t-1)	0.00	–0.58	0.01	1.08	0.00	–0.53	0.00	0.07	–0.02	–2.05	–0.01	–1.41
General fund expenditure ratio (t-1)	–0.06	–1.96	0.00	–0.16	0.25	6.29	0.04	1.38	0.04	1.00	0.16	2.70
Related socioeconomic factors												
Population change	0.01	0.14	–0.04	–0.63	0.03	0.30	0.08	1.09	–0.08	–0.80	0.19	1.35
Per capita personal income growth rate	–0.15	–1.80	–0.09	–0.95	–0.22	–1.81	–0.23	–2.08	–0.22	–1.56	–0.48	–2.25
Own-source welfare spending ratio	0.42	4.77	0.63	6.76	0.18	1.66	–0.04	–0.44	0.34	2.87	0.29	1.94
State unemployment rate ratio	0.00	0.25	0.01	0.91	0.00	0.22	0.01	0.92	0.05	2.86	–0.01	–0.42
Balanced budget requirement dummies												
Governor must submit a balanced budget	0.00	–0.02	0.00	–0.82	0.00	–0.18	0.00	–0.07	0.00	–0.42	0.00	0.14
Legislature must pass a balanced budget	0.01	0.87	0.01	1.52	0.01	1.27	0.01	0.75	0.00	–0.37	–0.01	–0.88
Governor must sign a balanced budget	–0.01	–1.98	–0.01	–1.48	–0.01	–1.01	0.01	0.58	0.00	0.02	0.00	–0.26
May carry over deficits	0.00	0.35	–0.01	–1.10	–0.02	–3.09	0.02	2.56	0.03	2.90	0.02	1.19
Sector contribution to GSP												
Durable goods manufacturing	0.33	1.98	–0.06	–0.35	–0.54	–2.54	–1.04	–5.21	–0.43	–1.51	–0.66	–1.65
Nondurable goods manufacturing	–0.34	–1.54	–0.69	–2.77	–0.09	–0.30	0.27	1.10	–0.09	–0.25	0.82	1.51
Mining	0.06	0.39	0.10	0.63	–0.33	–1.61	–0.48	–3.11	0.29	1.23	–1.01	–3.06
Agriculture, forestry, and fishing	0.11	0.44	0.05	0.20	–0.34	–1.00	–0.40	–1.62	0.17	0.51	–0.27	–0.51
Construction	0.51	1.78	0.80	2.56	0.24	0.57	0.06	0.18	1.10	2.20	–0.38	–0.50

(continued)

Table 6.4 (continued)

Column	(1)		(2)		(3)		(4)		(5)		(6)	
Phase of business cycle	Downturn years (negative exp gap)						Upturn years (positive exp gap)					
Dependent variable	GNE gap		OSE gap		GFE gap		GNE gap		OSE gap		GFE gap	
Independent variables	Coef.	z-stat	Coef.	z-stat	Coef.	z-stat	Coef.	z-stat	Coef.	z-stat	Coef.	z-stat
Finance, insurance, and real estate	–0.11	–0.72	–0.24	–1.42	–0.29	–1.54	0.01	0.03	0.18	0.63	0.32	0.93
Electronics and equipment	–0.28	–1.32	–0.28	–1.30	0.10	0.35	0.56	3.19	0.24	1.01	0.09	0.26
Government	–0.12	–0.47	–0.09	–0.31	–0.46	–1.27	–1.15	–3.93	0.07	0.16	–0.73	–1.22
Party politics												
Dummy: governor-legislature confrontation	0.01	3.61	0.01	2.10	0.00	0.05	0.01	1.89	–0.02	–3.00	–0.02	–2.10
Dummy: House majority is Democrat	–0.01	–1.41	0.00	0.51	–0.01	–1.78	0.00	0.53	0.01	1.22	0.00	0.16
Dummy: Senate majority is Democrat	0.01	2.20	0.01	2.17	–0.01	–1.14	0.00	0.10	–0.02	–2.14	–0.01	–0.69
House dominance ratio	0.00	2.44	0.00	1.19	0.00	0.97	0.00	1.31	0.00	–1.83	0.00	–1.22
Senate dominance ratio	0.00	0.18	0.00	0.11	0.00	0.96	0.00	0.20	0.00	–0.68	0.00	–1.25
Censored observations	479		408		470		549		620		538	
Uncensored observations	547		616		535		477		408		466	
Likelihood ratio test of independent equation X^2	2.01		3.02		2.28		5.86		1.96		5.17	

Note: Results of stage one are not reported

expenditures stay above the trends, existence of a BSF still "pushes up" state expenditures. The magnitude of the effects, however, is smaller than in a downturn. For general expenditure (GNE) gap, it is 0.13 (downturn year 0.65); for own-source expenditure (OSE) gap, it is 0.49 (downturn year 0.6); and for general fund expenditure (GFE) gap, it is 0.24, almost the same as in downturn years (0.25). These procyclical effects of BSF, however, are pseudo and should not be surprising because the size of BSF balance is capped by law, in most states at a level equal to 5% of the current-year general fund. When the economy has been continually strong and the state has more revenue streaming in than actual expenditures require, the state has to spend it somewhere once the BSF has reached its statutory limit. Therefore, instead of being "procyclical," this is really the cap effect of the BSF law reflected in state expenditures. The cap effect is especially obvious on own-source expenditure and general fund expenditure.

Comparing the magnitudes of the BSF coefficients in downturn years against those in upturn years reveals much more about where the actual uses of BSF balances go. Because BSF balances are always spent as own-source revenues, its effect on OSE gap is also the most obvious. But this effect in down years produces a chain effect on general expenditure – increases of own-source expenditure probably wins back more federal grants; therefore, the lean-year BSF coefficient on the general expenditure (GNE) gap is even larger than on the own-source expenditure (OSE) gap. However, this chain effect is not observed in upturn years when the BSF coefficient on GNE gap is only 0.13. The BSF coefficient on GFE gap is larger at 0.24, which may be more of the cap effect on the BSF balance than the chain effect of winning federal money.

Contrary to assumptions in some previous studies, general fund surplus does not display observable countercyclical effects on any of the three types of expenditure: GFS coefficients for none of the three dependent variables in downturn years are statistically significant. In the upturn-year regressions, though the GFS coefficients are positive, only the one on general fund expenditure (GFE) is statistically significant, further confirming a finding from the OLS model that GFS is first and foremost for use on general fund expenditure items. Further, the positive GFS coefficients in upturn years may be the residual effect of continued economic boom, similar to the cap effect for BSF—when the economy is continually strong and the state government has more revenues than needed to meet the spending demands, some revenue resides in the general fund as surpluses.

Results from the Heckman model reveal different effects of BSF on own-source expenditure (OSE) gaps in downturn years (0.60) from upturn years (0.49), both statistically significant, confirming results from the all-sample-year (OLS) model. In comparison, the coefficients of GFS are very small (downturn 0.02 and upturn 0.03) and are not statistically significant. Surprisingly, these results explain the ones from the OLS model that embrace the effects for both downturn and upturn years. The sum of the upturn-year BSF coefficient of 0.49 and that for the downturn year (0.60) is close to the 1.03 coefficient from the all-sample-year (OLS) model. And the sum of upturn and downturn GFB coefficients (0.03 and 0.02) is also close to that from the all-sample-year (OLS) model (0.04). In other words, the sample-selection model

Table 6.5 Summary of results in upturn- and downturn years

Phase of cycle	Downturn years			Upturn years		
Expenditure type	GNE	OSE	GFE	GNE	OSE	GFE
Budget stabilization fund	+	+	+	+	+	+
General fund surplus						+

decomposes the coefficients from the OLS model into two parts, one for downturn years and the other for upturn years. This decomposition is, however, observable only on own-source expenditure. The results are summed up in Table 6.5.

6.5.2 *Effects on Per Capita Expenditures: A Sensitivity Test*

Development of time-series econometrics in recent decades reminds us that economic data trend upward through time, causing a potential nonstationarity problem with state finance indicators. Some authoritative studies are offered in Fuller (1976), Granger and Watson (1984), Engle and Granger (1987), and Hamilton (1994). Though this author has tried hard to maintain technical vigor in developing the dependent variables, the measure of "expenditure gaps" may still not be free of nonstationarity. To handle the time-series property of the data and run a sensitivity test, this section transforms the three expenditures as well as BSF and GFB measures into comparable real (year-2000) per capita dollars and runs the OLS model again with the same specification as in Table 6.3. In this case, the dependent variables are per capita real expenditures of the three types in level instead of calculated gaps, and the two key explanatory variables, BSF and GFS, are also in real per capita dollars instead of percentages of general fund expenditures. Coefficients thus obtained will be the effects of each dollar of savings on actual-state expenditures.

Table 6.6 presents results from the all sample year, OLS with fixed-effects model, everything else being the same as in the expenditure gaps model (Table 6.3). F-tests show that the models are reliable; R-squares are reasonably high; t-statistics for coefficients of key variables are all statistically significant, an improvement on the expenditure gaps model. The effects of BSF are the largest with own-source expenditure (0.89), followed by general expenditure (0.67), and the smallest with general fund expenditure (0.16), presenting the same pattern of distribution of the effects as with the expenditure gaps.

GFS coefficients are the smallest with general expenditure (0.12), larger with own-source expenditure (0.18), and the largest with general fund expenditure (0.21), again presenting the same pattern of distribution as with the expenditure gaps model, confirming the previous finding that subnational governments treat and use the two major saving devices differently: BSF is focused on own-source expenditures; its use is much less on general fund expenditure of routine functions. In contrast, GFS is the major force on routine operations but much less on general expenditures. Thus, these two devices complement each other nicely.

Table 6.6 Prais-Winsten model with fixed effects. Dependent variables are real (year-2000) per capita expenditures

Column	(1)		(2)		(3)	
Dependent variable	GNE		OSE		GFE	
Independent variables	Coef	t-Stat	Coef	t-Stat	Coef	t-Stat
(Intercept)	2.56	4.18	0.45	0.75	−0.48	−1.03
CAFR-BSF real per capita (t-1)	*0.67*	3.36	*0.89*	4.13	*0.16*	0.96
Dummy: presence of BSF (t-1)	0.00	−0.17	−0.02	−0.67	0.01	0.52
CAFR-GFS real per capita (t-1)	*0.12*	2.06	*0.18*	2.93	*0.21*	4.40
Dummy: GFS on MAB of accounting (t-1)	0.00	0.04	−0.01	−0.34	0.01	0.61
General fund expenditure ratio (t-1)	0.11	1.19	0.19	1.82	−0.09	−1.07
Related socioeconomic factors						
Population change	−0.03	−0.28	−0.10	−0.68	0.10	0.87
Per capita personal income (,000)	0.03	2.86	0.06	4.98	0.06	7.02
Per capita personal income growth rate	−0.64	−2.62	−1.05	−3.91	−0.81	−3.80
Own-source welfare spending ratio	1.08	3.90	1.76	5.88	−0.14	−0.61
State unemployment rate ratio	0.08	2.12	0.07	1.66	0.07	2.13
Balanced budget requirement dummies						
Governor must submit a balanced budget	0.00	0.14	0.01	0.38	−0.01	−0.62
Legislature must pass a balanced budget	0.02	0.91	0.01	0.43	0.00	−0.09
Governor must sign a balanced budget	−0.02	−0.89	−0.02	−0.83	0.00	0.11
May carry over deficits	−0.01	−0.41	0.00	−0.11	−0.03	−1.84
Sector contribution to GSP						
Durable goods manufacturing	−1.04	−1.32	−0.64	−0.79	−0.10	−0.15
Nondurable goods manufacturing	−3.13	−3.22	−2.90	−2.92	−1.65	−2.13
Mining	0.95	1.42	1.67	2.56	−0.12	−0.23
Agriculture, forestry, and fishing	0.94	1.10	1.69	1.86	−0.43	−0.60
Construction	2.38	1.60	3.95	2.65	0.03	0.02
Finance, insurance, and real estate	−0.84	−0.98	−1.87	−2.30	−0.49	−0.78
Electronics and equipment	1.07	1.24	0.27	0.31	−0.14	−0.21
Government	0.87	0.57	1.73	1.16	1.30	1.13
Party politics						
Dummy: governor-legislature confrontation	0.00	0.19	0.00	0.17	0.00	−0.12
Dummy: house majority is Democrat	−0.01	−0.70	−0.01	−0.75	−0.02	−1.36
Dummy: senate majority is Democrat	−0.04	−2.33	−0.04	−2.05	0.02	1.54
House dominance ratio	0.01	1.13	0.00	−0.17	0.01	1.56
Senate dominance ratio	0.00	−1.28	0.00	−1.31	0.00	0.65
Prob>F	0.00		0.00		0.00	
R^2	0.76		0.89		0.79	
Adjusted R^2	0.74		0.88		0.76	
Observations	979		979		978	
Transformed DW	2.01		2.00		2.02	

6.6 More Tests of Effects on Own-Source Expenditure

Among the three types of state outlays, own-source expenditure should be more carefully examined for several reasons. First, in times of urgent, sharp spending increases, federal grants may not increase at proportionate pace. Second, state taxes, by far the largest source of own-source revenues, are procyclical. The rise and fall of tax revenue growth roughly follow that of state economy as indicated by gross state product (GSP). However, service demand is countercyclical. There exists a reverse relation between state economy and service demands on state governments. When GSP growth is positive, state unemployment rate goes down and state welfare spending is low. In downturn years, state unemployment rate goes high and states' own-source welfare spending rises accordingly. Finally, during recessions the federal government may increase welfare aid to states, which requires state matching funds, so state own-source welfare spending also increases during recessions. Therefore, it makes sense to separate state own-source welfare spending from federal welfare grants. In situations when spending demands rise sharply but the federal government does not provide grants proportionate to the increased demands, state own-source expenditure is of particular concern. This section conducts further tests on the effects of fiscal reserves on state total own-source expenditure in downturn years.

6.6.1 *Setup of Estimation*

Here I first adopt the residual-from-trend approach and then check the validity of the results with the first-difference growth rate approach. The underlying pattern (e.g., the trend line) of each state's OSE is obtained by a levels regression. To handle the time-series properties of state expenditure, annual figures are transformed into natural logs. The regression goes

$$\ln\left(\mathrm{E}_{\mathrm{it}}{}^{*}\right)=\alpha_{\mathrm{i}}+\beta_{\mathrm{i}}\mathrm{T}_{\mathrm{t}};$$

where $\ln(E_{it}{}^{*})$ is the predicted value of expenditure for state *i* in year *t*, α_i is the constant for state *i*, β_i is the linear trend parameter for state *i*, and T_t is value of the year in year *t*.

Then, the year-by-year variance of the actual expenditure from the trend is calculated by subtracting the trend from the actual expenditure. The variance then is divided by the trend, expressed as a percentage, which is the expenditure gap of state total own-source expenditure from the trend:

$$\begin{aligned}\text{Expenditure Gap} &= (\text{Actual Exp} - \text{Trend Exp}) / \text{Trend Exp}\\ &= \left(\ln(\mathrm{E}_{\mathrm{it}}) - \ln\left(\mathrm{E}_{\mathrm{it}}{}^{*}\right)\right) / \ln\left(\mathrm{E}_{\mathrm{it}}{}^{*}\right)\end{aligned}$$

The expenditure gap is the first dependent variable. This expenditure gap is procyclical. It is expected that in downturn years, fiscal reserves (GFS and BSF) would exert positive effects on state expenditure, thereby reducing the negative expenditure gap by drawing down the reserves to increase spending.

The empirical model is

$$\ln(\text{ExpGap}_{it}) = \lambda \text{Reserve}_{-1}(\text{BSF}_{-1} + \text{GFS}_{-1}) + \beta_k X_{kit} + \alpha_i + \gamma_t + \varepsilon_{it}$$

In the model, β_k is responses of expenditure to idiosyncratic (state-specific) changes in various factors ($X_{kit)}$ that influence state OSE besides fiscal reserves. α_i and γ_t are the state- and year-fixed effects to control for cross-sectional variation constant over the sample period and aggregate variation at the national level. The fixed effects also help correct for potential endogeneity.

As discussed in previous chapters, there are two data sources for BSF and GFS; they are the state *CAFR*s and NASBO's *Fiscal Survey of States* (FSS) series. The *FSS* lists six more states as having a BSF than the *CAFR* in the sample period (thus, the *FSS* source has more samples than the *CAFR* source). Year-end general fund balance (GFB) in the *FSS* series has been taken as GFS in previous studies (Sobel and Holcombe 1996a; Knight and Levinson 1999). In this section, I use both GFB and the unreserved undesignated balance of the general fund (UUB, which I name GFS) to test their respective effects. Both GFB and UUB are expressed as a percentage of current-year general fund expenditure.

As done in previous sections of this chapter, I use a dummy to account for the effect of BSF. Since *CAFR* UUB is on modified accrual basis of accounting and *FSS* GFB is on a budgetary basis, to correct any possible distortion by mixing the two kinds of accounting practices, a dummy variable for the modified accrual basis of accounting distinguishes the effects of the two kinds of balance figures. These two controls appear only in tests for the *CAFR* data. State general funds occupy varying portions of total state budgets, from less than 20% to over 90%. A general fund ratio controls for the state-to-state, year-to-year variation of general fund expenditure against general expenditure. This variable is used in testing data from both sources.

Control variables are about the same as in previous tests. *Social and economic factors* include population change, state own-source welfare spending as a percent of general expenditure, and growth in real per capita personal income, and state average monthly unemployment rate as a percent of the national average rate is included. *Balanced budget requirements* include four dummies: Governor must submit a balanced budget, the legislature must pass a balanced budget, the governor must sign a balanced budget, and the state may carry over deficits into the next fiscal year. *Economic structure* is proxied as share contribution to GSP of eight sectors. Six of these sectors are procyclical: manufacturing of durable goods, manufacturing of nondurable goods, mining industries, construction, electronics, and agriculture, forestry, and fishing. While five of these sectors decline over time in the sample period as a ratio of state GSP (electronics remains stable with slight increases), their procyclical nature is obvious, especially in manufacturing of durable goods and construction. The government sector is countercyclical because more people rely on welfare in recession years, and this changes dramatically in boom years. The finance, insurance, and real estate sector are also countercyclical. *Party politics* variables include political party confrontation between the governor and the majority in the state legislature, a majority of the house being Democrat, a majority of the senate being Democrat, dominance of the house by one party, and dominance of the senate by one party. The first three are dummy variables to capture the party effect, assuming that the two parties uphold different ideology. The last two variables are calculated from the number of seats in the two state legislative chambers; the number of seats one party holds is divided by the number of seats the other party holds, and the reverse operation is also done. Ratios smaller than one are deleted, leaving only those greater than one during the 21 years because only ratios larger than one are considered dominant. These two variables test the majority party's dominance of each chamber.

6.6.2 Methodology

As done previously, Alaska is excluded in the tests. Four other states also pose unique data issues. California, Illinois, and New York recorded deficits in their UUB for over 10 years in the sample period. Massachusetts changed its reporting entity of general fund twice during the last two decades. Besides the average balance level of BSF from both sources, GFB and UUB for each of the four states are far below the average level of these variables for the 49 states. Exclusion of these four leaves the data set with 45 states. See Table 6.7, Panel E.

I also need to examine the case with the 11 non-BSF states (by the strict definition, see Section 3.3). Because general fund surpluses historically played countercyclical roles and because these states did not have a BSF, they should have used the GFS for stabilizing purposes. If this was the case, then the effects should show up in the estimates. Therefore, regressions are also run with only the 11 non-BSF states. Tests are first done with the aggregate fiscal reserves, the sum of BSF and GFS, and then done with the reserves broken down into BSF and GFS for their separate effects on state spending. Again, I use the Heckman (1979) two-stage sample-selection model for the test. The first stage selects the downturn years for each state by calculating the likelihood of a state's spending falling below the trend line. The second stage obtains the effects of fiscal reserves on state actual spending during those downturn (below-trend) years. Variables used in the first stage to select the sample years include (apart from the socioeconomic factors, balanced budget requirements, and state politics) regional economic growth, sector contribution to gross state product, and state tax structure, all lagging 1 year. It is assumed that if the region had negative growth last year, then a state in the region may well have a below-the-trend expenditure in the current year. Along the same line of reasoning, the eight sectors' last-year contribution to GSP may help explain whether their current-year expenditure is below the trend. The three dummies for personal income, corporate income, and general sales taxes are controls for state revenue.

Table 6.7 Summary statistics for further tests on own-source expenditure

Source	Variable	Number of states	Number of observations	Mean	Standard deviation	Minimum	Maximum
Panel A							
FSS	BSF	49	675	0.027	0.035	0.000	0.310
		45	618	0.028	0.035	0.000	0.310
		11	118	0.010	0.022	0.000	0.104
CAFR	BSF	49	527	0.031	0.035	0.000	0.311
		45	472	0.033	0.036	0.000	0.311
		11	0	NA	NA	NA	NA
Panel B							
FSS	GFB	49	1028	0.052	0.075	–0.146	0.700
		45	944	0.056	0.077	–0.146	0.700
		11	231	0.064	0.069	–0.133	0.282
CAFR	UUB	49	1,028	0.039	0.090	–0.271	0.532
		45	944	0.047	0.085	–0.214	0.532
		11	231	0.044	0.094	–0.214	0.420
Panel C							
FSS	Reserve	49	675	0.069	0.077	–0.146	0.837
		45	618	0.074	0.078	–0.146	0.837
		11	231	0.058	0.051	–0.018	0.210
CAFR	Reserve	49	527	0.061	0.099	–0.271	0.398
		45	472	0.074	0.090	–0.192	0.398
		11	231	0.044	0.094	–0.214	0.420
Panel D							
ln(OSE gap)		49	1,029	–0.0003	0.009	–0.032	0.059
		45	945	–0.0002	0.009	–0.032	0.059
		11	231	–0.0004	0.008	–0.019	0.028
Panel E: Summary statistics of five states for further tests on own-source expenditure							
a. Alaska							
FSS	BSF	12	0.640	0.515	0.083	1.471	
	GFB	21	0.135	0.416	–0.070	1.882	
CAFR	BSF	8	0.826	0.514	0.225	1.509	
	UUB	21	–0.206	0.484	–1.464	0.657	
b. California							
FSS	BSF	17	0.015	0.019	0.000	0.054	
	GFB	21	0.018	0.046	–0.027	0.165	
CAFR	BSF	21	0.008	0.014	0.000	0.052	
	UUB	21	–0.005	0.053	–0.091	0.152	
c. Illinois							
FSS	BSF	10	0.000	0.000	0.000	0.000	
	GFB	21	0.031	0.018	0.009	0.063	
CAFR	BSF	21	0.000	0.000	0.000	0.000	
	UUB	21	–0.064	0.050	–0.171	0.011	
d. New York							
FSS	BSF	17	0.005	0.004	0.000	0.013	
	GFB	21	0.002	0.003	0.000	0.011	

(continued)

Table 6.7 (continued)

Source	Variable	Number of states	Number of observations	Mean	Standard deviation	Minimum	Maximum
	BSF	21	0.006	0.005	0.000	0.013	
	UUB	21	–0.158	0.096	–0.271	0.029	
e. Massachusetts							
FSS	BSF	13	0.023	0.024	0.000	0.076	
	GFB	21	0.007	0.033	–0.109	0.055	
CAFR	BSF	21	0.016	0.023	0.000	0.076	
	UUB	21	0.010	0.037	–0.111	0.074	

Notes
1. "BSF" is the BSF balance as a percentage of general fund expenditure. "GFB" and "UUB" are year-end balances as percentages of general fund expenditure
2. "CAFR" source reserve equals BSF + UUB (both from *Comprehensive Annual Financial Report* series)
3. "FSS" source reserve equals BSF + GFB (both from *Fiscal Survey of the States* series)
4. The log of OSE gap is the dependent variable, defined as the gap between log level actual and predicted real own-source expenditure as a percentage of predicted expenditure
5. NA = not applicable

6.6.3 Results and Discussion

Regression results are presented in Table 6.8. Panel A shows effects of the aggregate fiscal reserves on state spending in downturn years. Odd-numbered columns are estimates for the CAFR data and even-numbered columns for the FSS data. With only Alaska excluded from the sets, reserves from both data sources are shown to have positive effects on spending; however, the coefficient of CAFR data is statistically significant but the FSS coefficient is not (Columns 1 and 2). For the 45-state set (with California, Illinois, New York, and Massachusetts also excluded, Columns 3 and 4), the coefficients for reserves from both sources are statistically significant. For the 11-state group (according to the strict definition, since by the broad definition 6 of these 11 have a BSF) in Columns 5 and 6, neither coefficient is statistically significant. Interestingly, the CAFR reserve is positive while the FSS reserve is negative. In general, estimates in Panel A show that fiscal reserves did exert positive effects on state spending for most states during downturn years in the 1979–1999 period.

Estimates for disaggregated reserves are displayed in Panel B of Table 6.8. With only Alaska excluded from the samples (Columns 7 and 8), the estimates for the BSF from both sources are positive at significant levels; the estimates for UUB and GFB, however, are not significant though both are positive. This indicates that even with the extended general fund deficits from the four states, the BSF exerts positive effects on downturn spending. In Columns 9 and 10, when these states are taken out, coefficients on BSF from both sources become larger and significant at higher levels; also, the UUB coefficient doubles in size and turns significant.

For the 11-state group (Columns 11 and 12), estimates for both GFB and UUB are positive; the GFB is statistically significant and the UUB is not, hinting that the broadly defined GFB (with higher average balance levels) exerts a strong influence

Table 6.8 Results of Heckman sample-selection model for further tests on own-source expenditure

	Column	(1)	(2)	(3)	(4)	(5)	(6)
Source	Variable	AK excluded (49)		AK, MA, CA, IL, NY excluded (45)		Non-BSF states (11)	
Panel A: Effects of aggregate reserves (sum of BSF and GFS)							
CAFR	*Reserve* $_{t-1}$	0.006**		0.009***		0.010	
		(0.003)		(0.004)		(0.007)	
FSS	*Reserve* $_{t-1}$		0.007		0.012**		−0.010
			(0.040)		(0.006)		(0.035)
	Column	(7)	(8)	(9)	(10)	(11)	(12)
Source	Variable	AK excluded (49)		AK, MA, CA, IL, NY excluded (45)		Non-BSF states (11)	
Panel B: Effects of BSF and GFS							
CAFR	*BSF* $_{t-1}$	0.019*		0.030**			
		(0.011)		(0.015)			
	UUB $_{t-1}$	0.004		0.008**		0.010	
		(0.003)		(0.004)		(0.007)	
FSS	*BSF* $_{t-1}$		0.031**		0.034***		−0.142***
			(0.013)		(0.013)		(0.041)
	GFB $_{t-1}$		0.002		0.008		0.078***
			(0.012)		(0.006)		(0.023)

Notes
1. The dependent variable is the log of the level of own-source expenditure gap from trend
2. Standard errors are in *parenthesis*
3. Significance levels are marked by stars: * for 10%; ** for 5%; and *** for 1%
4. Estimates for control variables, fixed effects, and stage one are not reported but are available on request

(0.078) on state spending while the strictly defined UUB does not. Surprisingly, the estimate for BSF here is negative at highly significant levels and is much larger than GFB, which is why the aggregate reserve for the FSS source presents the negative sign (Column 6). One possible explanation for the negative BSF here is perhaps those six states (that do not have BSF by the strict definition) reported in the FSS series balances that they had to appropriate even in lean years but could not use for budget stabilization purposes; that is, probably, those were not a BSF.

In sum, fiscal reserves as an aggregate exert a positive influence on state OSE during downturn years. Breaking the reserves into the BSF and GFS components, the positive influence from the BSF is especially strong, and the magnitude of the BSF influence is similar for data from both sources. For most states, the UUB (or the GFS from the *CAFR* source) also exerts a positive influence on state spending but at a much lower magnitude; the GFB (the GFS from the *FSS source*) does not show this effect.

States that do not have a BSF by the strict definition (six of them claim to have a BSF and report BSF balances in the *FSS* series) relied on general fund balance as fiscal reserves. Their average GFB level (0.064) exceeds the 49- or 45-state averages (0.052 and 0.056) and did push up spending in downturns. The effect of their UUB (at 0.044, lower than the 45-state means of 0.047), however, is not significantly different from zero.

6.6.4 Cyclical Features of BSF and GFS

Estimation results of disaggregated reserves show that the BSF tends to exert larger effects on state downturn spending than GFS if GFS has a statistically significant coefficient, which hints that the two fiscal tools may possess different cyclical/structural features. A unique feature of the BSF is that it is protected by its enabling legislation against spending pressure during economic booms; thus, it can accumulate. GFS, in contrast, may have been much more subject to the manipulation of spending politics, and so it is difficult to last long. Table 6.9 shows results of regressing the BSF and the GFS against the state economy. The results show that the BSF, whether from the *CAFR* or *FSS* sources, roughly follows the growth of gross state product; that is, the BSF accumulates with positive GSP growth and decumulates with negative GSP growth. This pattern is true from the current year to lag-year five; that is, the BSF can stay untouched for at least 5 years (lag 4 to current). In contrast, the GFS accumulates for only 3 years. The negative sign on the lag-3 to lag-5 GSP is evidence. This cyclical difference between the BSF and the GFS may be an indication that since the widespread adoption of BSF in the states in the early 1980s, the countercyclical role of the GFS has probably been mostly taken over by the BSF.

6.6.5 Validity Check: An Alternative Dependent Variable and Results

In recent decades, the development of time-series econometrics has contributed substantially to our understanding of the unique features and potential problems in using time-series data. Of particular importance to this section is the measurement of cyclical variability of state expenditures. As shown by some recent research, state expenditures trend upward through time, with no tendency to return to an unconditional mean; herein is embedded the nonstationarity problem. Regressing expenditure against time generates coefficients that may have been subject to the problem. Besides, the coefficients from the time regression show merely the long-run growth but not the short-run variability (Sobel and Holcombe 1996b; Bruce et al. 2003). The natural log form of expenditure gaps used in the above test may have helped partially avoid, but probably not completely eliminate, the problem. For the purpose of this section, an alternative to the expenditure gap is the first-difference growth rate of own-source expenditure, which not only avoids the nonstationarity problem but also reveals cyclical variability of state expenditure patterns. Taking the first-difference growth rate of expenditure as an alternative dependent variable, this section reestimates the effects of fiscal reserves to check the validity of the above results.

Table 6.9 Cyclicality of BSF and GFS further tests on own-source expenditure

Panel A: BSF from two sources

	From *CAFR*		From *FSS*	
Dependent variable	Coefficient	t-statistic	Coefficient	t-statistic
Current GSP	0.054	2.56	0.044	1.26
GSP t-1	0.105	4.88	0.070	2.07
GSP t-2	0.075	3.82	0.092	2.97
GSP t-3	0.069	3.51	0.040	1.32
GSP t-4	0.031	1.70	−0.012	−0.43
GSP t-5	0.007	0.41	0.006	0.21
Observations	784		784	
Probability>F	0.00		0.08	
Adjusted R^2	0.02		0.01	
Transformed DW	1.87		2.06	

Panel B: GFS from two sources

	UUB (from *CAFR*)		GFB (from *FSS*)	
Dependent variable	Coefficient	t-statistic	Coefficient	t-statistic
Current GSP	0.299	4.47	fi0.272	4.65
GSP t-1	0.397	6.07	0.258	4.62
GSP t-2	0.142	2.40	0.047	0.95
GSP t-3	−0.053	−0.89	−0.093	−1.87
GSP t-4	−0.015	−0.27	−0.001	−0.02
GSP t-5	−0.001	−0.02	0.006	0.14
Observations	784		784	
Probability>F	0.00		0.00	
Adjusted R^2	0.06		0.07	
Transformed DW	2.02		1.85	

Notes
1. BSF, UUB, and GFB are all expressed as percentages of state general fund expenditure
2. GSP is the first-difference growth rate of real gross state product
3. The Prais-Winsten model is used for the estimation to correct for autocorrelation

First, the growth rates are regressed against gross state product to estimate their cyclicality. Presumably, state own-source expenditures should follow state economy (e.g., expenditures rise and fall with GSP). As shown in Table 6.10, OSE growth rate closely follows the state economy, and this relation is true from the current year to the third lag year. Thus, it is reasonable to assume that if fiscal reserves (BSF and GFS) present a positive coefficient, they exert positive effects on OSE growth rates. Second, a fixed-effects model is run to regress the fiscal reserves, with 1–5-year lags, respectively, against the OSE growth rate in all sample years. Results are shown in Table 6.11. The previous-year aggregate fiscal reserves from both data sources exert positive effects on current-year expenditure growth, and the results are statistically significant (Panels A and B). This is in general also true of the CAFR

Table 6.10 Cyclicality of growth rate of real own-source expenditure

	Coefficient	t-statistic
Current GSP	0.369	4.23
GSP t-1	0.293	3.33
GSP t-2	0.252	2.87
GSP t-3	0.144	1.70
GSP t-4	–0.062	–0.77
GSP t-5	0.092	1.20
Observations	784	
Probability > F	0.00	
Adjusted R^2	0.17	
Transformed DW	1.88	

Notes
1. The dependent variable is the growth rate of real own-source expenditure
2. The Prais-Winsten model is used for the estimation to correct for autocorrelation
3. Fixed effects are not reported

source BSF and UUB, with the BSF coefficients much larger than those of UUB (Panel C). For the FSS source BSF and GFB, however, the GFB coefficients are all positive, four out of the five at significant levels; the BSF coefficients are mostly positive, though not statistically significant (Panel D). Thus, estimates from this test to a large extent confirm the results from the variance-from-trend model.

6.6.6 *Summary*

This section provides evidence that fiscal reserves exert positive effects on state own-source expenditure in downturn years. The effects, however, are mainly from the BSF; the GFS coefficients, even when statistically significant, are only a quarter the size of those for the BSF. Nevertheless, states that do not have a BSF seem still to rely on the GFS. It appears that the BSF has taken over the countercyclical stabilizing function from the GFS.

6.7 Conclusion

This chapter has conducted some preliminary tests with regard to the distribution of the effects of countercyclical savings on three major types of state expenditures over the economic cycle. The chapter has found some evidence that states use their savings strategically across the three major expenditure types and that their strategy differs in downturn years from upturn years. The findings also provide evidence that there has appeared a "natural" division of work between the two saving devices: While the use of BSF concentrates mostly on own-source expenditure, its use in downturn years

Table 6.11 Effects on growth rates of real own-source expenditure, all years

Source	Variable	(1)	(2)	(3)	(4)	(5)
Panel A						
CAFR	*Reserve* $_{t-1}$	0.159***	0.192***	0.180***	0.173***	0.200***
		(0.223)	(0.033)	(0.035)	(0.038)	(0.041)
	Reserve $_{t-2}$		–0.052	–0.013	–0.013	–0.051
			(0.033)	(0.043)	(0.047)	(0.052)
	Reserve $_{t-3}$			–0.062	–0.039	–0.043
				(0.034)	(0.044)	(0.047)
	Reserve $_{t-4}$				–0.051	0.008
					(0.034)	(0.043)
	Reserve $_{t-5}$					–0.082**
						(0.034)
Observations		979	930	881	832	783
Adj R^2		0.11	0.10	0.10	0.11	0.11
Panel B						
FSS	*Reserve* $_{t-1}$	0.067**	0.186***	0.181***	0.176**	0.116
		(0.031)	(0.060)	(0.067)	(0.073)	(0.079)
	Reserve $_{t-2}$		–0.154***	0.087	0.032	0.063
			(0.056)	(0.083)	(0.095)	(0.102)
	Reserve $_{t-3}$			–0.269***	–0.111	–0.034
				(0.057)	(0.087)	(0.100)
	Reserve $_{t-4}$				–0.142**	–0.177**
					(0.060)	(0.090)
	Reserve $_{t-5}$					–0.013
						(0.061)
Observations		626	577	528	479	430
Adj R^2		0.08	0.07	0.11	0.11	0.12
Panel C						
CAFR	*BSF* $_{t-1}$	–0.101	0.308***	0.219*	0.209*	0.225*
		(0.066)	(0.120)	(0.126)	(0.128)	(0.129)
	BSF $_{t-2}$		–0.470***	–0.149	–0.182	–0.219
			(0.121)	(0.182)	(0.183)	(0.185)
	BSF $_{t-3}$			–0.291**	–0.074	–0.039
				(0.129)	(0.185)	(0.185)
	BSF $_{t-4}$				–0.209	–0.204
					(0.132)	(0.188)
	BSF $_{t-5}$					–0.022
						(0.134)
	UUB $_{t-1}$	0.205***	0.195***	0.190***	0.181***	0.212***
		(0.025)	(0.034)	(0.037)	(0.039)	(0.044)
	UUB $_{t-2}$		0.001	0.003	0.010	–0.031
			(0.034)	(0.044)	(0.048)	(0.053)
	UUB $_{t-3}$			–0.017	–0.026	–0.026
				(0.035)	(0.045)	(0.048)
	UUB $_{t-4}$				–0.013	0.034
					(0.035)	(0.044)
	UUB $_{t-5}$					–0.063*
						(0.036)
Observations		979	930	881	832	783
Adj R^2		0.08	0.13	0.12	0.13	0.13

(continued)

Table 6.11 (continued)

FSS	*BSF* $_{t-1}$	−0.104	0.110	0.127	0.117	0.039
		(0.075)	(0.114)	(0.124)	(0.132)	(0.137)
	BSF $_{t-2}$		−0.288***	−0.054	−0.080	−0.055
			(0.103)	(0.142)	(0.158)	(0.166)
	BSF $_{t-3}$			−0.226**	−0.023	0.037
				(0.105)	(0.150)	(0.164)
	BSF $_{t-4}$				−0.052	0.018
					(0.110)	(0.154)
	BSF $_{t-5}$					−0.133
						(0.118)
	GFB $_{t-1}$	0.157***	0.198***	0.211***	0.190**	0.133
		(0.047)	(0.070)	(0.076)	(0.084)	(0.094)
	GFB $_{t-2}$		−0.050	0.140	0.078	0.140
			(0.070)	(0.091)	(0.101)	(0.113)
	GFB $_{t-3}$			−0.240***	−0.110	−0.612
				(0.072)	(0.097)	(0.107)
	GFB $_{t-4}$				−0.188**	−0.236**
					(0.077)	(0.101)
	GFB $_{t-5}$					0.006
						(0.080)
Observations		626	577	528	479	430
Adj R^2		0.09	0.08	0.11	0.24	0.12

Notes
1. The dependent variable is the first-difference growth rate of real own-source expenditure
2. Standard errors are in *parenthesis*
3. Significance levels are marked by stars: *for 10%; **for 5%; and ***for 1%
4. Estimates for fixed effects are not reported

may generate a chain effect to increase general expenditure but not general fund expenditure that is used mostly to cover the routine operations. Use of GFS is more salient in upturn years, and its effect shows more clearly on general fund expenditure. A sensitivity test with per capita real expenditures validates these findings.

While providing evidence on a new aspect of the true implications of subnational countercyclical fiscal policy, this study is exploratory in nature: It discerns and reveals areas where much more work is needed for further study. Among issues to pursue, three are particularly prominent. First, what are the unspecified "strategic" considerations behind the states' behavior? The strategies may vary across states, across different functions, and over time. Second, if federal dollars are states' target in downturns (even in upturns), then it may impose other constraints on state spending because of the matching requirements. Finally, but not less important, there have been suggestions that unreserved but designated fund balance (UDB) may be used not entirely for its designated purposes; the remainder is instead carried into next fiscal year(s). For special purpose governments, for example, school districts, the difference between UUB and UDB may not be as distinct as for general purpose governments. For quasi-public organizations that use non-GAAP practices, designations may be even less enforceable; then the whole issue may turn into something different. Focusing on state governments, this chapter does not check the details into these issues. They are left for future research.

References

Bretschneider SI, Gorr WL, Grizzle G, Klay E (1989) Political and organizational influences on the accuracy of forecasting state government revenues. Int J Forecast 5(3):307–319

Bruce D, Fox WF, Tuttle MH (2003) Tax base elasticities: a multi-state analysis of long-run and short-run dynamics. Mimeo, University of Tennessee, Knoxville

Engle RF, Granger CWJ (1987) Co-integration and error correction: representation, estimation and testing. Econometrica 55(2):251–276

Finkler SA (2005) Financial management for public, health and not-for-profit organizations. Prentice Hall, Upper Saddle River

Fuller WA (1976) Introduction to statistical time series. Wiley, New York

Granger CWJ, Watson MW (1984) Time series and spectral methods in econometrics. In: Griliches Z, Intriligator MD (eds) Handbook of econometrics, vol 2. Elsevier Science Publishers BV, Amsterdam

Hamilton J (1994) Time series analysis. Princeton University Press, Princeton

Heckman J (1979) Sample selection bias as a specification error. Econometrica 47(1):153–162

Hou Y (2003) What stabilizes state general fund spending during downturns? Public Budg Finance 23(3):64–91

Hou Y (2005) Fiscal reserves and state own-source expenditure in downturns. Public Finance Rev 33(1):117–144

Knight B, Levinson A (1999) Rainy day funds and state government savings. Natl Tax J 52(3):459–472

National Association of State Budget Officers (NASBO 1977–2004) Fiscal survey of states series. NASBO, Washington, DC

National Association of State Budget Officers (NASBO). State budget processes. 1985, 1988, 1992, 1995, 1998 and 2002 editions. Washington, DC

National Governors' Association. The book of the states series. Various years. Lexington

Pollock R, Suyderhoud J (1986) The role of rainy day funds in achieving fiscal stability. Natl Tax J 43(4):485–497

Prais SJ, Winsten CB (1954) Trend estimators and serial correlation. Cowles Commission discussion paper no. 383, Chicago

Rivlin A (1987) Economics and the political process. Am Econ Rev 77(1):1–10

Ruppel W (2004) GAAP for governments. Wiley, New York

Sobel RS, Holcombe RG (1996a) The impact of state rainy day funds in easing state fiscal crises during the 1990–1991 recession. Public Budg Finance 16(3):28–48

Sobel RS, Holcombe RG (1996b) Measuring the growth and variability of tax bases over the business cycle. Natl Tax J 49(4):535–552

Wagner GA (1999) Essays on the political economy of state government saving and the role of budget stabilization funds. Ph.D. dissertation, University of West Virginia

Wildavsky A (1988) If you can't budget, how can you govern? In: Anderson A, Bark DL (eds) Thinking about America: the United States in the 1990s. Hoover Institute Press, Stanford, pp 265–275

Chapter 7
Effects of Boom-Year Savings on Bust-Year Budgetary Actions

Abstract This chapter examines the effects of boom-year savings on budgetary actions that states often take during a recession. Here I draw the link between countercyclical fiscal policy and the concept of countercyclical fiscal capacity (CCFC). I define CCFC as the accumulation of savings in boom years and the use of them during revenue shortfalls to maintain countercyclical spending and program stability. Because a basic challenge for state governments is to maintain budgetary stability and program predictability in face of economic downturns, states can best meet this challenge by developing the "countercyclical fiscal capacity." In this chapter, I operationalize CCFC in terms of fiscal reserves (BSF and GFS) and analyze the operation of such reserves over a period that includes recessions in 1991 and 2001. I find evidence of the efficacy of countercyclical fiscal capacity and argue for states to make greater investments in this aspect of governance capacity.

7.1 Introduction

This chapter continues with empirical tests on the effects of boom-year savings; here I set up the test on budgetary actions that state governments often have to take in bust years – tax hikes, fee increases, and outlay reductions – to see whether savings can effectively reduce these pro-cyclical budgetary actions and how large the effect can be. With this setup, I am looking in the area of government financial management: If a state government adopts the countercyclical fiscal policy and accumulates savings in boom years and then use these savings in bust years to mitigate the adverse effects of revenue shortfall on public service provision, then I say this

This chapter draws from data and analysis in Hou Y and Moynihan D (2008) The case for countercyclical fiscal capacity. J Public Adm Res Theory 18(1):139–159.

Y. Hou, *State Government Budget Stabilization: Policy, Tools, and Impacts*, Studies in Public Choice 8, DOI 10.1007/978-1-4614-6061-9_7,

government has developed and used countercyclical fiscal capacity (CCFC). To conduct the test, I take advantage of a panel data set on state budgetary actions from 1985 to 2003. The sample period covers the 1991 and the 2001recessions, which allows me to examine whether and how much state governments mitigated the impacts of revenue shocks during two recent recessions.

The rest of the chapter is organized as follows. Section 7.2 makes the extension from countercyclical fiscal policy to countercyclical fiscal capacity, also discusses BSF and GFS as tools of CCFC. Section 7.3 elaborates on the background to the several types of budgetary reactions that states often have to take in handling revenue shocks; here I also offer some descriptive analysis. Section 7.4 presents and tests a formal theory of how states reacted to revenue shocks in 1991 and 2001. The results are discussed in Section 7.5. The final section concludes by summarizing the importance and practicality of CCFC; some thoughts are given to avenues of future research.

7.2 Countercyclical Fiscal Capacity

As a step to link policies to the roles that the public sector should play, we can look at the countercyclical fiscal policy and boom-year savings from the perspective of government function at the state level: State governments are put in place to provide public services, and the demand for these services is persistent in the sense that whether the economy is in boom or in bust, the expectation by the general public is that the government should deliver reliable and continuous services at a roughly stable level without major disruption; thus, continuity and predictability of services over the economic cycle hold key to the quality and effectiveness of governance. In this respect, we can extend the countercyclical fiscal policy that we have discussed so far to the concept of countercyclical fiscal capacity (CCFC). A state government is said to possess high governance capacity if it can deliver the normal services at a relatively stable level without obvious disruption across the boom-bust cycles; otherwise, we say the capacity of this government is low with regard to mitigating the adverse impact of an economic downturn on budget stability. This countercyclical fiscal capacity is operative on many instruments. Here we focus on boom-years savings as fiscal reserves. We treat the use of such reserves to mitigate spending cuts and tax increases in downturns as part of a state's capacity to govern as reflected in stable service provision.

We have already discussed the working mechanism of the countercyclical fiscal policy, which is also true with CCFC: During economic downturns, governments typically face revenue shortfalls that are referred to as (negative) revenue shocks. In such cases, elected officials find in the middle of a fiscal year that revenues are not streaming in as have been budgeted. The demand for service at this time does not fall; it stays strong and may even go higher than during boom years. However, the balanced budget requirements are legally binding; so policy makers will have no other choice but to raise taxes and fees or cut programs, or do both. Either of the two causes instability in program delivery to citizens and businesses. Therefore, the benefits of predictability in the delivery of public goods cannot be overvalued. In economic theory, the utility and benefits of program continuity are evident from the efficiency explanation of tax smoothing and consumption smoothing. In public management theory, continuity and predictability are central to O'Toole and Meier's (1999) theory of effective public management, and to Provan and Milward's (1995) theory of network success. Thus, we can draw a direct link between a state government's ability to use financial reserves for maintaining a predictable flow of public services to its governance capacity.

The natural next question is what the tools are of countercyclical fiscal capacity.

As discussed in earlier chapters, this book focuses on the two major and most explicit policy instruments of CCFP; here I bring them to the tests for CCFC. Thus, the term "fiscal reserves" refers to total financial resources previously accumulated, that is, the sum of GFS and BSF ($reserve_{it} = bsf_{it} + gfs_{it}$). The operation of the accumulation and drawing down of fiscal reserves can be illustrated as how state governments respond to the revenue fluctuations across the economic cycle. During boom years, the tax base expands and thereby generates abundant revenues that exceed current outlay needs; so states can afford to provide more services, to spend more on capital projects with pay-as-you-go financing (for details, see appendix to Chapter 10), and to save (more) in the general fund and the budget stabilization fund. In downturn years, the tax base shrinks and tax revenues cannot satisfy the regular program outlays that have been budgeted for the ongoing fiscal year; therefore, states draw down their boom-year savings in an effort to maintain the planned service levels. When the revenue shortfall is drastically large or the recession is expected to last over a year, and prior accumulated reserves are believed to be inadequate to fill up the gap between current revenues and budgeted outlays, then service levels will have to be cut or program quality will compromise accordingly.

Dollars spent from the GFS and BSF are equivalent in terms of their economic impact – both are accumulated resources available for appropriation in the next fiscal year (Allan [GFOA] 1990; Pollock and Suyderhoud 1986; Sobel and Holcombe 1996, 32). But it is worth repeating here that there are three differences between the two kinds of fiscal reserves. First, a BSF is set up with enabling legislation that details rules (for its method of deposit, purpose of use, and approval procedures for use) as a means to protect it from spending pressure in boom years. As such, BSF is structurally different from GFS. Another and probably more important distinction between the two types of reserves is the legal restriction on their deposits and use. BSF are restricted with its use whereas GFS are at the discretion of policy makers. Finally, although fiscal reserves in general may be regarded as equivalent in their economic effects, they may function differently in the budgeting process. I have discussed this point in Chapter 6, and empirical results thereof support this proposition. Specifically, when decision-makers plan budgetary policies, they may treat the two kinds of reserves differently. Because BSF are usually restricted for use only in times of emergency – even then it is often subject to the politically loaded, time-consuming appropriations process (Hou 2004) – budget decisions during a recession may rely more on the discretionary, easy-to-use GFS. Because of these differences, I will need to separate in my analysis the respective effects of BSF and GFS in state

Table 7.1 Summary statistics of major variables

	Fiscal reserves			Budgetary responses to revenue shocks		
Variable	Budget stabilization fund	General fund surplus	Total reserve	Budget cut	Revtenue actions	Net revenue change
Sample years	1985–2003	1985–2003	1985–2003	1985–2003	1988–2003	1988–2003
No. of observations	930	931	930	950	800	800
Mean	$32.69	$62.86	$95.62	$13.77	$9.94	$23.80
Standard deviation	51.69	91.94	111.17	33.74	55.24	67.56
Minimum	0	−369.78	−369.78	0	−299.36	−289.89
Maximum	461.17	798.02	798.02	543.59	419.58	422.69

Notes
1. Data are from the Fiscal Survey of States series, published by NASBO
2. All financial figures are in real (year 2000) per capita dollars
3. Alaska is excluded because it is an extreme outliner with its budget stabilization fund and general fund balance

budgetary reactions to revenue shocks. Table 7.1 offers summary statistics of the three major variables that I am going to examine in detail – BSF, GFS, and total fiscal reserves. Also included are statistics of the three dependent variables – budget cuts, revenue actions (tax hikes), and net revenue change (sum of the first two). Financial figures have been converted into per capita year 2000 dollars for comparability purposes.

7.3 State Reactions to Revenue Shortfalls

As the name suggests, "countercyclical fiscal capacity" is put to use during times of "revenue shocks" (throughout the chapter, this term always refers to negative shocks, i.e., revenue shortfalls). The cross-state heterogeneity of fiscal conditions and policies lends a platform for empirical analysis of how states react to such shocks (Poterba 1994). Given the cyclical nature of the economy, revenue shocks are inevitable. However, because governments do not know when recessions will occur, they have limited ability to plan for them in advance. In lean years, revenue shocks cut the tax base so deep that revenue estimates, even revised ones, are frequently off target and often force decision-makers to re-budget for the current fiscal year and revise their plan for the next year. Revenues shocks include not only shocks to state own-source revenues (taxes and fees) but also grants and other forms of assistance from the federal government. Data limitations render this distinction very difficult to operationalize on a reliable basis; therefore, I address revenue shocks as a whole in the chapter.

Different from the federal government, states have more limited revenue sources (portfolio) and face legal restraints during a recession; they respond to revenue shocks in ways that reveal these restraints. For example, states have to cut spending and/or raise taxes to meet their statutory or constitutional requirement to balance the budget. Though borrowing is possible, most states are prohibited by their law operate on debt. If they do borrow to fund operations, as a few states have done in recent years, this unconventional practice will hurt these states' credit rating on the financial market. Therefore, budgetary reactions to revenue shocks are unavoidable. Immediate reactions to shocks tend to be unplanned and of a temporary nature, involving urgent budget cuts to programs and services in the current fiscal year. Here "budget cuts" are defined as program reductions that are enacted during the current fiscal year on the budget that was adopted last year and is now in the execution phase. Put another way, budget cuts are emergency measures that states take to cope with surprise revenue shortfalls from the economic cycle. These cuts are unplanned; they are deductions to the approved budget.

Once struck by a recession, state governments also need to react to revenue shocks by changing their revenue portfolio (types of taxes and fees) and/or revenue base/structure (rates). Such changes are usually tax hikes or fee increases. These measures to increase revenue are understandable and necessary because the adverse effects of any recession will last across a fiscal year, given that governments follow regular budget cycles. Unlike budget cuts, these "revenue actions" are planned and designed to increase revenue in the next fiscal year(s) as an effort to deal with the cyclical revenue shortfall. Revenue actions can be taken for multiple reasons; at least policy makers may make such claims. Some of the measures are taken for equity purposes, some on efficiency grounds, the rest for other prevailing political preferences. Whatever reason is given as the trigger for the measure, revenue shortfalls caused by a downturn in the economic cycle impose revenue actions on policy makers for the simple reason that more resources are needed to provide the demanded services. In such cases, even long planned revisions to a state's revenue system may have to be readjusted or rescheduled to fit the new reality of declining revenues.

Needless to say, program cutbacks may occur in any single year; service reductions may be pro-cyclical or acyclical; so there is wide variation among states in why they cut spending. Nevertheless, budget cuts tend to occur most frequently and intensely in recession years and in the 1 or 2 years immediately following a downturn. During the last two recessions, these were the years 1990–1993 and 2001–2004. In contrast, we observe very few cases of budget cuts in the boom years (e.g., 1998–2000); even when cuts did occur in boom years, such cuts tend to be minimal. Likewise, states take revenue actions in lean years as well as in boom years to increase revenues; but in aggregate, concentrated revenue increasing actions were also associated with recessions, taking place in years 1990–1994 and 2002–2004. Fiscal years 1995–2001 were marked with numerous revenue reducing actions, a result of the record-long economic expansion in the late 1990s. Among these revenue reduction years, 2001 was an extension of tax and fee abatement commitments made in earlier years when the economy was strong; these should not be taken as an indicator of inaction by the states in response to the recession. In many states, the impact of the recession was not yet apparent by the end of FY 2001.

Summing up budget cuts and revenue actions that occur in the same fiscal year obtains "net revenue changes." These net changes reflect turns of the economic cycle. Not surprisingly, years 1990–1993 and 2002–2004 saw remarkable net revenue increases as governments increased taxes and fees and cut programs; whereas 1996–2001 witnessed considerable revenue reductions. Table 7.2 presents summary statistics for each of the sample years on the three key variables (BSF, GFS, and total reserves) and the three dependent variables (budget cuts, revenue actions, and net revenue change). As indicated in the table, though states also make budget cuts and raise taxes and fees in boom years, most of such budgetary changes, especially drastic ones, are made in recession years: Over half of the states cut taxes and fees (made negative net revenue changes) each year between 1997 and 2001, and 24 states did so in 2001. In contrast, following the 1991 and 2001 recessions, fewer than five states made negative net changes; but over 70% of states raised taxes and fees (made net positive changes).

From Table 7.2 we can also infer that states employed different strategies in their response to the 1991 and the 2001 recessions. To cope with the 1991 downturn, states tended to rely more heavily on tax and fee increases rather than spending cuts. In years 1991–1994, the average size of budget cuts was just over $20 per capita, while the size of revenue actions was over $37 per capita. Budget cuts were minimal in the years prior to 2002, which indicates that states employed budget cuts quickly for the 1991 recession, but appear to have waited somewhat longer to react to the 2001 recession. When state governments did react in 2002, they appear to have been reluctant to repeal their tax reductions (see also Johnson 2002) and more willing to balance budgets through cuts to spending. In 2002–2003, average annual budget cuts were approximately $41 per capita, while average revenue actions were just over $12. Since actions to increase revenue tend to lag budget cuts, it is not appropriate to compare budget cuts with revenue actions that are taken in the same year. A more appropriate comparison would be to compare mean budget cuts in 2002 (an average of $40 per capita) with revenue increases ($24) in 2003 – it thus becomes clear that the reliance on budget cuts is striking.

The increasing preference for budget cuts over tax increases between 1991 and 2001 parallels changes in political attitudes toward taxes and spending. During this period, the Republican Party increasingly controlled state legislatures and governorships. Democrats had 1,542 more state legislators than Republicans in 1990, but only 288 more after the 2000 elections.[1] In the same period, elected officials came under increasing pressure to pledge not to increase taxes by conservative lobby groups, such as Americans for Tax Reform, and were given a lesson on the political costs of reneging on such pledges when George H. W. Bush lost his bid for reelection after backtracking on his "no new taxes" pledge. Conservative political rhetoric increasingly portrayed tax cuts as an economic stimulus that was necessary during recessions. Given these political changes, budget cuts appeared an increasingly acceptable alternative to tax increases, and our comparison of the 1991 and 2001 recession provides some evidence that changing political preferences have impacted how state governments deal with revenue shocks.

[1] National Council of State Legislatures, http://www.ncsl.org/programs/legman/statevote/statevote2000.htm

Table 7.2 Summary statistics of dependent and major variables by sample year

Fiscal year	1985	1986	1987	1988	1989	1990	1991	1992	1993	1994	1995	1996	1997	1998	1999	2000	2001	2002	2003
Dep. variable	*Budget cut*																		
Mean	$1	$10	$29	$7	$5	$16	*$36*	*$26*	*$13*	*$6*	$4	$11	$4	$3	$1	$0	$7	*$40*	*$42*
Positive/negative	3	16	23	11	12	19	28	35	22	10	8	12	7	2	3	1	17	36	42
Dep. variable	*Revenue actions*																		
Mean				$26	$6	$32	*$39*	*$53*	*$22*	*$28*	$2	–$11	–$11	–$9	–$21	–$9	–$13	*$1*	*$24*
Positive/negative				27/9	14/12	30/8	26/7	31/4	28/3	24/3	16/20	8/28	7/27	11/30	3/32	11/30	8/27	14/15	24/7
Dep. variable	*Net revenue change (budget cut + revenue actions)*																		
Mean				$33	$10	$48	*$75*	*$78*	*$35*	*$34*	$6	$0	–$6	–$6	–$20	–$8	–$5	*$42*	*$66*
Positive/negative				35/6	20/9	32/8	38/3	42/2	37/2	31/2	19/18	15/24	11/27	12/29	5/32	12/29	12/24	36/4	43/3
Key variable	*Budget stabilization fund balance*																		
Mean	$18	$16	$26	$27	$27	*$16*	$12	$10	$15	$20	$27	$31	$39	$61	$65	$70	*$71*	$35	$33
Key variable	*General fund surplus*																		
Mean	$71	$55	$55	$74	$81	*$59*	$31	$38	$46	$64	$60	$74	$84	$95	$80	$93	*$68*	$33	$33
Key variable	*Total reserves*																		
Mean	$89	$71	$81	$102	$109	$75	$44	$49	$60	$85	$87	$104	$124	$157	$145	$163	$139	$68	$66

Notes
1. Financial figures are per capita year 2000 dollars
2. Figures of "positive/negative" show number of states taking actions to increase (positive) or decrease (negative) taxes and fees
3. Alaska is excluded because it is an extreme outliner with its budget stabilization fund and general fund balance

Table 7.2 also shows a changing composition of fiscal reserves over the sample period, and the growing reliance on BSF as a tool of CCFC. Prior to the recession of the early 1990s BSF accounted for only 25% of the average per capita total reserves (in FY 89). As states faced revenue shocks, GFS declined, from $81 in FY 89 to $59 in FY 90, and further to $31 by the end of FY 91. GFS was the primary defense against the revenue shocks of the early 1990s recession. BSF was a minor tool in relative terms. However, by the 2001 recession (end of FY 01), BSF made up 43% of the $163 average per capita total reserves. Between FY 00 and FY 01, GFS fell from $93 in 2000 to $68 when at the same time BSF remained essentially unchanged at $71. However, by the end of FY 2002, both BSF and GFS fell to the mid-30s. These numbers suggest that while GFS may have been relied on more during the early stages of the 2001 recession, because its unrestricted nature makes it easier to access quickly, both instruments provided a major contribution to CCFC. This represents a different pattern from the previous recession.

7.4 Methodology and Model Specification

In this section I examine how reserves are used to impact the dependent variables defined above: budget cuts, revenue actions, and the sum of both – net revenue changes. Data for these variables are published regularly by the National Association of State Budget Officers (NASBO) in its biannual *Fiscal Survey of States*. Budget cut figures are available since fiscal year 1985, and figures of revenue actions are available since 1988. My sample years are from 1985/1988 to 2003. To operationalize the test, budget cuts and revenue raising actions are expressed as positive numbers because these are measures to increase state own-source revenue, while revenue decreasing actions are recorded as negative numbers. Both GFS and BSF data that come from the *Fiscal Survey of States* are cleaned of double counting.[2] For states that do not have a BSF, reserves refer only to their GFS.

To test the effects of fiscal reserves on budgetary reactions, I use the panel data method with state- and year-fixed effects. Alaska is excluded because it is an outlier in many aspects of fiscal behavior. The Prais-Winsten (1954) model is adopted to correct for autocorrelation.[3] All monetary figures are transformed into year 2000 per capita dollars. My key variables of interest are fiscal reserves from previous years, BSF and GFS. Dependent variables are budget cuts in the current year, revenue

[2] In this chapter I use the term GFS rather than GFB, see Section 3.2 for the rationale. GFB figures in the *i* often include BSF balances. Not excluding BSF from these GFB figures will cause double counting. Specifically, California's BSF balance is reported to be negative in 1991 (–1,715 millions) and 2002 (–3,535 millions), both much larger than the negative balance of the GFB. In such cases, we turn the BSF into zeros and these larger negative balances to be the revised GFB. For more information, see California Code 16418 (d).

[3] The annual balances of BSF and the annual GFS may be serially correlated, even after they are converted into per capita real levels. The Prais-Winsten (1954) model is chosen to correct for the serial correlation.

raising actions for the next fiscal year, and net revenue change in the next year. For each of the three dependent variables, I first test the effects of the aggregate reserves, then the effects of BSF and GFS, respectively.[4]

I use four groups of controls: socioeconomic factors, state tax structure, budgetary institutions, and state politics. Six variables are chosen to control for social and economic variation between the states. Per capita personal income (in thousands) captures effects of a state's wealth on its choice of reactions to revenue shortfalls, whether budget cuts or tax increases or both. Economic growth is the first-difference increase rate of real gross state product; it is to capture the effects of economic momentum on the dependent variables. Average annual unemployment rate captures the business cycle effect. Population (in millions) controls for the size of each state. Poverty rate controls for social services expenditures. And per capita general fund expenditure (in thousands) captures effects of a state's government size on its choice of fiscal reactions to revenue shocks.

Different revenue portfolios may have influenced states' revenue fluctuations and thereby their actions in face of shocks. I introduce binary variables to indicate the use of the three most important tax types – personal income tax, corporate income tax, and general sales tax.

State budgetary institutions influence fiscal and budgetary practices the most. This chapter pays special attention to this aspect. Of these institutions, balanced budget requirements (BBR) are among the most important in that they may necessitate budget cuts in years of unexpected revenue shocks followed by revenue raising actions in subsequent years. Four most frequently used BBR variables are (1) governor submitting, (2) legislature passing, (3) governor signing a balanced budget, and (4) no deficit carryover into the next budget cycle. They have been used as controls in almost all studies of fiscal and budgetary issues. Recently, Hou and Smith (2006) proposed a new, more elaborate framework of BBR which identifies nine BBR articles along a political-technical continuum. This framework carries the potential of more explanatory power. These nine articles are (1) the governor must submit a balanced budget; (2) own-source revenue must match (meet or exceed) current expenditures; (3) own-source revenue and (unspecified) debt (in anticipation of revenues) must match (meet or exceed) current expenditures; (4) the legislature must pass a balanced budget; (5) a limit is in place on the amount of debt for deficit reduction; (6) the governor must sign a balanced budget; (7) mechanisms are in place to control supplementary appropriations or limit re-budgeting; (8) within-fiscal-year managerial controls are installed to ensure deficits are not to be incurred; and (9) no deficit carryover is allowed. I include in the models eight of these indicator variables (with the first as the default comparison) to capture the effects of BBR on state revenue actions.

Besides BBR, I control for three other budgetary institutions. Statutory revenue limitations and expenditure limitations restrict state government's ability to increase

[4] One caveat to keep in mind with this model is that it does not include state-specific recessions, and so changes in the dependent variables, while dependent on cyclical fluctuations, may also arise from other factors.

tax or expenditure in any given year. As a budgetary institution, revenue limitations are expected to have a negative impact on revenue raising actions, while increasing the likelihood that state governments will turn to budget cuts to achieve balance. Expenditure limits are likely to also discourage the need for revenue increases and increase pressure to cut spending when it extends beyond revenue. Of all the 50 states, about 20 still use biennial budget cycles. This practice is carried over from the old times of part-time legislators; some states keep it partly for the reason of potentially more stable financial operations. I control for this variation to capture its influence on budgetary actions in times of revenue shocks.

Among state politics, I control for the effect of a gubernatorial election year. Even in a time of revenue shocks, politicians may be more inclined to limit budget cuts and tax increases to improve reelection chances. Thus, I expect a negative sign for the election year dummy. The dummy variable Democratic governor distinguishes an incumbent Democratic Party governor from other parties. The divided government variable indicates that the majority of the state legislature is of the different party from the governor, which may render contentious political action such as budget cuts and tax raises more difficult. To control for historical and political traditions of states, we use the (Berry et al. 1998) measures for citizen ideology and state government ideology. More details on variable definitions and sources are provided in the appendix. The full model is as follows:

$$\begin{aligned}&\textbf{Budget cut}_{\textbf{it}}\ /\ \textbf{revenue action}_{\textbf{it+1}}\ /\ \textbf{net revenue change}_{\textbf{it+1}}\\&\quad=\alpha+\beta_1(\textbf{reserve}_{it-1})+\beta_2\textbf{X}_{it}+\lambda_1(\textbf{state}_i)+\lambda_2(\textbf{year}_t)+\varepsilon_{it},\\&\text{or}=\alpha+\beta_1(\textbf{bsf}_{it-1})+\beta_2(\textbf{gfb}_{it-1})+\beta_3\textbf{X}_{it}+\lambda_1(\textbf{state}_i)+\lambda_2(\textbf{year}_t)+\varepsilon_{it}\end{aligned}$$

I = 49 (Alaska is excluded as an outlier)
T = 19 (budget cuts); = 16 (revenue actions and net revenue change)
X is the matrix of control variables.

7.5 Results and Discussion

Whether combined as aggregate reserves or as separate instruments, previously accumulated BSF and GFS are expected to exert negative influence on the dependent variables; that is, they reduce the magnitudes of budget cuts, revenue raising actions, and net revenue changes. Regression results as displayed in Table 7.3 show that all coefficients of these three key variables present the expected negative sign. The empirical evidence thus indicates that the presence of fiscal reserves in general seems to add to the operating certainty of state budgets. With these reserves in place, decision-makers are better able to avoid cuts to programs already being executed during the current fiscal cycle. The same reassuring effect is also seen in fiscal planning – the availability of reserves reduces the need for policy makers to take revenue raising actions for the next fiscal year. The impact of fiscal reserves is also significant for the combined measure of revenue changes and budget cuts; the net revenue changes for

Table 7.3 Effects of reserves on state responses to revenue shocks

Column	1		2		3		4		5		6	
Dependent variable	*Budget cuts$_t$*				*Revenue actions$_{t+1}$*				*Net rev change$_{t+1}$*			
	Coef	Std Err	Coef	Std Err	Coef	Std Err	Coef	Std Err	Coef	Std Err	Coef	Std Err
Reserves$_{t-1}$	***–*0.05*	0.01			***–*0.14*	0.03			***–*0.16*	0.03		
BSF$_{t-1}$			–0.02	0.02			***–*0.18*	0.05			***–*0.21*	0.06
GFS$_{t-1}$			***–*0.06*	0.01			***–*0.12*	0.03			***–*0.14*	0.04
Socioeconomic controls												
Per capita income (,000)	***2.69*	1.36	***2.67*	1.36	****8.89*	3.14	****8.88*	3.14	****11.92*	3.88	****11.92*	3.88
Economic growth	***–*98.31*	39.23	**–*97.95*	39.22	***–*355.48*	92.44	***–*355.85*	92.51	***–*550.50*	109.84	***–*550.92*	109.87
Unemployment rate	****4.24*	1.09	****4.09*	1.09	1.45	2.45	1.81	2.48	2.28	2.98	2.76	3.01
Population (million)	0.00	0.00	0.00	0.00	0.00	0.00	0.00	0.00	0.00	0.00	0.00	0.00
Poverty rate	–0.05	0.51	0.00	0.51	*–*2.00*	1.15	*–*2.12*	1.16	–1.80	1.38	–1.96	1.39
Per capita expenditure (,000)	11.12	7.26	11.32	7.26	*–*29.69*	16.14	*–*30.01*	16.17	–6.41	19.80	–6.82	19.83
State tax structure												
Personal income tax	0.52	40.26	3.06	40.27	25.85	169.80	35.89	96.58	1.08	210.63	–11.83	119.84
Corporate income tax	–16.56	37.00	–13.19	37.05	dropped		–24.64	88.80	dropped		–8.61	110.02
General sales tax	–21.60	22.25	–17.84	22.41	–29.54	167.80	–34.59	168.26	–73.48	208.06	–81.89	208.59

(continued)

Table 7.3 (continued)

Column	1		2		3		4		5		6	
Dependent variable	*Budget cuts$_t$*				*Revenue actions$_{t+1}$*				*Net rev change$_{t+1}$*			
	Coef	Std Err	Coef	Std Err	Coef	Std Err	Coef	Std Err	Coef	Std Err	Coef	Std Err
Balanced budget requirements												
Own-source revenue match expenditures	10.07	16.05	10.68	16.04	20.16	35.10	19.68	35.16	12.78	42.92	12.12	42.97
Own-source revenue plus debt meet expenditures	6.21	11.60	5.60	11.60	*******–54.57*	23.92	**–53.24*	24.02	**–49.12*	29.81	–47.33	29.91
Legislature pass balanced budget	–1.01	7.00	–0.44	7.01	****–42.13*	13.51	***–42.92*	13.57	****–42.66*	16.81	****–43.78*	16.87
Limit on debt for deficit reduction	16.75	17.65	17.86	17.66	1.56	53.63	–0.39	53.78	61.26	66.07	58.60	66.21
Governor sign balanced budget	–22.49	15.64	**–27.12*	16.00	–12.17	29.50	–5.53	30.44	–55.64	36.67	–46.38	37.78
With controls on supplementary appropriations	–2.40	6.85	–3.07	6.86	8.24	14.36	9.31	14.43	5.22	17.84	6.71	17.93
Within FY controls in place to avoid deficits	0.64	5.79	0.83	5.79	–9.32	12.10	–9.85	12.13	–8.94	14.97	–9.63	15.00

No deficit carryover	−3.37	11.09	−2.28	11.11	13.54	21.68	11.78	21.81	24.18	26.92	21.74	27.06
Other budgetary institutions												
Revenue limit	−1.53	4.68	−1.59	4.68	****20.21**	9.21	****20.30**	9.24	****23.93**	11.48	****24.05**	11.50
Expenditure limit	3.47	4.52	3.01	4.53	−8.99	9.26	−8.23	9.31	−7.99	11.49	−6.96	11.55
Biennial budget	****9.65**	5.04	****10.02**	5.05	−3.69	10.60	−4.00	10.62	−1.41	12.98	−1.85	13.00
State politics												
Election year	****−4.07**	2.03	****−4.05**	2.03	−6.18	5.41	−6.36	5.41	−3.62	6.31	−3.83	6.31
Democrat governor	5.70	3.63	5.69	3.63	−6.34	7.65	−6.32	7.67	−7.24	9.38	−7.19	9.39
Divided government	−0.59	2.04	−0.49	2.04	1.44	4.23	1.23	4.24	−1.75	5.20	−2.03	5.22
Citizen ideology	*****0.47**	0.19	*****0.48**	0.19	−0.37	0.44	−0.38	0.44	−0.26	0.53	−0.27	0.53
Government ideology	−0.16	0.10	−0.17	0.10	*****0.57**	0.22	0.58	0.22	****0.62**	0.26	***0.63**	0.27
No. of observations	832		832		734		734		734		734	
Adjusted R-squared	0.18		0.18		0.28		0.27		0.29		0.29	

Notes
1. Data are from the *Fiscal Survey of States* series, published by NASBO
2. Reserves, BSF and GFS figures, are all in real (year 2000) per capita dollars
3. Regressions are run with the Prais-Winsten model, state- and year-fixed effects
4. The reported R-squared is for the overall model. The within-state R-squared is higher
5. Significance levels are $^{***}p<0.01$, $^{**}p<0.05$, and $^{*}p<0.10$
6. Alaska is excluded as an extreme outlier

the next year. The results are consistent whether the test is conducted without fixed effects, with only state-fixed effects, or even with Alaska included.

The magnitude of the effects of fiscal reserves, however, differs substantially among the planned revenue actions and unplanned budget cuts. A $100 reserve reduces unplanned budget cuts by $5–$6 (columns 1 and 2). The effects of reserves on planned revenue actions are more than double the impact on budget cuts: a $100 reserve reduces tax hikes by $12–$18 (columns 3 and 4). Effects on net revenue change show that a $100 reserve can reduce the net change between $14 and $21 (columns 5 and 6).

This finding tells us that while fiscal reserves have a statistically significant relationship with middle-of-the-year spending cuts, the size of this impact is not especially large. When a recession hits, a state's revenue stream is adversely affected and the budgeted total revenue becomes an impossible target. As a result, decision-makers may have to immediately scale back programs to keep actual spending in line with revenues. In this process, fiscal reserves accumulated over past years help, but only by $5–$6 for each $100 of reserves. The reserves are more likely to be used when decision-makers plan for revenue actions for the next year. Put another way, reserves appear to offer a much better leverage against tax hikes in the next year than for program cuts in the current fiscal year.

Initially, this may not make intuitive sense. Since reserves are on hand, why can't state governments use them to avoid immediate cuts? There are two possible explanations. The first is caution under stress. During the early stages of a revenue shock, state governments may wish to use reserves sparingly out of a fear that the downturn may be prolonged or become worse. Recent research on the fiscal behavior of the state of Georgia during the 2001 recession supports this finding (Lauth 2003). The second explanation relates to political preferences. Emergency spending cuts may be seen as more politically and ideologically palatable than tax increases. As described in the previous section, such a preference for protecting tax cuts appearst to have become more dramatic in recent years.

While these effects of reserves on current-year budget cuts are not particularly large, the results reveal differences between BSF and GFS. For middle-of-the-year budget cuts, BSF is not statistically significant; that is, policy makers are "reserving" BSF for worse scenarios that may be on the way, while using GFS as the first line of defense (column 2). When budget makers plan for the next year, the comparative advantage, or real use of BSF, comes to the forefront (columns 4 and 6). This difference leads us to the question of whether BSF and GFS are really equivalent. As reserves, they should have the same effect on the budget, as previous studies have pointed out, but it is also reasonable to assume that the two types of fiscal reserves function differently. As discretionary reserves, GFS naturally serves as the first line of defense in cases of revenue shocks. BSF, on the other hand, are established as restricted reserves with its use subject to legislative approval and may function less promptly than GFS. This finding confirms Hou's (2003b) finding about the nature of BSF and GFS. The empirical results show that the relatively recent BSF have a larger effect on next-year budgets than GFS when controlling for other factors, suggesting that BSF are fulfilling their role of mediating these effects and providing the majority of the countercyclical fiscal capacity for states.

The control variables that are statistically significant suggest the following tentative interpretations. States with higher personal incomes are more likely to enact budget cuts and tax increases. A $1,000 difference in per capita personal income will lead to a variation of about $2.70 in current-year budget cuts, $8.90 in next-year tax increases, and $11.90 of net revenue change in the next year. This result echoes Joyce's (2001) argument that the amount of reserves each state maintains should be proportional to the composition of its revenue and expenditure portfolio. It suggests that richer states did not save enough to buffer recession effects; whereas less well-to-do states were less subject to dramatic swings in the business cycle. Further exploration of this question would require an investigation into the revenue volatility (tax elasticity) of each state's portfolios.

Economic growth, on the other hand, is shown to be the most solid buffer against budget actions, which makes perfect intuitive and theoretical sense. A one percentage point increase in state gross product will reduce the need for current-year budget cuts by about $98, next-year revenue action by nearly $356, and net revenue change in the next year by roughly $551. Vice versa, if the state economy goes the other direction, the reverse will be true. Unemployment is directly linked to current-year budget actions only. One percentage point increase in the unemployment rate triggers a budget cut of a little over $4 per capita in the same fiscal year. Why its effect on future revenue actions is not significant needs to be explored. Poverty rate and general fund expenditure are negatively associated with next-year budgets, significant on revenue actions but not on net revenue change. The negative sign is not expected; probably it is because the planning part has taken into consideration the social needs and the scale of expenditure. Further research is needed for better explanations.

Among the budgetary institutions, legislature passing a balanced budget is significant on planned budget actions. Presence of this article can reduce the magnitude of tax increases by about $42. The requirement of own-source revenue plus debt meeting expenditures can reduce the need for tax increase by over $50. Governor signing a balanced budget shows the expected negative sign but is significant only in one case. Revenue limits are positively related to revenue actions planned for the next year. When encountered with revenue shocks, governments with statutory revenue limits may have been forced to raise their next-year revenue by over $20 per capita. States with biennial budget may need to cut their current-year spending by about $10.

I do find that election years are negatively and significantly related to budget cuts. Ceteris paribus, the presence of an election year in our analysis reduced budget cuts by about $4. This is consistent with our expectations that elected officials will be reluctant to make painful budget cuts immediately prior to an election. Citizen ideology is positively related to current-year budget cuts, while government ideology is positively related to prior planned budget actions. These, however, are not consistent over the models; more detailed analysis is warranted for any further interpretation.

7.6 Conclusion

In this chapter I have extended countercyclical fiscal policy to countercyclical fiscal capacity and examined the utility of CCFC in mitigating budget cuts and tax hikes in bust years. Empirical tests offer several interesting findings on how reserves were used by state governments in their efforts to deal with revenue shocks. The standard caveat applies here that empirically observed correlation does not equal causation. Bearing this caveat in mind, the results offer support for the role of boom-year reserves to act as a tool of CCFC that improves state government performance in two ways. First, countercyclical savings help smooth and stabilize public spending and avoid tax hikes during recessions, at a time when the economy is weak and many more citizens particularly need additional government support than during boom years. Second, these reserves also help reduce emergency cuts in spending. In tandem, these two improvements contribute to budget stabilization; specifically they provide a measure of stability in program delivery.

The coefficients are small in magnitude, which suggests that reserves have a statistically significant relationship with the budget cuts and revenue actions, but this impact is not very large. Instead, state fiscal policy is largely driven by the revenue stream and the economic cycle rather than the other way around. When own-source revenues are sluggish, states will make middle-of-the-year expenditure cuts and plan tax/fee increases for the next year. The magnitude of the effects of reserves, however, is much larger on planning for the next fiscal year than on reducing emergency budget cuts. That is, fiscal reserves are more prominent in preplanned budgetary reactions to revenue shocks than for unplanned measures.

We have also seen differences in how state governments dealt with revenue shocks between the 1991 and the 2001 recessions. During the earlier recession, state governments were more likely to limit emergency spending cuts, while in later years there was a greater tendency to avoid tax/fee hikes. Both fiscal tools – mitigating tax hikes and mitigating spending cuts – are countercyclical in their nature. However, from a public management perspective, mitigating emergency spending cuts has the added advantage of maintaining program stability by avoiding unexpected cuts in the flow of program resources in the middle of the fiscal cycle. A policy recommendation that emerges from my empirical analysis – but appears to run counter to current state government preferences for the use of reserves – is that state governments recognize the dual benefits of limiting emergency spending cuts and be more willing to use reserves for this purpose.

The tests conducted in this chapter also add to our understanding of the evolution of fiscal reserves since the wide adoption of BSF in the 1980s. BSF have increasingly come to be relied on by states to mitigate budget cuts and avoid tax increases, but my analysis finds that GFS still plays a significant role in CCFC. The choice between BSF and GFS as a budgetary strategy relates to the nature of the two instruments. GFS is at the discretion of policy makers. Because of this flexibility, GFS acts as the first line of defense. BSF are restricted reserves under legal constraint intended to protect against boom-year spending pressure. Any use of BSF takes more time as legislators follow preset procedures; even so, it is an effective tool in the case of revenue shocks, increasingly relied upon by state governments. These confirm results from Chapter 6.

I find that statutory revenue and expenditure limitations have little impact on state's fiscal decisions with regard to their use of funds. This finding provides further support to the conclusions of Mullins and Wallin (2004), who survey previous studies of these budgetary rules. One possible reason for the weak impact of statutory tax and expenditure limitations is that many of these rules are "on the books" but routinely ignored. A useful direction for future research would be to differentiate between formal but inconsequential tax and expenditure limitations and those which offer real constraints. A similar research issue that this article raises but does not resolve is how variation between financial rules that shape the size and use of reserves impact CCFC, emergency spending cuts, and revenue actions. Some research already exists that suggests that structural differences in the operation of rainy-day funds impacts fiscal performance (Douglas and Gaddie 2002; Knight and Levinson 1999; Sobel and Holcombe 1996; Wagner and Elder 2005). Including measures of such variation would add greater depth to the empirical results presented here by taking into account that there are differences in how rainy-day funds operate across the states. Another potential application of our model and tools is to European Union (EU) member countries and prospective members. Efforts to integrate the EU economy and currency have led to specific rules designed to enforce budgetary discipline while removing some of the traditional fiscal tools these nations once enjoyed (e.g., currency devaluation and tariff policies). These changes have made the fiscal capacity challenges faced by EU states similar to those experienced by US states.

As governments seek different ways to improve public performance, the case of reserve funds as a form of public management capacity has some curious properties. All too frequently policy makers and researchers have great difficulty in establishing a clear link between government action and outcomes, but this is not the case here. Reserve funds have a clear and logical relationship with the goals of avoiding tax increases during recessions and reducing emergency budget cuts. This analysis finds empirical support for this relationship. In short, reserves work: They mitigate the need to raise taxes and make emergency cuts to spending during a recession. The curious aspect is that a predictable capacity-performance relationship has not received further support and investment by policy makers. Joyce (2001) wisely cautions that reserve funds should be contingent on the particular level of volatility in the state economy, but our analysis reveals that on aggregate reserve funds are not of sufficient size to overcome the effects of serious revenue shocks. During boom periods governments do not save adequate amounts to avoid the need to make emergency expenditure cuts or raise taxes/fees when the business cycle turns negative. One relatively straightforward policy recommendation, therefore, is for state governments to consider building up reserves that will be equivalent to the fiscal challenges that they will face during economic downturns. Given the inability of state governments to carry deficits, reserves are the only countercyclical fiscal tools on hand to influence, rather than be subject to, the revenue rollercoaster ride of the business cycle.

No doubt, setting aside money for an indefinite period incurs opportunity costs, and the political process is effective at identifying alternative uses of unspent revenues. Politicians, and the public, may grow concerned about maintaining large reserves that could be spent or returned to taxpayers and underestimate the relevance of such funds as the last recession recedes from memory. However, as has been shown elsewhere, state governments can design effective financial rules that guide the funding and spending of BSF to a set of preestablished guidelines (Douglas and Gaddie 2002; Hou et al. 2003), and more generally Posner and Gordon (2001) have shown that it is possible for other countries to follow self-imposed restrictions that allow them to save surpluses. Therefore, the question is not whether fiscal reserves improve state financial performance, the results have attested to the benefits; the question is neither whether states can devise rules to create countercyclical fiscal capacity, the prior chapters have showcased what many states have done to build up their fiscal capacity. The real challenge is whether state policy makers have the political will to do more in this line of policy for larger benefits.

Appendix

Variables used in the tests

Name	Definition	Data source
BSF	Actual BSF balance by end of fiscal year in real year 2000 per capita dollars	*Fiscal Survey of States*
GFS	Actual general fund balance (cleaned for double counting of BSF) by end of fiscal year in real year 2000 per capita dollars	*Fiscal Survey of States*
Reserves	BSF + GFS	
Personal income	Per capita personal income in thousands	Bureau of Economic Analysis
Unemployment rate	Average annual unemployment rate	Bureau of Labor Statistics
Expenditure	Per capita general fund expenditure of state government, in thousands	Census
Strict BBR	State may not carry over deficits into next fiscal year, dummy	*The Book of the States* series
Tax and expenditure limits	Tax and expenditure limitations on state government by referendum, two dummies, one for revenue limit and the other for expenditure limit	*Budget Processes of the States* series
Election year	Year for gubernatorial election, dummy	*The Book of the States* series
Democratic governor	Governor is a member of the Democratic party, dummy	*The Book of the States* series
Divided government	Governor and the majority of state legislature are of opposite party, dummy	*The Book of the States* series

References

Allan IJ (1990) Unreserved fund balance and local government finance. Research Bulletin of the Government Finance Officers Association (GFOA), Chicago

Berry WD, Ringquist EJ, Fording RC, Hanson RL (1998) Measuring citizen and government ideology in the American states 1960–93. Am J Polit Sci 42(1):327–348

Douglas JW, Gaddie RK (2002) State rainy day funds and fiscal crises: rainy day funds and the 1990–1991 recession revisited. Public Budg Finance 22(1):19–30

Hou Y (2003b) What stabilizes state general fund spending during downturns: budget stabilization fund, general fund unreserved undesignated balance, or both? Public Budg Finance 23(3):64–91

Hou Y (2004) Budget stabilization fund: structural features of the enabling legislation and balance level. Public Budg Finance 24(3):38–64

Hou Y, Smith DL (2006) A framework for understanding state balanced budget requirement systems: re-examining distinctive features and an operational definition. Public Budg Finance 26(3):22–45

Hou Y, Moynihan DP, Ingraham PW (2003) Capacity, management and performance: exploring the links. Am Rev Public Adm 33(3):295–315

Johnson N (2002) The state tax cuts of the 1990s, the current revenue crisis, and the implications for state services. Center on Budget and Policy Priorities, Washington, DC

Joyce PG (2001) What's so magical about five percent? A nationwide look at factors that influence the optimal size of state rainy day funds. Public Budg Finance 21(2):62–87

Knight B, Levinson A (1999) Rainy day funds and state government savings. Natl Tax J LII(3):459–472

Lauth TP (2003) Budgeting during a recession phase of the business cycle: the Georgia experience. Public Budg Finance 23(2):26–38

Mullins DR, Wallin BA (2004) Tax and expenditure limitations: introduction and overview. Public Budg Finance 24(4):2–15

O'Toole LJ, Meier KJ (1999) Modeling the impact of public management: implications of structural context. J Public Adm Res Theory 9(4):505–526

Pollock R, Suyderhoud JP (1986) The role of rainy day funds in achieving fiscal stability. Natl Tax J 43(4):485–497

Posner P, Gordon BS (2001) Can democratic governments save? Experience of countries with budget surpluses. Public Bud Finance 21(2):1–28

Poterba J (1994) State responses to fiscal crisis: the effects of budgetary institutions and politics. J Polit Econ 102(4):799–821

Prais SJ, Winsten CB (1954) Trend estimators and serial correlation. Cowles Commission discussion paper no. 383, Chicago

Provan KG, Milward HB (1995) A preliminary theory of interorganizational network effectiveness: a comparative study of four community mental health systems. Adm Sci Q 40(1):1–33

Sobel RS, Holcombe RG (1996) The impact of state rainy day funds in easing state fiscal crises during the 1990–1991 recession. Public Budg Finance 16(4):28–48

Wagner G, Elder E (2005) The role of budget stabilization funds in smoothing government expenditures over the business cycle. Public Finance Rev 33(1):439–446

Part III
Implications for Budgeting and Financial Management

Introduction

The emphasis of Part II was on the empirical effects of countercyclical fiscal policy (CCFP) and capacity (CCFC). In this part, I shift focus to the implications of CCFP for public budgeting and financial management. Chapter 8 carries forward the empirical results of Chapter 6 in theoretical exploration toward a new budgetary system that can better cope with uncertainty and instability, examining the annual balance as core of the modern budgetary theory to infer that the annual budget creates a mismatch between the budget cycle and the demand for continuity in public service provision. The chapter offers multiyear perspective on budgeting as a potential solution, with countercyclical fiscal reserves as the means to balance the budget through and across economic cycles. Based on results in Chapter 6, this chapter reiterates the following: States that had established a BSF can fair better in recessions than those that did not; states that established BSF earlier had better weathered recessions than those that adopted the fund late. That is, adopting the countercyclical fiscal policy and BSF has been a step in moving public budgeting from the annual to a longer-term perspective, which indicates progress toward building a new budgetary system for fiscal stability over the economic cycle.

Chapter 9 examines whether boom-year savings have had any effect on revenue forecasting. BSF as a tool of the countercyclical fiscal policy was created as precautionary savings against revenue shortfalls; however, public finance does not operate in vacuum; BSF cannot stay free of politics. Presence of savings inherently triggers complications in the politico-technical forecasting machine. This chapter examines whether adopting BSF has any impact on forecast errors and how the structural features and size of BSF influence the forecasting behavior in states with a BSF in place. No evidence is found that adopting a stabilization fund or the size of BSF reduces estimation errors. The results suggest that BSF as a formal savings device stays outside the forecasting process, but the level of general fund surplus may be part of the calculation in making revenue estimates.

Chapter 10 explores the use of debt as a fiscal tool for countercyclical use. It builds a model to incorporate long-term debt into budgetary policy. The proposition is to retire debt in boom years in order to preserve debt capacity and reduce borrowing costs and then incur debt at low interest rate in bust years in order to help maintain a state's service provision and pave the way for recovery. The chapter empirically tests the following: Do states in aggregate use debt pro- or countercyclically? What factors determine the cyclical patterns in states' use of debt? Will countercyclical debt issue and retirement be applicable and what may be the effects of this proposition. The chapter then simulates the effects of the proposed optimal debt policy with New York State; calibration shows that such a policy could have rendered the state a better position to encounter the Great Recession. The appendix to Chapter 10 provides details on pay-as-you-go financing of capital projects, its determinants of use, and its short-term and long-term implications on stability.

Chapter 8
Countercyclical Fiscal Policy and Multiyear Perspective on Budgeting

Abstract This chapter offers a theoretical exploration towards a new budgetary system to cope with uncertainty and instability. It begins by examining the practice of annual balance, core of the "modern" budgetary theory, and infers that annual budget creates a mismatch between the budget cycle and the continuity of public service provision. The chapter provides multi-year perspective on budgeting as a potential solution, with counter-cyclical fiscal reserves as the means to balance the budget through and across economic cycles. The chapter suggests that states have tried a multi-year perspective by adopting budget stabilization funds (BSF) and shifting annual surpluses from the general fund into BSF. By creating BSF legislation, states institutionalize the counter-cyclical fiscal policy. Then with sufficient fiscal reserves, states can better maintain trend-level public services during recessions. Through panel data (1979–1999) analysis, the chapter provides empirical evidence that BSF did help stabilize state general expenditure in downturns by releasing reserves to fill in spending gaps. Specifically, states that had established a BSF before the three sampled recessions fared better than those that did not; states that established a BSF earlier had better weathered the recessions than those that adopted the fund late. In other words, adopting the counter-cyclical fiscal policy and BSF is a step in moving public budgeting from the annual to a longer-term perspective, which indicates progress towards building a new budgetary system for fiscal stability over the economic cycle.

This chapter is based on and expanded from Hou Y (2006) Budgeting for fiscal stability over the business cycle. Public Adm Rev 66(5): 730–41, published by Wiley-Blackwell.

Y. Hou, *State Government Budget Stabilization: Policy, Tools, and Impacts*, Studies in Public Choice 8, DOI 10.1007/978-1-4614-6061-9_8,

8.1 Introduction

This chapter moves forward from the empirical tests done in Chapter 6 for a theoretical exploration toward a new budgetary system with which governments can better cope with economic uncertainty and financial instability. It begins by examining the practice of annual balance, which has been the core of the "modern" budget theory, and infers that the annual budget creates a mismatch between the budget cycle and the continuity of public service provision. The chapter offers the "multiyear perspective on budgeting" as a potential solution, with countercyclical fiscal reserves as one means to balance the budget through and across economic cycles. The chapter suggests that states have already experimented with the multiyear perspective by adopting the budget stabilization funds (BSF) and shifting annual surpluses from the general fund into BSF. By passing BSF legislation, states institutionalize the countercyclical fiscal policy. Then with sufficient fiscal reserves, states can better maintain trend-level public services during recessions. Based on results in Chapter 6, this chapter reiterates that states that had established a BSF fared better in recessions than those that did not and that states which established BSF earlier had weathered recessions better than those that adopted the fund late. In other words, adopting the countercyclical fiscal policy and the BSF has been a significant step in moving public budgeting from the annual to a longer-term perspective, which indicates progress toward building a new budgetary system for fiscal stability over the economic cycle.

During the Great Recession (2007–2009) and the subsequent years of sluggish recovery, state governments again came across many problems that are due to, or at least related to, the mismatch between the annual budget cycle and the need for a longer span of financial planning. In fact, during the 1980 recession, renowned budget scholar Naomi Caiden had already wisely warned, "[t]he task of public budgeting has become infinitely more complex, complicated, and worrisome. Current budget theory and practice lag behind operational requirements" (1981, 7). Since then, though many experiments with several aspects of budgeting have been made in practice, theoretical explorations remain below the desired level. This chapter attempts to fill in the inadequacy by examining the annual perspective in contrast to a multiyear perspective on budgeting.

The annual budget cycle of executive budgeting, which was a product and the most important achievement of the Budgetary Reform Movement (1890s–1910s), has well served the state and local sector for a century, and this annual cycle has produced many successes. Among its numerous successes, the annual budget has been very effective in controlling spending and in managing financial operations, because the 12-month period offers what seems to be the optimal span that facilitates legislative control for oversight while granting executive discretion for operational flexibility. A century's use, however, has also exposed some serious inadequacies of the annual cycle. Spanning for only 12 months, this cycle is not a sufficient device for financial planning, often leading to incurable cyclical deficits, which deprives governments of one of the means to maintain fiscal stability over the economic cycle. The mismatch has become increasingly protruding; each successive recession serves as a reminder. With the Great Recession as resounding alarm, it is time now to launch another round of public budgeting reform: to extend the perspective of budgeting from one fiscal year to a longer term so as to reinforce the planning function of public budgeting. One option that has been suggested is to adopt the multiyear budget window. However, multiyear budgeting relies heavily on accurate estimates of revenues and expenditures. Among other things to be solved, technical errors in forecasting are almost unavoidable, thereby making the multiyear budgeting cycle an unhandy tool. The theory of subnational countercyclical fiscal policy paves the way for the extended budgeting perspective, hence wider application of the multiyear budget. The theory advocates that subnational governments accumulate fiscal reserves during boom years and release the reserves in lean years as an effort to better maintain budgetary and fiscal stability. This chapter proposes that well-structured countercyclical fiscal policy and tool(s) be adopted as the core for the multiyear budgeting perspective, which is budgeting for fiscal stability over the economic cycle.

This chapter is organized as follows. The next section examines the annual budget cycle and offers analyses of its inadequacies. Section 8.3 provides a tripartite typology of deficits, leading to Section 8.4 – why the annual budget cannot solve cyclical deficits. Section 8.5 introduces multiyear budgeting to illustrate why the multiyear cycle is still not a handy tool for state governments, then brings in the theory of subnational countercyclical fiscal policy, and offers empirical analyses of the effects of CCFP on stabilizing state spending over the economic cycle. The chapter concludes with recommendations for state governments.

8.2 Dissecting the Annual Budget

The origin or acceptance of the annual budget as the most widely used budget cycle for government financial planning dates back to the Budgetary Reform Movement. At the turn of the nineteenth and the twentieth centuries, parallel to the movement for administrative reform went the Movement for Budgetary Reform in municipalities.[1] The latter achieved great success and was soon carried over to state governments. The concept of "budget" in the currently standard understanding was widely and strongly advocated in the Budgetary Reform Movement as an instrument for three purposes (Willoughby 1918b, 1–5). In the political sense, the budget was taken as an instrument of governance to promote democracy and to curb corruption then rampant in local governments because

> [The budget] at once serves to make known past operations, present conditions, and future proposals, *definitely locates responsibility and furnishes the means for control*. (Willoughby 1918b, 1–2; emphasis by this author)

[1] The two movements went separately. "It was not until the rise of the modern movement for budgetary reform that the connection between the two was seen" (Willoughby 1918b, 13). In this sense the budgetary reform can be taken as part of the administrative reform.

In the managerial sense, the budget was intended to coordinate the legislative and the executive branches in that

> ...When discretionary powers and authority are increased [to the executive branch] a corresponding increase should be made in the means of controlling and supervising [by the legislative branch] the manner in which these augmented powers are exercised. (Ibid, 3)

And in the technical sense, the budget was adopted to improve administrative efficiency:

> Government officers should ...be held up to the same standards of efficiency and honesty as...in the business world, ...[where] it is recognized that no undertaking of magnitude... can be efficiently administered which does not have a system of accounts and reports... (Ibid, 4)

The "budget" so conceived can be summarized as having three major "orientations" (Cleveland 1915) or "functions" (Schick 1966) – control, management, and planning. The control function is to make sure that public resources (tax dollars) are used to accomplish only, and exactly, the established (budgeted) goals. In the context of the budgetary reform, "the proper function of the budget is ... the presentation and adoption of a plan in fiscal affairs which will insure the most judicial use of the resources of the state for the purposes most desired by the citizens of the state" (Lowrie 1915, 47–63). The management function is to guarantee the technical and operational efficiency and effectiveness. The planning function is to decide on the objectives and policies, that is, the "acquisition, use, and disposition of the resources" (Cleveland 1915; Schick 1966). This theory of the three functions of the budget remains true even now, though the order of priority may have shifted from one to the other among the three in different periods. For example, during years of the Budgetary Reform Movement, effective control of expenditures to curb corruption was the priority; while during the Government Performance Review era (mid-1990s), management was the focus in an effort to improve performance (efficiency); in years of chronic deficits like now, more attention should be paid to financial planning so as to transition into sustainable budgetary operations.

The core of this standard budgetary theory has remained to be the concept and practice of keeping the annual budget in balance (Wildavsky 1978, 502); that is, recurring expenditures must not exceed recurring revenues. In Wildavsky's words, the budgeting process repeats itself each year, with the budgeted amount increasing marginally from previous year on a cash basis. The "annual" nature of the budget is made most explicit by Willoughby: "An estimate is made of expenditures.... required of the due conduct of governmental affairs during a period (this period being *almost universally fixed at one year*)" (Willoughby 1918a, 3; original parenthesis, italics by this author). In the context of the budgetary reforms, "it shall be the duty of the Mayor ... in each year to submit to the Council the annual budget of current expenses of the city..." (National Municipal League 1899). And "the expenditures of the city should be brought into direct relation to its possible or actual revenues and be based upon estimates and recommendations emanating from the spending departments" (Willoughby 1918b, 6).

This balanced budget requirement is not strange to us. All 50 states, by their constitution or statute, must balance their budget[2] – when the United States started with separate states, citizens (taxpayers) had seen the need to curb government spending to within the allowable means and to avoid corruption in the spending of tax dollars. State debt defaults in the 1830s instituted these requirements. The Budgetary Reform that occurred 100 years ago was a campaign to rid municipal governments of then rampant corruption. The reforms succeeded in restoring budgetary discipline to governmental finances. Therefore, the most important task for financial managers under this standard theory was to achieve structural balance – balancing annual recurring expenditures against annual recurring revenues. Even for those states that adopted biennial budgets, the focus stays on the annual balance either by readjusting the biennial plan near the end of the first year or by allocating appropriations into the annual time frame, though the span of planning stretches out one more year (PACH 1950, 25).[3] The three functions play out around this core of annual balance.

The annual cycle for budgeting delivers unique advantages that make it politically acceptable and technically operable. On the political front, spending checks and reviews are conducted on a regular basis at relatively short (annual) intervals so that the budget as a control system accounts for every cent of tax money. Oversight is comprehensive, with internal and external bodies set up for the whole government entity as well as its departments and component units. At the very basis is the appropriation system that guarantees financial assurance – not a single dollar can be spent without appropriation; and once appropriated, the specified dollar amounts can only be spent for the specified purposes. On the technical front, the fiscal year still allows 12-month planning into the future, though it is not as long as desirable for pure planning purposes. Thus, every aspect of the financing of government is ascertained before the start of government operations. It was in this sense that the budget becomes a plan for the whole government entity in the coming fiscal year. Till now, this annual perspective has served state (and local) governments for a century, with numerous successes, despite probably as many problems and challenges.

8.2.1 *Inadequacies of the Annual Perspective*

The term "balance" can be misleading. Conceptually, a pure balance with no surplus or deficit at the end of a fiscal year is not possible because neither revenue nor

---

[2] Some studies exclude Vermont from this category; while in fact Vermont is also under this legal obligation, though the statutory wording is a bit different, which requires the governor to balance the budget.

[3] The conferees to the Public Administration Clearing House (PACH) at Princeton Budget Theory Symposium, July 1949, pointed out that "the trend has been toward annual state budget", but "there is no magic about a year period. Stabilization of tax expectance [for businesses] is more important." Further, "longer projections and more frequent reviews by the legislative body are both desirable… [though] the longer the projection, the greater is the inertia built up against change in the budget estimates" (PACH 1950, 25).

expenditure pauses at the end of the fiscal year – that point of time is set for accounting purposes. Government operation (public service provision) is an ongoing process. A real "balance" can exist only in the account book, not in practice. For example, the state of Arkansas' *Comprehensive Annual Financial Report* each year (in my sample) from 1979 to 2001 reported zero for their unreserved undesignated balance of the general fund, which was really the result of post-year-end adjustments by reserving or designating surpluses for different purposes. Their general fund total balance is in fact not zero. On the other hand, balanced budget requirements in state finance laws (including state laws for local governments) prohibit deficits at the end of fiscal years. Thus, by definition, balanced budget requirements do not allow year-end deficits but require that governments end their fiscal years with "surpluses," here defined as the unreserved undesignated balance of the general fund at the end of fiscal year that is available for appropriation for the next fiscal year (see "list of terms" in the *Fiscal Survey of States* by NASBO). The "balance" therefore means positive balance, that is, surplus.

Such year-end surpluses must exist also for a practical reason. The continuous nature of public service provision requires working capital to pay for spending before tax dollars are collected and become available for outlays. Working capital is in this sense a lubricant to the government machinery; without it, the machine is difficult to run and the government has to borrow for eminent expenses; the interest thereby obligated adds to the cost. The recurring "spring borrowing" of the state of New York is one example. Working capital is kept in the general fund and as such adds to its "balance"; so zero or very small surplus of the general fund may indicate absence of, or insufficient, working capital.[4]

Maintaining structural balance as keeping general fund surplus on an annual basis is easier said than done due to political and economic reasons. The political reason is related to the budgetary process that is "intrinsically and irreducibly political" (Wildavsky 1964; Rubin 1999). As abundant literature on public expenditure and the much politicized budgetary process has revealed, taxpayers in general have a tendency to demand more current assumption of public services than their tax payments can support; when current assumptions are adequately satisfied but the government still possesses extra resources, requests for tax refunds often dominate (Proposition 13 is an example). Elected officials and legislators, following the taste and preference of voters, usually also prefer current spending or tax refunds so as to win reelection. Therefore, surpluses are often under spending pressure from key players in the budgetary process and thus are not easy to accumulate; once accumulated, they are difficult to sustain.

The economic reason is related to the economic cycle. Imagine there exists a gradually increasing trend line along which both governmental revenues and expenditures move. In normal years, revenues are enough to cover (i.e., larger than) expenditures, with marginal surpluses. During years of national recession or regional downturn, revenues fall short of budgetary estimates and thereby cannot cover the

[4] Some states, like Florida, keep a separate working capital fund for cash flow; even so, it is reported in the annual financial report under the general fund.

Table 8.1 Number and percentage of states with general fund UUB deficits 1979–2010

Year	*FY 1979*	*FY 1980*	*FY 1981*	*FY 1982*	*FY 1983*	*FY 1984*	*FY 1985*	*FY 1986*
Number	0	3	6	13	12	8	7	6
Percentage	0%	6%	12%	27%	24%	16%	14%	12%
Year	*FY 1987*	*FY 1988*	*FY 1989*	*FY 1990*	*FY 1991*	*FY 1992*	*FY 1993*	*FY 1994*
Number	5	9	9	15	19	18	11	9
Percentage	10%	18%	18%	31%	39%	37%	22%	18%
Year	*FY 1995*	*FY 1996*	*FY 1997*	*FY 1998*	*FY 1999*	*FY 2000*	*FY 2001*	*FY 20 02*
Number	11	13	9	6	5	4	6	10
Percentage	22%	27%	18%	12%	10%	8%	12%	20%
Year	*FY 2003*	*FY 2004*	*FY 2005*	*FY 2006*	*FY 2007*	*FY 2008*	*FY 2009*	*FY 2010*
Number	17	14	8	4	5	8	19	20
Percentage	35%	29%	16%	8%	10%	16%	39%	41%

a. Source: Compiled from the *Comprehensive Annual Financial Reports* (CAFR) of the states. For years before each state published CAFR, the *Annual Financial Report* on the budgetary basis is the source. Due to difference in the basis of accounting between the two sources, the number of states in deficit in the early and middle periods of the sample years is not comparable

b. Deficit is here defined as negative unreserved undesignated balance of the general fund

trend-line expenditure necessary for maintaining public services as needed. However, public service programs are not supposed to stop even though revenues have shrunk, and the general public is not happy about reduced services at times of critical needs. As a result, governments often have to exhaust surpluses to sustain service levels. When surpluses are not enough for this purpose, account books cannot balance and deficits inevitably emerge.

Governments and taxpayers have long been troubled by the recurring headache of deficits. Table 8.1 lists the number and percentage of states that ended their general fund in deficit for fiscal years 1979 through 2010. Although the percentage is in general higher during and immediately after recessions (1980, 1982, 1991, 2001, and 2008), there were states that ended in deficit in each year of this period except 1979, even in the record-long economic prosperity of the late 1990s as well as the mid-2000s. Two major reasons for this phenomenon could have been the political and economic ones as discussed above,[5] both being rooted in the annual budget format. Therefore, we can conclude that the annual perspective on budgeting, though successful in the control and management functions, falls short on planning. With only 1 year's span, the annual format cannot guarantee balanced budget but makes it more difficult for state and local governments to assure balanced budgets in the long run or to maintain stable spending for necessary service levels during lean years.

[5] Another possible reason for this phenomenon is management tradition. Specifically, 14 of the 50 states had no deficit years in the 1979–1999 period. These are mainly southern states such as Alabama, Arkansas (always 0 through figure manipulation), Florida, Mississippi, Oklahoma, Tennessee, and West Virginia and Midwestern and Western states such as Hawaii, Kansas, Montana, North Dakota, and Utah. Exceptions are New Jersey (Mid-Atlantic) and Ohio (Great Lakes). Another 14 states had only one to three deficit years. But 11 had ten deficit years and more, and the rest had between four to nine deficit years.

8.3 Typology of Deficits

Under a somewhat simplistic typology, deficits fall into three types – structural, managerial, and cyclical. Though distinction between them may not seem important to the ordinary observer, a clear separation of the three facilitates better understanding of the deficit problem and points out directions for solution.

8.3.1 Structural Deficits

These occur in cases where the size or amount of the revenue portfolio does not match that of expenditure so that recurring revenues are not adequate to cover the cost of promised public services. This is linked to the political reason mentioned above: Service level should be kept within affordable means; but the reality often goes other way due to political considerations. The cure for such deficits is either to raise the tax rate (or in the long term, to enlarge the tax base) or shrink the service promise. Neither is easy, given the nature of budgetary politics.

8.3.2 Managerial Deficits

Even when budgeted annual revenues and expenditures match in size, deficits can still occur due to poor fiscal management from ignoring the three fundamental functions of the budget (control, management, and planning). The cure for such deficits lies in hiring qualified financial managers, empowering them, and tightening daily management by enforcing the budget.

8.3.3 Cyclical Deficits

These by nature are not a result of structural mismatch or poor fiscal management; they occur even when the budget has been planned annually for structural balance (to avoid structural deficits) and well implemented on a year-by-year basis (to eliminate managerial deficits). Cyclical deficits indicate failure of the annual perspective of the current budgetary system. They occur because the planned annual recurring revenues are not streaming in at the expected amount due to a recession, while the demand for services does not decrease but may even increase when the economy is on the downturn, so that the annual revenues are far short of the needed annual expenditures. Mere success in achieving annual structural balance is far from enough to eliminate cyclical deficits. To cure such deficits requires more than the conventional budgeting concepts and practices in the annual perspective.

Table 8.2 Changes in state balanced budget requirements in selected years 1979–2008: number of states adopting the article

	1979	1984	1989	1994	1999	2002	2008
Governor must submit a balanced budget	23	43	44	43	44	45	44
Legislature must pass a balanced budget	21	39	38	39	39	41	41
Governor must sign a balanced budget	29	29	31	29	37	35	37
State may carry deficit over into next fiscal year	11	21	9	11	9	3	7

Source: Tabulated from *The Book of the States* series, various years. That series stopped reporting on state BBRs since 2005. Data source for 2008 is NASBO's *Budget Processes in the States*

8.4 Annual Budget and Cyclical Deficits

In their pursuit for solutions to the deficit problem, state governments have not conscientiously distinguished the three different types of deficits. In a generic approach, states instituted statutory or constitutional balanced budget requirements (BBR) dating back to the 1830/1840s that were based on the annual perspective, which have been classified into three categories, each state being bound by one, two, or all three of them: First, the governor must submit to the legislature a balanced budget; second, the legislature must pass a balanced budget; and third, the governor must sign into law a balanced budget (ACIR 1987; NGA series; NASBO 1992; Hou and Smith 2006). Designed for the annual budget, the BBRs may help directly avoid structural deficits and indirectly help harness managerial deficits; but since recessions are unpredictable in timing and may often be severe in magnitude, BBRs have not been sufficient to eliminate cyclical deficits. Table 8.2 offers a glimpse of the changes in BBR in selected years as reported in the *Book of the States* published by the National Governor's Association.

To be more exact, cyclical deficits occur not because the budget cannot be balanced annually in recession years with drastic fiscal measures like service reductions, hiring freezes (even layoffs), and tax increases but because these measures, though technically feasible, are "distasteful to taxpayers, uncomfortable with financial managers, and politically risky for elected officials" (Forsythe 1993). Although state governments often have to adopt such measures as they did in coping with the 2001 recession and especially the Great Recession, cyclical deficits are merely reduced to an acceptable (technically manageable and politically tolerable) extent but not eliminated. Furthermore, such drastic measures are procyclical: In years of recession, underfunding of social services (when demand is higher than in normal years), raising taxes, and freezing hires all go against the demand of citizens and the market, mitigating the overall effects of expansionary monetary and fiscal policies at the national level. This has turned out to be an especially protruding problem during the Great Recession and the slow recovery thereafter.

Tracing the causes of cyclical deficits, economists found that public expenditures and governmental revenues are two separate lines of activities, with distinct features of their own (White 1983). Public expenditures are service driven, which tend to increase when the economy is down and people need extra help from the government. After all, citizens, even businesses expect government to be the last resort in the worst economic scenarios regardless of their ideology. Tax revenues, on the other hand, can be more elastic to economic growth, depending on the specific portfolio of the tax structure (Misiolek and Perdue 1987) – states levying all of the three major tax types (personal income, corporate income, and general sales) have a more stable revenue stream while those without personal income tax suffer from high revenue volatility. A more recent study further reveals that even the same tax structure has inherently different long-run growth potential and short-run cyclical variability over the economic cycle (Sobel and Holcombe 1996). Therefore, the current focus of governmental budgeting on balancing the annual or biennial budget cannot solve the cyclical deficit problem without resorting to pro-cyclical fiscal measures. In Naomi Caiden's words, "traditional landmarks fade amidst uncertainty and instability" (1981, 18).

8.5 Multiyear Perspective on Budgeting

What is needed in addressing the cyclical deficit problem is to plan over a longer time span: Aim at maintaining structural balance through the peaks and troughs of the economic cycle. This is a fundamental change in the concept of public budgeting. Budget theorists like Naomi Caiden have long identified as a problem the mismatch between the annual/biennial budget cycle and the continuous nature of many service activities: "because annual budgeting uses a static framework to control a continuous and dynamic flow of activities, it may become a source of uncertainty" (1981, 15). Practitioners have from their firsthand experience spotted the problem of cyclical imbalance. A former New York state budget director succinctly said that surpluses and deficits as natural phenomena over the economic cycle are something that the traditional objective of the annual budget cannot balance well (Forsythe 1993). Alice Rivlin, former Director of the Office of Management and Budget and the Congressional Budget Office, also sees a necessity to assume "a longer planning horizon" (1987, 7–8). Here she was addressing mainly budget and fiscal policy at the federal level. Her suggestion, this author believes, is applicable to the state and local levels as well.[6]

Against this background, the multiyear budget cycle began to draw more attention and support from academics (Rivlin 1987; Forester 1991; Fisher 1997; Joyce 2000; Boex et al. 2000) as well as professional organizations (Guajardo 2000). Actual uses of this format can be found. Britain began conducting multiyear public expenditure surveys in 1961 (Heclo and Wildavsky 1974, 209). In the 1990s, it was a trend among

[6] Dr. Rivlin further points out that although it is true economists still cannot accurately forecast 2 years in advance, that does not erode the case for multiyear budgets (1987, 7–8).

OECD countries to reframe their annual budget process with a multiyear approach (OECD 1998). More recently, the Government Finance Officers' Association reports a success story of transition from the annual to the biennial format by local governments in the USA: A small city abandoned the traditional annual budget to embrace a biennial format; the city thereby has "improved its strategic planning capabilities and enhanced its overall financial condition" (Jackson 2002). The Government Performance Project (GPP) advocated the multiyear budgeting perspective, throughout its two phases (1998–2002 and 2005–2008) in assessing the management capacity of state and local governments.

A multiyear budget in simple words is a financial plan that budgets revenue and expenditure for multiyears. The GFOA definition of the multiyear cycle as "an operating budget… that spans two or more years" (Guajardo 2000, 1 and 15) is a very general classification. Boex et al. (2000, 92) put it as a "multiyear period" without specification. This author argues that a 2-year span is obviously not adequate to address the problem of cyclical deficits posed in this chapter. So far there has not been consensus on a uniform or standard definition or on the span, layout, and other technical details like adjustment and price volatility. That will emerge only after many more years of practice by many more governments at different levels. Before technical details are sought out and finalized, we may best depict multiyear budgeting as a perspective that aims at rectifying the inadequacies of the annual perspective by assuming a longer span of financial planning, which can be as long as 5–10 years, with its focus on achieving balance over the economic cycle.

Multiyear budgeting carries some potential but obvious and substantive benefits. For one, to assume the longer-term perspective, governments have to prioritize and state their policy goals explicitly and consistently. For another, current policies have to fit the multiyear fiscal strategy (Boex et al. 2000, 92), which helps limit short-term political games that dampen longer-term benefits. Most significantly, with a longer planning span, a multiyear perspective helps mitigate (if not eliminate) cyclical deficits.

The technical foundation for multiyear budgeting is accurate estimation of future revenues and expenditures (Guajardo 2000; Boex et al. 2000). However, accurate estimates do not come easily. As a "technically complex and administratively costly tool" (ibid), forecasts are developed by well-trained, experienced professionals using advanced computing equipment, working with data accumulated over time from many societal components (for details, see Chapter 9). It is a highly resource- and expertise-intensive enterprise, and the rate of accuracy is often not encouraging. Table 8.3 provides examples of error rates of state governments' revised estimation for the next fiscal year.[7] The error rates illustrate how far the estimates have gone from the actual revenues and expenditures.

---

[7] State governments as surveyed by the Government Performance Project conduct several estimates each year. The last estimate done before the budget is submitted to legislature is the final revised estimate and should be the one they believe to be the most accurate. In the *Comprehensive Annual Financial Reports*, these estimates are reported on the balance sheet of the general fund to compare with the actual revenues and expenditures. Error rates reported in Table 8.3 are calculated on these estimates.

Table 8.3 Error rates of revenue and expenditure estimates, 50 states

Item		1996 (%)	1997 (%)	1998 (%)	1999 (%)	4-year Avg. (%)
General fund revenue	Average	4.20	3.83	4.75	3.07	3.59
	Low	−8.10	−7.62	−12.61	−12.39	−11.03
	High	65.63	67.68	64.95	65.67	65.70
Total operating fund revenue	Average	1.75	3.35	3.94	1.64	2.79
	Low	−11.43	−15.73	−12.77	−12.91	−10.20
	High	29.46	77.64	80.24	41.73	47.23
General fund expenditure	Average	−2.03	−1.27	−2.09	−1.33	−1.67
	Low	−23.02	−28.38	−28.61	−29.14	−27.25
	High	14.50	26.30	15.35	13.42	16.62
Total operating fund expenditure	Average	−4.12	−2.63	−3.56	−4.33	−3.60
	Low	−41.89	−43.27	−43.90	−40.80	−42.23
	High	26.40	29.31	32.70	15.58	24.22

Notes: Error rate = (actual − estimate)/estimate. Positive revenue ratios indicate actual revenue was larger than estimated (underestimation of revenue), and negative ratios mean the actual revenue was smaller than estimated. Negative expenditure ratios indicate actual expenditures were smaller than estimated (overestimation of expenditure), and positive ratios mean the actual expenditures exceeded estimates. Smaller absolute values indicate better accuracy (smaller error) rates
Source: Government Performance Project state financial management survey 1998 and 2000

Estimation errors come in two types. One is intended protective error – "fiscal conservatism" in the forms of underestimation of revenue and overestimation of expenditures by financial managers and executive officials to guard against political pork barreling (Rodgers and Joyce 1996). In Table 8.3, fiscal conservatism is seen in the positive error rate of the 50-state average of the general fund as well as total operating fund revenues (actual exceeding estimation) but negative average error rate on the expenditure side of both funds (actual smaller than estimation). The other type is technical error in estimation due to uncertainty in economic operation and complexity of forecasting. While the former type may be reduced to the minimum (if financial managers and executive officials want to), the latter is very difficult to avoid. As Wildavsky succinctly put it: "Given economic volatility and theoretical poverty, the ability to outguess the future is extremely limited" (1978, 504). Therefore, multiyear budgeting alone cannot afford us the peace of mind; a built-in mechanism is necessary to facilitate fiscal stability in the longer term.

8.5.1 Countercyclical Fiscal Policy and Tools

Countercyclical fiscal policy fills in nicely by bridging the gap between the need for a longer-term perspective on budgeting and the unavoidable (technical) errors in forecasting. Suffering from recurring national and regional financial bumps, states have in fact been seeking a longer-term perspective on budgeting, and some of them have approached it, intentionally or unintentionally. Historically, the aggregate balance of the state and local sector accumulated surpluses in boom years and then released them in recession years (see Chapter 3 for details). Variation in the stringency of the balanced budget requirements is another example. On one hand, states require their governors and legislatures to submit, pass, and sign balanced budgets; on the other hand, some states choose to loosen the stringency of the implementation side of the requirements to allow deficit carry-over from the current into the next budget cycle (last row, Table 8.2). This measure is most probably out of the practical consideration for continuity of public service provision in downturn years, but it reflects the adoption of a more flexible attitude among state lawmakers toward cyclical deficits and a change from rigid to more flexible requirements on balancing the annual budget. Interestingly, the number of states allowing deficit carry-over increases with each recession and decreases after economic recovery.[8] The rise and fall of this number may indicate, among many other things, that the states have not found a satisfactory solution to the problem – but have been merely "muddling through."

Legislators in states that adopt a more volatile tax structure acutely realized the limitations of the annual budgeting process before those in many other states. One example is in the finance law of the state of Washington.[9] "The current budgetary system of Washington lacks stability. It encourages crisis budgeting and results in cutbacks during lean years and overspending during surplus years."[10]

The theory of subnational countercyclical fiscal policy (Gramlich 1987) paved the way for longer-term perspective on budgeting.[11] This theory opposes the use of procyclical fiscal measures because they are of a "perverse" policy: Balancing the budget annually in such manner amplifies the fluctuation from the economic cycles. The theory advocates the fiscal policy for stability: State governments can smooth the fluctuation of economic cycles by cutting spending during booms to accumulate more reserves and then releasing the reserves during downturn years to increase public expenditure.[12] This is to balance the budget through the economic cycle instead of the fiscal year. It serves as the theoretical basis for longer-term budgeting perspective.

The two major countercyclical fiscal devices are general fund surplus (GFS) and budget stabilization fund (BSF). The former used to dominate the scene; however, the expenditure limitation and tax revolt movement since the late 1970s, as typically

---

[8] Specifically, in 1979 only 11 states allowed deficit carry-over; after the 1980 and 1982 recessions, the number rose to 21. After the 1988 peak year, the number fell to a mere 9 but rose to 11 again after the 1991 recession, then falling to 9 again after the continuous prosperity in the 1990s. See Table 8.2, last row.

[9] Washington is one of the states with a more volatile tax structure: Not levying personal income tax, the state's finance relies on sales taxes and several business taxes.

[10] The Revised Code of Washington, Title 43, Ch 43.135.045. This article was adopted in 1981 as part of the enabling legislation for its BSF – the Emergency Reserve Fund.

[11] Although Gramlich's theory is more about economic stability, it is surely related to longer-term budgeting.

[12] Here I am referring to the weak version of his policy for stability. The strong version includes raising taxes during boom years and lowering them during recessions.

represented by Proposition 13, changed the scene. Tax revolts, an example of the political pressure on public spending, drastically reduced general fund surpluses. Then state policy makers increasingly turned to BSF as a legal haven for countercyclical reserves as a means to create operational buffer against revenue shortfalls[13]: The enabling legislation of a BSF usually dictates that BSF balances cannot be used unless in times of budgetary shortfall with special appropriations.

8.5.2 *Effects of Fiscal Reserves*

Empirical analysis can provide evidence on whether fiscal reserves have helped states during years of revenue downfalls. The tests are detailed in Chapter 6. For a brief summary here: First, trend expenditures of all 50 states are obtained using simple regression from their actual general expenditures from fiscal years 1979 through 1999. Then subtracting actual expenditure from the trends and dividing the differences by the trends yield gaps between the actual and the trend lines. The expenditure gaps are positive when actual expenditure was higher than the trend and negative when the actual was lower than the trend.

Then regressing real gross state product (GSP) in the current and past 3 years against the expenditure gaps offers a convenient examination of the cyclical properties of the gaps, which are positively correlated with the economy (national and regional): When the economy is strong, state actual expenditures tend to exceed the trend line, presumably because revenues stream often in larger amounts than have been budgeted. When the economy is down, actual spending tends to go below the trend because revenues fall short of expectation and accumulated surpluses are not adequate to fill in the gap. This is the time when cyclical deficits occur.

The empirical test is conducted with the expenditure gaps as the dependent variable and the Heckman sample selection model (Heckman 1979) as the empirical methodology to separate downturn years from upturn years of the economy. Controlling for social-economic factors, state economic composition, state party politics, and balanced budget requirements, the test produces evidence that BSF has been an effective countercyclical fiscal device in the three national recessions and more regional downturns that happened in the period from 1979 to 1999. During economic downturns in the 21-year sample period, when actual general expenditures of the states fell below their trend lines, each percentage point increase of the BSF balance as a percent of general fund expenditure in the previous fiscal year narrowed the negative expenditure gap in the next fiscal year by 0.65 percentage

[13] BSF and GFS data from state *Comprehensive Annual Financial Reports* (CAFRs) show that much of GFS shifted into BSF balances over the 1979–1999 period, while the sum of GFS and BSF remained at similar levels at the early and late years of that period. More details on this phenomenon, substitution and supplementation, are in Chapter 4.

points, ceteris paribus, the result being statistically highly significant[14] (see Table 6.4, Column 1, for details).

The widening adoption of BSF among the states outlines an (maybe unintentional) ongoing pursuit by the states for a better budgeting mechanism that crosses the annual/biennial cycle to a longer span. The pursuit started over six decades ago when the state of New York adopted the first BSF among the states (1946), followed by Florida in the 1950s. By 1999, finding that BSF was probably a usable mechanism to help achieve this longer-term structural balance, 39 states had established their BSF and made the first deposit into the fund. This number has further increased to 47 as of 2010 according to *Fiscal Survey of States* by NASBO. In some sense, adopting the countercyclical fiscal policy by these states can be said to have marked one very important step in the conceptual shift from the annual to the longer-term budgeting perspective.

8.6 Conclusion: Moving Toward Budgeting for Fiscal Stability

The annual budget cycle as heritage of the Budgetary Reform Movement has well served state (and local) governments for a century by tightening control over spending and strengthening daily management. But its 1-year span renders it an inadequate tool for financial planning, resulting frequently in cyclical deficits that are incurable with mechanisms available in the traditional budgetary system. As a consequence, subnational governments often have to adopt procyclical fiscal measures in recession years, as illustrated again during the Great Recession by hiring freezes, reduction of services, and/or higher taxes at the state and local levels.

The multiyear budget cycle looks appealing as a remedy to restore the tripod of the modern budgetary system, but the multiyear cycle is highly dependent on accurate estimates of revenues and expenditures in the coming years. On one hand, economic forecasts are very resource-intensive in terms of expertise, time, and equipment; on the other hand, the inherent uncertainty of economic activity and the complexity of forecasting make technical errors unavoidable (and other technical details are yet to be worked out), forming a barrier to wider adoption of multiyear budgets. This is a conundrum facing contemporary public budgeting.

The theory and practice of subnational countercyclical fiscal policy offer a possible intermediate relief before we obtain the final solution to the problem. By adopting such a fiscal policy and using effective policy tools, state and local governments can mitigate adverse effects of forecasting errors, narrow expenditure gaps in recession years, and thereby better maintain fiscal stability over the economic cycle. The policy tool at the state level used to be mainly general fund

[14] The results do not show that general fund surplus (GFS) exerted this countercyclical effect in the sample period, which is not a surprising finding since in the same period much of GFS had been transferred into BSF.

surpluses (GFS); since the 1980s, budget stabilization fund has taken on an increasingly stronger hold.[15]

Presence of enabling legislation is a necessary precondition for adopting a budget stabilization fund at the state level. What the BSF legislation does is much beyond merely creating a countercyclical reserve. By creating the BSF, the legislation institutionalizes the countercyclical fiscal policy, lifting the policy to a level above and beyond the whimsical power of any person. The policy becomes a permanent part of the government system. This, in the words of institutionalism, is capacity building. With well-structured features of institutionalized BSF, a state can accumulate high levels of fiscal reserves, which turns the potential countercyclical capacity into actual fiscal capacity – with higher level of fiscal reserves, a state can better manage public expenditures to provide services during recession years. This fills in the link from management capacity to performance (Ingraham et al. 2003).

Empirical analysis provides reliable evidence that from fiscal years 1979 through 1999, BSFs did increase state expenditures in downturn years by releasing the fiscal reserves to fill in the gaps between current revenue and trend-line public expenditures. States that had established a BSF before those three recessions fared better than those that did not; states that established a BSF earlier had better weathered the recessions than those that adopted the fund late. In other words, adopting the countercyclical fiscal policy and the BSF improved the potential and actual management capacity and enhanced the performance of those state governments during those three recessions. These states have in practice partially switched from the old annual budgeting perspective to a longer-term perspective by utilizing one of the tools to balance over the economic cycle. This is a significant step toward "a new budgetary system more in keeping with the new context of public finance" instead of continuously flowing back "to refinements to traditional budgeting" (Caiden 1981, 18).

8.6.1 Policy Recommendations

Policy recommendations are clear. Before all technical issues are clearly solved, multiyear budgeting may be best put as an approach (GPP, multi-years; Boex et al. 2000) that is used to improve and enhance, not to replace, the annual budget.[16] Crucial features of the approach include, but are not limited to, (1) shifting the focus from a "technical task" to strategic planning to link long-term goals with the financial planning process (Esser 2000, viii), (2) emphasis on multiyear estimation of revenues and expenditures to reinforce the budget as a financial plan that embeds the government's strategic plan, and (3) well-structured countercyclical fiscal policy and devices.

[15] Among metropolitans and large counties as surveyed by the Government Performance Project, however, general fund surplus remains the major countercyclical tool.

[16] Wildavsky (1978) offers a detailed analysis of the virtues and defects of the traditional budget format.

Adopting the countercyclical fiscal policy by creating a well-structured BSF will help a state better weather revenue shocks from recessions and downturns. With such a policy and policy tool, the state improves its management capacity and will enhance its performance by stabilizing provision of public services. Going through this process is a means to mitigate the limitations of the old annual perspective and to assume a longer-term perspective on budgeting. A longer-term perspective means much more than merely a countercyclical fiscal policy and a policy tool, but the latter is no doubt a very important step toward, and an essential component of, the former.

Using multiyear budgeting without adopting the countercyclical fiscal policy is an unreliable journey, as with a lame duck. Multiyear budgeting coupled with countercyclical fiscal policy and proper policy tool(s) stresses financial planning and is recession protective with a firewall against unexpected events. As such, subnational governments would be able to interact positively during a recession to the expansionary monetary and fiscal policy at the national level. This couplet is budgeting for fiscal stability over the economic cycle by state and local governments. It is my belief and hope that equipped as such, state and local governments will be able to better withstand economic fluctuations in the future.

References

Advisory Commission on Intergovernmental Relations (ACIR) (1987). Significant Features of Fiscal Federalism series. Government Printing Office, Washington, DC

Boex LFJ, Martinez-Vazquez J, McNac RM (2000) Multi-year budgeting: a review of international practices and lessons for developing and transitional economies. Public Budg Finance 20(2):91–112

Caiden N (1981) Public budgeting amidst uncertainty and instability. Public Budg Finance 1(1):6–19

Cleveland FA (1915) Evolution of the budget idea in the United States. Ann Am Acad Pol Soc Sci 62:15–35

Esser JL (2000) An elected official's guide to multi-year budgeting. GFOA, Washington, DC

Fisher L (1997) Biennial budgeting in the federal government. Public Budg Finance 17(3):87–97

Forrester JP (1991) Multi-year forecasting and municipal budgeting. Public Budg Finance 11(2):47–61

Forsythe DW (1993) State and local budgets and the business cycle. Paper presented at the annual conference of association of budgeting and financial management, Boston

Government Performance Project (GPP) (1998–2001) Survey instrument of the project used in state and local government surveys 1998–2001. Available at www.maxwell.syr.edu/gpp

Gramlich EM (1987) Subnational fiscal policy. In: Quigley JM (ed) Perspectives on local public finance and public policy, 3rd edn. JAI Press, Greenwich, pp 3–27

Guajardo SA (2000) An elected official's guide to multi-year budgeting. GFOA, Washington, DC

Heckman J (1979) Sample selection bias as a specification error. Econometrica 47:153–161

Heclo H, Wildavsky A (1974) The private government of public money: community and policy inside British political administration. Macmillan, London

Hou Y, Smith DL (2006) A framework for understanding state balanced budget requirement systems: re-examining distinctive features and an operational definition. Public Budg Finance 26(3):22–45

Ingraham PW, Joyce P, Donahue AK (2003) Putting management in the performance equation. The Johns Hopkins University Press, Baltimore

Jackson A (2002) Taking the plunge: the conversion to multi-year budgeting. Government Finance Review 22. www.gfoa.org/services/dfl/bulletin/budget-multiyearbudgetaug02.pdf. Accessed 14 June 2006
Joyce P (2000) Biennial budgeting: a tool for improving government management and oversight. Testimony before the House Committee on Rules, 16 Mar 2000
Lowrie SG (1915) The proper function of the state budget. Ann Am Acad Pol Soc Sci 62:47–63
Misiolek WS, Perdue DG (1987) The portfolio approach to state and local tax structures. Natl Tax J 40(1):111–114
National Association of State Budget Officers (NASBO) (1992) State balanced budget requirements: provisions and practice. National Association of State Budget Officers, Washington, DC
National Governors Association. The book of the states, series since 1935. Lexington, KY
National Municipal League (1899) Model municipal corporation act, Chicago
Organization for Economic Cooperation and Development (OECD) (1998) Statement by the Chairman at the 19th annual meeting of senior budget officials, Paris
Public Administration Clearing House (at Princeton) (1950) Symposium on budget theory. Public Adm Rev 10(1): 20–31
Rivlin AM (1987) Economics and the political process. Am Econ Rev 77(1):1–10
Rodgers R, Joyce P (1996) The effect of underforecasting on the accuracy of revenue forecests by state governments. Public Adm Rev 56(1):48–56
Rubin IS (1999) The politics of public budgeting. Chatham, New Jersey
Schick A (1966) The road to PPB: the stages of budget reform. Public Adm Rev 26(6):243–258
Sobel RS, Holcombe RG (1996) Measuring the growth and variability of tax bases over the business cycle. Natl Tax J 49(4):535–552
White FC (1983) Trade-off in growth and stability in state taxes. Natl Tax J 36(1):103–114
Wildavsky A (1964) The politics of the budgetary process. Little Brown, Boston
Wildavsky A (1978) A budget for all seasons? Why the traditional budget lasts. Public Adm Rev 38(6):501–509
Willoughby WF (1918a) The problem of a national budget. D. Appleton, New York
Willoughby WF (1918b) The movement for budgetary reform in the states. D. Appleton, New York

Chapter 9
Boom-Year Savings and Budgetary Forecasting

Abstract The forecasting of government expenditure and revenue is the outcome of complicated, often intense interaction between multiple key players in the budgeting process and multifarious aspects of government operations. The existing literature is very rich on the technical aspects but is relatively thin on the impact of institutions under the public choice perspective, especially those in financial administration, the budget stabilization fund (BSF) being a typical example. This chapter aims to fill in the niche by focusing on how BSF affects forecasting. BSF as a countercyclical fiscal policy tool was created as precautionary savings against revenue shortfalls, serving to reduce financial uncertainty from cyclical fluctuations. BSF is a formal institution with an underlying public choice motive to promote fiscal and budgetary transparency: BSF legislation is written to protect savings from political spending pressure and opportunistic electoral politics. However, public finance does not operate in vacuum; BSF cannot stay free of politics. Presence of savings inherently triggers complications in the politico-technical forecasting machine. This chapter examines state forecasts of their revenue with a BSF in place to see whether adopting BSF has any impact on forecast errors and how the structural features and size of BSF influence the forecasting behavior. I use a panel (49 states, 1979/1988–2007) plus details of state BSF features, with controls for state demographics, economy, politics, and other budgetary institutions. This chapter will contribute to the public choice literature by providing evidence on the effects of BSF on behavioral changes of state governments in their revenue forecasts.

9.1 Introduction

Forecasts of government expenditure and revenue are the outcome from the interaction between multiple key players in the budgeting process and multifarious aspects of government operations, including the economy, finance, politics, tradition, budgeting, and administration. Every one of these can be very complicated;

Y. Hou, *State Government Budget Stabilization: Policy, Tools, and Impacts*, Studies in Public Choice 8, DOI 10.1007/978-1-4614-6061-9_9,

it becomes especially tricky when these aspects come into hierarchical layers and reiterated rounds of interaction. The literature so far has well covered the political aspect, in particular the political business cycle implications; the literature is particularly rich on the technical dimensions such as models, data, and methods. The literature on the impact of institutions, especially institutions of financial administration, is growing but remains relatively thin, the budget stabilization fund (BSF) being a typical example. This chapter aims to fill in the niche by focusing on how boom-year savings affect budgetary forecasting.

Savings can accumulate via two major devices. The informal device is general fund surplus (GFS), which has been serving as stock of excess current year resources for a long time. The formal device to accumulate savings is by the budget stabilization fund (BSF) that is adopted with enabling legislation. The BSF is a countercyclical fiscal policy tool, created as the vehicle to store up precautionary savings against revenue shortfalls, serving to reduce financial uncertainty from cyclical economic fluctuations. BSF comes with an underlying public choice motive to promote fiscal and budgetary transparency: The BSF enabling legislation is written to protect savings from political spending pressure and opportunistic electoral politics. However, public finance does not operate in vacuum; BSF cannot stay free of politics. Presence of savings inherently triggers complications in the forecasting machinery that is politics laden and technically sophisticated.

This chapter studies revenue forecasts by US state governments; all of them use general fund surplus against the economic cycle in practice, and most of the states have adopted a BSF over the past several decades. I will examine whether the creation and adoption of BSF in the states has cast any impact on forecast errors and how the structural features and the size of the stabilization funds influence the forecasting behavior. In a similar fashion, I will pay attention to the potential impact of general fund surplus on forecasts. I will use a panel (49 states, 1979/1988–2010) plus details of state BSF features, with controls for state demographics, economy, politics, and other budgetary institutions. This chapter will provide evidence on the effects of boom-year savings on behavioral changes by state governments in their revenue forecasts. The next section reviews the literature on revenue and expenditure forecasts of governments, with emphasis on the revenue side; it links boom-year savings to public choice theory, tracing the evolution of countercyclical practices, thereby bridging the revenue side and the expenditure side of the fiscal account (Buchanan 1975). Section 9.3 offers details on empirical estimation. Results are discussed in Section 9.4. The last section concludes.

9.2 Revenue and Expenditure Forecasting: What Is Known?

9.2.1 Forecasting

Forecasting of revenue and expenditure is an exercise that governments at all levels must perform at least once each year in order to prepare and implement their budgets. Because the economy is dynamic and government finance fluctuates with the economy, budgetary forecasts are inherently an enterprise that almost always ends with some degree of errors. No reasonable person would expect a perfect forecast – one that has a zero error rate; it is simply impossible if not fabricated.

9.2.1.1 Unintended Versus Intended Forecasting Errors

Thus, inaccuracies in budgetary forecasts are only natural. They are discrepancy between the estimates made in the budgeting process and the outcomes from implementing the budget in a dynamic economic environment throughout the fiscal year. By the causes of their occurrence, we can categorize forecasting errors into two major types. Those due to economic fluctuations only are *unintended errors*. These are random, with the direction of the error being stochastic or uncertain; that is, the errors can be positive (surplus) or negative (deficit).

Since uncertainty abounds in the economy and errors are expected, but smooth operation of the budget is desirable, coping strategies have emerged over time from practice that are designed to constrain uncertainty and to bring possible negative errors (those that end the fiscal year in deficits) into positive ones (so that the fiscal year ends in surplus). In other words, it is to build *intended errors* into forecasts. Such intended errors are due to intervention as an effort to restrict the errors in the positive range or unidirectional. In this sense, they are systematic bias toward surplus in the budget that policy makers and other parties involved in the forecast use with a clear purpose.

9.2.1.2 Perceptions of Forecasting Errors

Forecasting errors are not treated equally; perceptions of them vary by the direction of the error – the treatment is asymmetric of surpluses and deficits: Being inevitable, errors that end in surplus are taken to be better than inaccuracies that land in deficit. This inequality makes sense from the making-your-ends-meet philosophy of ordinary citizens as well as the norm of balanced budget for governments (see Chapter 1), especially for state and local governments. From the technical point of view, surpluses serve to buffer against unexpected revenue shortfalls and expenditure increases, thus contributing toward smooth budgetary operations. In contrast, deficits pose difficulty in financial operations and embarrassment in public image. In the political perspective, surpluses are a witness of success and indication of capability that favors the political party and administration in office in front of voters for reelection, whereas deficits point to the exact opposite direction. In the early twentieth century when introducing budgetary principles from Europe into the United States, Wilner Sundelson (1935) observed, on accuracy in budget making, that an inaccurate forecast even from "deliberate falsification of revenue estimates" that leads to year-end surplus can better "serve the political and fiscal purposes of a budget" than a scientific estimate that ends up in deficits (257). More recent studies confirm that the political, economic, and administrative consequences of deficit are worse than those of surpluses (Bretschneider et al. 1989, 1992), which is confirmed again by the Tea Party movement in the past few years protesting against exploding federal deficits and debts.

9.2.1.3 Strategies Toward Surplus

Individuals, households, and governments have over time developed practices toward surpluses. I call these *strategies* to create firewalls against deficits – to underestimate revenue on the one hand and to overestimate expenditure on the other. The two, often termed *practical*, *conservative* methods in financial management, can be used separately or in tandem; any use of them is intentional *distortion* of the natural error rate, leading to systemic bias in budgetary estimation. Checking history, we can find that such bias dates as far back as the beginning of public budgeting.

9.2.1.4 Cyclical Patterns of Forecasting Error

Another feature of budgetary forecasting is that forecasts always fall behind their target, the economy that is constantly floating. This embedded lag displays a clear cyclical pattern: In the expansion phase of the economic cycle, revenue forecasts cannot catch up with revenue growth; in the contraction phase of the cycle, in contrast, forecasts on revenue turn out to be ahead of the curve. Policy makers and budgeteers tend to adjust their strategy by the phase of the economic cycle; but in boom years the economy gallops so that however optimistic forecasts have been adjusted to (being less underestimating), they still turn out to be underestimating; in bust years the decline of the economy may be so drastic that even underestimation appears to be overestimating. This cyclical pattern is related to and due partly to the revenue sources, the elasticity of each tax type.

Forecasts of expenditure embed a cyclical pattern as well, only in the opposite direction. Demands for public services can be both high in boom and in bust years, of different services. In boom years, forecasts may turn out to be above the board on basic services but below the board on better services – higher income has pushed residents toward the upper end of public services. In bust years, forecasts will turn out as below the bar on basic services – unemployment and reduced current income push residents toward the lower end of services. Linking revenue and expenditure, we find that governments can afford to fund the underestimated demand for extra services in a boom year with excess revenue from growth, but in a bust year, governments facing revenue shortfalls will have no other option but cut even the basic services. These should not be taken as surprises. After all, economic fluctuations are completely exogenous to state revenue forecasters whether they are politicians or experts in public finance. There has been empirical evidence of cyclical forecasting patterns and those in downturns different from upturns (Cassidy et al. 1989).

9.2.1.5 Evidence on Error Rates

The empirical literature on revenue forecasting is rich, though results are mixed. Some found no evidence of systemic error. Mushkin and Lupo (1967) review eight projections of state-local expenditures in six major studies; they conclude that those forecasts did not contain consistent bias, either underestimation of revenue or overestimation of expenditure. Plesko (1988) examines the accuracy of macroeconomic forecasts made by the President's Office of Management and Budget (OMB) and by the Congressional Budget Office (CBO) of the receipts, outlays, and deficits in an effort to examine the reliability record of each agency's estimates. He did not find systematic bias in short-run forecasts by either CBO or OMB (but he found rapid deterioration of projections over longer periods, especially of budget deficit).

Other studies do find evidence that policy makers budget precautionary room into revenue estimates. Gentry (1989), using time series data of major taxes of the state of New Jersey, finds that forecasters do not make full use of available information; their forecasts show a downward bias. Penner (2002) examines the record of CBO and finds the projections "extremely inaccurate" because the economic and technical assumptions used for the forecast were not right. He further finds that the errors grow quickly as the projection window is widened for periods longer than 5 years, because in such cases the projections are not substantively different from random noise. To continue on the Plesko (1988) test, Auerbach (1999) reexamines forecasts done by the OMB and the CBO. He finds that with the sample period broken into *pessimistic* and *optimistic* periods, the standard errors of forecast errors become too large for the forecasts to exhibit any underlying bias. But Auerbach believes that those forecasts fail statistical tests of efficiency and forecast revisions embed significant serial correlation and strong seasonality. Thus, the case remains wide open, calling for more explorations.

9.2.2 Budgetary Institutions

Here I use the term *institution* to refer to formal rules that heavily influence budgetary forecasts. The most important among such institutions are balanced budget requirements, tax and expenditure limitations, and budget cycles. I discuss these one by one in the following.

Balanced budget requirements (BBR) can work in two directions. On one hand, they help enforce fiscal discipline by requiring governors and lawmakers to avoid deficits, prompting the use of aforementioned forecasting strategies toward surplus; on the other hand, BBR may also forbid states from ending a fiscal year with big surpluses. This is the conventional version of balance, that is, a small positive balance (Hou 2006; see Chapter 8 for details). BBR interacts with budgeting strategies at least in three scenarios. First is the generic case of a normal, average year of the economy when the underestimated revenue is larger than or roughly equal to the overestimated expenditure; the budget is balanced and the outcome of budget execution is also balanced. But the BBR rules are static, with no consideration of the economic cycle. Policy makers, however, have to satisfy these binding rules in a dynamic economy; that is, they build their estimates of the economic trend into budget forecasts, applying the practical coping strategies. Thus, plugging in fluctuations of the economy, then we have two other situations. One is a boom year when the actual revenue turns out to exceed expenditure by a large margin; the governor and the state legislature can make midyear adjustments to either reduce taxes or increase expenditures or both; they can even put some extra revenue aside at the end of the fiscal year as savings for future downturns. The final outcome will be a small surplus balance, as in the first scenario. The other situation is a bust year when the actual revenue barely equals or is (far) short of the budgeted expenditure. In the latter case, midyear program cuts are necessary in order to end the year in balance because the strict BBR rule of *no deficit carry-over* binds (Bohn and Inman 1996). Midyear adjustments, in either direction with both revenue and outlay, are witness that budgeting strategies are not enough to guarantee even a small positive balance as demanded under BBR rules (see Chapter 7 for details on state budget actions in lean years).

The empirical evidence is mixed. Some studies do find evidence that the above is the case (Krause et al. 2006), while others do not (Cassidy et al. 1989; Poterba 1994). Bretschneider and Gorr (1992, 457) describe an optimal forecast as "one that generates a small surplus, not large enough to cause political embarrassment but still sufficient to provide a buffer against the vicissitudes of economic cycles and expenditure needs." However, this so-called optimal surplus is still taken as an error in arithmetic.

Tax and expenditure limitations (TEL) are citizen initiatives since the late 1970s that impose binding limits on the total size of revenue and expenditure of state and local governments. Tax limits are typically constructed to constrain the growth of government revenue, designed as a cap on annual tax rates using a formula or index of personal income, inflation, or population. Expenditure limits restrain outlay to some formula or index, even if the said government has managed to raise extra revenue to spend under the tax limits; these limits can appear as restrictions on appropriations to a percentage of the revenue forecast. By its working mechanism, TEL erodes the use of budgeting strategies by shrinking the room available for underestimation of revenue and overestimation of expenditure, leaning toward a bare-bones balance of the annual budget.

Empirical evidence on the effects of the TEL since the 1980s suggests that revenue limitations are more real (Bails 1982) than expenditure limitations because expectation of taxpayers/residents for services did not fall with the passage (adoption) of the TEL. In fact, demand for services has persisted – taxpayers/voters somehow assume (unrealistically) that state governments should be able to do as much with less by cutting waste and downsizing or privatization; states respond to TEL by pushing responsibilities down to local governments (Shadbegian 1999), and localities simply cut programs (Hou 2010). Brennan and Buchanan (1980) postulate that TEL would eliminate waste and thus have no adverse effects on the quality of public services; Stocker (1991) finds that Proposition 13 had cut not only taxes but also public services. Downes and Figlio (1999) summarize the literature to conclude that the imposition of tax and expenditure limitations resulted in long-run reductions in the performance of public school students.

The *budget cycle* refers to the length of period for an adopted budget to be in effect; it is divided into 1-year (annual) and 2-year (biennial) cycles at the state level. The latter is remnant of the old days when legislators were part time; with reform of state governments in the 1960s–1970s that installed full-time state law-makers, over half of the 50 states shifted from biennial to annual cycles. As of now, 29 states operate on annual cycles. States with biennial budgets may operate on different assumptions about their budget window, thereby budget more leeway into their estimates than those with annual budget cycles; but recent studies (Hou 2005; Hou and Brewer 2010; Krausc et al. 2006) found no such evidence. These three budgetary institutions will be incorporated into the analytical framework for empirical analysis.

9.2.3 Political Business Cycle

Since Nordhaus' (1975) seminal study, the theory of political business cycles has been widely applied and tested. For example, the institutions discussed above may also serve as incentives for elected officials to develop forecasts in order to shape the political context for better chances of winning elections and reelections. One typical phenomenon is that governors may overspend in the year or two prior to their reelection so as to generate a rosier economic and financial picture (Nordhaus 1975; Rogoff 1990). Another assumption is that Republicans prefer lower taxes and spending than Democrats do; the revenue forecasts by Republicans thus may be intentionally made conservative so as to exert downward pressure on spending. However, studies have generated mixed results in this regard; the few mentioned in the above subsection do not find any effect of the party composition of government on revenue forecasts.

Along the same lines, state politics plays into the strategic manipulation of forecasts, which will be easier and more pronounced when both the governor and the legislative majority are from the same party than when the two branches are controlled by different parties (Bretschneider et al. 1989). Likewise, Democratic or Republican control of the lower house of the legislature may lead to drastically different forecasts.

9.2.4 Budget Stabilization Funds and Forecasting

Governments have long followed practices by private citizens of outlay smoothing, relying on savings that have accumulated in the general fund in boom years (Rafuse 1965; Fisher 1984; see Section 3.2 for details), but there has been constant political spending pressure on such savings, which made financial managers look for alternative saving devices, giving rise to the budget stabilization fund (BSF) in the mid-twentieth century (Hou 2004; Section 3.3); as of the 2000s, 47 states have adopted these funds (NASBO 2007). Many of these states adopted their BSF following a deep recession so as to become better prepared for the next downturn (Gold 1983;

Douglas and Gaddie 2002). Wagner and Sobel (2006) argue that some states adopt their BSF in response to the tax and expenditure limitations since the late 1970s because TEL make it difficult to accumulate general fund surpluses. In fact, the double-dip recession of the 1980s and unemployment and the Medicaid programs were also behind the wide spread of BSF in those years.

Recent studies show evidence that budget stabilization funds do increase the amount of countercyclical savings: Adoption of a BSF is associated with a substantial increase in total savings, especially in states that use formulas for deposit into, and for withdrawal from, their BSF (Knight and Levinson 1999; Wagner 2003; Hou 2004; Hou and Duncombe 2008; see Chaps. 4 and 5 for details). Increased savings in turn are shown to remarkably reduce fiscal stress during recessions (Sobel and Holcombe 1996; Levinson 1998; Douglas and Gaddie 2002; Hou 2003, 2005; see Chapter 6). Leaving the savings in lawmakers' control seems to be less effective than formulas in promoting savings (Hou 2004; Knight and Levinson 1999). Hou (2004, 44) notes that "general fund surplus results as much from political manipulation as from overall economic strength and proper financial management… surpluses will not occur if the governor or the legislators, or both, want to spend more to win popular support."

In a similar way, lawmakers can easily evade rules from BSF enabling legislation that BSF can be used only for revenue shortfalls; they do so by engineering a budget gap through budget forecasts. Politicians may be able to evade even the strictest formulas in order to use these funds for purposes other than budget stabilization. For example, lawmakers may manage to withdraw more money in election years than in nonelection years, all else equal, even when the fund is governed by deposit and withdrawal formulas. As Hou (2004, 47) explains, there are many ways to circumvent legal restrictions on budget stabilization fund withdrawals – the existence of a formula merely "adds to the complexity of political manipulation."

9.2.4.1 Revenue Forecasting Authority

Given that BBR and TEL are binding legal requirements in public finance, who and which agency in a state holds *revenue forecasting authority* will directly impact forecasts. Such authority can be in the hands of the governor or the legislature; forecasts can also be done through consensus of the two branches or a board or commission of representatives from the two branches, with experts in public finance and from the private sector. Errors in forecasts might be larger when forecasting authority lies solely with the executive or the legislative branch than when forecasts are conducted by consensus (Bretschneider et al. 1989; Bretschneider and Gorr 1992) or with participation of outside experts. More recent studies by Mocan and Azad (1995) and by Krause et al. (2006), however, do not generate evidence in support of the above findings. Thus, the case remains open for further exploration. It is also reasonable to assume that this revenue forecasting authority will interact with TEL, gubernatorial elections, as well as the party affiliation of the governor and the legislative majority of state general assembly.

9.2.4.2 Research Questions

In this chapter I examine the following research questions. First, does the adoption of a formal savings device like the budget stabilization fund reshape the forecasting behavior of state policy makers? Since a BSF is created with enabling legislation to protect the boom-year savings from spending pressure within and outside the government and since in most states, the savings are useable only or mainly for recessionary shortfalls, a BSF should NOT cast observable influence. But who knows? So far there has not been a single study on this topic. Related to BSF, the potential impact of general fund surplus (GFS) is also examined. Different from BSF, GFS is usually more discretionary to policy makers than BSF. Thus, I assume GFS may exert observable impact in revenue forecasting. Second, in the case that adopting a BSF leads to some changes in revenue forecasts, how do the structural features of the BSF enabling legislation affect the change in forecasting behavior? This question makes sense and demands our attention because the variation in BSF across states derives from differences in the structure of each state's legislation, as discussed in the above review. Finally, does the level/amount of savings in the BSF affect the extent of change in state forecasting behavior? These three questions will be answered through empirical estimation; details are deliberated in the next section.

9.3 Empirical Estimation

Empirical estimation is done with the most care with regard to data selection, length of the sample period, construction of the dependent variable, as well as model specification. Details are provided in the following.

9.3.1 Data and Sample Years

I put together a panel data set of all 50 states from 1979 to 2010 on variables of boom-year savings including BSF and GFS balances, respectively, and also state budgetary forecasts from 1988 to 2010 which is the longest possible series for revenue forecasts at the state level for such a study. By the most recent account from the National Association of State Budget Officers (NASBO 2007), 47 of the 50 states have adopted a budget stabilization fund. From earlier chapters, we know that the earliest BSF state was New York in 1946 but most other states began adoption after the 1980s double-dip recessions, so this data set includes all the necessary contrasts between those with BSF and without, for those with a BSF, the ex ante years versus the ex post years. The sample period covers three full business cycles and two half cycles. I will also run models without the years of the 2008–2010 recession because, among other reasons, not all variables are yet available for these 3 years and the Great Recession has also been very different from the other downturns in the sample period.

Because of the substantive differences between Alaska and other states in its revenue structure and savings levels, I exclude Alaska even though Alaska is not necessarily very different from other states in their cyclical or countercyclical fiscal behavior. Features of each state's BSF legislation are coded as binary variables. This is by far the most comprehensive coding of BSF features, taken from Hou (2004) updated till 2010 (see Section 3.3 and General Appendix 1 for details). These features cover sources of BSF balance, balance levels allowed in the fund, rules on fund withdrawal from BSF, and purposes of fund use. BSF balances and general fund surplus are both taken from each state's *Comprehensive Annual Financial Report* (CAFR) from 1979 to 2010. As the audited official financial report that is subject to the generally accepted accounting principles, the CAFR series are the most accurate record for both variables. Another source of BSF data is NASBO's *Fiscal Survey of States*, a source that is consistent but relies solely on states' self-reporting. This author uses care in comparing the two data sources; in cases where misreport or maltreatment is identified, I handle it with care by comparing the two sources for accuracy.

9.3.2 Dependent Variable

The dependent variable is forecasting error of state general fund revenue, *Z*. The general fund is the single largest fund for a government, covering all operational expenses and some capital outlays. I choose *general fund revenue* instead of *total revenue* because the former (general fund revenue) is the amount within the control of the state, whereas the latter (total revenue) includes intergovernmental transfer from the federal government and borrowings from the market. The error rate is calculated as

$$Z = (\text{actual revenue} - \text{mid-year changes} - \text{appropriation}) / \text{appropriation}$$

In most forecasting studies, the dependent variable is the difference between actual revenue and appropriations divided by appropriations. Here I insert the revenue actions made by state legislature in the middle of the fiscal year because these changes are the revenue actions that are designed and taken to cope with up-to-date economic fluctuation. Omitting them from the equation leads to serious endogeneity problems. Poterba (1994 and several related studies) uses this midyear change in his design of shocks, which has since been taken as a most appropriate measure to capture revenue changes. These temporary changes are typically tax reductions in a boom year and tax hikes in a bust year; in other words, they are the measures to reduce forecasting error: When the economy is strong, revenues tend to go high so that reducing the rate will level off the peak. When the economy is sour, temporary tax hikes increase taxes to make up part of the loss from the shrunk tax base.

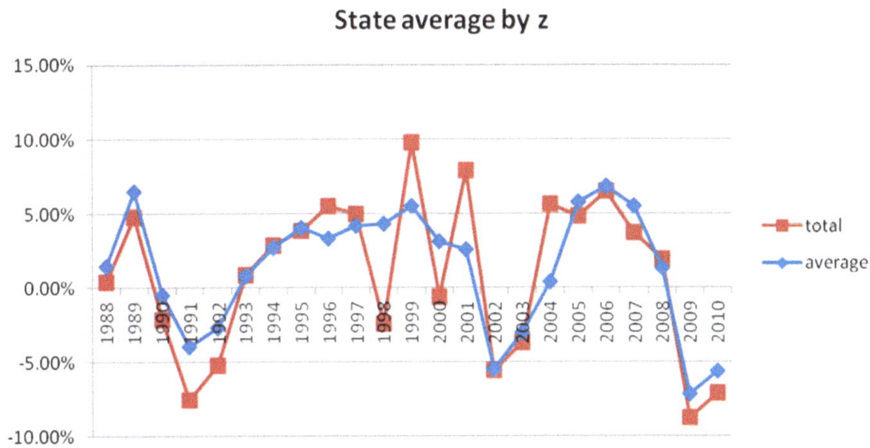

Fig. 9.1 Forecasting error over time

From this construct of the dependent variable, positive Zs reflect underestimation of revenue. Summary statistics of the dependent variable shows that even though its mean is only 1% (i.e., it is a surplus of about 1% of the budgeted outlay by the end of the budgeted fiscal year), its standard deviation is large, and this ratio ranges between –0.37 and +0.57, indicating that systematic under- and overestimation exist as a widespread phenomenon among the states in the sample period. Overall, the dependent variable shows a reasonable size that is within the professional 5% range set by NASBO and the Government Finance Officers' Association (GFOA) as *good* in revenue forecasting.

This error rate in fact stands much in line with the existing literature. Rodgers and Joyce (1996) find that between 1975 and 1992, states underestimated their revenues by 2.1%. Voorhees' (2006) estimate for the period from 1979 to 2002 was 1.5%. These average errors are in fact very small, in the range of *excellent* practices by the standard set by GFOA. Some papers sample selected states during recession periods to find that estimate errors may be even smaller. Cassidy et al. (1989) survey 23 states between 1978 and 1987 to find a modest bias of only 0.5%. Bretschneider and Gorr (1992) examine forecasts of sales tax revenues in 24 states between 1980 and 1985; they found no evidence of systematic *overestimation*. Mocan and Azad (1995) check 20 states between 1986 and 1992 and found no evidence of systematic underestimation either.

Figure 9.1 shows the graph of two measures of the dependent variable. The line marked as *average* is the mean of Z for all 49 states (Alaska, the outlier is excluded): $average = \sum z_t / 49$, where i is state and z_t is the DV. The line marked as *total* is the national level Z for each year. Both curves show a clear pattern of procyclicality of the forecasting error: They follow but fall behind the phases of the economic cycle, confirming what has been discussed in the literature review. In other words, the dependent variable developed for this study well depicts the behavior of state forecasts in the sample period. In the empirical tests, a positive coefficient of point estimates will indicate that the variable tends to push the outcome up toward surplus, and a negative coefficient tends to drag the outcome down toward deficits. To obtain the net effect of any variable on pure error rate, I will need to use the absolute values of this calculated error rate.

9.3.3 Model Specifications

The empirical model is specified to include several groups of explanatory variables. They are key variables about boom-year savings and state forecasting authority, state economic condition, state budgetary institutions, and state politics.

The *budget stabilization fund* is constructed in three forms for use in different specifications respectively. The first is a binary of the BSF fund, 1 for a state and year with BSF and 0 for none. This construct captures the differences between with and without the BSF and between years of ex ante and ex post adoption of the fund. The second form brings in features of the state BSF legislation under four categories: (1) sources of BSF balance, (2) cap levels, (3) withdrawal rules, and (4) purposes of BSF use. Each state can set any combination of five sources for its BSF: (a) as required balance, (b) by a preset formula, (c) from general fund surplus, (d) from the general fund by appropriations, or (e) from a special revenue source. The BSF balance level can be capped at (a) a low of 2% of expenditure level, (b) a medium of 2–5% level, or (c) a high of 7% and above level. Alternatively, a state can (d) set no limit to the balance level or (e) set a minimum requirement for this balance. The BSF withdrawal rules are either (a) by legislative appropriation or (b) by executive action or (c) by a preset formula free of legislative or executive discretion. BSF fund can be used, from the strictest to the most loose, (a) for cases of revenue shortfall, (b) for cash flow, (c) for an emergency, or (d) for any purpose.

The third form of the BSF key variable is a ratio – the level/amount of BSF balance at the time of budget preparation against the budget year expenditure ($BSF_{t-2}/GFexp_t$). The ratio is constructed carefully to fully consider the length of the budget cycle: If boom-year savings accumulated prior to a recession exert any impact, this ratio of BSF available at the time of a particular year's budget preparation (t–2) against the budget expenditure (t) will be able to capture it. The BSF balances are lag-2 figures for the reason that when the budget is being prepared, policy makers know what they have as savings from the previous year; thus, lag 2 is the only reasonable base. Without taking this lag, the relation between savings and outlay is not properly handled. Further, the lag-2 treatment also helps cut off potential endogeneity between budget year outlay and prior year savings. Another detail about the BSF ratio is that I distinguish two kinds of zeros in the BSF account. One is the zeros before a state adopts BSF; the other is after BSF adoption. These two are different in that the former is in the absence of the mechanism, whereas the latter indicates years when a state has used up its BSF balance in this fund. This treatment is a reasonable and reliable treatment, seen in the literature (Hou 2003).

With the first specification, BSF binary, all 49 states and all sample years are included. With the second specification, only states that have BSF legislation are included. With the third, only states that have a BSF and years when these states have a BSF balance are included. In general we may expect that adoption of BSF tends to reduce underestimation of revenue; but the magnitude of effects will depend on the size of savings and the rules governing BSF deposits and withdrawals.

In all three specifications, a second saving device, general fund surplus (GFS) is included. As Hou (2003) reports, GFS has always been a countercyclical saving device, with or without the budget stabilization fund. After a state adopts a BSF as a formal saving device to protect boom-year savings against spending pressure, there have been supplementation and substitution between BSF and GFB as coexisting policy tools (as detailed in Chapter 4). The former is increase of savings; the latter is shifting of savings from GFS into BSF, not real increase in savings. In Chapter 4, I have shown evidence that supplementation is about 85 cents for each dollar of BSF and substitution about 15 cents. GFS come under different formats; the best measure is the *unreserved undesignated balance* (UUB) from each state's *Comprehensive Annual Financial Report*. This is the amount that is not under any legal reservation or any administrative designation; it is the amount that can be used for reappropriation or at the full discretion of policy makers. As with the BSF level, I calculate a ratio between UUB at the time of budget preparation (t–2) and budget year general fund expenditure; it is ($UUB_{t-2}/GFexp_t$). This ratio is included in each of the three specifications to capture the effects of GFS on revenue forecasting before and after the adoption of budget stabilization funds.

Since recessions are completely exogenous to state economies and finance and countercyclical savings are designed as precaution against cyclical revenue shortfalls that often occur as surprises to state forecasters, those savings in stabilization funds are not expected to cast observable, statistically significant effect on forecasting error. The reason is probably not intuitive but understandable – these savings are outside the loop of regular, normal budgets. Savings that are kept as general fund surplus differ from BSF; they are expected to cast at least some influence on forecasts.

Another key variable is *state revenue forecasting authority*. This authority can be vested with (a) the governor, (b) the state legislature, (c) a legislative-executive consensus forecasting body, or (d) a board/commission composed of experts and representative from the two branches. Based on the discussion in the literature review, forecast error tends to increase when the estimation process is dominated by either the legislative or the executive branch; consensus forecasting or the involvement of boards with wider participation may reduce the error rate. These variables potentially carry a lot of weight because in the operating environment with binding balanced budget requirements, revenue forecasts to a large extent determine the size of outlay, thereby arises the room and incentive for manipulation of forecasts. The information source is NASBO's *Fiscal Survey of States* series and the National Council of State Legislatures (NCSL). The data, however, are not consistent or reliable; besides, the series is short. I choose to drop this variable in the study. This brings in a drawback that I need to address once data become available.

Under *state economy* I include seven variables. GSP growth rate reflects on the overall state economy. Unemployment rate is to capture the impact of cyclical economic fluctuations. Real per capita income measures differences in wealth between states and between states under varying economic conditions; it also helps to place states on a comparable bar. Poverty rate among each state's population is meant to capture impact of widespread poverty on state budgeting forecasts since higher poverty rates demand higher percentage of state outlay on welfare programs. These three variables may seem correlated, but they are not necessarily endogenous because they reflect different aspects of economic life. Shares of gross state product from three sectors (manufacturing, agriculture, and finance, insurance, and real estate or FIRE) help reveal the possible impact of state economic composition on forecasting practices. In general, I assume higher shares of FIRE are linked to more volatile revenue and therefore higher need for buffer against shortfalls. Higher shares of manufacturing may be linked with more fluctuation in GSP. Shares of agriculture are associated with lower GSP but more stable economy.

To fully and accurately capture the effects of a recession on forecasts, I create several binaries. The first is for all years during a recessionary period, including 1980–1983, 1990–1992, 2001–2002, and 2008–2010. It is reasonable to assume that during a recession, revenue is a falling target and forecasts cannot catch up with the shrinkage of the tax base; so the coefficient will be negative. However, this binary may turn out to be too blunt because the shock from a recession that states cannot predict is different from the second and even the third year after the start of a recession; for these into-recession years, states have had an expectation of fallen revenue and a slump recovery. So it is necessary to make the distinction. For this reason, I create dummies for the first, second, and third years of a recession. The first-year dummies include 1980, 1982 (double dip), 1991, 2001, and 2008. The second-year dummies are 1981, 1983, 1992, 2002, and 2009. The third-year dummies are 1993, 2003, and 2010. In coding these recession years, I take into consideration of differences between state fiscal years (NY, TX, MI, and AL), to match their fiscal year with the dates of national recessions as determined by the National Bureau of Economic Research (NBER).

For state *budgetary institutions*, I control first for the biennial budget cycle. Though most states (29) have already shifted from the traditional biennial budget to the annual, the rest (21 states) still use the biennial cycle that is expected to influence forecasting practices in ways different from those using the annual cycles. Tax and expenditure limitations (TEL) that are imposed by citizen initiatives or legislative action are divided into those on revenue and those on expenditure. As discussed in the literature review, the two types pose different reactions on the part of policy makers and budget agencies. They both impact forecasting in substantive ways. These three are all binaries, with presence of the variable being 1 and absence being 0.

State politics plays heavily into revenue forecasting, as discussed in Section 9.2. I use two binaries: gubernatorial election year and divided government between the governor and the legislature. Judging from past research, approaching gubernatorial elections tend to incentivize an incumbent governor to manipulate revenue forecasts, thereby aggravating forecasting errors. Two other often used political variables are Democratic control of the House and Republican control of the House; but in most of the literature, dominance of the House by either party may not be statistically significant. So I choose not to include these two variables. Definitions, data sources, and summary statistics of all variables are provided in Table 9.1.

9.3.4 *Estimation Strategy*

Because some of the binary variables for budgetary institutions like the adoption of BSF, TEL, and budget cycle tend not to change back to their previous status (0) once it is adopted (1) (but as I said in earlier chapters, BSF features and BBR rules do show changes over time), we have reason to suspect that use of the fixed-effects estimator may generate inconsistent error terms; in such cases, the random effects estimator is the natural choice. I do use fixed effects as well as random effects estimators as sensitivity tests; contrast between the with- and without-year fixed effects will add to the results. Besides, year fixed effects control for unobservable factors that are common to all states but vary over years.

9.4 Results and Discussion

In this section I present and discuss the results from estimation. I will discuss by the order of effects from (1) BSF adoption, (2) structural features of the BSF fund, (3) levels of the BSF, and (4) the recession broken into separate years. In all specifications, the level of general fund surplus (UUB) is used as a control variable. These results are presented in Tables 9.2, 9.3, 9.4, 9.5, and 9.6, respectively. Of the results, all models are robust with F statistics highly significant. I will start from the key variables.

9.4.1 *Effects of Boom-Year Savings*

Though it may be taken for granted that BSF adoption by each state and BSF levels may exert some influence on revenue forecasting, as discussed above, it turns out that it is not the case. Adoption of the budget stabilization fund does not seem to influence the outcome of revenue forecasting; the difference between the ex ante and ex post is not significantly different from zero (Table 9.2, dummy for BSF); this pattern is consistent across the fixed effects and random effects estimators, with- or without-year fixed effects. Of the structural features of the stabilization fund (Tables 9.3 and 9.4), only *minimum requirement* of the fund balance presents statistically significant effects: If a state has a BSF in place that operates under this feature, the forecasting error may go up toward the positive direction by around 6%.

Table 9.1 Summary statistics (no Alaska, 1978–2010)

Variable	Description	Mean	SD	Min	Max	Data source
z_ratio	*DV*, forecasting error as a ratio	0.01	0.08	−0.37	0.57	Author calculation
bsfd	Dummy, presence of real BSF	0.62	0.49	0.00	1.00	Hou 2004
UUB ratio	(GFSt−2/exp)	0.04	0.09	−0.25	0.53	CAFR
BSF ratio	(BSF balance t−2/ expenditure)	0.03	0.05	0	0.83	CAFR
recession	Dummy, for recession years	0.36	0.48	0.00	1.00	
Unem	Unemployment rate	5.88	2.08	2.30	17.40	BEA
gsprate	GSP growth rate	2.35	3.65	−15.65	19.88	BEA
pcinc	Real per capita income, 000	22.73	10.28	5.77	56.90	BEA
poverty	Poverty rate	12.92	3.87	2.90	27.20	Census
Bien	Dummy, biennial budgeting	0.41	0.49	0.00	1.00	NASBO
revlmt	Revenue limit dummy	0.28	0.45	0.00	1.00	Shadbegian 1999
explmt	Expenditure limitation dummy	0.38	0.48	0.00	1.00	Shadbegian 1999
elecyr	Dummy, governor election year	0.28	0.45	0.00	1.00	The Book of the States
Div	Dummy, divided government	0.48	0.50	0.00	1.00	The Book of the States
agrratio	(Agriculture value/GSP)	2.35	2.52	0.14	19.19	BEA and author calculation
manuratio	(Manufacturing value/ GSP)	16.42	7.33	1.78	37.33	
finanratio	(Financial services value/GSP)	17.39	5.35	6.18	47.56	
BSF structural features						
reqbal	Required balance	0.06	0.24	0.00	1.00	Hou 2004
formula	By formula	0.06	0.23	0.00	1.00	
gfsurp	General fund surplus	0.43	0.50	0.00	1.00	
gfappro	General fund by appropriations	0.21	0.41	0.00	1.00	
sperev	Special revenue	0.01	0.11	0.00	1.00	
low	2 up to 4%	0.07	0.25	0.00	1.00	
medium	4 up to 7%	0.31	0.46	0.00	1.00	
high	7 up to 12%	0.16	0.36	0.00	1.00	
nolimit	No limit to balance level	0.05	0.23	0.00	1.00	
minreq	Minimum requirement	0.09	0.28	0.00	1.00	
approp	By appropriation	0.34	0.47	0.00	1.00	
execut	By executive action	0.16	0.37	0.00	1.00	
byfmla	By formula	0.04	0.19	0.00	1.00	
revsht	For revenue shortfall	0.52	0.50	0.00	1.00	
cashflow	For cash flow	0.12	0.33	0.00	1.00	
emgy	For emergency	0.1	0.30	0.00	1.00	
any	For any purpose	0.04	0.20	0.00	1.00	

Table 9.2 Effects of BSF fund adoption

	(1)	(2)	(3)	(4)
Estimator	FE	FE	RE	RE
BSF dummy	−0.0071	−0.0034	−0.0080	−0.0040
	(0.0090)	(0.0091)	(0.0063)	(0.0064)
UUB ratio	−0.0501	−0.0229	−0.0265	0.0024
	(0.0345)	(0.0350)	(0.0280)	(0.0296)
Dummy: recession years	−0.0339***	−0.0717***	−0.0339***	−0.0686***
	(0.0054)	(0.0244)	(0.0053)	(0.0175)
Annual average unemployment rate	−0.0177***	−0.0138***	−0.0166***	−0.0106***
	(0.0019)	(0.0030)	(0.0017)	(0.0024)
Real per capita income (1,000)	0.0077**	−0.0050	0.0034	0.0006
	(0.0032)	(0.0064)	(0.0022)	(0.0028)
GSP growth rate	0.0010	0.0042***	0.0019**	0.0046***
	(0.0009)	(0.0010)	(0.0008)	(0.0009)
Poverty rate	0.0019	0.0003	0.0026***	0.0012
	(0.0014)	(0.0014)	(0.0010)	(0.0010)
Dummy: biennial budgeting states	0.0112	0.0130	0.0066	0.0083
	(0.0136)	(0.0132)	(0.0057)	(0.0058)
Dummy: state revenue limitations	−0.0158	−0.0102	−0.0002	−0.0006
	(0.0127)	(0.0124)	(0.0060)	(0.0061)
Dummy: state exp. limitations	0.0091	0.0155	0.0102*	0.0074
	(0.0141)	(0.0141)	(0.0058)	(0.0059)
Dummy: year of governor election $_{t-1}$	−0.0084*	−0.0051	−0.0084*	−0.0050
	(0.0049)	(0.0059)	(0.0049)	(0.0058)
Dummy: divided government	−0.0133***	−0.0138***	−0.0106**	−0.0115***
	(0.0046)	(0.0045)	(0.0044)	(0.0043)
Agriculture/GSP ratio	0.0077**	0.0034	−0.0006	−0.0012
	(0.0034)	(0.0036)	(0.0015)	(0.0016)
Manu./GSP ratio	0.0020*	0.0011	−0.0004	−0.0007
	(0.0011)	(0.0012)	(0.0005)	(0.0005)
Fin services/GSP ratio	0.0011	0.0024	−0.0013*	−0.0007
	(0.0017)	(0.0017)	(0.0007)	(0.0007)
Constant	−0.0396	0.1003	0.0798**	0.0972**
	(0.0568)	(0.0882)	(0.0326)	(0.0428)
Year dummies	No	Yes	No	Yes
Observations	1,121	1,121	1,121	1,121
R^2	0.252	0.324		

Significance levels: *10%; **5%; ***1%.

That is, if a state sets a minimum balance to its BSF, policy makers tend to *budget* this floor requirement into their forecasts by underestimating revenue, leading to larger, positive error margin. Recall from earlier chapters the floor effect of BSF, the result is linked to it. The level of balance of the stabilization fund does not seem to cast any observable influence (BSF ratio, in Tables 9.5 and 9.6); the only exception is a negative effect significant at 10% level (Table 9.6), but it is not consistent across estimators and is sensitive to year dummies. Thus, it is safe to conclude that the

Table 9.3 BSF features, without recession year dummy

	(1)	(2)	(3)	(4)
Estimator	FE	FE	RE	RE
UUB ratio	*–0.091****	–0.0275	*–0.0707***	–0.0084
	(0.0352)	(0.0355)	(0.0296)	(0.0311)
Required balance	–0.0345	–0.0308	–0.0133	–0.0079
	(0.0252)	(0.0240)	(0.0130)	(0.0133)
By formula	0.0474	0.0345	–0.0014	0.0006
	(0.0949)	(0.0903)	(0.0241)	(0.0241)
General fund surplus	0.0672	0.0432	0.0080	0.0069
	(0.0904)	(0.0861)	(0.0129)	(0.0131)
General fund by appropriations	0.0248	0.0067	–0.0038	–0.0010
	(0.0340)	(0.0324)	(0.0105)	(0.0106)
4 up to 7%	–0.1145	–0.0291	0.0047	0.0066
	(0.1340)	(0.1279)	(0.0131)	(0.0133)
7 up to 12%	–0.0343	0.0532	0.0216	0.0247
	(0.1330)	(0.1269)	(0.0157)	(0.0160)
No limit to balance level	–	–	–0.0021	0.0026
	–	–	(0.0198)	(0.0204)
Minimum requirement	*0.0630****	*0.0618****	–0.0027	0.0009
	(0.0221)	(0.0210)	(0.0114)	(0.0114)
By appropriation	0.0095	–0.0254	0.0027	0.0019
	(0.0580)	(0.0554)	(0.0090)	(0.0092)
By formula	–	–	0.0025	–0.0062
	–	–	(0.0314)	(0.0319)
For revenue shortfall	0.0288	0.0107	–0.0205	–0.0191
	(0.0692)	(0.0656)	(0.0156)	(0.0156)
For cash flow	0.0438	0.0233	0.0047	0.0029
	(0.0617)	(0.0585)	(0.0112)	(0.0112)
For any purpose	0.0903	0.0601	–0.0058	–0.0073
	(0.1070)	(0.1019)	(0.0197)	(0.0199)
Annual average unemployment rate	–0.0219***	–0.0133***	–0.0213***	–0.0111***
	(0.0018)	(0.0030)	(0.0016)	(0.0025)
Real per capita income (,000)	0.0041	–0.0033	0.0030	0.0006
	(0.0032)	(0.0065)	(0.0024)	(0.0032)
GSP growth rate	0.0030***	0.0044***	0.0035***	0.0045***
	(0.0009)	(0.0010)	(0.0008)	(0.0009)
Poverty rate	0.0022	0.0002	0.0031***	0.0013
	(0.0015)	(0.0014)	(0.0011)	(0.0011)
Dummy: biennial budgeting states	0.0176	0.0156	0.0029	0.0052
	(0.0153)	(0.0147)	(0.0072)	(0.0073)
Dummy: state revenue limitations	–0.0270*	–0.0239*	–0.0043	–0.0060
	(0.0142)	(0.0137)	(0.0080)	(0.0081)
Dummy: state exp. limitations	0.0045	0.0115	0.0125*	0.0091
	(0.0153)	(0.0150)	(0.0070)	(0.0071)
Dummy: year of governor election $_{t-1}$	–0.0053	–0.0052	–0.0049	–0.0053
	(0.0049)	(0.0059)	(0.0049)	(0.0058)

(continued)

Table 9.3 (continued)

	(1)	(2)	(3)	(4)
Estimator	FE	FE	RE	RE
Dummy: divided government	–0.0117**	–0.0123***	–0.0110**	–0.0119***
	(0.0048)	(0.0046)	(0.0045)	(0.0044)
Agr./GSP ratio	0.0033	0.0010	–0.0006	–0.0001
	(0.0036)	(0.0037)	(0.0019)	(0.0020)
Manu./GSP ratio	0.0011	0.0003	–0.0002	–0.0004
	(0.0011)	(0.0012)	(0.0006)	(0.0006)
Fin. services/GSP ratio	–0.0003	0.0015	–0.0013	–0.0003
	(0.0018)	(0.0018)	(0.0009)	(0.0009)
Constant	0.0118	0.0224	0.0841**	0.0218
	(0.0602)	(0.0931)	(0.0377)	(0.0527)
Year dummies	No	Yes	No	Yes
Observations	1,121	1,121	1,121	1,121
R^2	0.237	0.337		

Significance levels: *10%; **5%; ***1%.

stabilization fund as a formal savings device in general stays out of the budgetary forecast loop; neither the presence of the fund nor its balance level is considered in making revenue forecasts.

General fund surplus displays some different impact than does BSF. Table 9.3 shows evidence that *UUB ratio* does cast statistically significant, negative influence on the forecasts. This effect is consistent across estimators (–.09 in FE and –.07 in RE); that is, the amount of GFS available at the time of budget preparation may be taken into consideration in the forecasting process as readily useable resources. However, this effect is sensitive to year fixed effects; that is, GFS overall tends to exert some impact but once placed in specific years, its effect is sucked up by other factors. This result is not completely surprising because, as pointed out in Chapter 6, general fund surplus is the first line of defense in case of any needs because these surpluses are at the discretion of policy makers. Further evidence is that this effect also disappears when the recession year dummies are included in the model (Table 9.4). Overall, the results seem to indicate that boom-year savings tend to be outside the loop of revenue forecasting; errors in revenue forecasts are not directly related to the presence or size of such savings.

9.4.2 *Effects of Control Variables*

Of the variables on the economic condition of each state, unemployment rate is significant at the 1% level with a negative sign. Each percentage point increase of unemployment reduces forecast error by 1.1–1.8%. This resonates with findings from previous study that revenue forecasts in downturn years tend to be more conservative, that is, with smaller margins/room of discretion for policy makers. Thus,

Table 9.4 BSF features, with recession year dummy

	(1)	(2)	(3)	(4)
Estimator	FE	FE	RE	RE
UUB ratio	–0.0547	–0.0275	–0.0352	–0.0084
	(0.0351)	(0.0355)	(0.0296)	(0.0311)
Dummy: recession years	–0.0336***	–0.0618**	–0.0342***	–0.0666***
	(0.0054)	(0.0242)	(0.0054)	(0.0177)
Required balance	–0.0404	–0.0308	–0.0146	–0.0079
	(0.0247)	(0.0240)	(0.0127)	(0.0133)
By formula	0.0566	0.0345	0.0046	0.0006
	(0.0932)	(0.0903)	(0.0235)	(0.0241)
General fund surplus	0.0701	0.0432	0.0069	0.0069
	(0.0888)	(0.0861)	(0.0126)	(0.0131)
General fund by appropriations	0.0123	0.0067	–0.0046	–0.0010
	(0.0334)	(0.0324)	(0.0102)	(0.0106)
4 up to 7%	–0.0902	–0.0291	0.0046	0.0066
	(0.1318)	(0.1279)	(0.0128)	(0.0133)
7 up to 12%	–0.0140	0.0532	0.0254*	0.0247
	(0.1307)	(0.1269)	(0.0153)	(0.0160)
No limit to balance level	–	–	–0.0002	0.0026
	–	–	(0.0193)	(0.0204)
Minimum requirement	0.0593***	0.0618***	–0.0018	0.0009
	(0.0217)	(0.0210)	(0.0112)	(0.0114)
By appropriation	0.0019	–0.0254	0.0027	0.0019
	(0.0570)	(0.0554)	(0.0087)	(0.0092)
By formula	–	–	–0.0109	–0.0062
	–	–	(0.0307)	(0.0319)
For revenue shortfall	0.0104	0.0107	–0.0232	–0.0191
	(0.0680)	(0.0656)	(0.0152)	(0.0156)
For cash flow	0.0302	0.0233	0.0028	0.0029
	(0.0607)	(0.0585)	(0.0109)	(0.0112)
For any purpose	0.0809	0.0601	–0.0070	–0.0073
	(0.1052)	(0.1019)	(0.0193)	(0.0199)
Annual average unemployment rate	–0.0176***	–0.0133***	–0.0171***	–0.0111***
	(0.0019)	(0.0030)	(0.0017)	(0.0025)
Real per capita income (,000)	0.0071**	–0.0033	0.0047**	0.0006
	(0.0032)	(0.0065)	(0.0024)	(0.0032)
GSP growth rate	0.0012	0.0044***	0.0018**	0.0045***
	(0.0009)	(0.0010)	(0.0009)	(0.0009)
Poverty rate	0.0019	0.0002	0.0029***	0.0013
	(0.0014)	(0.0014)	(0.0011)	(0.0011)
Dummy: biennial budgeting states	0.0145	0.0156	0.0019	0.0052
	(0.0151)	(0.0147)	(0.0070)	(0.0073)
Dummy: state revenue limitations	–0.0307**	–0.0239*	–0.0083	–0.0060
	(0.0140)	(0.0137)	(0.0078)	(0.0081)
Dummy: state exp. limitations	0.0026	0.0115	0.0119*	0.0091
	(0.0150)	(0.0150)	(0.0068)	(0.0071)

(continued)

Table 9.4 (continued)

	(1)	(2)	(3)	(4)
Estimator	FE	FE	RE	RE
Dummy: year of governor election $_{t-1}$	–0.0089*	–0.0052	–0.0087*	–0.0053
	(0.0049)	(0.0059)	(0.0049)	(0.0058)
Dummy: divided government	–0.0121**	–0.0123***	–0.0114**	–0.0119***
	(0.0047)	(0.0046)	(0.0045)	(0.0044)
Agr./GSP ratio	0.0063*	0.0010	0.0010	–0.0001
	(0.0035)	(0.0037)	(0.0018)	(0.0020)
Manu./GSP ratio	0.0016	0.0003	–0.0000	–0.0004
	(0.0011)	(0.0012)	(0.0006)	(0.0006)
Fin. service/GSP ratio	0.0002	0.0015	–0.0011	–0.0003
	(0.0018)	(0.0018)	(0.0009)	(0.0009)
Constant	–0.0351	0.0775	0.0588	0.0884*
	(0.0596)	(0.0890)	(0.0371)	(0.0481)
Year dummies	No	Yes	No	Yes
Observations	1,121	1,121	1,121	1,121
R^2	0.264	0.337		

Significance levels: *10%; **5%; ***1%.

it confirms the idea that forecasting bias is procyclical: When the economy is strong, the bias grows; then it declines as the economy dips into recession. On the other hand, it adds to the argument that forecasting error is more of a function of the economy. The recession year dummy is significant at the 1% level, consistent across estimators and year dummies (Table 9.2). This remains mostly true even when I break each recessionary period into first, second, and third recession years – point estimates remain negative and statistically significant (Table 9.6).

Personal income shows a significant positive relation with forecasting error, though not consistent across model specifications: Each $1,000 rise in real per capita personal income may reduce estimation bias by 0.5–1.4% (Tables 9.2, 9.5, and 9.6). This result is not expected: Why does a wealthier state need to budget extra buffer relative to lower-wealth states? Probably this is reflection of higher service demand in revenue forecasts. If a state has a higher proportion of residents under the poverty line, it will have to prepare for welfare programs in each of its budgets regardless of its mean income and the phase of the economic cycle. This effect, when it is statistically significant, is small at about 0.3% for each percentage point increase of the poverty rate (Tables 9.2, 9.5, and 9.6). The tests do not generate reliable evidence that composition of state economy, as proxied with shares of the agriculture, manufacturing, and financial services sectors in state gross product, is consistently related to forecasting error. The overall position of state economy, as shown by GSP growth rate, shows consistent and positive relation with forecasting error; each percentage point increase of state economy pumps up the error rate by 0.2–0.5%, which is in line with our expectation, as discussed in the literature review that revenue forecasting follows (fall behind) the economy.

Table 9.5 Effects of controlling for recession years

	(1)	(2)	(3)	(4)
Estimator	FE	FE	RE	RE
BSF ratio	–0.0896	–0.0440	–0.0116	0.0012
	(0.0580)	(0.0579)	(0.0496)	(0.0488)
UUB ratio	–0.0523	–0.0111	0.0041	0.0385
	(0.0426)	(0.0432)	(0.0331)	(0.0346)
Dummy: recession years	–0.0338***	–0.0358*	–0.0341***	–0.0747***
	(0.0063)	(0.0192)	(0.0062)	(0.0190)
Annual average unemployment rate	–0.0162***	–0.0106***	–0.0162***	–0.0085***
	(0.0021)	(0.0035)	(0.0018)	(0.0027)
Real per capita income	0.0138***	0.0014	0.0048**	0.0025
	(0.0038)	(0.0079)	(0.0024)	(0.0029)
GSP growth rate	0.0010	0.0042***	0.0021**	0.0049***
	(0.0010)	(0.0012)	(0.0010)	(0.0011)
Poverty rate	0.0027*	0.0008	0.0029***	0.0014
	(0.0016)	(0.0016)	(0.0011)	(0.0011)
Dummy: for biennial budgeting states	–0.0018	–0.0044	0.0071	0.0071
	(0.0148)	(0.0145)	(0.0064)	(0.0064)
Dummy: state revenue limitations	–0.0031	0.0045	0.0010	–0.0002
	(0.0201)	(0.0197)	(0.0069)	(0.0070)
Dummy: state expenditure limitations	0.0097	0.0264	0.0075	0.0054
	(0.0204)	(0.0204)	(0.0064)	(0.0064)
Dummy: year of governor election $_{t-1}$	–0.0077	–0.0016	–0.0082	–0.0019
	(0.0054)	(0.0063)	(0.0054)	(0.0063)
Dummy: divided government	–0.0119**	–0.0134**	–0.0093*	–0.0108**
	(0.0054)	(0.0053)	(0.0049)	(0.0048)
Agr./GSP ratio	0.0050	0.0014	–0.0019	–0.0021
	(0.0039)	(0.0041)	(0.0017)	(0.0017)
Manu./GSP ratio	0.0033**	0.0022	0.0000	–0.0003
	(0.0013)	(0.0015)	(0.0006)	(0.0006)
Fin. service/GSP ratio	0.0008	0.0020	–0.0013*	–0.0008
	(0.0019)	(0.0019)	(0.0007)	(0.0007)
Constant	–0.1362**	–0.0474	0.0451	0.0555
	(0.0681)	(0.0873)	(0.0357)	(0.0448)
Year dummies	No	Yes	No	Yes
Observations	872	872	872	872
R^2	0.270	0.346		

Significance levels: *10%; **5%; ***1%.

Of state budgetary institutions, the tests do not generate evidence that the biennial budget cycle bears statistically significant difference from its annual cycle counterpart. Intuitively we may assume that states still using a 2-year window for arranging their budgets may possess an advantage over states using the annual budget cycle; but there is no support for this opinion. Effects of TEL are not consistent across model specifications; they are significant mostly in models that

Table 9.6 Recession broken into separate years

	(1)	(2)	(3)	(4)
Estimator	FE	FE	RE	RE
BSF ratio	−0.0946*	−0.0440	−0.0199	0.0012
	(0.0570)	(0.0579)	(0.0489)	(0.0488)
UUB ratio	−0.0474	−0.0111	0.0087	0.0385
	(0.0422)	(0.0432)	(0.0328)	(0.0346)
Dummy: first year of recessions	−0.0468***	−0.0196	−0.0476***	−0.0224
	(0.0076)	(0.0154)	(0.0075)	(0.0150)
Dummy: second year of recessions	−0.0457***	−0.0707***	−0.0497***	−0.0805***
	(0.0086)	(0.0197)	(0.0084)	(0.0181)
Dummy: third year of recessions	−0.0196**	−0.0612***	−0.0234***	−0.0747***
	(0.0085)	(0.0211)	(0.0082)	(0.0190)
Dummy: fourth year of recessions	0.0026	0.0031	0.0025	0.0055
	(0.0084)	(0.0147)	(0.0083)	(0.0142)
Annual average unemployment rate	−0.0146***	−0.0106***	−0.0140***	−0.0085***
	(0.0024)	(0.0035)	(0.0021)	(0.0027)
Real per capita income (,000)	0.0135***	0.0014	0.0056**	0.0025
	(0.0037)	(0.0079)	(0.0024)	(0.0029)
GSP growth rate	0.0018*	0.0042***	0.0028***	0.0049***
	(0.0010)	(0.0012)	(0.0010)	(0.0011)
Poverty rate	0.0026	0.0008	0.0028**	0.0014
	(0.0016)	(0.0016)	(0.0011)	(0.0011)
Dummy: biennial budgeting states	0.0003	−0.0044	0.0077	0.0071
	(0.0147)	(0.0145)	(0.0065)	(0.0064)
Dummy: state revenue limitations	0.0007	0.0045	0.0006	−0.0002
	(0.0199)	(0.0197)	(0.0070)	(0.0070)
Dummy: state expenditure limitations	0.0127	0.0264	0.0073	0.0054
	(0.0201)	(0.0204)	(0.0065)	(0.0064)
Dummy: year of governor election $_{t-1}$	−0.0012	−0.0016	−0.0016	−0.0019
	(0.0053)	(0.0063)	(0.0053)	(0.0063)
Dummy: divided government	−0.0116**	−0.0134**	−0.0092*	−0.0108**
	(0.0053)	(0.0053)	(0.0049)	(0.0048)
Agr./GSP ratio	0.0047	0.0014	−0.0015	−0.0021
	(0.0038)	(0.0041)	(0.0017)	(0.0017)
Manu./GSP ratio	0.0026**	0.0022	−0.0001	−0.0003
	(0.0013)	(0.0015)	(0.0006)	(0.0006)
Fin. service/GSP ratio	0.0008	0.0020	−0.0012*	−0.0008
	(0.0019)	(0.0019)	(0.0007)	(0.0007)
Constant	−0.1341**	−0.0063	0.0280	0.0555
	(0.0672)	(0.1067)	(0.0364)	(0.0448)
Year dummies	No	Yes	No	Yes
Observations	872	872	872	872
R^2	0.291	0.346		

Significance levels: *10%; **5%; ***1%.

include BSF features (Tables 9.3 and 9.4). Limitations on revenue show a negative sign that is significant only in fixed effects; the point estimate is about 3%. Limitations on expenditure show a positive sign, in random effect models that is statistically significant when year effects are excluded, which is an overall average effect. The point estimate is about 1%, much smaller than their revenue limit counterpart. Inconsistent as these coefficients are across specifications, they point to an overall direction of their potential impact on forecasts: Revenue limitations may work to reduce the positive error margin, whereas outlay limitations may increase it.

With regard to state politics, in the literature, years of gubernatorial elections are associated with larger than usual outlays in an effort to boost the state economy thereby the chance of reelection by incumbents. In the results, this variable consistently shows a negative sign in both fixed and random effects estimators, all specifications; it becomes statistically significant, across estimators, when recessions are controlled with a dummy and year effects are not included (Tables 9.2 and 9.4). In such cases, a gubernatorial election year reduces the forecasting error margin of the next year by close to 1%. This result points to the possibility that larger outlays in the election years reduce the difference between revenue estimates and the actual revenue, that is, less revenue underestimation. This is in line with the existing literature. Divided government shows a negative sign statistically significant across both estimators and all specifications, which confirms that different party affiliation between the governor and the majority of the state legislature tends to reduce forecasting error margin, here by about 1%.

9.5 Conclusion

In this chapter I have examined the impact of boom-year savings on outcome of state government revenue forecasting, which fills a niche in the literature. I have set up empirical estimation to check whether the presence of savings in the expansion phase of the economic cycle casts any observable impact on revenue forecasts by state policy makers. In particular, I have checked effects of the adoption of the budget stabilization, savings in general, and size of BSF balance as well as unreserved general fund balances.

This study has found no evidence that adopting a stabilization fund and the size of BSF balance help reduce the error margin of revenue estimation. The results suggest that BSF as a formal countercyclical savings device stays outside the revenue forecasting process; policy makers may not consider them in making forecasts. But the level of general fund surplus is different; it may have been part of the calculation in making revenue estimates, which is in line with my finding in Chapter 6. Together these findings offer new insight into the behavior of policy makers in the public choice literature; they may serve as a timely suggestion to policy makers against the background of the Great Recession when the general public has shown frustration, even anger, over financial distress and all subnational governments are seeking solutions to the old and new problems. What this chapter has done may also point to directions for future research. Obviously there remains a lot more to explore along the line of this research with regard to the minute details.

References

Auerbach AJ (1999) On the performance and use of government revenue forecasts. Natl Tax J 52(4):765–782

Bails D (1982) A critique of the effectiveness of tax and expenditure limitations. Public Choice 38:129–138

Bohn H, Inman RP (1996) Balanced-budget rules and public deficits: evidence from the U.S. states. Paper read at Carnegie-Rochester conference series on public policy. NBER working paper no. 5533, Rochester, NY

Brennan G, Buchanan JM (1980) The power to tax: analytical foundations of a fiscal constitution. Cambridge University Press, Cambridge

Bretschneider S, Gorr W (1992) Economic, organizational, and political influences on biases in forecasting state sales tax receipts. Int J Forecast 7(4):457–466

Bretschneider S, Gorr W, Grizzle G, Klay E (1989) Political and organizational influences on the accuracy of forecasting state government revenues. Int J Forecast 5(3):307–319

Bretschneider S, Bunch B, Gorr W (1992) Revenue forecasting errors in Pennsylvania local government budgeting: sources of variation. Public Budg Financ Manag 4(3):721–743

Buchanan JM (1975) Public finance and public choice. Natl Tax J 28(4):383–394

Cassidy G, Kamlet MS, Nagin DS (1989) An empirical examination of bias in revenue forecasts by state governments. Int J Forecast 5(3):321–331

Douglas JW, Gaddie RK (2002) State rainy day funds and fiscal crises: rainy day funds and the 1990–1991 recession revisited. Public Budg Finance 22(1):19–30

Downs TA, Figlio DN (1999) Do tax and expenditure limits provide a free lunch? Evidence on the link between limits and public sector service quality. Natl Tax J 52(1):113–128

Fisher RC (1984) "Statement before the Intergovernmental Relations and Human Resources Subcommittee of the Committee on Government Operations." In U.S. Congress (1985), 101–107

Gentry WM (1989) Do state revenue forecasters utilize available information? Natl Tax J 42(4):429–439

Gold SD (1983) Preparing for the next recession: rainy day funds and other tools for the states. Legislative Finance paper no. 41, National conference of state legislatures, Denver, CO

Hou Y (2003) What stabilizes state general fund spending during downturns? Public Budg Finance 23(3):64–91

Hou Y (2004) Budget stabilization fund: structural features of the enabling legislation and balance levels. Public Budg Finance 24(3):38–64

Hou Y (2005) Fiscal reserves and state own-source expenditure in downturns. Public Finance Rev 33(1):117–144

Hou Y (2006) Budgeting for fiscal stability over the business cycle. Public Adm Rev 66(5):730–741

Hou Y (2010) Local fiscal behavior under subnational provisions: do local governments smooth revenue from booms across busts? J Public Finance Public Choice XXVIII(1):3–27

Hou Y, Brewer G (2010) Supplementation and substitution between two saving devices. Public Adm Rev 70(6):14–24

Hou Y, Duncombe WD (2008) State saving behavior: effects of two fiscal and budgetary institutions. Public Budg Finance 28(3):48–67

Knight B, Levinson A (1999) Rainy day funds and state government savings. Natl Tax J 52(3):459–472
Krause GA, Lewis DE, Douglas JW (2006) Political appointments, civil service systems, and bureaucratic competence: organizational balancing and executive branch revenue forecasts in the American states. Am J Polit Sci 50:770–787
Levinson A (1998) Balanced budgets and business cycles: evidence from the states. Natl Tax J 51(4):715–732
Mocan HN, Azad S (1995) Accuracy and rationality of state general fund revenue forecasts: evidence from panel data. Int J Forecast 11(3):417–427
Mushkin SJ, Lupo GC (1967) Is there a conservative bias in state-local sector expenditure projections? Natl Tax J 20(3):282–291
National Association of State Budget Officers (1995) Budget processes in the states, various years. Washington, DC
National Association of State Budget Officers (1977–2010). The Fiscal Survey of States. Various years. Washington, DC
National Governors Association. The book of the states, series (since 1935). National Governors Association, Lexington
Nordhaus W (1975) The political business cycle. Rev Econ Stud 42:169–190
Penner RG (2002) Dealing with uncertain budget forecasts. Public Budg Finance 22(1):1–18
Plesko GA (1988) The accuracy of government forecasts and budget projections. Natl Tax J 41(4):483–501
Poterba J (1994) State responses to fiscal crises: the effects of budgetary institutions and politics. J Polit Econ 102(4):799–821
Rafuse RW (1965) Cyclical behavior of state-local finances. In Musgrave RA (ed) Essays in fiscal federalism, 118. The Brookings Institution: Washington, D.C
Rodgers R, Joyce P (1996) The effect of underforecasting on the accuracy of revenue forecasts by state governments. Public Adm Rev 56(1):48–56
Rogoff K (1990) Equilibrium political budget cycles. Am Econ Rev 80(1):21–36
Shadbegian RJ (1999) The effect of tax and expenditure limitations on the revenue structure of local government 1962–87. Natl Tax J 52(2):221–238
Sobel RS, Holcombe RG (1996) The impact of state rainy day funds in easing state fiscal crises during the 1990–1991 recession. Public Budg Finance 16(3):28–48
Stocker FD (ed) (1991) Proposition 13: a ten-year retrospective, introduction. Lincoln Institute of Land Policy, Cambridge, MA
Sundelson JW (1935) Budgetary principles. Polit Sci Q 50:236–263
Voorhees W (2006) Consistent underestimation bias, the asymmetric loss function and homogeneous sources of bias in revenue forecasting. J Public Budg Account Financ Manag 18(1):61–76
Wagner GA (2003) Are budget stabilization funds only the illusion of savings: evidence from stationary panel data? Q Rev Econ Finance 43(2):213–238
Wagner GA, Sobel S (2006) State budget stabilization fund adoption: preparing for the next recession or circumventing fiscal constraints? Public Choice 126(1):177–199

Chapter 10
Debt as a Countercyclical Fiscal Tool

Abstract This chapter builds on existing literature, in particular Robert Barro's "transitory income and government expenditure" theory, and formulates a model for the countercyclical use of long-term full faith and credit debt by state governments to finance infrastructure. The model incorporates long-term debt into budgetary policy, bringing into consideration debt capacity, purposes and security of debt, as well as equity issues. The proposition is to retire debt in boom years in order to preserve debt capacity and reduce borrowing costs and then incur debt at a lower interest rate in bust years in order to help maintain state government's service provision and pave the way for recovery. The chapter conducts several empirical tests. First, do states in aggregate use debt pro- or countercyclically? Second, what factors determine the cyclical patterns in states' use of debt? Third, will the proposed optimal path of debt issue and retirement be applicable? And what may be the effects of this proposition? My results show that overall states do not tend to use debt against the economic cycle; however, I obtain some weak evidence that at least some states have adopted countercyclical debt policies. Finally, I simulate the effects of the proposed optimal debt policy with New York state; calibration shows that such a policy could have rendered the state a much better situation to encounter the Great Recession. Findings and results of this study will provide timely insight into this important issue to scholars and policy makers.

10.1 Introduction

The use of debt generates huge utility by promoting productivity growth and living standards improvement; such effects were especially obvious from the financing opportunities made possible by advances of the financial market in the twentieth century. On the other hand, the steady decline in savings rate in couplet with rapidly increasing public debt against the background of electoral politics has caused deep concern among the general public about the sustainability of our current financial system.

Y. Hou, *State Government Budget Stabilization: Policy, Tools, and Impacts*, Studies in Public Choice 8, DOI 10.1007/978-1-4614-6061-9_10,

This problem has become particularly protruding in the 2008–2010 round of deep recession. By the start of the Great Recession, state and local government debts in the USA had reached $2.6 trillion. In specific terms, it was $8,500 per capita, or 18% of GDP, or 96% of all state-local annual revenue, of which 39% were by states; annual interest payment on the debt was 3.8% of state-local revenue in 2008 (Wassmer and Fisher 2011).

Barro (1974) formulated the seminal "debt neutrality" proposition that whether government finances its expenditure with current taxes or with debt does not make much difference, because the value of government bonds is equal to the present discounted value of the interest and principal of the bonds. This theory was named the "Ricardian equivalence theorem" by James Buchanan (1976). Since then, this line of literature has been increasing with consensus that even though the Ricardian equivalence may not hold under uncertainty (Barro 1974; Buchanan 1976), finite life span (Weil 1987), liquidity constraint, or credit market imperfection (Barro 1989), the equivalence theorem is empirically a better description of the reality than the traditional Keynesian model.

The theorem per se, however, does not offer a theory of public debt creation. To fill in the hole, Barro (1979) proposes such a theory to identify factors that determine an average government's choice between tax finance and debt finance. In that paper, Barro tested three hypotheses. First, debt issue exerts a positive effect on temporary increase in government spending during war years and postwar recovery efforts. Second, debt issue imposes a negative effect on temporary income increase, which is a countercyclical response to the economic cycle (issue in bust years and retirement in boom years). And third, there exists a one-to-one effect of expected inflation on the growth rate of nominal debt. These propositions carry two implications: One, the growth rate of debt is independent of the debt-income ratio and the other, the growth rate of debt is not affected, or at most in a minor way, by the level of government expenditure.

Lewis Kimmel (1959, Chapter 2) succinctly reminded us in his discussion of federal fiscal policy from the Civil War to 1929 that "part of sound budget policy, with balanced budgets, is to preserve the credit and standing of a country and the national wealth." This author believes that a countercyclical model of debt use works exactly in this direction for all governments at the national and subnational levels. Thus, given recent financial crisis, findings of the Barro paper confirmed his hypotheses and the results were stable over variation of sample years. The only exception is the excess of the countercyclical response of debt issue over the theory, which indicates that the federal government heavily used debt between 1922 and 1976 as a stimulus fiscal policy tool in recession years. In other words, the optimal debt issue path was confirmed; and the US federal government purposely used debt issue as a countercyclical fiscal policy.

The purpose of this chapter is to extend the Barro (1979) propositions to the subnational (state) level. Specifically, I will build upon and extend Barro's "transitory income and government expenditure" theory and a countercyclical model specification. My research questions are the following: Do American state governments in aggregate use debt countercyclically? Does each individual state also use their debt against the economic cycle? And how much may such countercyclical use of debt help an average state on the margin in fighting a recession? The rationale behind these questions is boom-year savings as BSF and GFS are necessary as a tool to stabilize the budget but not sufficient to facilitate recovery. For the latter purpose, another fiscal policy tool is needed. It is debt for capital construction. Potential contribution of this chapter is twofold, as an extension of Barro's theory to the subnational level and policy implications for state governments in preparing for and thereby potentially better handling future recessions.

10.2 Economic Theories on Debt

Checking the history of economic thought and recent literature on debt use, I found the following components pertinent to my topic. I briefly review them below on the parts of these ideas that are closely related to this study. In sections on Empirical Analyses, I will visit the empirical literature on their findings as related to this study and compare their results with mine for similarities and differences, confirmation, or negation.

10.2.1 Debt as a Fiscal Policy

The use of credit on the financial market was invented in the fourteenth century in northern Italy to facilitate trade; in this sense debt was a great invention that promoted economic development. Later on, debt was adopted by governments, based on market information with regard to the creditworthiness of the debtor. Economic theory supports the use of long-term debt to finance capital projects with lasting useful lives. The most obvious benefits from using debt are at least threefold: to achieve higher efficiency by lowering and smoothing tax rates over a longer period of time, to reserve some current revenue for cash flow/working capital, and to achieve greater intergenerational equity by charging all who will benefit from the constructed projects over time (Musgrave 1959). These have been the foundation for the popularity of debt use as a public finance tool that is technically practical and politically appealing to most members of the society.

There had been cases of overborrowing in history. With the public sector, Irving Fisher (1911, in particular 1933) raised warnings with his theory on debt: Boom-year overborrowing is one of two major causes of all great depressions (the other being deflation in the depression following the deep indebtedness).[1] John Maynard Keynes (1936) enriched economic theory by proposing countercyclical fiscal policy (CCFP) at the national level. Keynesianism proposes heavy use of debt in downturn years to pull up aggregate demand, to be retired in boom-years. More recently Roy

[1] For a most recent exposition on Fisher's theory, see Robert Shiller's 2011 ASSA conference paper.

Bahl (1984) proposes that debt can also be a fiscal policy tool by state governments. Edward Gramlich (1987) formally extended CCFP to the subnational level (for details, see Chapter 2).

10.2.2 Pay-Go Versus Pay-Use Financing of Capital Projects

In fact, governments do not always finance capital projects by borrowing; instead, pay-as-you-go (pay-go) financing is common for infrastructure investment at the national and subnational levels. The President's Commission to Study Capital Budgeting (1999) found that "states often dip into general revenues to pay for capital items, although the extent to which they are allowed or choose to do so varies."[2] Pay-go financing has been a long-standing practice in some parts of the United States as an effective means to lower debt burdens. In recent decades rating agencies have even been using it as a necessary supplement to debt financing (Fitch 2000); scholars and professional organizations (GFOA 1999; NASBO series) have recommended pay-go as one of the best practices in public budgeting. There is an especially strong case for pay-go financing when the economy is strong and/or a government or its entity has extra resources available.

Wang et al. (2007) develop a model that considers the preferences of voters and politicians on capital financing decisions. They conduct tests using a panel data set of 48 states over 16 years and Tobit random- and fixed-effects models. They find that income level, economic conditions over the business cycle, and political as well as budgetary institutions are the key determinants of the use of pay-go financing. In particular, they find that lower borrowing costs may reduce the use of pay-go and lead to higher debt. Wang and Hou (2009) examine state experience in capital outlay volatility over two recent economic cycles; they find evidence which suggests that pay-go is associated with lower capital spending in the long run though it may increase short-run variability. They recommend that states adopt a countercyclical strategy by combining pay-go in boom years with pay-use in lean years. They believe these two mechanisms in unison can reduce aggregate volatility and increase long-run stability of capital expenditures. The appendix to this chapter provides details of these two studies.

10.2.3 Countercyclical Infrastructure Investment

Infrastructure investment can play a key role in stabilizing a downturn economy. The Swedish government experimented with it from the 1950s to the 1970s, with strong success in the early years (Lindbeck 1974). Detailed studies dissected its

[2] *Report of the President's Commission to Study Capital Budgeting* (1999, 19).

initial success and trickling ending (Bergstrom 1981). John Taylor's (1982) seminal econometric analysis of the underlying theoretical model illustrates how countercyclical infrastructure investment works. Hou (2010) makes a further step from Taylor (1982); he suggests designing countercyclical federal transfers for infrastructure investment, service maintenance, and business tax relief as incentives for states to save in boom years then build from recession into recovery.

10.2.4 Countercyclical Use of Debt

Barro's (1979) public debt theory, in particular its component on "transitory income and government expenditure," is in line with the Ricardian invariance theorem. This theory promotes an *optimal time path of debt issue*, which means the amount of deficits vary from year to year across the boom and bust phases of the economic cycle in order to maintain the expectation that tax rates stay constant across the whole economic cycle. In this fashion, there is an optimal time path of debt issue, that is, temporary increases of government debt in bust years raise the current level of spending, which poses positive effect; then debt is retired in boom years. This is a countercyclical response of government debt to temporary income movement; that is, more debt is issued when current income is low (recession) and more debt is retired when income is high (peak). Debt issue is invariant with the outstanding debt-income ratio or with the level of government spending.

The Barro (1979) model was built for national governments where most variables can be safely assumed to be exogenous. This chapter extends the Barro model to the subnational level (states in the USA). This extension from the national to the subnational level is based on the following arguments. First, the size of population is exogenous to state governments, so are the demand for services as reflected in total state government expenditure and the size of state economy, gross state product (GSP). Second, the effects of state debt policy on inter-state migration are negligible or at least not substantial in the short run. This point was luminously illustrated when Edward Gramlich (1987) extended the economic stabilization function of government from the national to the subnational level. Third, the revenue portfolio of states, that is, composition of taxes and fees, is not correlated with debt policy. And finally, interest rates, nominal and real, are not within the control of state governments, thereby nor is the cost of borrowing in general. Berne and Schramm (1986) in their classic analysis of government debt (Chapter 6) provide a list of the factors that affect the effective interest cost of a debt issue, among which a state can at most control the maturity period and security behind the debt (whether it is general obligation bond [GO] or revenue bond) and call provision or not. They can influence but not control the number of underwriters competing for the issue, whether the issue is negotiated or bid competitive; states cannot even control the size of the issue. The rest of the factors are completely outside the reach of state governments, like the overall interest rate, the overall financial condition, and the factors in the regional market.

State governments differ from the federal government in several important ways in their fiscal behavior. States are under strict restraint of balanced budget requirements and debt limit; states use a capital budget that is separate from the operating budget; and states issue debt mostly if not only for capital projects. From the literature, we know that capital construction brings the largest multiplier effect to the economy; so it is among the best tools to boost the economy during a recession. Thus, it is reasonable to assume that states differ from the federal government in fundamental ways, but the countercyclical use of debt should be only more obvious and could be more heavily used.

Most recently, Balázs Égert (2012) examines the case of the Organization for Economic Cooperation and Development (OECD) in their reaction of fiscal policy to the economic cycle. The study finds that the amount of debt may have led to different cyclical patterns in fiscal policy. Nations that have incurred more than average level of public debt and have been using above-the-bar level of deficits tend to adopt procyclical fiscal policies; whereas countries that have incurred lower than average level of debt and have kept surpluses show a higher probability to (or can afford to) use countercyclical fiscal policies. This adds further credibility to Barro's and our advocated proposition.

10.3 A Model of Countercyclical Debt Issue

In the following I borrow from Barro's (1979) debt theory and Hamilton's (1989) two-state regime change proposition and develop a model for countercyclical debt use in the context of state fiscal and budgetary institutions. The logarithms are adapted from or based on those of Barro and Hamilton.

States must balance their budget each year; they divide annual total outlays into two parts, the operating budget for the regular provision of services (O) and the capital budget for construction of capital projects with long useful life (C). States are allowed to issue debt for the latter but not the former; such debt usually is long-term, guaranteed with the full faith and credit (FFC, or GO bond) of the taxing power of the state, with maturity in most cases longer than 10 years for intergenerational equity—thus, whoever benefits from the facilities in the long run should pay for it—and economic efficiency, to smooth the tax rate across phases of the economic cycle. To prevent abuse of borrowing, debt issues are subject to statutory debt limits. Thus, the annually balanced *budget equation* is

$$(O_t + C_t) + rb_{t-1} = \tau_t + (b_t - b_{t-1}), \tag{10.1}$$

where O is state operating expenditure, C is capital expenditure excluding interest payments on previous debt, b is the stock of total long-term debt outstanding at the end of year t, r is the real rate of return on debt, and τ_t is the real tax revenue in year t.

With the annual budget balancing restraint in the equation, I assume that debt service payments for each fiscal year are planned ahead and incur at the beginning of the fiscal year, which fits the reality of budgeting. Tax rate is the total tax revenue, τ, as a fraction of total income (tax base), Y. Total tax revenue is a function of this ratio, $\tau_t f(\tau_t / Y_t), f' > 0$. For efficiency reasons, we assume this function to be invariant over the economic cycle.

Taxation incurs costs, Z. By the Ramsey rule of taxation, dead weight loss from taxes is a quadruple positive function of tax rates. Thus, Z_t is positively related to tax revenue (τ_t) with a positive second derivative and negatively related to the contemporaneous tax base, Y_t. Again for efficiency reasons, an objective of the government is to minimize taxation costs, part of which is to minimize the revenue-raising costs, such that the marginal cost for raising taxes, $\partial Z_t / \partial \tau_t$, is to stay constant over the economic cycle.

Let us express the economic cycle as a regime that switches between two states (S): $S_{0,1}$, 1 = recession, duration 1–2 years; 0 = boom, duration of 4–6 years. The expected mean duration of booms and busts in American macroeconomy is taken from Hamilton (1993) and Gordon (2010). Suppose we are now in a boom period (S_0), income grows at a trend (constant) rate ρ, so that

$$Y_t = Y_0(1+\rho)^t \text{ and } \tau_1 = \tau_0(1+\rho), r > \rho;$$

and that government program outlays grow at rate γ, so that

$$(O+C)_t = (O+C)_{t\text{-}1}(1+\gamma)^t, \gamma \leq \rho < r.$$

Now suppose we are in a recession (S_1), Y temporarily falls below the trend by a fraction of μ (< 0), for n periods (N = 1, 2), such that

$$Y_1 = (1+\mu)\,Y_0(1+\rho);$$

and that capital outlay (C) rises above its trend by a fraction of $\in$ (> 0) for k periods (K = 1, 2, 3), $C_1 = (1+\in)\,G_0\,(1+\rho)$. Here I assume operating expenditure remains unchanged during the recession. Thus, the increase of debt in a recession year over that of a boom year can be expressed as

$$\begin{aligned} b_t - b_{t-1} &= (O+C)_t + rb_{t-1} - \tau_t \\ &\cong \left[(1+\rho)/(1+r)\right]^k \left[(O_{t-1} + \in C_{t-1})(1+\rho)\right] \\ &\quad - \left[(1+\rho)/(1+r)\right]^n \left[(O+C)_{t-1}(1+\rho) + rb_{t-1}\right]\mu + \rho b_{t-1}. \end{aligned} \tag{10.2}$$

Then let $(\overline{O}_t + \overline{C}_t) = (O+C)_{t-1}(1+\rho)$ be the trend level of program outlays and $\overline{Y}_t = Y_{t-1}(1+\rho)$ be the trend level of income, and combine outlays as an aggregate, G, the above can be rewritten as

$$\begin{aligned} b_t - b_{t-1} &\cong \left[(1+\rho)/(1+r)\right]^k (G_t - \overline{G}_t) \\ &\quad - \left[(1+\rho)/(1+r)\right]^n (\overline{G}_t + rb_{t-1})\Big]\Big[(Y_t - \overline{Y}_t)/\overline{Y}_t\Big] + \rho b_{t-1}. \end{aligned} \tag{10.3}$$

Next divide both sides of the equation by previous debt; it becomes the growth rate term of debt use across years:

$$(b_t - b_{t-1}) / b_{t-1} \cong [(1+\rho)/(1+r)]^k (G_t - \overline{G}_t)/b_{t-1} - [(1+\rho)/(1+r)]^n \left[(\overline{G}_t + rb_{t-1})/b_{t-1}\right]\left[(Y_t - \overline{Y}_t)/\overline{Y}_t\right] + \rho. \tag{10.4}$$

With this debt growth rate, I will be able to identify the cyclical pattern in the use of debt by the states. I will be able to explain changes in the level of debt use with the two variables on the right-hand side of the equation. One variable is how much each state's program outlays deviate from its trend, $(G_1 - \overline{G}_1)$, relative to previous year's debt level. In this setup, the coefficient of the outlays, $[(1+\rho)/(1+r)]^k$, is expected to be < 1 since $r > \rho$. The other variable is the extent of income deviation from its trend, $(Y_1 - \overline{Y}_1)/\overline{Y}_1$, multiplied by the trend level of program outlays (including interests on previous debt) relative to previous debt level. The coefficient of this variable, $[(1+\rho)/(1+r)]^n$, is also expected to be < 1.

Let *P* stand for price, π for inflation, *R* for nominal interest rate, and *B* for nominal debt. At the subnational level, price changes are exogenous with inflation; unexpected changes in price are shocks indicated as $P_t = P_{t-1}(1+\pi)^t$; nominal interest rate is $r+\pi$; nominal debt is $b_{t-1} = B_{t-1}/P_1$; and growth rate of nominal income is $\rho+\pi$. Thus, Eq. 10.4 becomes

$$B_1 - B_{t-1}/B_{t-1} = [(1+\rho)/(1+r)]^k P_1(G_1 - \overline{G}_1)/B_{t-1} - [(1+\rho)/(1+r)]^n \left[(P_1\overline{G}_1 + rB_{t-1})/B_{t-10}\right]\left[(Y_1 - \overline{Y}_1)/\overline{Y}_1\right] + \rho + \pi. \tag{10.5}$$

By the Barro theory of debt issue, I can arrive at the following: Though the overall ratio of debt to income would stay constant across an economic cycle, the ratio could rise in recession years (S_1 of the two-state regime) when the aggregate income falls sharply short of the trend and states increase infrastructure outlays to a level high above the trend (Barro 1979, 950–2). Thus, integrating the Barro (1979) theory of debt issue and Hamilton's (1989) two-state regime switching, we can set up a dynamic stochastic general equilibrium (DSGE) model. In summary terms, total expenditure is the sum of operating and capital outlays:

$$O_t + C_t = R_t - rD_{t-1} + S_tD_t, \quad S = 0,1. \tag{10.6}$$

During recession (S_1, lasting 1–2 years),

$$O_{t,s=1} + (1+2\varphi)C_{t,s=1} = R_t + D_t - rD_{t-1}. \tag{10.7}$$

Operating outlays ideally remain constant (with reserves that have accumulated in boom years, BSF and GFS) in order to maintain trend level public services, whereas capital outlays increase so as to accelerate planned projects by 2 times φ, a fraction of about 0.2–0.25 of a state's debt capacity, for stimulus. Thus, current revenue that is already short of the trend is far from enough; it is supplemented with extra issue of debt. Meantime, payment of interest on previous debt stays.

During expansion (S_0, lasting 4–6 years),

$$O_{t,s=0} + C_{t,s=0} = R_t - rD_{t-1} - (1+\varphi)D_{t-1}. \tag{10.8}$$

Capital outlays resumes the trend level whereas accumulated debt is retired at the rate of $(1+\varphi)$. Thus, the practice of annual budget balancing may change to cross-cycle balancing, assuming the average length of a whole cycle is about five to eight years. The overall budget constraint is

$$\sum_1^8 \left[(O_t + C_t)/(1+r)^t\right] + b_{t-1} = \sum_1^8 \left[\tau_t/(1+r)^t\right]. \tag{10.9}$$

The present discounted value (PDV) of program outlays except interest payments, and the previous debt is set to equal the present discounted value of current tax revenue. The PDV of outlays and the previous debt level are exogenously given. Together they determine the required size of current year tax revenue in PDV.

10.4 Cyclicality of Debt Issue by States: An Empirical Analysis

In this section I conduct empirical tests about the historical cyclical patterns of debt issue by state governments. My first test is whether state governments in aggregate and by region used long-term debt countercyclically; the second test is whether each individual state used their debt capacity against the economic cycle. These two tests are done with time-series methods. The third test uses panel data methods for verification of results from the first two. I will focus on long-term debt, using it as my dependent variable; this choice is supported by the literature. For example, a recent study by Wassmer and Fisher (2011) shows that among state-local debt since 1992, the bulk of debt increase was long-term debt for public capital projects—in line with this study's argument; long-term debt for private purposes stayed stable at about 4% of GDP since 1997; long-term debt for public purposes rose from 10.4% of GDP in 1992 to 13.4% in 2007. I check debt in annual change rates and real per capita terms, respectively. These are the most widely accepted and most easily understood and most frequently used measures in policy making.

10.4.1 Test 1: Did Aggregate State Debt Use Go Countercyclical in the Past?

To test the historical trend of debt use by the 50 states, I use time-series methods for the analysis. The sample period is chosen to run from 1950 to 2006. This choice is based on two reasons. The first is data availability: The earliest year for which a continuous annual series of data on new debt issues and total debt outstanding is available is 1950. The data source is the 2010 version of the *State Government*

Finance (SGF) annual series from the US Census. The most recent year of data availability in this series is 2006, right before the Great Recession. The second is the length of the sample period. I believe this 57-year window is broad enough to reveal trends of state debt use.

The dependent variable is the annual growth rate of debt use. The estimation equation is borrowed from Barro (1979), with necessary modifications to fit the state sector, so that I can use Barro's findings on the US federal government as a benchmark in interpreting results from my tests. The equation takes the following form:

$$\log(B_t / B_{t-1}) = \alpha_0 + \alpha_1 \pi_t + \alpha_2 \left[P_t (G_t - \bar{G}_t) / \bar{B}_t \right] - \alpha_3 \left[log(Y_t / \bar{Y}_t)(P_t \bar{G}_t) / \bar{B}_t \right] \quad (10.10)$$

where B_t is the stock of nominal debt at the end of fiscal year t (Barro's original test takes the calendar year for the federal government), $\bar{B}_t$ is the average amount of debt outstanding during year t, π_t is the average anticipated inflation rate during year t, P_t is the average price level for year t, G_t is the state total expenditure during year t excluding interest payments on debt, Y_t is the aggregate personal income for year t, and $\bar{Y}_t$ is the level of normal income during year t.

These variables are measured in the following fashion: Nominal debt B_t is the stock of state debt (total amount) at par value at the end of each fiscal year as reported in the *SGF* series. I choose to use the total instead of any smaller (narrower) category for this first test in order to capture the big picture. The bulk of state debt (about 94%) is long term; short-term debt is small (Wassmer and Fisher 2011). Thus, it is safe to assume that combining the two categories into one lump sum will not blur the big picture. In the next test, I will use long-term debt as the measure. $\bar{B}_t$ is measured as the square root of the product of total debt outstanding in the current year and that in the previous year ($\sqrt{B_t \cdot B_{t-1}}$).

The choice of the average anticipated inflation rate, π_t, needs some explanation. In his test of federal debt, Barro (1979) estimated an after-tax nominal rate on corporate bonds and used the estimates to proxy the anticipated rate of inflation over the average period of the bonds if the anticipated after-tax real rate of return were fixed. Obviously the Barro estimates do not fit my need in this study. A readily available index is the implicit price deflator (IPD) for purchases by the state-local sector which is standard calculation by the Bureau of Economic Analysis (BEA) based on a basket of goods for that sector, different from the basket for calculating the consumer price index (CPI). The IPD series is widely used in all research, but it is not a good proxy for anticipated inflation or return on investments. Better fitting this study is the 20-Bond Buyer Index (20BBI). This index is developed by the bonds market; it is composed of 20 general obligation (GO) bonds with 20-year maturity.[3] The 20BBI is a simple average of the average estimated yields of the included GO bonds. As such, it serves as indication of theoretical yields, not actual price or yield quotations.

P_t is the consumer price index (CPI) for each year. Normal state expenditure, $\bar{G}$, is calculated from state expenditure that includes interest payments as a part of

[3] According to the Bond Buyer website, the average rating of the 20 GO bonds included in the index is Aa2 by the Moody's and AA by the Standard and Poor's.

government expenditure; the purpose is to take account of the long-term growth rate of real state spending.[4] Barro (1977, 1978) calculated $\overline{G}$ as a distributed lag of total spending using an adaptation coefficient of 0.2 per year. In this study I use a time trend formula, $\overline{G}_{it} = \alpha_i + \beta_i T_i$. Normal real personal income, $\overline{Y}$, is also calculated as a time trend using the same formula, from the aggregate personal income series. As a time trend, these two calculated variables are linear, not counting for fluctuations during recessions, whereas the actual spending and personal income are subject to cyclical shocks. Thus, when the actual is deducted from the linear time trend, as in Eq. 10.1, there will be negative numbers, which will drop out during log operation. But since the 57-year sample period is long; the loss of a few years does not necessarily compromise validity of the variable.

In addition, the sample period includes periods of extraordinary growth in personal income and government spending, the former being years 1950–1975 and the latter being years 1973–1982. To account for these special cases, I create two separate dummy variables for each year in these two periods in alternate model specifications to allow for a higher rate of growth and for a different (higher) anticipated real rate of return, respectively. Variables calculated by Eq. 10.10 and used in the estimation of the 50-state aggregates are tabulated into Table 10.1. Summary statistics (of the 50-state aggregate, the eight Census regions, and each of the 50 states) are in Table 10.2.

Based on Barro (1979), the theory behind Eq. 10.10 and results thereof are expected to carry the following implications for the coefficients: The constant, α_0, would equal the growth rate, ρ, if real income and state expenditure have been growing at the same rate. If government spending, $G = O + C$, has been growing faster than income, Y, for some period (which was the case for most states in the sample period), there would be a downward effect on the constant as indicated in a general way $(\rho - \gamma)$. Second, α_1, the expected return rate, should equal unity because anticipated inflation rate exerts a one-to-one effect on the growth rate of nominal debt. Coefficients α_2 and α_3 are expected to be below unity.

Results of the 50-state aggregate test are shown in Table 10.3, Panel A. The constant, α_0, is statistically significant in all four specifications; its magnitude ranges from 3.7% to 4.9%, which is roughly the growth rate. Since government spending in most states grew faster than personal income in the sample period, there shows a downward restraint on the point estimate. Coefficient on the expected return rate, α_1, is significant at the 10% level in the two specifications with special period dummies; its magnitude is 0.64, close to the expected unity level. The key here is from the other two coefficients that are neither statistically significant in any of the specifications, which indicates that states' use of debt in aggregate does not show any pattern across the economic cycles – they are acyclical. In other words, the states did not take the boom or the bust of the economy into the consideration of their debt issuance.

---

[4] By Barro's calculation, the average annual growth rate of federal government spending was 5.6% from 1890 to 1976.

Table 10.1 Values of independent variables for test 1

Year	π	$\log(Y/\bar{Y})$	$P\bar{G}/\bar{B}$	$P(G-\bar{G})/\bar{B}$	$P\bar{G}*\log(Y/\bar{Y})/\bar{B}$	$G/\bar{Y}$
1950	0.019					
1951	0.020		−3.488	3.692		
1952	0.022		−0.675	0.722		
1953	0.027		−0.212	0.229		
1954	0.024		−0.157	0.173		
1955	0.025		0.056	−0.064		
1956	0.028		−0.166	0.192		
1957	0.033		−0.271	0.331		
1958	0.032		−0.167	0.221		
1959	0.036		−0.026	0.039		
1960	0.035		−0.036	0.066		
1961	0.035	0.931	−0.007	0.025	−0.006	0.204
1962	0.032	0.265	0.005	0.012	0.001	0.103
1963	0.032	−0.102	0.021	0.002	−0.002	0.074
1964	0.032	−0.326	0.032	−0.010	−0.010	0.059
1965	0.033	−0.475	0.052	−0.024	−0.025	0.051
1966	0.038	−0.577	0.109	−0.058	−0.063	0.047
1967	0.039	−0.663	0.131	−0.074	−0.087	0.047
1968	0.044	−0.704	0.192	−0.112	−0.135	0.046
1969	0.057	−0.731	0.262	−0.155	−0.191	0.046
1970	0.063	−0.762	0.286	−0.169	−0.218	0.047
1971	0.055	−0.782	0.223	−0.128	−0.175	0.050
1972	0.053	−0.775	0.159	−0.091	−0.123	0.050
1973	0.052	−0.742	0.302	−0.175	−0.224	0.050
1974	0.062	−0.720	0.532	−0.303	−0.383	0.052
1975	0.070	−0.701	0.431	−0.228	−0.303	0.057
1976	0.066	−0.666	0.257	−0.126	−0.171	0.062
1977	0.057	−0.625	0.278	−0.139	−0.174	0.061
1978	0.060	−0.564	0.313	−0.157	−0.177	0.062
1979	0.065	−0.503	0.446	−0.214	−0.224	0.065
1980	0.086	−0.442	0.514	−0.224	−0.227	0.070
1981	0.114	−0.375	0.377	−0.149	−0.141	0.076
1982	0.116	−0.353	0.215	−0.084	−0.076	0.077
1983	0.095	−0.332	0.106	−0.040	−0.035	0.079
1984	0.101	−0.270	0.132	−0.050	−0.036	0.079
1985	0.091	−0.242	0.101	−0.034	−0.024	0.084
1986	0.073	−0.227	0.048	−0.015	−0.011	0.088
1987	0.077	−0.205	0.087	−0.025	−0.018	0.091
1988	0.077	−0.167	0.097	−0.026	−0.016	0.093
1989	0.072	−0.127	0.111	−0.027	−0.014	0.097
1990	0.073	−0.099	0.121	−0.024	−0.012	0.103
1991	0.069	−0.098	0.090	−0.013	−0.009	0.109
1992	0.064	−0.068	0.062	−0.005	−0.004	0.118
1993	0.056	−0.063	0.060	−0.003	−0.004	0.122
1994	0.062	−0.042	0.050	−0.002	−0.002	0.124

(continued)

Table 10.1 (continued)

Year	π	$\log(Y/\overline{Y})$	$P\overline{G}/\overline{B}$	$P(G-\overline{G})/\overline{B}$	$P\overline{G}*\log(Y/\overline{Y})/\overline{B}$	$G/\overline{Y}$
1995	0.060	–0.019	0.055	0.000	–0.001	0.130
1996	0.058	0.011	0.056	0.000	0.001	0.130
1997	0.055	0.042	0.043	0.001	0.002	0.131
1998	0.051	0.087	0.029	0.001	0.003	0.133
1999	0.054	0.111	0.040	0.003	0.004	0.139
2000	0.057	0.163	0.059	0.008	0.010	0.148
2001	0.052	0.172	0.048	0.010	0.008	0.158
2002	0.050	0.166	0.025	0.007	0.004	0.167
2003	0.047	0.173	0.034	0.011	0.006	0.173
2004	0.047	0.209	0.037	0.013	0.008	0.174
2005	0.044	0.241	0.045	0.017	0.011	0.179
2006	0.044	0.287	0.041	0.017	0.012	0.184

Table 10.2 Summary statistics of 50-state aggregate test

Variables	N	Mean	SD	Min	Max
π	46	0.061	0.020	0.032	0.116
$\log(Y/\overline{Y})$	46	–0.232	0.381	–0.782	0.931
$P\overline{G}/\overline{B}$	46	0.146	0.141	–0.007	0.532
$P(G-\overline{G})/\overline{B}$	46	–0.060	0.082	–0.303	0.025
$P\overline{G}*\log(Y/\overline{Y})/\overline{B}$	46	–0.071	0.099	–0.383	0.012
$G/\overline{Y}$	46	0.098	0.045	0.046	0.204

This finding is contrary to Barro's with regard to the federal government's use of debt that is countercyclical. The two special period dummies are not significant, implying that their impacts are not statistically different from zero.

10.4.2 Test 2: Did Individual State Debt Use Go Countercyclical?

Next I broke the country into the eight Census regions, summed up the variables of states into each region's total, and ran the same regression. To do so is to reveal any regional patterns that might have been concealed by the national features. Results of the full model specification for each region are shown in Table 10.3, Panel B. The results show much variation across the eight regions. The constant, α_0, is statistically significant in only three regions: the Great Lakes and the Southeast show a growth rate of 5–6% while the Rocky Mountains had an 18% growth. The expected return on debt, α_1, is significant only for New England and Mid-Atlantic, though at the expected magnitude of about 1%. Coefficients α_2 and

Table 10.3 Results of time-series test of debt use cyclicality

	α_0		α_1		α_2		α_3							
	Constant		π (20BBI)		P(G-Gbar)/Bbar		[PGbar*log(Y/Ybar)]/ Bbar		1950–1975 dummy		1973–1982 dummy		R^2	N
Panel A														
50-state	*0.0491******	(0.017)	0.0047	(0.0029)	0.00409	(0.0044)	–0.00429	(0.0035)					0.179	46
Aggregate	*0.0481****	(0.018)	0.0049	(0.0030)	0.00385	(0.0045)	–0.00425	(0.0036)			–0.00518	(0.0174)	0.181	46
	*0.0369**	(0.021)	*0.00637**	(0.0033)	0.00335	(0.0044)	–0.00335	(0.0037)	0.0139	(0.0134)			0.200	46
	*0.0365**	(0.021)	*0.00641**	(0.0034)	0.00345	(0.0045)	–0.00328	(0.0037)	0.0152	(0.0152)	0.00369	(0.0195)	0.201	46
Panel B: States in Census region aggregates														
New England	0.0130	(0.0328)	*0.0102****	(0.0051)	0.00158	(0.0081)	–0.00215	(0.0070)	0.00963	(0.0232)	–0.00305	(0.0330)	0.159	47
Mid-Atlantic	0.0212	(0.0275)	*0.00733**	(0.0043)	*0.0173******	(0.00614)	*–0.0213******	(0.00611)	0.00837	(0.0203)	*–0.0554****	(0.0254)	0.374	47
Great Lakes	*0.0555****	(0.0244)	0.00460	(0.00371)	0.00228	(0.00310)	–0.00333	(0.00319)	–0.0219	(0.0190)	0.00366	(0.0220)	0.226	48
Plains	0.0585	(0.0377)	0.00401	(0.00567)	0.00107	(0.00294)	–0.00125	(0.00267)	–0.0290	(0.0288)	*0.0745****	(0.0327)	0.360	47
Far West	0.0417	(0.0313)	0.00581	(0.00488)	–0.00233	(0.00525)	0.00387	(0.00426)	*0.0438**	(0.0235)	*0.0597**	(0.0343)	0.133	46
Rocky Mountains	*0.180******	(0.0600)	–0.0124	(0.00900)	*–0.0212******	(0.00632)	*0.0157******	(0.00436)	0.00229	(0.0448)	0.0751	(0.0734)	0.455	45
Southwest	0.0805	(0.0786)	0.000940	(0.0125)	–0.00635	(0.00662)	0.00398	(0.00487)	0.0374	(0.0553)	–0.0972	(0.0844)	0.066	45
Southeast	*0.0535**	(0.0270)	0.00319	(0.00428)	–0.00126	(0.00388)	0.00203	(0.00293)	*0.0410****	(0.0194)	*0.0436**	(0.0257)	0.152	46
Panel C: Results of time-series test by state														
Alabama	*0.0345******	(0.00936)	4.78e-05	(0.0113)	0.00707	(0.00931)	*0.155******	(0.0421)	*0.124**	(0.0631)	*–0.159****	(0.0597)	0.350	46
Alaska	*0.0215****	(0.00997)	*0.0214******	(0.00582)	–0.0114	(0.00713)	*0.214******	(0.0607)	*0.216******	(0.0521)	–0.107	(0.0670)	0.588	43
Arizona	*0.0410****	(0.0182)	–0.00191	(0.00156)	*0.00238**	(0.00128)	*0.185****	(0.0867)	0.234	(0.160)	–0.104	(0.120)	0.269	44
Arkansas	0.00528	(0.00722)	*–0.0102******	(0.00305)	*0.00871******	(0.00256)	–0.0282	(0.0358)	–0.00199	(0.0590)	0.0467	(0.0474)	0.548	46
California	0.00552	(0.00717)	–0.00460	(0.00536)	0.00549	(0.00469)	0.0241	(0.0303)	–0.000160	(0.0547)	0.0623	(0.0446)	0.160	46
Colorado	–0.0115	(0.0138)	–0.00451	(0.00600)	0.00353	(0.00373)	–0.0864	(0.0645)	0.145	(0.113)	*0.199****	(0.0912)	0.235	45
Connecticut	0.0144	(0.00861)	0.00200	(0.0147)	–0.00670	(0.0147)	0.0233	(0.0368)	–0.0656	(0.0588)	–0.0231	(0.0550)	0.109	47
Delaware	0.00914	(0.0118)	–0.0412	(0.0363)	0.0421	(0.0329)	0.0666	(0.0478)	0.0935	(0.0781)	–0.0126	(0.0739)	0.134	46
D.C.	–0.0131	(0.0290)	0.00250	(0.00196)	*–0.00762****	(0.00164)	0.0772	(0.0620)	0.0813	(0.0966)	0.109	(0.156)	0.883	27

Florida	0.00864	(0.0101)	0.00395	(0.00467)	−0.000918	(0.00329)	0.0619	(0.0428)	0.0805	(0.0603)	0.0465	(0.0621)	0.084	45
Georgia	0.0124	(0.0103)	0.00323	(0.00838)	0.00148	(0.00631)	*0.0769***	(0.0374)	0.0965	(0.0665)	0.0118	(0.0617)	0.180	45
Hawaii	0.0119	(0.00929)	0.0131	(0.0174)	−0.0210	(0.0179)	0.0607	(0.0444)	−0.0354	(0.0529)	−0.0280	(0.0587)	0.283	44
Idaho	−0.00969	(0.0163)	−0.00516	(0.00330)	0.00451	(0.00269)	0.0588	(0.0902)	*0.190***	(0.0915)	0.160	(0.109)	0.181	46
Illinois	−0.00671	(0.00705)	−0.000628	(0.00646)	−0.000927	(0.00622)	−0.0363	(0.0356)	0.0594	(0.0388)	*0.123***	(0.0466)	0.169	48
Indiana	*0.0269****	(0.00833)	−0.000957	(0.00432)	0.00280	(0.00520)	−0.00194	(0.0407)	−0.0230	(0.0675)	−0.0528	(0.0551)	0.331	48
Iowa	−0.00169	(0.0185)	−0.00259	(0.00562)	0.00303	(0.00547)	−0.0186	(0.0891)	0.0354	(0.125)	0.132	(0.124)	0.027	48
Kansas	−0.0189	(0.0208)	0.0128	(0.00815)	−0.0126	(0.00777)	*−0.183***	(0.0743)	0.0221	(0.0963)	*0.254***	(0.122)	0.217	47
Kentucky	−0.00140	(0.0148)	−0.00103	(0.00828)	*0.0170**	(0.00981)	*0.180***	(0.0732)	0.0743	(0.0910)	0.0767	(0.0968)	0.224	47
Louisiana	0.0136	(0.00969)	−0.0148	(0.0145)	0.0146	(0.0114)	0.0821	(0.0496)	0.0545	(0.0602)	−0.0336	(0.0645)	0.177	47
Maine	*0.0150**	(0.00750)	*0.0136**	(0.00730)	*−0.0131***	(0.00627)	−0.00172	(0.0367)	−0.00755	(0.0411)	−0.0230	(0.0486)	0.213	47
Maryland	0.000118	(0.00778)	0.0104	(0.0173)	−0.00821	(0.0133)	0.0154	(0.0363)	0.0328	(0.0474)	0.0580	(0.0490)	0.113	46
Massachusetts	*0.0130**	(0.00739)	*0.0236**	(0.0134)	−0.0169	(0.0114)	0.00576	(0.0338)	0.00523	(0.0472)	0.00810	(0.0478)	0.137	47
Michigan	*0.0134***	(0.00560)	*0.00876***	(0.00409)	*−0.00744**	(0.00395)	−0.0140	(0.0278)	0.0218	(0.0346)	0.00652	(0.0371)	0.269	48
Minnesota	0.000894	(0.00907)	0.00136	(0.00825)	−0.00376	(0.00673)	−0.0280	(0.0437)	0.0142	(0.0465)	0.0450	(0.0587)	0.252	46
Mississippi	0.00901	(0.0197)	0.0194	(0.0145)	−0.0142	(0.0120)	−0.0105	(0.0773)	−0.000111	(0.0944)	0.0474	(0.115)	0.077	46
Missouri	*0.0111***	(0.00546)	*−0.00297**	(0.00164)	*0.00361***	(0.00149)	0.0313	(0.0294)	*0.203****	(0.0322)	0.0165	(0.0366)	0.718	47
Montana	0.0121	(0.0144)	−0.00125	(0.00830)	0.00309	(0.00769)	−0.0301	(0.0642)	0.0951	(0.105)	0.0380	(0.0961)	0.143	48
Nebraska	*0.0532***	(0.0241)	0.00153	(0.00333)	−0.00181	(0.00361)	0.108	(0.0989)	−0.0950	(0.170)	−0.237	(0.161)	0.108	47
Nevada	−0.0174	(0.0217)	*−0.0410****	(0.0129)	*0.0234****	(0.00706)	0.0807	(0.119)	0.145	(0.139)	0.195	(0.147)	0.320	43
New Hampshire	0.00369	(0.00998)	−0.0216	(0.0166)	0.0125	(0.00960)	−0.0235	(0.0462)	0.0957	(0.0571)	0.0499	(0.0636)	0.328	45
New Jersey	*0.0142***	(0.00654)	−0.000262	(0.00583)	−0.00761	(0.00612)	−0.0106	(0.0326)	*−0.0715**	(0.0402)	−0.0216	(0.0433)	0.353	47
New Mexico	*−0.0228**	(0.0124)	−0.0111	(0.00777)	0.00998	(0.00599)	0.0135	(0.0687)	0.147	(0.0927)	*0.233****	(0.0824)	0.239	46
New York	0.00801	(0.00591)	*0.0209****	(0.00731)	*−0.0244****	(0.00802)	0.0274	(0.0283)	−0.0437	(0.0354)	0.0155	(0.0383)	0.325	48
North Carolina	−0.000716	(0.0137)	0.00355	(0.00815)	−0.00332	(0.00607)	−0.0768	(0.0558)	−0.0242	(0.0925)	0.113	(0.0845)	0.062	45
North Dakota	0.0197	(0.0145)	0.00100	(0.00144)	*−0.00185**	(0.000977)	−0.0111	(0.0684)	0.0535	(0.0787)	−0.0437	(0.0973)	0.171	49
Ohio	*0.0128***	(0.00518)	0.000835	(0.00457)	−0.00559	(0.00559)	−0.0154	(0.0272)	*−0.0766***	(0.0321)	−0.0130	(0.0338)	0.328	48

(continued)

Table 10.3 (continued)

	α_0		α_1		α_2		α_3							
	Constant		π (20BBI)		P(G-Gbar)/Bbar		[PGbar*log(Y/Ybar)]/ Bbar		1950–1975 dummy		1973–1982 dummy		R^2	N
Oklahoma	−0.0135	(0.0179)	*−0.0452***	(0.0198)	*0.0315**	(0.0169)	0.0486	(0.0819)	*−0.251***	(0.123)	0.151	(0.116)	0.139	47
Oregon	−0.00323	(0.00783)	*0.0363***	(0.0154)	*−0.0317***	(0.0128)	−0.0109	(0.0435)	*0.171****	(0.0386)	0.0538	(0.0517)	0.510	46
Pennsylvania	−0.00141	(0.00452)	*0.0121****	(0.00434)	*−0.0189****	(0.00465)	−0.0298	(0.0196)	*−0.110****	(0.0246)	*0.0814****	(0.0281)	0.439	48
Rhode Island	−0.00431	(0.00828)	*−0.0276***	(0.0127)	*0.0285***	(0.0114)	0.0423	(0.0386)	*0.166****	(0.0554)	0.0886	(0.0548)	0.286	47
South Carolina	0.00234	(0.0114)	0.00582	(0.0128)	−0.00722	(0.0104)	−0.0510	(0.0575)	0.0630	(0.0544)	0.0491	(0.0726)	0.222	46
South Dakota	*−0.0286**	(0.0156)	0.00214	(0.00384)	−0.00116	(0.00383)	−0.00757	(0.0880)	*0.269****	(0.0708)	*0.258***	(0.105)	0.288	47
Tennessee	−0.00237	(0.00883)	−0.000952	(0.00565)	0.000195	(0.00446)	0.0605	(0.0413)	0.0216	(0.0428)	0.0585	(0.0563)	0.226	46
Texas	0.0133	(0.0182)	0.000483	(0.00739)	−0.000827	(0.00567)	0.0484	(0.0778)	−0.0762	(0.105)	0.00483	(0.113)	0.048	45
Utah	−0.0234	(0.0226)	−0.0191	(0.0133)	0.0149	(0.00917)	0.128	(0.118)	0.184	(0.156)	0.242	(0.149)	0.145	45
Vermont	0.00421	(0.00912)	0.00108	(0.0146)	−0.0125	(0.0122)	0.0455	(0.0446)	*−0.138****	(0.0490)	0.0342	(0.0574)	0.373	46
Virginia	−0.00594	(0.00886)	−0.00608	(0.00603)	0.00290	(0.00412)	−0.0542	(0.0438)	0.0752	(0.0481)	0.110*	(0.0572)	0.358	46
Washington	*0.0201****	(0.00594)	0.00590	(0.00480)	−0.00247	(0.00374)	0.0446	(0.0305)	0.0497	(0.0423)	−0.0395	(0.0389)	0.250	45
West Virginia	*−0.0168***	(0.00728)	−0.00588	(0.00503)	−0.00635	(0.00466)	*−0.0624**	(0.0356)	0.00591	(0.0342)	*0.148****	(0.0480)	0.256	49
Wisconsin	−0.00478	(0.00839)	*0.00340***	(0.00140)	0.00235	(0.00204)	*0.156****	(0.0466)	*0.0942***	(0.0455)	*0.130***	(0.0558)	0.419	47
Wyoming	−0.00786	(0.0216)	0.00727*	(0.00360)	−0.00405	(0.00379)	0.110	(0.120)	*0.371****	(0.125)	0.0775	(0.145)	0.241	47

Significance levels: *10%; **5%; ***1%.

α_3 are significant at the 1% level for only the Mid-Atlantic and the Rocky Mountains regions with opposite signs; so we cannot make much out of this result. The high growth rate dummy (1950–1975) is significant only for the Far West and the Southeast regions at the magnitude of about 4%. The high inflation dummy for 1973–1982 is significant for four regions. Three of them are as expected, higher inflation pushes up borrowing at a range from 4.4% to 7.5%; but one is negative, showing variation. In summary, checking the census regions does not show consistent patterns of debt use. Probably debt use is not necessarily of any regional pattern either.

I made the extra step of checking on each state in this time-series setup. The full model results are shown in Table 10.3, Panel C. Here we can observe much more heterogeneity. The growth rate (constant) has some in the negative. The 20BBI ranges from less than 1% to 4.5%, indicating that the national level response of debt use to the state level is not relevant at all; each state has its own, different set of considerations in the consideration of debt issue. The other variables also display opposite signs and very different range of response.

Thus, we can safely conclude that state governments, whether in total aggregate, by Census region groups or by individual entity, have not necessarily considered the phases of the business cycle in their issuance of debt. The states are subject to a different set of fiscal and budgetary institutions than the federal level. To further the exploration, I resort to the panel data methods.

10.4.3 Test 3: Determinants of State Debt Use

Now I refine the test to examine the determinants of states' use of debt over the economic cycle in a panel setting. The dependent variable is narrowed to total long-term debt outstanding by the end of fiscal year, which is total debt outstanding without short-term use (maturity within 12 months); this measure better fits the proposition of debt financing for countercyclical purposes.

Explanatory variables are carefully chosen, based on previous literature, to be the causal factors that have been widely used in existing studies. These fall into five groups. *Demographics* include the proportions of population aged 65 and over and that in school age, assuming most of them attend public K-12 schools. *State politics* is proxied with the Berry et al. (2010) liberal citizen ideology index 1960–2008. I use four variables to capture effects of *state economy and finance*; they are personal income, unemployment rate, federal intergovernmental transfer to states, and budget balance as percent of expenditure. I control for two *fiscal and budgetary institutions* that are widely believed to affect state use of debt: One is the budget stabilization fund (dummy and level in alternate model specifications); the other is the presence of tax-expenditure limitations (as two binaries). For the *borrowing cost* indicator, I choose not to use state bond rating due to technical reasons that Clingermayer and Wood (1995) have elaborated on.[5] As stated in the previous

[5] Clingermayer and Wood (1995, note 7) provide detailed reasons of not using bond ratings.

Table 10.4 Summary statistics of variables in the panel data test

Variables	N	Mean	SD	Min	Max
ln(debt)	1,850	0.042	0.124	–0.517	1.417
ln(issued)	1,802	0.062	0.962	–9.161	8.614
ln(ffc)	1,050	0.023	1.208	–7.359	7.097
ln(ng)	1,642	0.066	1.118	–7.821	8.125
Ratio 12k	1,850	27.751	3.775	12.560	40.040
Ratio 65+	1,850	11.694	2.289	2.250	18.500
Liberal citizen ideology	1,850	47.342	15.748	7.042	95.972
ln(income)	1,850	10.173	0.215	9.488	10.819
Unemployment rate	1,850	5.932	2.575	2.000	74.000
ln(fed transfer)	1,850	6.763	0.399	5.731	8.252
fund balance %	1,850	7.649	10.615	–39.207	181.586
Stabilization fund (dummy)	1,850	0.468	0.499	0	1
Revenue limit (dummy)	1,850	0.208	0.406	0	1
Expenditure limit (dummy)	1,850	0.278	0.448	0	1
Bond Buyer Index	1,850	6.617	1.792	4.400	11.640
ln(bsf level)	732	10.565	1.722	–0.501	15.841

section, I believe the Bond Buyer's 20 index is among the best composite indicator: It is inflation-adjusted and calculated from a basket of issues with different bond ratings (grades) and of varying maturities. As such, this index is exogenous to any potential strategic behavior by the states and can well capture any minute contemporaneous effects thereof.

The variables are measured in the following fashion. The dependent variable still takes the growth rate form, as in the previous test, $\log(B_{it} / B_{it-1})$. To further remove potential endogeneity and handle nonstationarity, I convert all level variables into per capita terms, then turn them into real terms using either the IPD (for debt, federal transfer, and budget balance) or the CPI (for personal income); finally, take the natural log of them. The final measure also facilitates interpretation of results as a percent-to-percent relationship. Budget balance is calculated as percent of previous year balance against current year expenditure. Data availability reduces the sample period by 20 years to 1970. Summary statistics are provided in Table 10.4. I believe this parsimonious approach toward variable selection can well handle multicollinearity and endogeneity.

Because each state's revenue and expenditure limit dummies do not change from year to year, nor does the BSF binary once it has been instituted, and the 20 bond buyer index is the same each year for all states, the model with these variables are run with the random effects estimator. The estimation equation is

$$Debt\,growth = f\left(\text{demographics, ideology, economy, institutions, bondindex}\right).$$

Then I replace the BSF dummy with its level (in real per capita log form; sample period shrinks to 1979–2006), drop the revenue and expenditure dummies as well as

Table 10.5 Results of panel data tests. DV is the annual growth rate of long-term debt

Fixed effects	No.		State		State and year	
Sample years	1970–2006	1970–2006	1970–2006	1979–2006	1970–2006	1979–2006
	(1)	(2)	(3)	(4)	(5)	(6)
Ratio 12k	−0.00136	−0.00150	-0.00905^{***}	−3.60e-05	−0.00117	−0.00256
	(0.00165)	(0.00164)	(0.00228)	(0.00385)	(0.00289)	(0.00398)
Ratio 65+	−0.00307	-0.00369^{*}	-0.0208^{***}	−0.00330	-0.0141^{***}	−0.00691
	(0.00210)	(0.00204)	(0.00473)	(0.00703)	(0.00544)	(0.00810)
Liberal citizen ideology	-0.000459^{*}	−0.000413	-0.000830^{**}	-0.00101^{**}	4.15e-05	-0.00123^{**}
	(0.000251)	(0.000256)	(0.000397)	(0.000499)	(0.000428)	(0.000595)
ln(income)	0.0390^{*}	0.0367	0.0457	0.153^{**}	0.108^{*}	−0.0877
	(0.0224)	(0.0224)	(0.0469)	(0.0747)	(0.0626)	(0.117)
Unemployment rate	0.000945	0.000771	0.00276^{**}	0.0104^{***}	−0.000240	0.00648^{*}
	(0.00140)	(0.00132)	(0.00137)	(0.00327)	(0.00150)	(0.00367)
ln(fed transfer)	-0.0181^{*}	-0.0184^{*}	-0.0519^{***}	-0.0631^{**}	0.00710	0.0515
	(0.0104)	(0.0103)	(0.0179)	(0.0262)	(0.0239)	(0.0372)
Fund balance %	−1.01e-06	−1.64e-05	−0.000163	0.000238	−0.000123	0.000114
	(0.000373)	(0.000378)	(0.000309)	(0.000383)	(0.000353)	(0.000496)
Stabilization fund (dummy)	0.00182	0.00125				
	(0.00860)	(0.00839)				
ln(bsf level)				−0.00129		−0.00303
				(0.00252)		(0.00248)
Revenue limit (dummy)		0.0128				
		(0.00833)				
Expenditure limit (dummy)	-0.0175^{*}	-0.0197^{**}				
	(0.00916)	(0.00850)				
Bond buyer index	0.00557^{**}	0.00567^{**}				
	(0.00265)	(0.00265)				
Constant	−0.176	−0.143	0.446	−1.064	−0.976	0.766
	(0.272)	(0.274)	(0.465)	(0.721)	(0.692)	(1.230)
Observations	1,850	1,850	1,850	732	1,850	732
R-squared			0.028	0.034	0.127	0.167
Number of id	50	50	50	46	50	46

Robust standard errors in *parentheses*
$^{***}p<0.01$; $^{**}p<0.05$; $^{*}p<0.1$

the bond buyer index, and run the model with fixed-effects estimator, first with state effects only, then with both state- and year-fixed effects. The estimation equation is

$$Debt\,growth = f\left(\text{demographics, ideology, economyn, bsf}\right),$$

$$i = 1 \text{ to } 50 \text{ and } t = 1970 \text{ to } 2006$$

Results of the random effects model, state-fixed effects model, and the state- and year-fixed effects model are reported in Table 10.5, side by side for clearer comparison. The sample period shrinks to 1979–2006 when the balance level of budget stabilization fund is used to replace the BSF dummy.

Of demographics, both the ratio of school age children and the ratio of seniors in state population present a negative effect. School age population is statistically significant only in the state-fixed effects model; each percent increase of the young reduces debt growth rate by about 1%. Senior population is statistically significant in all three model specifications; each percent increase in this ratio reduces debt growth by 1–2% in the fixed-effects models but only 0.4% in the random effects model. These are counter intuitive: In the literature these two variables represent high demands for public services; they are both expected to add to debt.

The index of liberal citizen ideology also shows a negative relationship with debt growth: Each 10 points increase on this index reduces debt growth by about 1% in the fixed-effects models; the magnitude is slashed by half in the random effects model. Personal income shows a strong positive correlation with debt use, which is in accord with existing literature and intuition: 1% increase of income can push up debt growth by 11–15% by the fixed-effects models; in other words, a $1,000 increase in per capita income can raise borrowing by $110–$150. Again, the magnitude is much smaller in the random effects model.

Unemployment rate, as indicator of the economic cycle, is as expected positively related to debt growth. It is significant only in the fixed-effects models, with marginal magnitude: Each percentage point increase of unemployment pushes up state debt growth by a mere 0.3–1%. Put in another way, states do not tend to respond to economic downturns with more borrowing; this corresponds to my preliminary findings from test one discussed above.

Federal transfers do relieve pressure on states to borrow; the result is statistically significant in the random and the state-fixed effects model: Each percent increase of federal transfer reduces state debt growth by a range of 2–6%. This result is in agreement with Barro's 1979 finding that the federal government does tend to incur deficits in recession years. It is not significant in the year-fixed effects model: Once the year dummies are included in the model, the effects are caught up by the year dummies. State budget balance is not statistically different from zero in any of the models.

Of the budgetary and fiscal institutions, the budget stabilization fund is not significant whether as a dummy or in level, nor is the revenue limitation. Expenditure limitation does show a significant, negative effect: Adoption of this clause in the state finance law reduces debt growth by close to 2%. On the effects of borrowing costs, the bond buyer index presents a significant and positive point estimate of 0.6%; that is, each percentage point increase in the borrowing cost increases borrowing by about a little over half a percent. This is on the one hand partial confirmation of the Barro (1979) proposition and the finding in the previous section; it is on the other hand indication that states do borrow less when the cost soars. This finding fits in well with the direction of this study's proposition countercyclical use.

The state-fixed effects model generates some interesting findings but the model's explanatory power is low, with R-squared at 0.3. That of the state- and year-fixed effects model is 0.13 and 0.17, indicating that year effects are a factor to consider. Checking the coefficients on the year dummies, I find the following worth of attention. The base year used for comparison (default) is 2005, the economically best year in the boom prior to the most recent recession. Years 1976–1986 were a long stream of high growth rate in debt use, which probably reflects the high inflation in that period, plus potential effects from the recessions of 1975, 1980, and 1982. Years 1991 and 1992 also each saw an increase of 8%, which was most probably also a recession effect; so were years 2001 and 2002. Meanwhile, some boom years also posted strong positive growth against the base year; they are 1971 and 1989. Years 1996 and 1998 post 5% and 7% growth, respectively; years 2000 and 2004 were 4.5% and 5%. This irregularity points again to the fact that states do not necessarily follow any cyclical pattern in issuing long-term debt.

To go further along this test, I add three narrower dependent variables; they are (1) total long-term debt issues each year, (2) total full faith and credit (FFC) long-term debt issues each year, and (3) total nonguaranteed long-term debt issues each year. They are configurated also as growth rate; then I run the same random effects and state-fixed effects models, with the same specifications as above except that the revenue limitation is dropped—it is not significant in any of the specifications. The sample size is smaller than for the previous tests due to nonuse of these debts by some states or absence of data thereof, but the sample size and sample years remain representative and randomly distributed and selected. The results are shown in Table 10.6.

Among the variables that generate statistically significant coefficients, unemployment rate stands out to provide new and important information. It is positive and substantially larger, especially with state-fixed effects. For each percentage point increase of unemployment, total long-term issue increases on average by 7% (46 state sample); so does nonguaranteed debt (43 state sample); GO (FFC) debt new issue increases by 14.5% (35 state sample), which is clear indication that at least in the three recent full economic cycles (1979–2006), states did use long-term debt as a countercyclical fiscal policy tool. This result is different from that from the time-series test; it confirms the weak inclination that I got from the panel test on total long-term debt outstanding. Teasing out accumulated debt and focusing on new issues, I have been able to capture a more accurate estimate of the research question. The result is of course much smaller than the full sample.

Expenditure limit remains statistically significant, for total new issues and nonguaranteed new issues, and negative, confirming previous results but the magnitude of the estimate doubles from 1.75–2.0% to 3.5–4%, which further illustrates the impact of this variable. Worth mentioning is that though it remains negative for FFC new issues, it is not statistically significant, suggesting that the impact of this limitation article may lose its punch for FFC debt. Thus, the statistically insignificant estimate may become "significant" by lending more power to the countercyclical use of long-term FFC debt.

Also worth mentioning is that federal transfer remains significant and negative for FFC in the random effects model, as in previous test (Table 10.5, columns 1 and 2) but its magnitude jumps from less than 2% to 10%. Placing it into the context of a downturn economy, then the complimentary or crowding-out effect of federal transfers becomes apparent. Besides, the bond buyer index also corresponds with results in the time-series and panel tests with an expected negative sign. Its magnitude also jumps from less than 1% to over 3%, indicating that states care very much for the cost of borrowing: In the same model, one percentage point increase in the unemployment rate pushes up FFC new issues by 1.7%, whereas one percentage point increase of the bond buyer index can reduce FFC

Table 10.6 Determinants of long-term debt issues. DVs are growth rate of long-term debt issued each year

DV	Total		FFC		Nonguaranteed	
Fixed effects	No.	State	No.	State	No.	State
Sample years	1970–2006	1979–2006	1970–2006	1979–2006	1970–2006	1979–2006
Ratio12k	–0.00386	0.0388	–0.00906	–0.00246	–0.00915	0.0409
	(0.00612)	(0.0327)	(0.0120)	(0.102)	(0.00643)	(0.0472)
Ratio 65+	–0.00245	0.0223	–0.0161	0.0623	–0.00287	–0.0174
	(0.00667)	(0.0596)	(0.0177)	(0.171)	(0.00878)	(0.0760)
Liberal citizen ideology	–0.00150	–0.000664	0.000225	–0.00466	–0.00172	–0.00390
	(0.000960)	(0.00423)	(0.00125)	(0.0120)	(0.00117)	(0.00507)
ln(income)	–0.0520	0.566	–0.00519	1.718	–0.0545	0.871
	(0.0775)	(0.634)	(0.170)	(1.656)	(0.0899)	(0.805)
Unemployment rate	0.00993	*0.0705***	*0.0171**	*0.145**	0.00853	*0.0684***
	(0.0104)	(0.0277)	(0.00944)	(0.0762)	(0.0122)	(0.0332)
ln(fed transfer)	–0.0494	0.0769	*–0.102**	–0.261	–0.0286	0.0733
	(0.0334)	(0.222)	(0.0562)	(0.574)	(0.0396)	(0.272)
Budget balance	–0.000249	0.00227	–5.89e-05	0.00215	0.000517	0.00525
	(0.00128)	(0.00325)	(0.00164)	(0.00872)	(0.00175)	(0.00407)
BSF dummy	–0.00121		*0.0951**		–0.0126	
	(0.0210)		(0.0569)		(0.0311)	
Expenditure limit	*–0.0350**		–0.0467		*–0.0402**	
	(0.0190)		(0.0428)		(0.0240)	
Bond buyer index	–0.0122		*–0.0343***		–0.00604	
	(0.0109)		(0.0140)		(0.0126)	
ln(BSF level)		–0.00768		0.0217		–0.0247
		(0.0214)		(0.0546)		(0.0257)
Constant	1.166	–7.880	1.277	–17.41	1.184	–10.24
	(1.023)	(6.115)	(2.162)	(16.22)	(1.113)	(7.979)
Observations	1,802	732	1,050	414	1,642	643
R-squared		0.014		0.011		0.014
Number of id	50	46	43	35	50	43

Robust standard errors in *parentheses*

***$p<0.01$; **$p<0.05$; *$p<0.1$

new issues by 3.4%, offsetting the former effect by 100%. Finally, interesting is the statistically significant (at 10% level) and positive coefficient of the stabilization fund dummy. It is large at 9.5%: With a stabilization fund adopted, a state may issue more FFC debts by almost 10%. It points to a potential, indirect link of a state's fiscal capacity that is boosted by adopting BSF to improved credit rating, which reduces borrowing cost.

10.4.4 Empirical Evidence in the Literature

How do my results compare against empirical results in the existing literature? In the following I select some relevant studies for comparison and contrast. Bahl and Duncombe (1993) examine the determinants of state indebtedness in a 3-year window (1988–1990). Their dependent variable is debt ratio against state total personal income; their independent variables include population and income differences for public service demand, per capita spending by category and state debt limitations as proxy for expansionary government preferences, percent of public and private revenue bonds in total debt, and historic debt burden from 1977. They found positive effects on debt ratio from population size and density, historic debt level, school enrollment, and current government expenditure; they did not check cyclical patterns of debt. They found negative effect on debt ratio from private purpose debt and debt limit; the latter shares some connection with my finding of negative effects from expenditure limitations.

Temple (1994) estimates the effects of public service demand and optimal financing mix (between taxes and debt) on the use of debt by states. She assumes that if policy makers choose the debt level that minimizes cost to taxpayers, the optimal debt-cash ratio equals marginal costs of debt and tax mix. Among her main findings, two are relevant to mine. Higher personal income pushes up demand for capital projects, leading to more debt issue and hence higher share of debt; my finding on personal income's positive effect on debt agrees with this result of hers. Sun Belt states tend to use more tax financing (less debt) than states in other regions of the country, which is in agreement with my finding in test 1 on the eight Census regions.

Clingermayer and Wood (1995) use a panel (48 continental states, years 1961–1989) and the pooled-data, first-difference approach to examine debt use by the states. Under economic factors, they include income, own-source state and local revenue, federal transfer, bond buyer index, and a dummy for the 1986 tax reform. Their political and institutional controls include federal debt, political liberalism (constant across states each year), electoral competition, divided government, fiscal decentralization (ratio of state revenue to total state-local revenue), tax and expenditure limitation dummy, and a dummy for debt limit in place. They found, among those relevant to this study, liberalism and electoral completion increase the use of debt, which is contrary to my finding of the negative sign on the Berry et al. citizen liberalism ideology index. But probably we have covered different things and their sample period is shorter and earlier. They found positive association between tax and expenditure limitations and debt use; that is, the limitation actually crowded state spending to debt but was not effective in reducing either revenue or spending. This study uses two dummies (a measure sharper than theirs); tax limitation is not statistically significant and expenditure limitation exerts downward pressure on debt use. A possible explanation is again the sample period: Over time probably the limitation has become effective in reducing not only spending but also debt use. Their estimate of the bond buyer index is also significant and negative; my finding confirms that higher borrowing cost reduces debt.

Ellis and Schansberg (1999) use weighed debt measures (by population or state-local spending) in a panel (years 1966–1994, all 50 states) to check variation in long-term debt use with the one-way error component model, which is to subtract from each observation the 50-state mean of each variable in each year, which is effectively equal to including a set of state dummies in the regression; thus, their results may show resemblance with my state-fixed effects results (Table 10.5, columns 3 and 4). They found positive effects from young people on debt but negative effect from old people; we conflict on the former and agree on the latter. The difference is probably because debt for school construction was heavy in their sample years but not in mine. They found positive effect of income on changes in debt, which my result confirms.

Wassmer and Fisher (2011) use four rounds of Census data (1992 and 1997, 2002 and 2007) to identify the determinants of heterogeneity in states' use of debt. They found consistently positive effect of K-12 enrollment on state-local debt, contrary to my finding. But their debt is state-local aggregate; the fact that school districts now hold a larger share of total debt than before may explain this difference between us. They also found some evidence that state-local debt is substitute for federal aid (especially among localities), which my finding of the negative sign on federal transfer confirms. Besides, they found many state dummies are statistically significant, indicating that state-specific factors not picked up by independent variables are important. In this study, I found year dummies equally important, because state debt use is equally influenced by the macro economy. In this sense, the two studies complement on our results.

Cogan and Taylor (2010) check the implementation of the American Recovery and Reinvestment Act (ARRA, the 2009 stimulus package) to reexamine the multiplier of government purchases in countercyclical fiscal policy. They found that the multiplicand was only 2%: Infrastructure investment increase was made mainly by the federal government; states did not increase their share of investment. They received large federal grants but reduced borrowing. This result fully agrees with my finding in this study that there exists a substitution effect between state borrowing and federal transfer. Thus, this study has generated findings that confirm existing evidence on some aspects; some results are new and not reported in the literature. Some disagreements between my results and existing evidence may be explained with differences in measurement, sample years, and sample size.

10.5 Calibrations of New York State

In this section, I extend my proposition of countercyclical debt issue into application. I will calibrate state debt limits and their actual issue of long-term debt into a simulation exercise to generate a counterfactual: If states had followed the *optimal time path of debt issue*, that is, borrowing more in recession years for infrastructure and accelerating the retirement of these debts in boom years, could they have been better prepared for downturns? More specifically, the simulation may provide some clue as to how countercyclical debt policy may help an average state in mitigating the adverse impact of a recession on the margin. This exercise makes full technical sense: On one hand, results from tests 1 and 2 above show that states' use of long-term debt has been in general acyclical across six decades; on the other hand, I do have some evidence from test 3 that at least some states (70% of the sample) may have practiced countercyclical use of long-term debt, with both GO bonds and revenue bonds, more with GO than with revenue bonds, which offers some clue that it is politically acceptable and administratively doable. This exercise is no doubt timely as an applicability test.

The states are very diverse in their tradition, policy, and use of debt. A full simulation will have to go through each state, which is beyond the scope of this study. For practicality, I choose New York state, the oldest advanced economy and leader of innovation in financial management in public finance history of the country.

10.5.1 State Debt Limits

Of all the states, 48 have both a constitutional and a statutory debt limit; two (Connecticut and Vermont) have statutory but no constitutional debt limits (Bunch 1991). The sources of this variable are National Association of State Budget Officers Association (NASBO) *Budget Process in the States* series (1981, 1992, and 2008). These limits are among the commonly seen "debt burden measures" classified in the debt literature (Berne and Schramm 1986) and set within the professional benchmarks.

New York's policies are the following: The limit on annual debt service is 5% of the state's overall budget; the limit on authorized debt is 4% of total personal income. This limit of amount is below the 15% line for caution set by the Standard & Poor's.

Meanwhile, the state stipulates that its new debt must use level debt service for the useful life of the facilities to be constructed, which is equal to or shorter than 30 years. Berne and Schramm (1986) suggest 10–15 year as the acceptable range of maturity for outstanding long-term debt, to boost bond rating. Though both the state law and the professional opinion emphasize smoothing debt service, with strong efficiency consideration, New York's debt service window is twice as long as the one recommended. The difference, seemingly insignificant, can be substantial if we factor in cyclical rippling of debt service. The point is to balance the trade-off between efficiency and cyclical maneuvering of debt retirement for countercyclical operations.

10.5.2 Variables of Focus

I focus on long-term debt (LTD), which is the bulk of all debt and mainly for capital projects, especially infrastructure. Of long-term debt, I further focus on issues of full faith and credit (FFC, or GO bonds) rather than nonguaranteed (NG or revenue bonds) because FFC is subject to statutory debt limit and voter approval whereas NG is not—NG debt is usually for projects that will generate revenue and thus self-finance in the long run; in some cases states also use NG for private purposes.

I will check new issues of FFC and NG debts then the retirement of them. For this purpose, ratios are calculated for (a) total LTD outstanding against own-source revenue or debt limit, (b) total debt service (interest payment plus FFC debt retirement) against own-source revenue or against service limit, and (c) LTD retirement against total LTD outstanding of previous year.

10.5.3 Operationalization

To simulate the countercyclical operation of debt issuance and retirement as indicated in the model, I divide debt capacity into three regions—low, middle, and high of each state's total debt capacity or limit. The low region is the first quarter (0–25%) of the debt limit; it is the room for regular operation of debt use. The middle region is the two intermediate quarters (25–75%) of debt limit. The high region is the top quarter (75–100%) of debt limit; it is reserved mainly for long and deep recessions or extreme emergencies that cry for extra funding.

The countercyclical operation of debt issuance and retirement is designed to rise and fall mainly within the middle region under normal circumstances; in long periods of expansion, the lower region of outstanding debt can be further retired at a slower annual rate. Variation of debt use is supposed to occur over the economic cycle. Once a recession has been identified, the bust signal triggers on accelerated path of long-term debt for infrastructure, according to the pre-prepared capital budget that has listed shovel-ready projects. New debt can increase over a 1- or 2-year window to 75% of the debt capacity at the rate of 25% of capacity each year. This is the time when the interest rate is low; also by this time the state should have raised its credit rating by retiring previous debt thus having reserved extra debt capacity. If the recession is short, 1-year increased issuance will be adequate to address the need. If the recession is long, the 2-year window will help. In extreme cases, the remaining 25% (high region) of debt capacity will be utilized.

At the identification of recovery, debt issue for recession may continue because reversing the direction may take some time. This does not necessarily create any problem since more investment at the initial stage of recovery will be of extra help. Then with surpluses in tax revenue, retirement of debt will start at the pace of 10–12.5% of the debt capacity per year of the expansionary phase. At this speed of retirement over the average 4–6 year range of the boom, outstanding debt will abate to the 25% level of debt limit. So doing harvests the benefits of avoiding the high interest rates in the boom years thus reducing costs on borrowing, reserving debt capacity for the next round of recession, thereby raising the credit rating of the state.

The state of New York has long been a leader in financial management innovations; its fiscal and budgetary institutions are the most comprehensive among the states; and its use of debt has been "liberal," in recent decades, under strong electoral politics. I use the parameters of New York for calibration to showcase the possible (on-paper) effects of the proposed optimal path of debt issue and retirement. Results are shown in Table 10.7.

10.5.4 Simulation Results

The preliminary calibration shows that by following the proposed path of debt issue and retirement, New York could have obtained the counterfactual that may have been fiscally better than the actual policy outcome in the 1980s double-dip recession, the 1990 and 2001 recessions, as well as the Great Recession.

The actual use of the state's debt limit and debt service limit was both low, the former below 51% and the latter below 30% in most years. The proposed retirement path is moderately active but always stays within the limit, whereas the issue path is *actively bold* in order to take full advantage of the limit. Combined, the two sides work in a way that is exactly what countercyclical debt use means in this context. Thus, in boom years, more debt is retired so that the state can issue more new debt in each forthcoming recession for 2–3 years in a row. The proposed path allows much more debt capacity in all recession and subsequent years (except 1992 by a 4.8% margin).

Under electoral politics, policy makers have tended to adopt procyclical tax cuts in boom years and then procyclical tax hikes in recession years. Plugging in the actual (available since 1988), I found that the optimal countercyclical policy path could have absorbed all the boom-year tax cuts and made all recession-year tax hikes unnecessary. The added debt capacity under the proposed policy path could have done much better than the procyclical policies. This proposed path could have rendered the state a much more favorable scenario prior to the Great Recession.

10.6 Remaining Issues

To adopt and implement the optimal path of debt issue and retirement, we have to discuss some relevant issues. The first is efficiency. The current practice as has been used by most states is procyclical, with frequent changes to tax rates. The optimal path will eliminate such inefficiency, wiping out dead weight loss thereof. If states can incorporate the proposed policy into their finance law, thereby turning the policy into one that is time consistent, it is possible to minimize political muddling with tax rates. If the federal government can institute countercyclical matching grants to boost recessionary infrastructure spending, then it will help avoid moral hazard by

Table 10.7 Simulation of New York State optimal path of issue and retirement of long-term full faith and credit debt

Fiscal year	1 = bust; 0 = boom (calendar yr)	Unemployment rate (calendar yr)	Optimal path as % debt limit	Outstanding/debt limit: Actual	Outstanding/debt limit: Proposed	Retired/service limit: Actual	Retired/service limit: Proposed	New issue/ debt limit: Actual	Add-on to actual: Proposed	Procyclical tax cuts*/ debt limit: Actual	Effect on tax cuts: Proposed	Procyclical tax hikes*/ debt limit: Actual	Effect on tax hikes: Proposed
1977	0	9.1	*–0.125*	0.510	0.385	0.174	0.684	0.057					
1978	0	7.7	*–0.125*	0.500	0.260	0.184	0.739	0.066					
1979	0	7.1	*–0.125*	0.482	0.135	0.196	0.763	0.049					
1980	**1**	7.5	*0.250*	0.392	0.385	0.190		0.027	*0.223*				
1981	0	7.6	*0.250*	0.382	0.635	0.177		0.029	*0.221*				
1982	**1**	8.6	*0.250*	0.339	0.885	0.171		0.013	*0.237*				
1983	0	8.6	*0.100*	0.285	*0.985*	0.165		0.054	*0.046*				
1984	0	7.2	*0*	0.244	0.985	0.158		0.023					
1985	0	6.5	*–0.125*	0.227	0.860	0.161	0.749	0.029					
1986	0	6.3	*–0.125*	0.214	0.735	0.145	0.742	0.026					
1987	0	4.9	*–0.125*	0.205	0.610	0.134	0.719	0.061					
1988	0	4.2	*–0.125*	0.195	0.485	0.139	0.739	0.026		–0.0225	*For debt retire-ment*		
1989	0	5.1	*–0.125*	0.167	*0.360*	0.138	0.741	0.022		–0.00025			
1990	**1**	5.3	*0.250*	0.182	0.610	0.135		0.047	*0.203*			0.035	*No need with large new debt issues*

1991	0	7.3	*0.250*	0.263	0.860	0.148		0.103	*0.147*			0.097
1992	0	8.6	*0.100*	0.355	*0.960*	0.165		0.148	*−0.048*			0.045
1993	0	7.8	*0*	0.406	0.960	0.170		0.106				0.017
1994	0	6.9	*−0.125*	0.454	0.835	0.482	0.619	0.133				0.022
1995	0	6.3	*−0.125*	0.438	0.710	0.162	0.617	0.038		−0.02	*For debt retire-ment*	
1996	0	6.2	*−0.125*	0.419	0.585	0.169	0.641	0.040		−0.05		
1997	0	6.4	*−0.125*	0.395	0.460	0.277	0.663	0.051		−0.11		
1998	0	5.6	*−0.125*	0.364	0.335	0.317	0.678	0.055		−0.08		
1999	0	5.2	*−0.125*	0.335	0.210	0.224	0.669	0.035		−0.045		
2000	0	4.6	*−0.0625*	0.300	*0.148*	0.185	0.342	0.019		−0.01		
2001	**1**	4.9	*0.250*	0.278	0.398	0.193		0.024	*0.226*	−0.0003		
2002	0	6.1	*0.250*	0.250	0.648	0.109		0.008	*0.242*			
2003	0	6.3	*0.125*	0.229	0.773	0.276		0.057	*0.068*			
2004	0	5.8	*−0.125*	0.187	0.648	0.093	0.557	0.012				
2005	0	5.0	*−0.125*	NA**	0.523	NA	0.581	NA		−0.0002	*For debt retire-ment*	
2006	0	4.5	*−s*	NA	0.398	NA	0.593	NA		−0.0003		

Notes

a. Debt service limit is capped at 5% of overall budget

b. Debt limit is capped at 4% of personal income. New debt must use level debt service for useful life, = <30 years

c. Source of tax cuts and hikes is NASBO, various years, available only since 1988

d. FFC debt data are not available for 2005 and 2006

state politicians in making and implementing policies with regard to state saving and borrowing.

Another factor is cost. Retirement of debt ahead of schedule necessitates a call option into the debt structure, which adds to the borrowing cost. This cost, however, may be offset by the savings from early retirement and from improved credit rating that a state may achieve with abundant debt capacity.

Gain on efficiency, however, may imply some loss on the equity side. As Lewis Kimmel (1959, Chapter 2) wisely pointed out, "retirement of debt with current tax collections on long-term debt involves an equity issue." In this case, the countercyclical early retirement may create some necessary evil onto intertemporal or intergenerational equity. This may be some of the price we have to pay.

10.7 Policy Suggestion and Conclusion

A policy suggestion is a natural product of this study: Rewrite state debt legislation to provide a clause for countercyclical use of debt capacity, such that financing of capital projects is a combination of pay-go and debt in boom years but solely by debt in bust years. Related to this, routine boom-year outlays need to include accelerated retirement of (though not all of them) debt to accumulate debt capacity for downturns. Alternatively, such legislation could even divide total debt capacity into two parts, one acyclical and the other countercyclical. The acyclical part is the lower region in my tripartite scheme (0–25% of debt capacity), which is to be used during any phase of the economic cycle. The countercyclical part is the middle region plus the high region, which is to be used exclusively in recession years. With such a rule in place, it will be an automatic, time consistent policy that can be free of political muddling and discretionary manipulation by politicians. Needless to say, real implementation of such a policy will be possible only after many experiments and refinement. But it is time now to start serious consideration and policy design.

References

Bahl RW (1984) Financing state and local governments in the 1980s. Oxford University Press, New York

Bahl RW, Duncombe W (1993) State and local debt burdens in the 1980s: a study in contrast. Public Adm Rev 53(1):31–49

Barro RJ (1974) Are government bonds net wealth? J Polit Econ 82(6):1095–1117

Barro RJ (1977) Unanticipated money growth and unemployment in the United States. Am Econ R 67(1):101–115

Barro RJ (1978) Unanticipated money, output, and the price level in the United States. Journ Pol Econ 86(4):549–580

Barro RJ (1979) On the determination of the public debt. J Polit Econ 87(5):940–971, Part 1

Barro RJ (1989) The Ricardian approach to budget deficits. J Econ Perspect 3(2):37–54

Bergstrom V (1981) Studies in Swedish post-war industrial investments. Ph.D. dissertation, Uppsala University

Berne R, Schramm R (1986) The financial analysis of governments. Prentice Hall, New York
Berry WD, Fording RC, Ringquist EJ, Hanson RL (2010) Measuring citizen and government ideology in the U.S. states: a re-appraisal. State Polit Policy Q 10(2):117–135
Buchanan JM (1976) Barro on the Ricardian equivalence theorem. J Polit Econ 84(2):337–342
Bunch BS (1991) The effect of constitutional debt limits on state governments' use of public authorities. Public Choice 68(1):57–69
Clingermayer JC, Wood BD (1995) Disentangling patterns of state debt financing. Am Polit Sci Rev 89(1):108–120
Cogan JF, Taylor JB (2010) What the government purchases multiplier actually multiplied in the 2009 stimulus package? NBER working paper series, w16505
Égert B (2012) Fiscal policy reaction to the cycle in the OECD: pro- or counter-cyclical? CESIFO working paper no. 3777
Ellis MA, Schansberg DE (1999) The determinants of state government debt financing. Public Financ Rev 27(6):571–587
Fisher I (1911) The purchasing power of money. MacMillan, New York
Fitch IBCA (2000) Impact of management practices on municipal credit. Special report in its Public Financ Newsl, 4 May 2000. http://www.fitchibca.com. Accessed 10 Jun 2000
Gordon RJ (2010) Okun's law and productivity innovations. Am Econ Rev 2:11–16
Government Finance Officers Association (GFOA) (1999) Recommended budget practices. Government Finance Officers Association, Chicago
Gramlich EM (1987) Subnational fiscal policy. In: Quigley JM (ed) Perspectives on local public finance and public policy, vol 3. JAI Press, Greenwich, pp 3–27
Hamilton J (1989) A new approach to the economic analysis of nonstationarity time series and the business cycle. Econometrica 57(2):357–384
Hamilton J (1993) Estimation, inference, and forecasting of time series subject to changes in regime. In: Maddala GS, Rao CR, Vinod HD (eds) Handbook of statistics, vol 11. North-Holland, New York
Hou Y (2010) Business cycle, federal transfer and infrastructure – a fiscal framework to coordinate federal-state policies for economic stability. Paper presented at the conference of the Association for Budgeting and Financial Management (ABFM). 7–9 Sept 2010, Omaha
Keynes JM (1936) The general theory of employment, interest and money. Harcourt Bruce, New York
Kimmel LH (1959) Federal budget and fiscal policy 1789–1958. The Brookings Institution, Washington, DC
Lindbeck A (1974) Swedish economic policy. University of California Press, Berkeley
Musgrave RA (1959) Theory of public finance. McGraw-Hill, New York
National Association of State Budget Officers Association (NASBO) (1981, 1992, and 2008) Budget process in the states series. Washington, DC
President's Commission on Capital Budgeting (1999) Report of the President's Commission to Study Capital Budgeting. Government Printing Office, Washington, D.C.
Shiller RJ (2011) Irving Fisher, debt deflation and crises. Paper presented at the Allied Social Sciences Association (ASSA) conference, Denver
Taylor JB (1982) The Swedish investment funds system as a stabilization policy rule. Brookings Pap Econ Activ 13(1):57–99
Temple J (1994) The debt/tax choice in the financing of state and local capital expenditures. J Reg Sci 34(4):529–547
Wang W, Hou Y (2009) Pay-go financing and stability of capital spending. Public Budg Financ 29(4):90–107
Wang W, Hou Y, Duncombe W (2007) Determinants of pay-as-you-go financing of capital projects: evidence from the states. Public Budg Financ 27(4):18–42
Wassmer RW, Fisher RC (2011) Determinants of state-local government debt in the United States. Paper presented at the 67th annual congress of the International Institute of Public Finance (IIPF), 8–11 Aug 2011, Ann Arbor
Weil P (1987) Love thy children: reflections on the Barro debt neutrality theorem. J Monetary Econ 19:337–391, June

Appendix: Pay-as-You-Go Financing and Its Impact on Capital Outlay Volatility*

Wen Wang, Yilin Hou, and William Duncombe

A10.1 Introduction

Although public finance theory suggests that capital projects are best financed through pay-as-you-use (pay-use) mechanisms, that is, debt, so as to spread out the payments of large one-time spending and to achieve greater intergenerational equity (Fisher 1984; Musgrave and Musgrave 1989), state governments do not always finance their capital projects by borrowing. In fact, pay-as-you-go (pay-go) financing, defined as allocating general fund revenues for capital projects, is often used for infrastructure investment. As pay-use became the standard means of capital financing, pay-go remains a necessary supplement to pay-use and has even been recommended by professional organizations (GFOA 1999; NASBO series) and scholars as a best practice, especially when the economy is booming and/or the government has extra resources available.

The use of pay-go financing is potentially affected by factors different from those affecting debt usage, which has been a focus of the existing literature. For example, the political composition and electoral cycle may affect particularly the use of taxes for capital financing. Budgetary institutions may influence the relative use of pay-go financing. The availability of intergovernmental aid may also have a crucial impact on the choice of financing mechanisms for capital projects. Socioeconomic characteristics of voters could affect their preferences for government services and capital financing mechanisms. Therefore, the investigation of the determinants of pay-go financing may contribute substantially to the understanding of factors affecting prevalent capital financing practices in the states.

Capital outlays are large sums of expenditure on one-time projects for long-term facilities; therefore, their use is much more sensitive to the impact of economic cycles than that of recurring, current expenditure on daily operations of government finance. State governments often cut their capital expenditures during economic downturns (McGranahan 1999). The cut is politically easier and popular and technically realistic since the benefits of capital projects are less immediately apparent than those of maintaining current programs. Such cuts occur during lean years also because capital spending is less likely to arise from entitlement programs. Therefore, states may delay their capital spending so as to alleviate pressure on the operating budget.

---

*This appendix draws from data and analysis in Wang W, Hou Y, Duncombe W (2007) Determinants of pay-as-you-go financing of capital projects: evidence from the states. Public Budg Finance 27(4): 18–42, and Wang W, Hou Y (2009) Pay-as-you-go financing and capital outlay volatility: evidence from the states over two recent economic cycles. Public Budg Finance 29(4): 90–107, published by John Wiley & Sons Ltd.

On the other hand, state governments may, as long as they have enough debt capacity remaining, make full use of long-term debt in a recession to maintain or even increase capital spending as a means to stimulate the growth of economy. In this scenario, the two financing mechanisms can be used in a complementary manner: more pay-go during boom years and more pay-use in lean years. More pay-use in recessions entails less use, and more retirement, of debt in boom years so as to reserve debt capacity. This argument for the complementary use of pay-go and pay-use was first proposed in the 1940s as a countercyclical fiscal policy by Hansen (Hou 2004). This practice, if adopted by states, may help mitigate the impact of business cycle on the volatility of capital expenditures. This is especially important during an economic recession because relatively stable capital spending can help the state economy (Peng 2005).

This appendix provides empirical evidence on when and under what circumstances states may opt to use pay-go financing. Based on previous research on government capital finance decisions, we develop a model that considers the preferences of voters and politicians for the type of capital finance tool when they make capital financing decisions in a given institutional setting. We also test the effects of pay-go financing on the cyclical stability of state capital expenditures. The complementary use of pay-go and pay-use may benefit the smooth operation of state financial administration and avoid drastic fluctuations in capital expenditures over the business cycle. While there have been some studies on the stabilization of state operating budget (Sobel and Holcombe 1996; Knight and Levinson 1999; Wagner 2003; Hou 2003, 2005; Wagner and Elder 2005), little is known about the effect of pay-go on the stability of state capital spending. This study fills in a gap in the literature.

This appendix chapter is organized as follows: The next section reviews existing literature related to pay-go and pay-use. Section A.3 presents theoretical models for analyzing the determinants of states' use of pay-go as well as the effects of pay-go on capital expenditure stability over the business cycle. Section A.4 is data and methodology, with results and discussion offered in Section A.5. The last section concludes with directions for further exploration.

A10.2 Pay-Go Versus Pay-Use Financing: A Brief Survey

At the start of the commercial and market system, cash payment for all transactions was the norm for individuals, businesses, and government, both very small in the early centuries. Later, due to the fact that cash transaction was far too restrictive and inadequate for [working] capital needs and investment for production expansion, the idea of "credit and debt/borrowing" was invented and put into practice. Credit and debt greatly boosted productivity, economic growth, and the market system.

In the early nineteenth century, debt defaults occurred in several states and cities because state and local governments borrowed heavily in the absence of regulation (Fisher 1996; Kiewiet and Szakaly 1996). As part of the correction efforts, the practice of, and requirement for, "cash payment" for large items returned, under the new name of "pay-as-you-go" in the mid-nineteenth century.[6] The term crept into finance terminology unnoticed by public finance scholars [7] yet has since occupied a permanent place in the public finance literature (Bazuin 1941). As another correction effort in reaction to debt defaults, balanced budget requirements and debt limitations were subsequently added into state constitutions and laws (Hou and Smith 2006; Kiewiet and Szakaly 1996). Occasional defaults by state and local governments also prompted the passage of state constitutional restrictions upon debt financing during the twentieth century (Clingermayer and Wood 1995). Thus, during much of the US history, public debt has been considered as a threat to the solvency of governments and should therefore be avoided as much as possible. Though the balanced budget norm was often violated when governments had no choice but to borrow in order to finance large capital projects and wars, it has been widely held by the general citizenry and elected officials that state and local governments should in principle balance their budgets annually.

With the increasing demand for public expenditures and the existence of a well-developed financial market, the amount of state debt increased in the 1950s to finance higher education and the improvement and replacement of roads and bridges. The tax revolts in the late 1970s and early 1980s restricted state/local access to guaranteed debt; nonguaranteed debt (revenue bonds) boomed. During the 1980s downturns, many states resorted to issuing debt when they were faced with declining revenues but increased program responsibilities. Therefore, states have become more reliant on long-term debt and also shifted from reliance on general obligation debt to nonguaranteed debt as a means to circumvent the restrictive limits on general obligation debt (Bahl and Duncombe 1993). In more recent years, the indebtedness of states has nearly reached record levels (Robbins and Dungan 2001).

A10.2.1 Theories of State Capital Financing

Most early studies of government capital finance started from the Ricardo-Barro equivalence theorem that builds upon the assumptions of (1) a single rational agent, (2) a single benevolent social planner, and (3) the neutrality of institutions. It is assumed that both the agent and the government, a benevolent social planner whose objective is to maximize the welfare of the agent, have an infinite time horizon and thus do not consider the intergenerational aspects of debt or the finite terms of office for governments. The agent, knowing that debt increases imply tax raises in the future, will adjust his bequests to offset the implied changes in future tax liabilities. Thus, he is indifferent to the debt-tax choice because the two mechanisms are

---

[6] New York state comptroller used it in his 1843 annual report.

[7] It cannot be ascertained "by whom this term was invented [or] when it was first advanced in application to the policy of financing permanent improvements from current revenues..." (Studensky, 1930, p.19)

equivalent – debt (long-term) and taxation (current) have no differential impact on personal wealth (Imbeau 2004).

Scholars have proposed explicit theories that offer a framework for studying what determines the relative use of pay-go versus debt by relaxing one or more of the theorem's assumptions. The negative bequest theory arises from relaxing the single rational agent assumption (Imbeau 2004). Assuming multiple "rich" and "poor" agents, the Cukierman-Meltzer model (1989) suggests that rich and poor agents have differential preferences for borrowing: The rich are indifferent because they intend to leave positive bequests anyway; in contrast, the poor favor borrowing because they prefer to leave negative bequests. Another line of research, the tax arbitrage view, explores the effect of income levels and tax rates on individual decisions on this issue. A voter prefers tax financing when the federal tax rate facing him is greater than the implicit tax rate that equates the after-tax returns on taxable and tax-exempt bonds. Similarly, the same voter prefers debt financing when the federal tax rate for him is below the implicit tax rate (Holtz-Eakin 1991). Since tax rates are correlated with income level, it follows that low-income individuals would favor tax-exempt debt, whereas high-income individuals who itemize their tax returns and therefore are eligible for tax deductions would favor tax financing.

The political business cycle theory (Nordhaus 1975) arises from relaxing the assumption of a single benevolent social planner. These models investigate the effects of a pending election on public spending (Kirchgassner 2002). In order to win elections, opportunistic politicians tend to increase public spending or lower taxes when elections get close. The theory predicts that more debt financing will be used in anticipation of elections. Empirical findings on electoral cycles suggest that partisan effects are significant and persistent in formulating policies, but the two major parties tend to adopt identical positions when an election is pending and adapt their policies to win uncommitted voters (Mueller 2004).

Relaxing both assumptions one and two leads to the partisan cycle theory, which takes politicians as ideologists who base their decisions on the preferences of their party and their voters. In its simplest form, the theory predicts that public spending will be higher when the left is in power and lower when the right is in power (Imbeau and Tellier 2004), but the theory is less clear as to which financing mechanism will be preferred by the left and the right.

Finally, relaxing the assumption of neutral institutions together with assumptions one and two opens the field of research about budgetary institutions (Imbeau 2004). Institutions influence the making of collective choices and thus have important effects on policy outcomes (Bails and Tieslau 2000; Buchanan and Tullock 1965). Numerous studies have investigated the effects of budgetary institutions, such as balanced budget requirements (BBR), tax and expenditure limitations (TEL), borrowing constraints, and the gubernatorial line-item veto power, on budgetary outcomes, and empirical results suggest that budgetary institutions do matter (Bohn and Inman 1996; Poterba 1997). Thus, as Buchanan (1976) suggested, the tax-debt equivalence is illusory. An investigation of the determinants of pay-go financing for capital projects will have to consider the impact of voters, self-interested politicians, and institutions on budgetary outcome.

A10.2.2 Volatility of State Capital Expenditures

The effects of using pay-go or pay-use financing on the volatility of state government capital outlay over the business cycle are an area that has drawn almost no scholarly attention; there has been very little literature on this topic. A few studies we have found barely related to this topic are reviewed as below.

States often decrease their general fund expenditures during economic downturns by, among other measures, drastically reducing capital expenditure, which helps them to achieve budget balance (McGranahan 1999). Cuts in capital spending may be politically more acceptable than those in other areas because capital spending presents immediate costs but only longer-term benefits.

Own-source revenues of state government are expected to be positively correlated with the business cycle since most of them rely on income-elastic taxes such as personal and corporate income taxes and sales taxes. Empirical evidence also indicates that state revenues are procyclical (Wibbels and Rodden 2005). Sorensen and Yosha (2001) find that federal grants appear to provide some insurance against state-specific downturns, controlling for US-wide effects with the inclusion of time-fixed effects. However, Wibbels and Rodden (2005) argue that countercyclical flows of federal grants to the states are not compatible with the central government's incentives. Because tax increases and expenditure cuts are costly in political terms, central governments will face incentives to shift the costs of adjustment to subnational levels. The central government may borrow to smooth expenditures or even use "unfunded mandates" to shift their responsibilities to the states. Therefore, federal grants to the states are mostly expected to be procyclical. Given the procyclical properties of state own-source revenues and federal grants, the option left for the states is to use borrowing to smooth expenditures in downturns. Empirical studies suggest that fiscal institutions such as balanced budget requirements and debt limitations may have an impact on state fiscal decisions. If these fiscal rules are effective, they may prevent state governments from using debt issuance to smooth expenditures (Wibbels and Rodden 2005).

A10.3 Modeling Pay-Go Financing and Cyclical Stability of Capital Outlay

A10.3.1 Determinants of Pay-Go Financing

Relaxing the three assumptions of the Ricardo-Barro equivalence theorem, we develop a model with demographic, socioeconomic, political, and institutional variables to capture the behavioral patterns of voters and politicians when making capital financing decisions in a given institutional setting.

A10.3.2 The Voters

The logical extension to the assumption of a single rational agent is the median voter model, which assumes that government decisions are based on the preferences of a decisive voter. Median voter models have often been used in public finance to model demand for public services as a function of income, intergovernmental aid, tax prices, and preference factors (Ladd and Yinger 1991; Rubinfeld 1985). We modify the median voter model by examining socioeconomic and demographic factors that may be related to preferences of the median voter for capital financing mechanisms, such as the decision to finance capital outlays via pay-go versus debt.

Income and prices are key measures typically included in median voter models. The negative bequest and tax arbitrage theories suggest that the income of the median voter and his likelihood of itemizing returns will affect preferences for capital finance mechanisms. Lower-income individuals are apt to prefer debt financing of capital, while, according to the tax arbitrage view, voters with higher income are likely to prefer pay-go financing (the negative-bequest theory suggests they are indifferent). Therefore, the higher the income level and share of itemizers in a state, holding other factors constant, the more likely there will be support for pay-go financing. Interest rates are the key price associated with the issuance of debt and are significantly influenced by the credit ratings received by the government on general obligation debt.

The median voter's preference for pay-go or pay-use may depend on what state services and infrastructure he uses and how long he thinks he will be able to use them. For example, a high (per thousand residents) highway mileage could affect voters' decisions on state investment in transportation and related service areas. Since highway infrastructure is more apt to be funded with earmarked gasoline taxes and federal aid from the Federal Highway Administration (Congleton and Bennett 1995), in such a case, the demand for pay-go financing from the state general fund should be lower.

Demographic differences across states may also affect voters' preferences over how public infrastructure is financed. The long useful life of some capital assets implies that younger voters could disproportionately benefit from capital spending compared to older voters. Thus, we would expect that the higher the share of older (younger) residents, the less (more) supportive voters will be of pay-go finance. In addition, an individual expecting to move out of a state may prefer borrowing so as to postpone taxes until after his departure (Adams 1977). Therefore, states with higher percentages of senior citizens and mobile population are less likely to gain support for pay-go.

Federal grants for service areas that require commitment of considerable state revenue might affect decisions about pay-go versus debt financing, especially if the grants require state matching. Medicaid is a major federal-to-state matching grant that does not require a lot of state investment in infrastructure. Therefore, in states with heavy commitments to Medicaid, voters may be more likely to support the use of debt since a significant amount of tax revenue is already covering health and social services. Since the state share of Medicaid spending is based on its resources as well as its poverty rate, the level of poverty may be a good proxy for a state's commitment of its tax revenue for public health and social services. An increase in federal infrastructure grants is likely to reduce pay-go finance since states may substitute capital grants for the use of own-source current revenue.

A10.3.3 The Politicians

Once we relax the assumptions of a single rational agent and a single benevolent social planner, we need to consider the impact of self-interested politicians with opportunistic and ideological motives on state financial policies. In our representative democracy, elected officials weigh the perceived interests of their constituencies and adjust policies accordingly to maximize their probability of winning reelection (Downs 1957); their choice of capital financing mechanisms may be affected by considerations to provide services for their constituencies while avoiding tax increases so as to maximize their electoral votes. According to the political business cycle theory and the partisan cycle theory, the gubernatorial election year and party majority in the Senate and the House may be important determinants of a state's use of pay-go. In addition, a divided government is more likely to incur higher deficits and accumulate debts – and thus use less pay-go spending – because it is more difficult for either side to increase taxes, while both sides like to increase spending.

Capital spending is more sensitive to the business cycle than current expenditure. Thus, pay-go financing may be heavily influenced by the cyclical variability of state revenues. In an upturn when there is a budget surplus, states are more likely to use pay-go because they do not have to raise taxes or issue bonds to finance capital projects. States with more volatile revenues might be more likely to use pay-go during economic expansion and less apt to use debt (Pagano 2002). Therefore, measures of economic cycles and state revenue volatility are expected to affect politicians' decisions to use pay-go as opposed to debt.

In addition, politicians may have to balance the benefits of debt financing against the costs of financial distress when making capital spending decisions. Financial distress usually depends on a state's tax capacity and the level of its outstanding debt. Higher debt ratios would increase financial risk and therefore increase the cost of financial distress and bankruptcy, which creates disincentives for politicians to rely too much on debt.

A10.3.4 The Institutions

Relaxing the neutrality of institution assumption opens research about the impact of budgetary institutions on fiscal outcomes. Researchers point out that models of fiscal policy that treat institutions as mere neutral communicators of voter preferences have severely limited explanatory power (Crain 2004). As Poterba (1997) argues, institutions are not simply veils pierced by voters but rather important constraints on political bargaining regarding public spending and taxation. Given the difference between the short-term timeframe of politics and the long-term timeframe of capital investments, there may be a tendency to shift spending onto future generations without institutional constraints. A number of budgetary institutions could have a significant impact on states' relative use of pay-go financing; these include balanced budget requirements, tax and expenditure limits, debt limitations, and the line-item veto. For example, strict limitations on general obligation or revenue debt should encourage the use of alternative capital financing mechanisms, such as pay-go. Tax rate limitations, on the other hand, may encourage state governments to use debt to reduce volatility of tax rates. The effects of balanced budget requirements on capital financing decisions could depend on the nature of the requirement. Thus, the decisions of voters and politicians regarding the relative use of pay-go capital financing can be modeled as

$$\text{Pay} - \text{go} = f(\text{V}, \text{C}, \text{P}, \text{I}) \tag{A10.1}$$

That is, pay-go is a function of factors affecting voter preferences (V), the economic cycle (C), the state political environment (P), and the budgetary institutions in the state (I).

A10.3.5 Cyclical Stability of Capital Outlay

Capital outlay as big items expenditure is more sensitive to the economic and revenue boom-bust cycle than current expenditure, whereas one important function of government is to maintain fiscal stability through policy design and implementation; thus, it is important to investigate whether prevalent capital financing mechanisms would promote, and by how much, the stability of capital spending over the business cycle. The ideal policy design would be such that the annual capital outlay is smooth with little fluctuation despite the ups and downs of the economy and the government revenue stream; that is, the flow of capital spending is "ideally" neutral to the business cycle. However, this theoretical scenario is possible only on paper, with the purely countercyclical fiscal policy as originally proposed by Hansen (1941): In boom years, tax rates go high or remain stable; surplus revenue finances capital outlay in the pay-go fashion, while debt is retired or issued less, reserving the borrowing capacity for the downturn. In bust years, tax rates will be reduced while borrowing increased to provide economic stimulus; capital outlay will be financed with the pay-use mechanism. By this design, the capital stream would remain smooth, symmetrical over the expansion as well as contraction phases of the cycle.

The real world poses various restraints on the best policy design; two restrictions are eminent. First, boom-year tax hikes are next to impossible with mounting electoral pressure for tax reductions; thus, budget surpluses will be far from adequate to cover capital outlay and debt will be necessary to maintain the capital stream required by infrastructure needs. Second, the issuance of long-term debts, with a flat debt service structure, does not consider the business cycle effect on government revenue. Whether the revenue stream is up or down, a prearranged equal amount has to be budgeted each year as debt service. In this scenario, the boom-year capital outlay consists of partly pay-go and partly debt; the bust-year capital spending carries more debt but little or no pay-go. The policy thereby becomes asymmetrical over the business cycle.

Besides, the practice of capital financing in the states also varies with their different tradition. For example, a fiscally liberal state may opt to use only a little pay-go mingled with debt in a boom and then issue more debt in lean years for infrastructure financing. In contrast, a fiscally conservative state may choose to go all out for pay-go in a boom, then uses little debt and foregoes pay-go in a lean year.

The practice of capital financing is further complicated with changing composition of the major funding sources. State capital financing mainly comes from four sources: (a) long-term debt or borrowing, (b) other state funds or dedicated revenues, (c) federal grants, and (d) the general fund. Long-term debt is either in the form of general obligation bonds or revenue bonds that usually come with an annually flat debt service schedule. Dedicated revenues include state gasoline taxes, tolls, or fees from bridges or other facilities. As dedicated funds, they are usually reserved or designated for capital use only, with no regard to cyclical fluctuations of state revenue. The largest federal grant is for highway construction and is financed by the federal tax on gasoline. As discussed in the Literature Review section, federal grants are usually procyclical, in a similar way as the general fund, subject to the business cycle impact at the federal and state levels. In sum, the asymmetry of capital financing policy, different fiscal traditions of each state, and varying compositions of the funding sources are the three major factors that contribute to the cyclicality of state capital outlay. Our modeling is to be based on this analysis.

We first hypothesize, about an average state's long-run volatility for capital outlay, that the use of pay-go may help reduce the volatility or maintain the stability of capital expenditures in the long run. More use of surpluses (pay-go) in boom years and less in downturn years may contribute toward a smooth stream of capital investment. Debt (pay-use), in contrast, may increase the long-run volatility because of the asymmetrical distribution of its use over the cycle. Its impact on the stability of state capital outlays depends on how effective fiscal rules are in restricting states' debt issuance.

Long-run volatility and short-run cyclical variability are distinct concepts and capture different attributes of capital spending over the business cycle. Our second hypothesis is to test the effects of pay-go financing on the short-run cyclical variability of capital spending over the bust-boom of the economy and decline and rise of state revenue collections. We hypothesize that the asymmetric distribution of pay-go and pay-use will pose opposite signs from the long run: In the short run, pay-go financing may increase the cyclical variability of capital expenditures and pay-use may decrease it. Dedicated state funds may increase volatility in both the long run and the short run because they have been legally reserved or administratively designated for capital financing regardless of the economic cycle. Federal grants, being procyclical, will also be raising the volatility of capital outlay for both the long and the short runs.

A review of literature indicates political factors and fiscal rules matter in states' response to fiscal shocks and other fiscal outcomes (Poterba 1997). Besides examining the effects of the major financing mechanisms on the stability of state capital outlays, we also include relevant variables of state politics and budgetary institutions so as to empirically test their impact. We develop two empirical models of long-run and short-run state capital outlay stability over the business cycle. The general structure of the two models is as follows, with long-run capital outlay volatility ($LGap$) or short-run variability ($SGap$) as the dependent variable, respectively:

$LGap\,/\,SGap = f$ (funding sources, socioeconomics, demographics, politics, institutions)

A10.4 Data and Empirical Methodology

A10.4.1 Dependent Variables

To better analyze the determinants of pay-go financing, we calculate the share of capital expenditures from the general fund (pay-go) against state total capital spending and use this share as our dependent variable. The rationale for this choice is that our interest is in what determines the use of pay-go relative to other financing methods. Data for pay-go and total capital spending are from NASBO's *State Expenditure Report* series, which is the best available source for state capital spending over an extended period, 1988–2003. The pay-go share is calculated from actual figures of state capital expenditures. Alaska, being an obvious outlier in capital spending with its mean level of pay-go spending way above that of all other states, is excluded from the analysis. Wisconsin is also excluded because its capital expenditure data are not available. [8]

For the analysis on the effects of pay-go financing on the stability of capital outlay, we construct two dependent variables to capture the long-run volatility and short-run cyclical variability of state capital expenditures, respectively. The long-run dependent variable is the absolute value of the deviation from the long-term trend of state capital outlay. We first use the ordinary least squares (OLS) estimator to regress capital spending against the time trend (year), assuming random distribution of expenditure data around the trend line. The model used for this regression is represented as

$$Exp^*_{it} = \alpha_i + \beta_i T_t$$

[8] Connecticut, Montana, New York, Pennsylvania, and Vermont reported they did not use pay-go for capital financing over the sample period. They are kept in the sample because these states were not legally prohibited from using pay-go financing; they chose not to use pay-go.

where Exp^*_{it} is the predicted value of capital expenditure for state i in year t, α_i is the constant for state i, β_i is the linear trend parameter for state i, and T_t is the value of the year in year t. Deviations of actual capital expenditures from the trends are calculated by subtracting the trends (Exp^*) from the actual expenditures (Exp). The deviations are expressed as a percentage after being divided by the trends. Then the long-run dependent variable is constructed as the absolute value of this percentage:

$$LGap_{it} = \left|(Exp_{it} - Exp^*_{it}) / Exp^*_{it}\right|.$$

We use the change in state capital expenditures from the immediate past year to capture its short-run variability. Thus, the short-run dependent variable is constructed as the absolute value of the first difference of capital expenditures:

$$SGap_{i,t} = \left|Exp_{i,t} - Exp_{i,t-1}\right|.$$

Similar to the analysis on the determinants of pay-go financing, data of pay-go and other sources of capital spending are from NASBO's *State Expenditure Report* series for the 1989–2004 period. Alaska and Wisconsin are excluded from the analysis for the same reason as mentioned above.

A10.4.2 Independent Variables

Table A10.1 offers details about variables used for analyzing the determinants of pay-go financing. The sample years are 1988–2003, the longest time series for which we can obtain reliable data. Variables related to voter preferences include three demographic variables: share of population 65 years old or older, share of the population 18–24 years old, and population mobility rate. Since annual data on in-migrants and out-migrants of each state is not available for all sample years, we approximate population mobility with total population change in a state minus births and plus deaths.

Socioeconomic variables include per capita income and the percentage of income from capital gains (dividends, interest, and rent). The latter proxies for the share of tax itemizers in the state. Poverty is expected to be associated with a greater commitment of state revenues for Medicaid and other social services. Including per capita federal capital grants may cause concerns about endogeneity (Knight 2002); but most categorical aid is allocated through formulas that are results of political bargaining at the federal level (Hale and Palley 1981), and the chance is very slim that states can substantially increase grants by fine-tuning their fiscal policy (Matsusaka 1995). Thus, treating the federal grant as exogenous may not seriously bias the estimates.

Other preference variables include highway mileage per thousand population and two dummy variables for state GO bond ratings: states with an AAA rating and states with no rating. AAA ratings indicate lower prices for debt, while no rating for GO bonds may be positively related to interest rates and the pay-go share.

Table A10.1 Variable definitions and data sources for determinants of pay-go financing

	Variable	Definition	Data source
Key variables	Total state capital spending		*State Expenditure Report* annual series, by NASBO.
	Capital spending from general fund	Pay-as-you-go financing of state capital projects	
Preference variables	% of population 18–24 years old	College-age residents	US Census Bureau
	% of population aged 65 and older	Senior residents	
	Population mobility rate	Population change minus births plus deaths over total population	
	Highway mileage	State highway mileage per 1,000 population	
	Per capita real income (,000)		US Bureau of Economic Analysis (BEA)
	% of income from capital gains	Percentage of income from dividends, interest, and rent	
	Federal funds per capita	Federal grants for capital projects	*State Expenditure Report*, annual series by NASBO
	Poverty rate	Percentage of population in poverty	Census
	AAA bond rating	1 for states with GO bond rating of AAA, 0 otherwise	Moody's Investor Services
	No bond rating	1 for states with no GO bond rating, 0 otherwise	
	Debt burden	State total debt outstanding divided by personal income	Census and BEA
Economic cycle	Business cycle	Deviation from the mean of GSP growth rate, in 3-year lags	BEA
	Economic volatility	Absolute deviation from the mean of GSP growth rate, in 3-year lags	
State politics	Gubernatorial election year	1 for election year, 0 otherwise	*Book of the States*
	Senate Democratic majority	1 for Senate Democratic majority, 0 otherwise	
	House Democratic majority	1 for House Democratic majority, 0 otherwise	
	Divided government	1 if governor and majority of both chambers of the legislature are of different parties, 0 otherwise	
Budgetary institutions	Governor submit a balanced budget	1 for yes, 0 otherwise	*Book of the States*
	Legislature pass a balanced budget	1 for yes, 0 otherwise	
	Governor sign a balanced budget	1 for yes, 0 otherwise	
	No deficit carryover	1 for no deficit carryover, 0 otherwise	
	Revenue limit	1 for revenue limit, 0 otherwise	Mullins and Wallin, 2004
	Expenditure limit	1 for expenditure limit, 0 otherwise	

We construct two business cycle variables by following the Morgan-Rime-Strahan (2003) approach of regressing the growth rate of gross state product (GSP) in each state-year on state (c_i) and year (c_t) dummies. Thus, the business cycle indicator equals the error term from the regression, and state economic volatility equals the absolute value of the error term, as

$$GSPGROWTH_{it} = c_i + c_t + \nu_{it}; \text{Cycle} = \nu_{it}; \text{and Volatility} = |\nu_{it}|$$

With state dummies included in the regression, the mean GSP growth rate is subtracted for state *i* over time. To "demean" by the state average removes long-term GSP growth differences across states. With year dummies included, the mean growth rate is subtracted across states in year *t*. To demean by the national average each year helps control for aggregate business cycle fluctuations. The business cycle variable will capture the deviations from the average GSP growth rate for each state in each year; it is expected to be positively associated with pay-go share since a state in boom years is more likely to be able to finance capital projects with general fund revenue. The volatility measure as the absolute value of these deviations is also likely to be positively correlated with pay-go share, as suggested by Pagano (2002).

To capture the effects of the state political environment, we include four dummy variables from the *Book of the States*. Gubernatorial election year is hypothesized to be negatively associated with pay-go share. Senate Democratic majority and House Democratic majority are included to capture the party effects. Because it is theoretically unclear whether Democrats would prefer to finance their higher expenditures through debt or taxation, the expected signs of these two variables remain an empirical question.

As a divided government may be less successful in making difficult budgetary adjustments, such as raising taxes, we hypothesize that they will have higher accumulated debt and a lower share of pay-go financing.[9] The divided government variable is set as one if the governor and the majority of both legislative bodies are from different parties.

We include measures of two budgetary institutions in the model: balanced budget requirements (BBR) and tax and expenditure limitations (TEL).[10] To reflect different types of BBR, four dummy variables are used in the model: (1) The governor must submit a balanced budget, (2) the legislature must pass a balanced budget, (3) the governor must sign a balanced budget, and (4) the state may not carry deficits into the next budget cycle. As the most stringent retrospective constraint, no deficit carryover is likely to be the most effective among the four measures in reducing pay-go share. TEL is separated into indicator variables for revenue limitations and expenditure limitations. Both are hypothesized to be negatively associated with pay-go share, with the revenue limits likely to be more restrictive than expenditure

[9] Nebraska is coded 0 for divided government since it has a nonpartisan unicameral legislature. The exclusion of Nebraska does not significantly affect the empirical results.

[10] Debt limits and line-item veto are excluded from the analysis based on fixed-effects models because they are time invariant.

Table A10.2 Descriptive statistics (1988–2003) of pay-go determinants

	Variable	Mean	Std Dev	Maximum	Minimum
Dependent variable	Pay-go share	7.76	11.68	93.75	0.00
Preference variables	% of population 18–24 years old	10.06	0.96	14.19	7.79
	% of population aged 65 and older	12.72	1.71	18.55	8.41
	Population mobility rate	0.54	1.10	10.69	–2.25
	Highway mileage	26.72	25.83	137.01	3.45
	Per capita real income (,000)	25.81	4.26	41.72	16.17
	% of income from capital gains	18.74	2.34	29.80	12.17
	Federal funds per capita	77.02	74.00	943.84	0.00
	Poverty rate	12.68	3.80	27.20	2.90
	AAA bond rating	0.18	0.39	1	0
	No bond rating	0.20	0.40	1	0
	Debt burden	7.89	4.65	24.66	0.68
Economic cycle	Business cycle, lag 3 years	–0.02	2.60	20.53	–17.31
	Economic volatility, lag 3 years	1.80	1.88	20.53	0.00
State politics	Gubernatorial election year	0.27	0.44	1	0
	Senate Democratic majority	0.54	0.50	1	0
	House Democratic majority	0.60	0.49	1	0
	Divided government	0.47	0.50	1	0
Budgetary institutions	Governor submit a balanced budget	0.88	0.33	1	0
	Legislature pass a balanced budget	0.76	0.43	1	0
	Governor sign a balanced budget	0.63	0.48	1	0
	No deficit carryover	0.17	0.38	1	0
	Revenue limit	0.31	0.46	1	0
	Expenditure limit	0.43	0.50	1	0

Notes

1. Financial variables are adjusted with the price index for state and local government consumption expenditures provided by the Bureau of Economic Analysis
2. Number of observations is 696

limits (Mullins and Wallin 2004; Rafool 1997). Table A10.2 provides summary statistics of the variables.

For the analysis on the effects of pay-go financing on the stability of capital outlay, some of the independent variables are similar to the ones used for the study on the determinants of pay-go financing. Socioeconomic variables include per capita income, poverty and unemployment rates, and state highway mileage per thousand population. Demographic variables include population density, population growth, percent of seniors in the population, and percent of out-migration (the out-migration data is available only since 1989). Political variables include the gubernatorial election cycle, the majority of the Senate being Democrat, the majority of the House being Democrat, and the divided government. All financial figures are adjusted by the price index for state and local government consumption expenditures provided by the US Bureau of Economic Analysis. Budgetary institutions include balanced budget requirements (BBR) and tax and expenditure limits (TEL). Table A10.3 offers definitions and data sources of the variables used, and Table A10.4 provides summary statistics of the variables.

Table A10.3 Variable definitions and data sources for pay-go volatility tests

Variable	Specification (data source)
Pay-go	State per capita capital spending from General Fund (NASBO)
Other state funds	State per capita capital spending from other state funds (NASBO)
Bonds	State per capita capital spending from bonds (NASBO)
Federal fund	State per capita capital spending from federal fund (NASBO)
Per capita real income	Per capita income, in thousands (BEA)
Poverty rate	Percentage of population in poverty (Census)
Unemployment rate	Percentage of population unemployed (Census)
Highway mileage	State highway mileage per 1,000 population (Census)
Population growth	Percentage of population growth (Census)
Population density	Population per square mile (Census)
Percentage of population over 65	Percentage of population aged 65 and above (Census)
Percentage of out-migration	Percentage of out-migration in the population (Census)
Gubernatorial election cycle	1 for governor's election year, 0 otherwise (Book of the States)
Senate Democrat majority	1 for Senate Democrat majority, 0 otherwise (Book of the States)
House Democrat majority	1 for House Democrat majority, 0 otherwise (Book of the States)
Divided government	1 if governor and majority of both chambers of the legislature
	being different parties, 0 otherwise (Book of the States)
Submit a balanced budget	1 for submission of a balanced budget, 0 otherwise (Book of the States)
Pass a balanced budget	1 for submission of a passed balanced budget, 0 otherwise (Book of the States)
Sign a balanced budget	1 for submission of a signed balanced budget, 0 otherwise (Book of the States)
No deficit carryover	1 for no deficit carryover, 0 otherwise (Book of the States)
Revenue limit	1 for revenue limit, 0 otherwise (Mullins and Wallin, 2004)
Expenditure limit	1 for expenditure limit, 0 otherwise (Mullins and Wallin, 2004)

A10.4.3 Estimation Methodology

Because some states do not use pay-go for capital financing or do not use it each year, over 20% of the observations for the dependent variable of pay-go share are zero. To handle this case, we estimate a state- and year-fixed effects Tobit model, estimated by maximum likelihood, which is defined as

$$y_{it}^{*} = x_{it}'\beta + \varepsilon_{it} + \alpha_i + \delta_t \tag{A10.2}$$

$$y_{it} = Max\left(0, y_{it}^{*}\right);\ \varepsilon_{it} \sim N\left(0, \sigma_{\varepsilon}^{2}\right)$$

Table A10.4 Descriptive statistics (1989–2004) of pay-go volatility tests

Variable	Mean	Standard deviation	Minimum	Maximum
Long-run stability of capital outlay	24.00	42.51	0.00	808.38
Short-run cyclical variability of capital outlay	51.63	137.22	0.13	3,193.08
Pay-go	20.64	75.83	0.00	1,348.87
Other state funds	100.72	120.07	−28.07	1,624.11
Bonds	71.73	100.70	0.00	913.73
Federal fund	78.17	80.57	0.00	944.21
Per capita real income	26.15	4.23	16.90	41.72
Unemployment rate	5.22	1.41	2.20	11.40
Poverty rate	12.63	3.70	2.90	26.40
Highway mileage	25.66	26.60	3.42	137.09
Population growth	1.06	2.19	−49.77	11.55
Population density	179.79	243.96	4.67	1,170.98
Percentage of population over 65	12.74	1.70	8.53	18.55
Percentage of out-migration	3.57	1.00	1.83	8.00
Gubernatorial election cycle	0.27	0.44	0.00	1.00
Senate Democrat majority	0.53	0.50	0.00	1.00
House Democrat majority	0.58	0.49	0.00	1.00
Divided government	0.46	0.50	0.00	1.00
Submit a balanced budget	0.87	0.33	0.00	1.00
Pass a balanced budget	0.76	0.42	0.00	1.00
Sign a balanced budget	0.63	0.48	0.00	1.00
No deficit carryover	0.17	0.38	0.00	1.00
Revenue limit	0.32	0.47	0.00	1.00
Expenditure limit	0.45	0.50	0.00	1.00

Notes

1. Financial variables are adjusted by the price index for state and local government consumption expenditures provided by the Bureau of Economic Analysis
2. Number of observations is 648

where α_i represent the state-fixed effects and δ_t the year-fixed effects. It is assumed that y_{it} and x_{it} are observed for $i = 1,2,\ldots,n$ in every period, but the latent variable y^*_{it} are unobserved if $y^*_{it} \leq 0$. One advantage of the fixed-effects model is that the error term ε_{it} may be correlated with the individual effect α_i. It is a more robust specification than the random effects estimator (Greene 2002).

Given the panel structure of the dataset, autocorrelation and heteroskedasticity may be present in the error terms ε_{it}. In the presence of autocorrelation and heteroskedasticity, the usual standard errors and test statistics are inaccurate. Thus, statistical inferences based on these test statistics will be misleading. We use the Newey-West estimation procedure to explicitly deal with the problems of autocorrelation and heteroskedasticity. This procedure computes OLS estimates with heteroskedasticity and autocorrelation consistent (HAC) standard errors (Newey and West 1987). State- and year-fixed effects will also be included in the Newey-West regression.

For the analysis on the effects of pay-go financing on the cyclical stability of capital outlay, we attempt to address two empirical challenges. First, the model may suffer from autocorrelation of the error terms due to the time-series nature of the data. The results of a test for autocorrelation in panel data suggest that first-order autocorrelation (AR1) is present in the models.[11] We use robust estimation; results show that first-order autocorrelation is corrected and the statistics are robust. The second challenge, despite our efforts to develop measures for the important variables in the capital expenditures stability model, is omitted variables bias. We add in the models state-fixed effects to control for time-invariant unobservable factors and year-fixed effects to control for nationwide unobservable changes. These may help reduce the bias to a certain extent. The two empirical models for long-run volatility and short-run variability are presented as below:

$$LGap_{it} = \alpha_i + \gamma_t + \beta' x_{it} + \varepsilon_{it}$$

$$SGap_{it} = \alpha_i + \gamma_t + \beta' x_{it} + \varepsilon_{it}$$

where α_i represents the state-fixed effects and γ_t the year-fixed effects.

A10.5 Results and Discussion

A10.5.1 Results from Fixed-Effects Tobit Model and Newey-West Regression

Table A10.5 presents the results from the fixed-effects Tobit model and the fixed-effects model with Newey-West estimation. The share of senior citizens is negative but not statistically significant in the fixed-effects models. Population mobility is positive in both models and is statistically significant in the Tobit model. Per capita income is positive and significant in both models; a $1,000 increase in income is estimated to raise the pay-go share by 1.25 percentage points in the Newey-West regression. The results are consistent with the prediction of the negative bequest theory and tax arbitrage view. Income from capital gains shows a negative sign in both models, and it is significant at the 0.10 level in the fixed-effects Tobit model. Federal grants do not appear to have a significant impact on the use of pay-go in the fixed-effects models.

Highway mileage is statistically significant in these models and has the expected negative sign. A 1 mile increase is associated with a reduction of the pay-go share by 0.26 percentage points according to the Newey-West regression. This result may not be surprising, because highway expenditures have their own dedicated tax base from other state funds, and highway is one of the major components of state capital

[11] The F statistics are 11.164 and 4.807 for models with the two dependent variables, respectively; the null of no first-order autocorrelation is rejected.

Table A10.5 Determinants of pay-go use from two-way fixed-effects models

	Explanatory variables	Tobit	t-stat	Newey-West	z-stat
Preference variables	% of population 18–24 years old	–0.72	–0.79	0.27	0.28
	% of population aged 65 and older	–0.34	–0.25	–0.15	–0.10
	Population mobility rate	*1.68*	2.16**	1.31	1.51
	Highway mileage	*–0.30*	–1.68*	*–0.26*	–1.88*
	Per capita real income (,000)	*1.96*	3.08***	*1.25*	2.08**
	% of income from capital gains	*–1.22*	–1.75*	–0.97	–1.50
	Federal funds per capita	–0.01	–1.43	–0.01	–0.68
	Poverty rate	–0.02	–0.08	0.04	0.19
	AAA bond rating	*–4.65*	–2.19**	–3.91	–1.17
	No bond rating	1.27	0.43	1.43	0.66
	Debt burden	–0.30	–1.00	–0.19	–0.59
Economic cycle	Business cycle, lag 3 years	*0.36*	2.64***	*0.33*	2.25**
	Economic volatility, lag 3 years	0.34	1.50	0.25	1.37
State politics	Gubernatorial election year	0.40	0.38	0.47	0.66
	Senate Democratic majority	1.44	0.91	0.50	0.41
	House Democratic majority	*2.95*	2.08**	*2.78*	1.85*
	Divided government	*–3.34*	–3.51***	*–2.35*	–3.17***
Budgetary institutions	Governor submit a balanced budget	3.41	1.61	*3.67*	2.13**
	Legislature pass a balanced budget	–2.36	–1.06	*–2.83*	–1.90*
	Governor sign a balanced budget	1.79	1.20	0.77	0.67
	No deficit carryover	*–2.76*	–1.85*	–1.54	–1.18
	Revenue limit	–1.82	–0.76	–2.04	–1.13
	Expenditure limit	*4.91*	2.05**	*3.96*	2.15**
	Constant			–10.63	–0.36
	Sigma	*8.81*			
	Log likelihood	*–1,998.76*			
	F			*8.90*	
	Prob>F			*0.00*	
	Centered R^2			*0.58*	
	No. of observations	*696*		*696*	

Notes

1. Statistical significance levels are * 0.10; ** 0.05; *** 0.01
2. Alaska is excluded as an extreme outlier and Wisconsin excluded due to missing observations
3. Financial variables are adjusted using the BEA price index for state and local government expenditures
4. State- and year-fixed effects are not reported but available from the authors at request
5. Dependent variable is a share of pay-go in total capital spending (48 states, 1988–2003)

budgets. AAA bond rating is significant at the 0.05 level in the fixed-effects Tobit model. Business cycle and economic volatility are positive but only business cycle is statistically significant. The results suggest that states are more likely to use pay-go financing when they are in better economic conditions and thus do not have to raise taxes or issue bonds to finance capital projects. We include 3-year lags for both variables to capture the lagging effects of economic cycles and economic volatility on a state's fiscal and budgetary decisions.[12]

Among political variables, Democratic majority in either chamber is positively related to pay-go financing but only the House is statistically significant, which warrants further investigation. Divided government is negative and statistically significant; this variable is estimated to decrease the share of pay-go by 2.35 percentage points in the Newey-West regression. Of budgetary institutions, no-deficit-carryover variable is negative and significant at the 10% level in the fixed-effects Tobit model but is not significant in the Newey-West regression. Governor submitting and legislature passing a balanced budget both are significant in the Newey-West estimation, with positive and negative signs, respectively. Spending limits do not appear to be effective in restricting the use of pay-go to finance state capital expenditures. The coefficient for revenue limits is not statistically different from zero.

A10.5.2 Results from the Stability Models

Table A10.6 reports the effect of pay-go spending on long-run volatility of capital expenditure. Model 1 includes the four sources of capital outlay and controls for socioeconomic variables; model 2 adds in state politics and fiscal institutions. Results from the two model specifications are consistent; the signs and magnitudes of the coefficients are not sensitive to changes in the specification, indicating that the empirical results are in general reliable. The pay-go variable is statistically significant at the 10% level. Its negative sign confirms our hypothesis that the use of pay-go may help reduce long-run volatility. Each dollar of pay-go can reduce long-run volatility by 4.4%. Given that the mean value of the long-run volatility is 24% and the 48-state average per capita pay-go is about 20 dollars, this magnitude of the pay-go effect is remarkable. The coefficients on "other state funds," "bonds," and "federal fund" are all positive and statistically significant at 1% level, suggesting that the use of these financing sources are associated with higher volatility of capital outlays in the long run. Further, these three coefficients are all larger than that of pay-go, by a margin from 14% (other state funds) to 77% (federal fund) to 107% (debt). Considering that their mean values are 2.5–5 times higher than that of pay-go, these funding sources push up capital spending as a trend and their effects can overwhelm that of pay-go. Against this possible scenario, the "cooling" effect of pay-go to "pull down" the uprising trend may become very valuable. No doubt, the

[12] We tried 1- to 3-year lags and moving averages for the business cycle and economic volatility variables; the results are similar to what is reported here.

Table A10.6 Effects of pay-go on long-run capital outlay volatility (48 states, 1989–2004)

	Model 1		Model 2	
Variable	Coefficient	t-stat	Coefficient	t-stat
Pay-go	–0.044	(–1.67)*	–0.043	(–1.63)*
Other state funds	0.051	(2.42)**	0.053	(2.5)***
Bonds	0.091	(4.72)***	0.090	(4.67)***
Federal fund	0.078	(2.75)***	0.078	(2.71)***
Per capita real income (,000)	–0.079	–0.04	–0.381	(–0.21)
Unemployment rate	1.469	0.89	1.567	0.94
Poverty rate	–0.108	–0.18	–0.083	–0.14
Highway mileage	–2.519	(–3.5)***	–2.359	(–3.23)***
Population growth	0.094	0.24	0.091	0.23
Population density	0.103	0.7	0.128	0.87
Percentage of population over 65	1.349	0.31	1.859	0.43
Percentage of out-migration	–0.782	–0.12	–0.442	–0.07
Gubernatorial election cycle			1.984	0.96
Senate Democrat majority			–5.922	–1.22
House Democrat majority			–0.496	–0.12
Divided government			–2.230	–0.8
Submit a balanced budget			–2.664	–0.35
Pass a balanced budget			–2.830	–0.36
Sign a balanced budget			0.294	0.05
No deficit carryover			–1.387	–0.33
Revenue limit			–4.421	–0.44
Expenditure limit			10.969	1.09
Constant	26.818	1.65	22.603	1.38
R^2	0.13		0.13	
No. of observations	648		648	

Notes

1. Statistical significance levels are *0.10; **0.05; *** 0.01
2. Alaska is excluded as an extreme outlier and Wisconsin excluded due to missing observations
3. Financial variables are adjusted using the BEA price index for state and local government expenditures
4. Coefficients for state and year dummies are available on request from authors, but are not included in the table

real world is much more complicated than these models can reveal; and further explorations are warranted.

The socioeconomic variables are not statistically significant except highway mileage. The negative coefficient of the variable indicates that states with higher highway mileage are likely to experience less long-run volatility. Model 2 is more fully specified with the inclusion of state political and budgetary institutions to see whether these variables affect the long-run volatility. Though none of them bears a statistically significant effect on the dependent variable, this full specification as a sensitivity test does not generate any flip of signs or drastic fluctuations in the magnitudes of the coefficients on the key variables of the four major capital financing sources.

Table A10.7 reports estimation results of pay-go on short-run cyclical variability of capital expenditures, our second hypothesis. Here we focus on the sign and magnitude

Table A10.7 Effects of pay-go on short-run capital outlay variability (48 states, 1989–2004)

	Model 3		Model 4	
Variable	Coefficient	t-stat	Coefficient	t-stat
Pay-go	1.616	(20.16)***	1.620	(20.04)***
Other state funds	0.325	(4.83)***	0.318	(4.68)***
Bonds	–0.171	(–3.19)***	–0.177	(–3.28)***
Federal fund	0.309	(3.73)***	0.319	(3.79)***
Per capita real income (,000)	14.069	(1.73)*	12.920	1.58
Unemployment rate	10.757	(2.13)**	11.316	(2.21)**
Poverty rate	1.855	1.18	2.086	1.31
Highway mileage	3.300	1.01	3.032	0.92
Population growth	–0.944	–0.79	–0.909	–0.75
Population density	0.102	0.12	0.057	0.07
Percentage of population over 65	19.234	0.45	23.174	0.54
Percentage of out-migration	66.240	(3.05)**	64.025	(2.93)***
Gubernatorial election cycle			0.940	0.11
Senate Democrat majority			0.755	0.06
House Democrat majority			–4.288	–0.36
Divided government			0.529	0.07
Submit a balanced budget			21.404	1.09
Pass a balanced budget			6.185	0.27
Sign a balanced budget			–7.738	–0.52
No deficit carryover			–32.182	(–2.83)***
Revenue limit			1.844	0.07
Expenditure limit			28.600	0.80
Constant	67.04	6.12	37.53	1.34
R^2	0.77		0.77	
No. of observations	591		591	

Notes

1. Statistical significance levels are *0.10; **0.05; ***0.01
2. Alaska is excluded as an extreme outlier and Wisconsin excluded due to missing observations
3. Financial variables are adjusted using the BEA price index for state and local government expenditures
4. Coefficients for state and year dummies are available on request from authors but are not included in the table

of the pay-go variable. The two models are specified in the same fashion as with the two long-run volatility models in Table A10.6. The pay-go coefficient is positive and significant at 1% level in both models, consistent and robust, not sensitive to changes in model specification, indicating that the use of pay-go tends to increase the cyclical variability of capital expenditures in the short run – this cyclical fluctuation comes with strong revenue streams in boom years and goes away with a sour economy. Each dollar of pay-go adds to the cyclical fluctuation by 1.62 dollars, about 3 percentage points (coefficient 1.62 divided by 51.63, the mean of the dependent variable).

Other state funds and federal funds also present a positive sign, which suggests that these two financing sources may also contribute to increasing the short-run cyclical variability. Their magnitudes, however, are much smaller at only about 20% of the pay-go coefficient. Debt (bonds) stands out as the only financing source that may help reduce the short-run variability (negative sign), which is consistent to the findings of an earlier study (McGranahan 1999). The size of it looks very small: Each dollar of bonds may reduce the variability by only 17 cents or 3/10ths of a percent, but since the state average of debt is about 72 dollars per capita, the cumulative effect can be as large as 23.6 dollars, near half of total short-run fluctuations. Among the socioeconomic variables, unemployment rate and out-migration both pose positive results significant at the 5% or 1% level, respectively, suggesting that states with higher unemployment rates and out-migration ratios are more likely to experience higher cyclical variability in their capital outlays.

Similar to model 2, we test the effects of political and budgetary institutions on the short-run variability in model 4. The estimated coefficients of the variables for the four capital financing sources are similar to those in model 3. No deficit carry-over has a negative coefficient and is highly significant, which indicates that this budgetary rule has been effective in maintaining the short-run stability of state capital outlays. Other political and budgetary institutional variables do not seem to create a significant impact on the stability of capital expenditures.

A10.6 Conclusion and Recommendations

Although a standard recommendation in public finance is that capital projects are best financed through pay-use mechanisms such as long-term debt, pay-go financing remains a common supplement to debt financing. However, so far little is known about the use of pay-go financing. The literature has been inadequate on the mechanisms and benefits of pay-go financing, especially on the effects of pay-go financing on the cyclical patterns of capital spending. Growing state borrowing in recent decades has raised concerns about intergenerational equity and state debt management policy (Brecher et al. 2003). This study fills in a gap in the literature on determinants of states' use of pay-go to finance capital projects; it also contributes to the literature by proposing a model that examines the effects of pay-go on the long-run volatility and the short-run cyclical variability of capital expenditures.

Relaxing the assumptions of the Ricardo-Barro equivalence theorem, this study has developed a model that considers the preferences of voters and politicians making capital financing decisions in a given institutional setting. The analysis improves our understanding of what factors promote or discourage the use of pay-go. Not surprisingly, use of pay-go finance is sensitive to the economic cycle. States with more volatile economies are more apt to use pay-go finance, particularly several years after the start of economic expansion.

This study has generated empirical evidence to suggest that pay-go financing is associated with lower volatility in capital spending in the long run, but it contributes to cyclical variability in the short run. Although the results seem a little detached from practice in a debt-dominated world, they still bear indirect implications for policy makers. Professional organizations recommend pay-go as a best practice in public financial administration for more "rational" use of extra cash in boom years;

such use of cash as a supplement to already dedicated debt financing adds to the cyclical variability of capital outlay over the economic cycle. However, pay-go helps maintain long-run stability of capital expenditures by reducing its volatility. The issuance of bonds could help reduce short-run variability, but it appears to contribute to increasing the volatility of capital spending in the long run. Therefore, we strongly recommend that states consider more use of pay-go with less pay-use in boom years; the reserved debt capacity will then be released more intensively in lean years. In this way, pay-go will serve as a real complement to pay-use; the two mechanisms for financing infrastructure may work in unison to reduce the aggregate volatility and thereby improve the long-run stability of capital expenditures. That will be moving in the direction of the tax-smoothing approach and a symmetric countercyclical fiscal policy.

References

Adams RD (1977) Individual preferences as supply determinants in the municipal and federal bond markets. Public Finance Q 5:175–202

Bazuin JB (1941) A study of the financing of the construction of municipal permanent improvements out of current revenues contrasted with the traditional method of borrowed funds and a practical evaluation of the principles evolved through an analysis of the pay-as-you-go plans of three American municipalities. Michigan State College (Unpublished dissertation)

Bahl RW, Duncombe WD (1993) State and local debt burdens in the 1980s: a study in contrast. Public Adm Rev 53(1):31–49

Bails D, Tieslau MA (2000) The impact of fiscal constitution on state and local government expenditures. Cato J 20(2):255–277

Bohn H, Inman RP (1996) Balanced budget rules and public deficits: evidence from the U.S. states. NBER Working paper no. 5533

Brecher C, Richwerger K, Wagner MV (2003) An approach to measuring the affordability of state debt. Public Budg Finance 23(4):65–85

Buchanan JM (1976) Barro on the Ricardian equivalence theorem. J Polit Econ 84(2):337–342

Buchanan JM, Tullock G (1965) The calculus of consent: logical foundations of constitutional democracy. University of Michigan Press, Ann Arbor

Clingermayer JC, Wood BD (1995) Disentangling patterns of state debt financing. Am Polit Sci Rev 89(1):108–120

Congleton RD, Bennett RW (1995) On the political economy of state highway expenditures: some evidence of the relative performance of alternative public choice models. Public Choice 84(1–2):1–24

Crain WM (2003) Volatile states: institutions, policy, and the performance of American state economies. University of Michigan Press, Ann Arbor

Cukierman A, Meltzer AH (1989) A political theory of government debt and deficits in a neo-Ricardian framework. Am Econ Rev 79(4):713–732

Downs A (1957) An economic theory of democracy. Harper & Row, New York

Fisher RC (1984) Statement before the intergovernmental relations and human resources subcommittee of the committee on government operations. In: U.S. congress, federal and state roles in economic stabilization. Washington, DC, pp 101–107

Fisher RC (1996) State and local public finance. Irwin, Chicago, IL

Government Finance Officers Association (GFOA) (1999) Recommended budget practices. Government Finance Officers Association, Chicago, IL

Greene WH (2002) LIMDEP version 8.0 econometric modeling guide, 4th edn. Econometric Software, Plainview
Hale GE, Palley ML (1981) The politics of federal grants. Congressional Quarterly Press, Washington, DC
Hansen AH (1941) Fiscal policy and economic cycles. WW Norton, New York
Holtz-Eakin D (1991) Bond market conditions and state-local capital spending. Natl Tax J 44(4):105–120
Hou Y (2003) What stabilizes state general fund expenditures in downturn years-budget stabilization fund or general fund unreserved undesignated balance? Public Budg Finance 23(3):64–91
Hou Y (2004) Budget stabilization fund, structural features of the enabling legislation and balance levels. Public Budg Finance 24(3):38–64
Hou Y (2005) Fiscal reserves and state own-source expenditure in downturns. Public Finance Rev 33(1):117–144
Hou Y, Smith D (2006) A framework for understanding state balanced budget requirement systems: re-examining distinctive features and an operational definition. Public Budg Finance 26(3):22–45
Imbeau LM (2004) The political-economy of public deficits. In: Imbeau LM, Petry F (eds) Politics, institutions, and fiscal policy. Lexington Books, Lanham, pp 1–20
Imbeau LM, Tellier G (2004) The political-economy of budget deficits in the Canadian provinces, 1968–2000. In: Imbeau LM, Petry F (eds) Politics, institutions, and fiscal policy. Lexington Books, Lanham, pp 89–111
Kiewiet DR, Szakaly K (1996) Constitutional restrictions on borrowing: an analysis of state bonded indebtedness. J Law, Econ Organ 12(1):62–97
Kirchgassner G (2002) The effects of fiscal institutions on public finance: a survey of the empirical evidence. In: Winer SL, Shibata H (eds) Political economy and public finance: the role of political economy in the theory and practice of public economics. Edward Elgar, Cheltenham, pp 145–177
Knight B (2002) Endogenous federal grants and crowd-out of state government spending: theory and evidence from the federal highway aid program. Am Econ Rev 92(1):71–92
Knight B, Levinson A (1999) Rainy day funds and state government savings. Natl Tax J 52(3):459–472
Ladd H, Yinger J (1991) America's ailing cities. Johns Hopkins University Press, Baltimore
Matsusaka JG (1995) Fiscal effects of the voter initiative: evidence from the last 30 years. J Polit Econ 103(3):587–623
McGranahan L (1999) State budgets and the business cycle: implications for the federal balanced budget amendment debate. Econ Perspect 23(3):2–17
Morgan DP, Rime B, Strahan PE (2003) Bank integration and state economic cycles. NBER working paper no. W9704
Mueller DC (2004) Public choice: an introduction. In: Rowley CK, Schneider F (eds) The encyclopedia of public choice, vol 1. Kluwer, Dordrecht/Boston, pp 32–48
Mullins DR, Wallin BA (2004) Tax and expenditure limitations: introduction and overview. Public Budg Finance 24(4):2–15
Musgrave RA, Musgrave P (1989) Public finance in theory and practice, 5th edn. McGraw-Hill, New York
National Association of State Budget Officers (NASBO) (1990–2004). State expenditure report. Washington, D.C.
Newey WK, West KD (1987) A simple, positive semi-definite, heteroskedasticity and autocorrelation consistent covariance matrix. Econometrica 55(3):703–708
Nordhaus WD (1975) The political business cycle. Rev Econ Stud 42(2):169–190
Pagano MA (2002) Municipal capital spending during the 'boom'. Public Budg Finance 22(2):1–20

Peng J (2005) The state capital funding structure: its effect on the operating budget and capital spending growth. Munic Finance J 26(2):1–18

Poterba JM (1997) Do budget rules work? In: Auerbach AJ (ed) Fiscal policy: lessons from economic research. MIT Press, Cambridge, MA, pp 53–86

Rafool M (1997) State tax and expenditure limits. State Tax Notes 12:115–135

Robbins MD, Dungan C (2001) Debt diligence: how states manage the borrowing function. Public Budg Finance 21(2):88–105

Rubinfeld D (1985) The economics of the local public sector. In: Auerbach A, Feldstein M (eds) Handbook of public economics. North-Holland, Amsterdam, pp 87–161

Sobel RS, Holcombe RG (1996) The impact of state rainy day funds in easing state fiscal crises during the 1990–1991 recession. Public Budg Finance 16(3):28–48

Sorensen BE, Yosha O (2001) Is state fiscal policy asymmetric over the business cycle? Econ Rev, Third Quarter. Federal Reserve Bank of Kansas City

Wagner GA (2003) Are state budget stabilization funds only the illusion of savings? Evidence from stationary panel data. Q Rev Econ Finance 43(2):213–238

Wagner GA, Elder EM (2005) The role of budget stabilization funds in smoothing government expenditures over the business cycle. Public Finance Rev 33(4):439–465

Wibbels E, Rodden J (2005) Fiscal decentralization and the business cycle: an empirical study of eight federations, working paper. Seattle, University of Washington

Part IV
Retrospect and Prospect on Budget Stabilization

Introduction

In this part, I look into the future at how the government system should coordinate for better stabilization of public services, even the whole economy. In doing so, I am drawing a complete circle from the beginning of the book. Chapter 11 examines the theory behind the design of fiscal transfers – an important part of the intergovernmental relations network. It identifies acyclicality as a drawback in the design of transfer programs and proposes countercyclical design as an optimal fiscal framework to mitigate cyclical economic fluctuations. It further advocates countercyclical transfers for infrastructure investment and service maintenance as incentives for states to save in boom years then build from recession into recovery. It also advocates business tax relief as an incentive for businesses to invest into production and to retain their workforce during downturns. The framework focuses on fiscal policy; it does not discuss the political dynamics or details in implementation.

Chapter 12 concludes the book as a nonconclusion. It first briefly summarizes the key points of the whole book then reviews the performance of countercyclical savings in the Great Recession, thereby touches upon a few issues indirectly related to budget stabilization at the subnational level that this book has not discussed. Finally, the chapter offers the caveat that boom-year savings are merely one of the devices for financial management and budget stabilization in recession years. Savings per se are not enough; whether savings can accumulate in boom years and whether they can be used most efficiently and effectively in bust years is part of fiscal discipline which is the bottom line that we should hold at any time.

Chapter 11
A Framework for Fiscal Policy Coordination and Economic Stability: Countercyclical Transfer for Infrastructure

Abstract This chapter examines the theory behind the design of fiscal transfers; it identifies acyclicality of transfers as a drawback and proposes countercyclical design as an optimal fiscal framework to mitigate cyclical economic fluctuations. It further advocates countercyclical transfers for infrastructure investment, service maintenance, and business tax relief as incentives for states to save in boom years then build from recession into recovery. The framework is set to operate on time-consistent policy rules, as automatic stabilizers with triggers from key economic indicators. It advocates dynamic equity to compensate boom-year donor states during recession for more effective macroeconomic stabilization. This chapter focuses on fiscal policy; it does not discuss the political dynamics or details in implementation.

11.1 Introduction

The Great Recession (December 2007 to June 2009) caused tremendous economic damage and also invoked unprecedented quick counteractions by most central governments. The huge damage has set policy makers and scholars in deep thinking again about the role of government in stabilizing the macroeconomy and about the policy rules and tools that are available and should be fully employed. In macroeconomics, there have long been debates about the necessity and efficacy of the government economic stabilization role as well as the choice between monetary and fiscal policies as the major tool for this function. As fiscal policy dominated from the mid-1930s to the 1960s under Keynesianism (Stein 1996), so did monetary policy from the 1970s to 2000 under monetarism (Blinder 2006). During this recession, central governments did not hesitate in fully exploiting both types of policies. Robert Solow (2002) famously regretted that "there has not been any serious discussion of fiscal policy"; this Great Recession has offered the prime occasion for "new economic thinking" on what is the most appropriate policy mix to stabilize

Y. Hou, *State Government Budget Stabilization: Policy, Tools, and Impacts*, Studies in Public Choice 8, DOI 10.1007/978-1-4614-6061-9_11,

macroeconomy[1]; it is also the best occasion for serious reexamination of fiscal policy. This chapter echoes the call for a balanced view of monetary and fiscal policies – both types are essential (Seidman 2003; Blinder 2006) – mutually reinforcing; we can afford to drop neither for macroeconomic stabilization.

This chapter focuses on the optimal design of transfer programs in fiscal policy; its central research question is how fiscal transfers by central governments can be designed for best use to stabilize the budget of subnational governments and thereby help stabilize the macroeconomy. This author advocates that fiscal policy should be countercyclical in design – to be rule-based and time consistent and to accumulate savings in boom years for stabilizing power in recession years – and that central fiscal policy should be designed to coordinate vertically national-subnational actions and horizontally the spending behavior of both government and businesses to render policies the utmost efficacy in mitigating recessions. The proposed framework includes three parts – a national infrastructure trust fund, an antirecession public service reserve, and a corporate income tax reduction – all to run countercyclical as new mechanisms of fiscal policy. I will not discuss how such a proposal can be accepted in current political systems; I will also avoid details of an implementation plan. This omission is not out of political naivety or technical ignorance; they are to be treated at full length in separate studies.

This chapter is organized as follows. The next section explores the relationship between economic cycles, fiscal policy, and the need for policy coordination in mitigating the adverse effects from economic fluctuations. Section 11.3 elaborates on federal transfer as a fiscal institution, the procyclicality of current programs, and the need for dynamic cross-cycle equity in granting transfers. Section 11.4 brings infrastructure investment into the countercyclical perspective and discusses how to incorporate it into federal and state policies. Section 11.5 puts together the proposed framework in three parts, with Section 11.6 on the operation of the three parts, paying special attention to moral hazard issues. The last section concludes with a summary of the framework, its caveats, limitations of the current version of the framework, and directions for future research.

11.2 Economic Cycle and Fiscal Policy

Business cycles are inherent in the economy. Recessions can be taken positively as occasions for correcting inefficiencies that have emerged in the economy, especially during the expansionary phase of the cycle; the corrective action then is to reallocate resources in the economy through voluntary or involuntary means by businesses. Involuntary resource reallocation during a recession in most cases means drastic

[1] George Soros: "The crisis was generated by the system itself." See the Institute for New Economic Thinking, available at http://ineteconomics.org/.

decline that often causes tremendous damage to productivity and disruption to normal living. Amelioration of such damage falls at least partly on government as the macroeconomic stabilization function: Government can act against the phases of the economic cycle by implementing countercyclical monetary and fiscal policies. Monetary policy is designed to run against the cycle; there has rarely been any doubt about their countercyclical practice. In contrast, fiscal policy simultaneously pursues tripartite goals: to control government size (allocation), to strive for equity (redistribution), and to ameliorate cyclical fluctuations of the economy (stabilization). Goal multiplicity of fiscal policy often places stabilization in conflict with the other goals of fiscal policy, seriously compromising its countercyclical practice and outcome. The fact that central governments worldwide launched stimulus packages to mitigate the Great Recession reconfirms that fiscal policy should be applied against the economic cycle. The basic idea is common sense: Save while harvests are bountiful for use in years of famine. In contemporary context, it is to apply taxation, public expenditure, and debt against the boom-bust cycles: Save surplus tax revenues and retire debt during booms in order to increase public expenditure during busts, holding tax rate constant.

To be effective in stabilizing a downturn economy, stimulative public expenditure must be large in size. The benchmark obtained from empirical analysis is 1% of GDP a year; increased expenditure shy of this size is not adequate to pull up the aggregate demand. Effective stabilization requires coordinated fiscal policies: When the central government increases expenditure, the policy outcome will be reinforced with supplements if subdivisions increase their shares; the outcome will be less effective if subdivisions maintain their usual shares; the worst is when subnational entities reduce their own shares. The last scenario was unfortunately true in the past few years in the USA: While the federal stimulus package was being implemented, states cut their programs, hiked taxes and fees, and laid off employees. States drew down their general fund balances (from 0.39% of GDP in 2006 to 0.05% in 2009) but kept their budget stabilization funds at about the same level (from 0.24% of GDP in 2006 to 0.21% in 2009). Effective stabilization also calls for tax incentives for businesses to increase capital investment. The private sector accounts for the bulk of the economy; without their active participation, stimulative efforts can hardly meet expectations.

Subnational governments operate under balanced budget requirements, face revenue and expenditure limitations, and are restrained by statutory debt limits. They rely on the central government for a large share of their recurring outlays and have long taken transfers as a regular component of their budget. From 2000 to 2009, the annual average all state own-source expenditure in the USA was 6.99% of GDP, which was supplemented with federal transfers that averaged 3.33% of GDP. In order to explain how to reverse the procyclicality of subnational outlays, we need to examine the rationality, design, and cyclical features of federal transfer programs.

11.3 Transfer as a Fiscal Institution

Conventional wisdom offers four economic justifications for a central government to distribute resources to subnational entities: (1) economic efficiency, to mitigate effects of externalities; (2) substitution in tax administration, to reduce inefficiencies from duplication and inequity; (3) redistribution, for equity across the country; and (4) stabilization of local economies. So far, national economic stability is not among the major factors to justify fiscal transfers; however, central governments of major economies have long used this policy tool during almost every deep recession, the most recent and noticeable example being the Great Recession. This author argues that macroeconomic stability justifies central-to-subnational/local transfers as a major fiscal institution.

The US federal government gives most of its transfers to the states, only a small amount directly to local governments: From 1951 to 2006, federal-to-state grants averaged $358 (per capita, in year-2000 dollars; the same in the following); federal-to-county grants, in contrast, averaged only $21 from 1973 to 2004, while in the same period, state-to-county grants were $151. Thus, it suffices to focus on federal-state transfers in this chapter. Most transfers are for education, highways, and public welfare. A brief historical summary of the composition of federal grants reveals this pattern. Of the total per capita federal-state grants of $358, the largest single item is welfare, at over $178, about half the total. The next item is education, at $61, only about one-third of welfare. The third largest item is for highways at $45. Health and hospitals come at $18, followed by employment security ($6.9), natural resources ($6.7), and housing and community development ($5.4). Purposes and distribution of federal grants in these items indicate upward shifting of responsibilities from localities and states to the federal level. Over the gradual course of economic integration and freer flow of production factors, the federal government plays an increasingly more active role in correcting externalities and achieving equity. A summary of 1951–2006 federal-state grants is provided in Table 11.1. In sum, federal transfers have long been a fiscal institution in the United States.

11.3.1 Procyclicality of Current Transfer Programs

However, cyclicality of the economy is not considered in creating grants; most transfer programs so far have been designed to be acyclical by default. But economy fluctuates, tax revenues rise and fall with their base, and state expenditure on public services also fluctuates, thus leading to a mismatch between the design of transfer programs and the macroeconomy. Some federal programs even tend to be procyclical, federal medical assistance being a typical example.

Federal Medical Assistance Percentage (FMAP) is the federal share of the total cost in financing the Medicaid program; it starts at 50% and rises inversely with a state's per capita income relative to the national average, with a statutory maximum

Table 11.1 A historical summary of American federal-state transfers

Variable	Mean	Std. Dev.	Min	Max
Total federal grants	358.21	529.77	0.73	4,870.47
Welfare grants	178.17	279.48	0.25	1,874.35
Education grants	60.73	87.68	0.06	699.94
Highway grants	44.82	68.76	0.00	702.93
Health and hospitals grants	18.08	31.21	0.02	314.78
Employment security grants	6.87	8.42	0.00	119.21
Natural resources grants	6.72	17.97	0.01	346.71
Housing and community development	5.37	12.59	0.00	112.32
Revenue sharing	0.59	1.41	0.00	9.34

Notes
a. All figures are in per capita, year-2000 dollars
b. Sample years, 1951–2006, all 50 states included; number of observations (N) = 2,790
c. Data source: the Census *State Government Finances Historical Database*

(cap) at 83%. The federal share is determined annually; so it should respond negatively to the decline in income. A state's position to the national average brings in volatility of its economy in the structure of any particular recession. In general, states with more manufacturing jobs encounter higher volatility; agrarian states fare better in this regard. The FMAP that is used for any particular year in calculating state Medicaid transfers lags the actual date by several years: FMAP is calculated as the average of the three most recent calendar years of data available from the Bureau of Economic Analysis (BEA). It is calculated and published each November for use in the next federal fiscal year. For example, the federal percentages effective for FY 2008 were calculated in 2006 using income data of 2003, 2004, and 2005 that were available from BEA in October 2006; the percentages for each state were then published in the November 2006 issue of the *Federal Register* (Grady 2008). It was thus 4 years behind the economic cycle.

If we look at California and Michigan, it becomes clear that the base years used for the calculation (2003–2005) were a time period when the economy of these two states was strong and their personal incomes higher than during the Great Recession. By the time of the calculation (late 2006), the two states had no reason to be unhappy about their assistance percentages. But in 2008 when the 2006 calculated percentages were in use for federal money allotment, officials of these two states must be in dismay and there was nothing they could do about it. Their situation in 2009 would not improve either: They had to pay a higher own-sources ratio on Medicaid expenses during the depth of the Great Recession when their unemployment rates topped the nation and millions more of their residents became eligible for Medicaid than in normal years. But in a few years when their economy has recovered from the recession, their federal percentage will go up!

Another example is transportation outlay. The Transportation Equity Act for the twenty-first century (TEA-21, enacted in 1998 and renewed in 2002) authorizes the collection of fuel and excise taxes (18.4 cents/gal on gas and 24.4 cents/gal on diesel), their placement into the Highway Trust Fund (HTF), and distribution of federal highway grants to states via formulas as federal highway grants. States get a large portion of funding for highway construction, some for maintenance, from federal highway grants that (the TEA-21 Act) on the one hand allow 6-year contract authority as minimum funding levels in order to smooth cash flows and to protect multiyear construction from "unpredictable annual appropriations cycles" (ibid). On the other hand, these grants, in a fashion similar to FMAP, do not consider the economic boom-bust cycles. The Federal Highway Administration uses many factors and weights in calculating its annual apportionments to states;[2] some are to protect interests of small states, with minimums or floors. But none of the factors or weights is related to the economic cycle; the acyclical design again leads to procyclical outcome on funding: States have to pay more in a downturn (or construct/maintain less) when their own sources are low; federal dollars are bountiful when state own revenues are high.

From 1973 to 1986 the *General Revenue Sharing* (GRS) program was the hallmark of federal-state fiscal relations. The program was authorized by the state and Local Fiscal Assistance Act of 1972; the act did not factor cyclical economic fluctuations into its allocation formula. According to a recent study, the "rationale behind GRS in 1972 cannot be traced to a single… economic objective such as economic stimulus" (Maguire 2009), definitely not "as a primary tool to provide counter-cyclical assistance"; "[t]he amount was flat throughout the whole life of the program across business cycles, with no changes in the amount" (Maguire 2009, p. 1 and Table 1, respectively). The main factor was tax effort based on population and per capita income: The size of grants to states and localities increases with their tax efforts.[3] "Two states with the same ability to pay and the same amount of taxes collected receive equal score. If one of the two raised more taxes, it receives a higher tax effort score" (Maguire 2009, note 6). Thus, it may well go against the economic cycle, worsening the situation in a state (procyclical).

The above examples and analyses lead us to the conclusion that federal grant programs are designed by default to be acyclical, but may have produced procyclical outcome on recipient governments, which is probably fine in boom years but goes against the countercyclical policy orientation of the federal government in recession years. To test the cyclicality of federal grants, I use personal income growth and unemployment rates of the 48 continental states as regressors to run ordinary least squares (OLS) with state- and year-fixed effects, against federal grants total and in four major categories, using the current and lags 1–4 terms of the regressors. The sample period is from 1950 to 2006. Results are shown in Table 11.2, Panel 1 on personal income growth and Panel 2 on unemployment.

---

[2] For details, see "Federal Highway Trust Fund Apportionment Formulas," available at http://www.fhwa.dot.gov/reports/financingfederalaid/appd.htm.

[3] The formula of the GRS program was $State_i$'s share of GRS = A_{us} * [(pop_i * $GTEF_i$ * RIF_i)/sum of 51(pop_i * $GTEF_i$ * RIF_i)], where A = total appropriation, RIF = relative income factor = national average per capita income/state per cap income, and GTEF = general tax effort factor = taxes collection/total personal income.

Table 11.2 Cyclicality test of federal-state transfers

Panel A: federal transfer against personal income

OLS estimator with robust standard errors, year- and state-fixed effects

DV = annual growth rate of federal grants per capita; N = 2,496; t = 1950–2006, 48 continental states

Summary stats of IGR growth rate: mean = 0.1114; std dev = 0.927; min = –0.415; and max = 0.468 (N = 2,688)

Summary stats of income growth rate: mean = 0.09; std dev = 0.049 min = –0.114; and max = 0.331 (N = 2,688)

	Total grants			Welfare			Education		
Dep. V	Coef	Std err	P>t	Coef	Std err	P>t	Coef	Std Err	P>t
Δrate of income	–0.063	0.098	0.518	–0.033	0.097	0.732	0.056	0.138	0.687
L1	*–0.143*	0.088	0.103	–0.103	0.091	0.255	0.109	0.142	0.443
L2	0.042	0.089	0.640	–0.040	0.097	0.679	–0.150	0.161	0.354
L3	–0.055	0.089	0.540	–0.024	0.101	0.814	–0.170	0.117	0.144
L4	–0.082	0.101	0.418	*–0.234*	0.091	0.010	*–0.194*	0.102	0.057
Cons	0.154	0.018	0.000	0.084	0.023	0.000	0.119	0.029	0.000
Prob>F	0.000			0.000			0.000		
R-squared	0.349			0.305			0.307		

	Highway			Health and hospitals			Employment Security		
Dep. V	Coef	Std err	P>t	Coef	Std err	P>t	Coef	Std err	P>t
Δrate of income	1.518	1.627	0.351	0.192	0.290	0.508	–1.001	0.994	0.314
L1	1.449	1.807	0.423	0.189	0.296	0.524	0.365	0.484	0.450
L2	1.656	1.519	0.276	0.269	0.297	0.365	0.451	1.079	0.676
L3	1.566	1.415	0.269	*–0.450*	0.266	0.091	–0.035	0.514	0.945
L4	0.474	0.599	0.429	–0.155	0.249	0.534	–0.500	0.345	0.147
Cons	–0.338	0.497	0.497	0.129	0.063	0.042	0.112	0.101	0.267
Prob>F	0.000			0.000			0.000		
R-squared	0.045			0.100			0.051		

Panel B: federal transfer against annual average unemployment rates

N = 1,728; t = 1967–2006; other parameters are the same as Panel a

Summary stats of unemployment rate: mean = 5.693; std dev = 2.02; min = 1.8; and max = 18 (N = 1,920)

	Total grants			Welfare			Education		
Dep. V	Coef	Std err	P>t	Coef	Std err	P>t	Coef	Std err	P>t
Unemployment	0.0002	0.002	0.931	–0.0019	0.003	0.564	–0.001	0.004	0.831
L1	0.0010	0.003	0.762	0.0052	0.004	0.200	0.005	0.004	0.269
L2	–0.0006	0.003	0.846	–0.0003	0.004	0.931	0.001	0.005	0.851
L3	0.0037	0.003	0.202	–0.0006	0.004	0.887	–0.001	0.005	0.914
L4	–0.0029	0.002	0.202	0.0012	0.003	0.689	0.002	0.003	0.616
Cons	0.1108	0.020	0.00	0.1192	0.022	0.00	0.048	0.028	0.09
Prob>F	0.000			0.000			0.000		
R-squared	0.394			0.288			0.158		

(continued)

Table 11.2 (continued)

	Highway			Health and hospitals			Employment security		
Dep. V	Coef	Std err	P>t	Coef	Std err	P>t	Coef	Std err	P>t
Unemployment	−0.035	0.037	0.341	0.012	0.009	0.173	0.029	0.027	0.268
L1	0.070	0.085	0.412	−0.016	0.012	0.162	−0.023	0.030	0.431
L2	−0.058	0.073	0.428	−0.004	0.012	0.712	0.038	0.037	0.293
L3	0.053	0.049	0.283	0.013	0.010	0.204	−0.083	0.079	0.295
L4	−0.046	0.033	0.166	−0.002	0.008	0.789	0.021	0.039	0.587
Cons	0.216	0.201	0.282	0.229	0.073	0.002	0.182	0.115	0.112
Prob>F	0.452			0.000			0.000		
R-squared	0.050			0.102			0.060		

Results show that in all cases with state unemployment and all but one case with income growth, the coefficients are not statistically different from zero, that is, grants are acyclical, which may have fitted the design purpose but fell short on fulfilling federal goals in recession years. In other words, these major federal-state transfers do not contribute toward stabilizing the macroeconomy or accelerating the recovery. The exception, statistically significant at 10% level, is the lag 1 year of income growth (= 2 years from the start of a recession): When income growth falls, total federal grant per capita increases by 14 cents. This is our desired outcome, but it may have come too late for a short recession.

Three cases with income growth show statistically significant (at 1, 5, and 10% levels, respectively) negative coefficients: welfare at 23 cents in lag 4 year, education at 18 cents in lag 4 year, and health/hospital at 45 cents in lag 3 year. The signs are right, countercyclical effects; the magnitudes are large. But unfortunately they come too late, 4–5 years after the start of a recession. That is, federal money comes in large amounts when probably you do not need it as much or any more. These are evidences of the several types of lags, potential loopholes of CCFP, that Friedman (1948) and Blinder (2006) discuss. These also confirm my previous theoretical analyses of the transfer programs. Thus, I can conclude with certainty that, regardless of the specific purpose of any program and its underlying rationale, the current design of transfers cannot deliver on the countercyclical policy side. Even for economic efficiency, there is no reason why efficiency is higher during a recession so that less money is enough. A new, dynamic design is badly needed that takes into consideration the temporal aspect of the grant programs.

11.3.2 Equity of Transfers: From Static to Dynamic

There has been a rich body of literature on the equity of federal tax burdens and federal grants (e.g., Buchanan 1950, 1952; Jenkins 1951; Scott 1950; Bradford and Oates 1971; Weingast et al. 1981; Albouy 2009). Existing literature mostly focuses on the (re)distribution function of government – equity – often horizontal (between jurisdictions of the same level): taking from the rich to give to the poor at one snapshot of time. Conventional models of grants focus on social equity, political business cycle, pork barrel politics, bureaucratic politics, grantsmanship, and recipient behavior (Rich 1989). This is a static, one-dimensional perspective on redistribution. From a policy stand, static transfer programs redistribute resources exclusively from cross-sectional considerations, with no thoughts given to cyclical fluctuations of state economies. While relatively easy to design and implement, static transfers embed an inherent problem – donors are always donors. In fact, given the larger size and the wider range of volatility of their economy in contrast to receiver states, donors may face bigger expenditure gaps than receiver states during recessions because these wealthier states have more volatile economies over the cycle (with higher shares of the manufacturing and the services sectors; for resource-rich states that rely on severance taxes, resource prices are high in boom but low in bust), while the economies of poor state are less volatile (with higher shares of agriculture).

To address this issue, we need to consider macroeconomic operation and fluctuations of state economies and place equity in a two-dimensional frame, both cross-sectional and cross-cycle, to handle horizontal equity and cyclical equity: In boom years, distribution leans toward the poor, as in the static model; in bust years, distribution leans toward the more volatile as well as the needy, the absolute poor and the relative poor because of the bust. The cross-cycle dimension places countercyclical design into federal grants, a new component that seeks to compensate boom-time donor states during recessions. This dynamic element of equity can help quell calls from donor states for "fairness." Since these states have larger and more volatile economies, spending more resources to stabilize them contributes more to macroeconomic stabilization. Broadly speaking, this countercyclical arrangement can add rigor to democratic politics, because the conventional rich-to-poor static transfers are maintained to win support from the poor; the new rich-to-rich, cross-cycle transfers are the new element to win support from the rich. The overall efficiency and social welfare is improved.

11.4 Countercyclical Infrastructure Investment

Infrastructure is the system of public works of a country; it includes all large capital projects. The strong, positive link between infrastructure and economic development has long been established and confirmed in academic studies. All phases of major economic growth rely on and demand infrastructure as the foundation for development, productivity growth, and standards of living improvements (Duncombe and Hou 2011). Infrastructure investment can play a key role in stabilizing a downturn economy to maintain the prerecession standards of living for the general public and to prepare for postrecession recovery and development. This is the policy of countercyclical infrastructure investment. An ideal option is to seek economic stability with countercyclical infrastructure investment. The Swedish government experimented with it from the 1950s to the 1970s, with strong success in the early years (Lindbeck 1974); there have been studies dissecting its initial success and trickling ending (Bergstrom 1981). Econometric analysis of the underlying theoretic model by John Taylor (1982) illustrates how countercyclical infrastructure investment works. A brief description of the model follows.

11.4.1 Taylor's Model for Multi-period Construction Projects

We can take existing infrastructure as capital stock and building new infrastructure as accumulating the stock. Depreciation reduces capital stock; deterioration requires reserves for replacement or current year outlay for maintenance of existing structure and facilities. Since infrastructure is expensive, governments try to minimize the expected cost of building them. Demand for infrastructure is exogenously driven and determined by demographic and other factors. The infrastructure-GDP ratio is assumed to be constant since we consider the cyclical (short-term) changes in the relative cost of investment into infrastructure. Thus, there is a U-shaped cost of having too little or too much infrastructure relative to the demand. Demands for infrastructure, capital stock, investment, project starts, and cost are all cyclical deviations from their secular growth trend; so their long-run averages are zeroes. In order to minimize the cost, we choose a level of project starts. It is reasonable to assume most projects are normally completed within 3 years; census data on construction projects show that this is a reasonable assumption. Project starts in any year are determined by the estimated future demands; estimates are done in the infrastructure improvement process, given in the capital budget. This estimated number of project starts is also the discounted and expenditure-weighted sum of investment costs in the next few years. In other words, we can discount the expected gap in infrastructure some years into the future; the optimal level of starts is a weighted average of the infrastructure gap and the infrastructure outlay to close the gap.

We can design an infrastructure investment stabilization policy to handle drastic cyclical shocks. As infrastructure demand fluctuates around the long-run trend, the effective price of investment goods moves in the same direction. We can separate net investment from replacement of capital stock depreciation: Net investment materializes via a linear accelerator mechanism; the accelerator coefficient is positively related to the desired infrastructure ratio and negatively related to the depreciation rate. The accelerator and its response to the stabilization policy both depend on the length of construction. Thus, the stabilization policy shows different total and marginal effects for each value of the length. Infrastructure in a year is now a distributed lag of starts over a few years. Appendix, Section 11.1 provides the logarithms of the model.

11.4.2 Two-State Regime Switching

Economic cycles are nonlinear, with regime switching at turning points of the cycle (Burns and Mitchell 1946). Forecasts on infrastructure demand are done with autoregressive models and data from past years; such incremental forecasts are the best the federal and state governments can do, but they are not in line with shocks to demand from cyclical fluctuations. Advances in time series techniques in the 1980s provide tools for the breakthrough. In autoregressive forecasting, infrastructure demand deviates above or below the secular trend; the deviations are expected to gradually return to the trend over time. That is, assuming demand deviations are due from a simple first-order autoregressive process, which is a gradual, continuous process, typical of normal years in a boom but not characteristic of the economic cycle. From a cyclical perspective, infrastructure demands embed "turning points" that are transition from the expansionary phase (peak) into the contraction phase (trough) and then from contraction back into expansion (Burns and Mitchell 1946). These turning points are regime switching from boom to bust and back to boom. Hamilton (1993) and Kim and Nelson (1999) provide the logarithms for such a model. The Hamilton (1989) tractable approach to modeling regime changes uses the parameters in an autoregression as the outcome of a discrete-state Markov process; it draws probabilistic inferences on the unobservable regime changes with a nonlinear iterative filter that he devised an algorithm for. Research prior to this assumed linear stationary process in the first difference of the log of key macroindicator series; Hamilton proposed that these series follow a nonlinear stationary process. The macroeconomy switches between a fast growth phase and a slow, even negative growth phase of the cycle; the switch is governed by a Markov process. The Kalman filter is a linear logarithm for continuous unobserved state vectors; the Markov filter Hamilton devised provides nonlinear inferences which can well handle the phase switches of economic cycles. Appendix, Section 11.2 provides details of this approach.

Model Integration. To link the two-state Markov regime switching to the identification of actual economic cycles, Diebold and Rudebusch (1996) provide a transition probability matrix that treats regime switching as different probabilistic objects: The path of the observed time series, in our case the macroeconomic indicator, GDP, or infrastructure investment depends on the state. The density of the former is conditional on the latter. They proposed a multivariate dynamic factor model with Markov regime switching. The conditional density summarizes the probabilistic dependence of the two. The key factor moves around two means, recession and boom. Thus, econometricians have shown that a time-consistent stabilization policy can work in theory on infrastructure investment. Appendix, Section 11.3 offers details on the integration.

11.4.3 Fitting Infrastructure into Federal/State Programs

To put countercyclical infrastructure investment to practice necessitates long-term national and subnational infrastructure programs. This chapter proposes that the federal government adopts a National Infrastructure Program (NIP), with several key features. First, it forecasts needs for infrastructure at the national level in human and economic development. For the former, further improvement of living standards, human capital of the nation, and future demographic changes may demand facility upgrades or new constructions. For economic development, the next generation of industries, changing patterns of industrial composition, and future energy needs cry for large infrastructure. Therefore, the NIP focuses on the medium and long term, to be compiled every 12–20 years, which is longer than presidential and senatorial terms. Once composed and adopted as a law, the NIP stays for implementation for its planned duration. Subsequent presidents and Congresses may make revisions or adjustments but probably not overhauls. Third, the NIP is to be compiled, under presidential leadership, by an independent panel of experts and policy makers from the public and private sectors, deliberated by the general public as well as the Congress in order to achieve consensus. The private sector keeps adequate voice for their needs; federal departments (like DoT, Energy, Interior, and USDA), relevant congressional committees, and the Council of Economic Advisers fully participate. Last but not least, the NIP offers a blueprint for national development in the future, serving as a guideline for state and local governments in compiling their capital budgets. A special trust fund is to be established (see Section 11.5). The NIP serves to assure businesses that their future needs for infrastructure will be addressed. To private citizens, the NIP offers prospect of higher living standards by way of assured public investment into future productivity growth.

States will continue with their current practice of compiling capital budgets on a rolling basis, each covering the current year and five out years. States will incorporate the NIP into their capital budgets as an important component. On one hand, the national program helps states clarify what is to put into their own capital list for economic development and better life quality. On the other hand, full incorporation of the NIP into their capital budgets offers potential cash input as a contingency plan during recessions for accelerated realization of their planned projects. The latter part materializes through the countercyclical financing scheme of the federal NIP. The national program is designed for two paces of implementation: In boom years, the program stays on a normal scale and speed; during a recession, the program switches into an accelerated pace, to return to normal scale upon economic recovery.

11.5 The Framework

Discussions in Sections. 11.2, 11.3, and 11.4 can be integrated into a coherent countercyclical fiscal framework to coordinate federal and state policies for budgetary and thereby economic stability. The framework consists of three tiers of stabilization policy rules: (1) infrastructure investment, (2) (state-local) public services maintenance, and (3) business tax relief and investment. The first two are for the public sector, and the third for the private sector. All three rely on federal transfer as a countercyclical fiscal institution, the first two on federal-state transfers and the third on federal tax expenditure to assist businesses. The three tiers are independent but mutually reinforcing; they can be applied separately in a shallow recession or used simultaneously in a deep recession.

11.5.1 Budget Neutral Boom-Year Savings Mechanism

The starting point is statutory countercyclical savings, to be created via congressional action as permanent authorization. The core of this mechanism is budget neutral, to save during boom years and to draw down the savings in recessions to increase spending so that the countercyclical spending does not increase deficits or national debt. The source of revenue for the savings is mainly the corporate income tax; the amount to save each boom year is 0.5% of current year GDP. In an average economic cycle with 4–6 boom years,[4] savings can accumulate to 2–3% of GDP; then the savings will be released 1–1.5% of GDP each year for one or two consecutive years during a recession.

The choice of the CIT as source of savings is based on two considerations. The CIT is a proportional tax; its share in the federal revenue portfolio has been declining over the decades. Since the mid-1990s its share has been around 2–2.5% of GDP in a boom year and 1–1.5% of GDP in a bust year. To link this tax to a permanent stabilization device may help revive its status. The CIT is a good candidate also because the federal government is in a better position than the states to reserve and use some portion from this source for exclusive placement into a national savings account, and improved infrastructure will better serve businesses.

Another possible source of savings is the federal gasoline tax, by increasing the current federal tax rate and earmarking the increment as countercyclical savings, with the newly increased revenue deposited also into the savings account as specified below. Energy use taxes are a good candidate for several reasons. First, fuel taxes are already a federal tax; inclusion of it under the savings account may cause less public outcry than creating a new tax. Second, the federal-state combined rate may be progressive among and between states in any given year; but across the economic cycle they may become flat. At the individual and business level, they are a benefit tax. Better infrastructure will benefit everyone and all firms.

11.5.2 National Infrastructure Trust Fund

We need to create a National Infrastructure Trust Fund (NITF), into which 50–75% of the boom-year savings will be placed. The against-cycle saving and spending makes the NITF an automatic stabilizer in general: More payouts are made than collections during a recession, and more taxes are collected than payments during an expansion. This is true even in the case that several states may be in a regional downturn any year in the absence of a national recession. The next step is to design and adopt an infrastructure stabilization policy that makes capital expenditure

[4] For the estimated average length of business cycles in the twentieth century, see Hamilton 1993 and Robert Gordon 2010.

cheaper during a recession. This price effect is intended for federal-state policy coordination, by inducing states to accelerate their capital spending to counter the recession, in line with the federal macropolicy. The working mechanism is to use the federal fund as a policy tool to reduce the effective price of infrastructure investment during recessions. We know from microeconomic principles that price effects will exert larger impact than income effects. It works in a way that the temporary price will be higher during boom years and lower in bust years relative to the average price over the cycle.

If we decide to add a gasoline part in the NITF, it may be constructed like the current Highway Trust Fund (HTF). At the current fuel tax rates, the annual federal collection is about 50% of the state-local share. The new NITF fuel tax will double the current HTF in size, in order to serve as a stabilizer. In combination with the current HTF, we will have two parts for infrastructure, one regular and the other countercyclical. The regular part is the HTF, serving a partially redistributive role for horizontal equity, with economically more developed states as donors to underdeveloped receiver states. The countercyclical part, the NITF, is linked to cyclical fluctuations of state economies, such that boom-year donor states may receive more grant dollars in a recession than their current year contribution into the fund (but over the whole cycle they may still end up as donors) because their economies experience larger fluctuation. In this way, dynamic equity is served. Donor state economies are more volatile during recessions; more funding for such states will produce larger effects on the national economy than on smaller, more stable state economies. Funding formula will be based on key indicators of the national and state economies, on multiyear authority from Congress.

11.5.3 National Antirecession Trust Fund

The second tier is a countercyclical grant to help stabilize state-local public services, as a further step in stabilizing public expenditure in a downturn. It functions like the General Revenue Sharing program in the 1970s, only to be launched once a recession is announced as ongoing.[5] Creation of this tier requires an additional 0.5% of GDP as savings each boom year; this part of the savings will be deposited into a National Anti-recession Trust Fund (NATF), designed as a national fund for state-local budget stabilization. When a recession besets the country, the federal government can release 0.5–0.75% of GDP a year for up to 2 years as matching grants to the budget stabilization fund of each state. This measure will provide strong incentive for all states to create a BSF and to save more during boom years.

[5] McGuire 2009 notes that the Congress held discussions about a new version of the GRS program to help state and local governments handle the budget crisis they were facing in 2009.

Box 11.1 Summary of the Fiscal Framework

Tier	Institution	Source	Target	Matching requirement	Incentive	Magnitude
Infrastructure investment	Federal transfer	Boom-year savings	Growth, productivity potential, jobs	State capital projects fund, debt proceeds	States use more pay-go in boom years and more debt in recession	0.5–1% of GDP, plus state own funds
Public service	Federal transfer	Boom-year savings	Basic services and jobs	State budget stabilization fund	States save and go countercyclical	0.5–0.75% of GDP, plus state BSFs
Business tax reduction	Federal tax expenditure	Current year tax	Jobs	(State CIT)		0.5–1% of GDP

11.5.4 CIT Reduction or Exemption in Recession

The third tier, for use when a recession is judged to be deep and prolonged, allows for temporary reduction, even exemption of the corporate income tax so that businesses with reduced tax burden may be able to retain jobs rather than laying off workers. An alternative method of implementing this tier is to allow business investment tax credit. These measures will be triggered off by key indicators when the economy is back to its normal trend. An addition to this tier is for each state to consider whether they will also reduce or forgo their share of the corporate income tax, in line with the federal policy. Box 11.1 is a summary of the framework.

11.6 Operation of the Framework

11.6.1 Automatic Stabilization Policy and Time-Consistent Policy Rule

The framework is designed as a time-consistent policy, its governing rule being automatic application with triggers embedded in key economic indicators. The rationality for an automatic instead of discretionary policy rule has solid support from theoretical and empirical research (Kidland and Prescott 1977), with three major advantages. The first is to minimize lags. Public sector intervention in the economy encounters three types of lags that arise in (1) recognition of recession, (2) taking countercyclical action, and (3) showing effect of the policies (Friedman 1948; Blinder 2006). The recognition lag can now be handled much better than before with more data as well as analytical/computing power. The showing-effect lag is inherent in and varies with policies; in general the earlier the policies are made and implemented, the earlier they will show the designed effect. The lag in taking actions lies in the political system. An automatic policy rule with triggers can minimize this lag by avoiding delays in the policy making process. As long as we can make policies that are technically sound and politically acceptable and pass them in advance for permanent authorization, countercyclical intervention can be much more effective than before.

The second advantage of automatic policy rule is its time consistency, leaving no room for guesswork, which maximizes certainty (minimizes uncertainty and speculation). Policy rules of this nature help reestablish public trust during and after a recession in the economic system and in government policy. The comparative edge and hence more success of monetary policy against fiscal policy has been the rule-based certainty of the former vis-à-vis the discretionary nature of the latter (Taylor 1993). It has been the consensus among (Keynesian) macroeconomists that the direction of any countercyclical fiscal policy is automatic policy rule (Solow 2002; Seidman 2003; Blinder 2006). The third, related to and derived from the first two, is to minimize the space for moral hazard behavior. Any economic intervention causes distortion, out of which moral hazard behavior occurs. With premade, transparent, time-consistent policy rules, we can avoid moral hazard to the minimum.

11.6.2 Infrastructure Stabilization: Formula with Trigger

The infrastructure transfer is designed to stabilize national (50 state total) outlays on infrastructure across expansions and contractions. This policy works through a federal transfer program with regime switching between the boom and bust phases of the economic cycle: Federal transfers subsidize infrastructure investment in recessions but not in expansions, which affects the timing of state capital outlay over the cycle. In years when state economies present strong growth, countercyclical subsidies are put on hold; as a result, state infrastructure outlays will be on a normal scale (lower than it would have been without the stabilizer). Once the economy falls to slow or negative growth, the stabilization program is triggered on. Federal transfers flow in to lower the effective price of infrastructure investment; thus, state spending on capital projects will be higher than in the absence of the federal transfers.

These countercyclical infrastructure transfers can be designed to function as matching grants in order to induce states into policy coordination with federal policy orientation. The hope is that, the federal money being an incentive, states may over time move toward more use of pay-go financing in boom years and more debt in bust years, with more efficient use of their boom surpluses and debt capacity (Wang and Hou 2009; see Appendix to Chapter 10). When a recession hits and federal dollars become available, states can match with own sources from their reserved capital project funds and increased new debt proceeds.

This arrangement does not interrupt, increase, or reduce the overall level of infrastructure investment; it only accelerates such outlay in recession years by advancing some infrastructure investment from the expansionary phase to the contraction phase of the cycle. It reverses current state practices of reducing capital construction (even maintenance) in bust years and smoothes the cyclical fluctuations in capital outlay. The intention is to turn recessions into preparations for future growth, to assimilate state policy with federal macrostabilization policy, and to provide an effective means of cutting cyclical unemployment.

The current Highway Trust Fund stays, keeping its minimum funding as contract authority for continuity of projects. The countercyclical NITF will work through an automatic mechanism. In boom years, the regular part is in use, with the stabilizer shelved. Once the economy slows to the (regime switching) turning point, the predesigned automatic indicator will get the measure and trigger on the stabilizer. As discussed earlier, a National Infrastructure Program will have been created and incorporated into state capital budgets; thus, state and federal agencies have "shovel-ready" projects; businesses as rational economic agents hold reasonable expectations – they will have prepared for such projects as the economic indicators turn sour. In this fashion, the usual adverse effects of jump-starting construction projects (like worker relocation) can be minimized.[6] Capital projects typically last 1–3 years; transfer subsidized projects will be ongoing during early recovery as reinforcement, with little adverse effects because such spending authority will be divided into two types, one for 1-year projects and the other for 2-year projects, to fit the average length of a deep recession.

The issue of moral hazard is omnipresent, in particular when a federal countercyclical transfer program is created to reduce the real cost of infrastructure to states. Thus, if a state expects the cost of investment will fall in the near future, then they have full incentive to reduce their current period investment by postponing projects to a later period in order to take advantage of the federal subsidy. In this case, the result of the countercyclical policy can be destabilizing. Fortunately, in the operation of the macroeconomy, uncertainty is constantly present, with demand for infrastructure being completely exogenous to the states; the timing of triggering on the countercyclical stabilizer and its duration are beyond the forecasting ability of any

[6] Seidman (2003) notes that public works projects are more likely to shift workers from their current jobs to public works jobs, thus leading to dislocation (xv). The proposed NIP with planned infrastructure work will not run into this problem.

state. Therefore, moral hazard may not be a serious issue in most cases of this framework. As Taylor (1982) analyzes, the most probable case of moral hazard is within a very short time frame when the onset of a recession is almost certain; but then the state will have too little time for any realistic and practical readjustment to their preset strategies. Further, the preset transparent policy rule helps further reduce moral hazard behavior.

11.6.3 Public Service Stabilization

The transfers for public service stabilization will be available only for recession years, to be triggered on with signals from key indicators, thereby serving as an automatic stabilizer for deep recessions when the economy is so sluggish and state own-source revenues are so low that their budget stabilization funds are not adequate to fill in the hole. Then, this countercyclical "revenue sharing" will start as matching grants for state own reserves in their budget stabilization funds. The BSF matching requirement is to encourage states to save by themselves in boom years in order to reduce moral hazard behavior. This matching requirement creates a "semi-antirecession insurance market" that states are free to opt in or stay out. Availability of federal dollars will induce all states to save and keep more reserves, which helps restore fiscal discipline among policy makers and state legislatures. The matching for bust year spending can help avoid hoarding of federal transfers that occurred with the recent stimulus package.[7]

Related to and as part of public service stabilization, the calculation method of the Federal Medical Assistance Percentage (FMAP) for the Medicaid program should be changed to using most up-to-date data instead of 3-year averages of old data. The change will convert FMAP from a seemingly acyclical setup with procyclical outcome into a truly countercyclical structure so that federal contribution increases with recession and declines with recovery, better fitting the cyclical needs of the states.

11.6.4 Antirecession Business Tax Reduction

The private sector tier of the framework is also an automatic stabilizer. By the policy rule, this part is triggered on when key indicators show that the recession is deep and the two public sector tiers are not adequate, or the duration of the recession is known

[7] As of the end of FY 2009, states still held BSF balances equal to 2.1% of GDP, which indicates that federal stimulus dollars had to a large extent replaced state own resources – a concern explicitly expressed by President Obama.

to be long. This private sector tier may work in at least two ways. One is corporate income tax reduction or exemption for 1 year with the possibility of extending for another year. Each state may choose to forgo their share of the tax for coordination with the federal policy. This measure will help firms retain their workforce by reducing their tax burden. An alternative is to provide "investment tax credit" (ITC) on production facilities. In the 1950–1960s, an earlier version of ITC was used. This current proposal differs fundamentally from the earlier ITC in at least two important aspects: The earlier ITC was not a time-consistent rule, while this new version will be; the earlier ITC was under the discretion of politicians, open to much manipulation from lack of transparency and subject to heavy moral hazard. The proposed one is an automatic policy rule, governed by a trigger mechanism, placed under transparent policy rule. Risk of moral hazard is set to be minimal.

11.7 Concluding Remarks

Macroeconomists since the 1930s have conducted several rounds of explorations in the line of research this chapter is engaged in, making tremendous theoretical and policy contributions. As Milton Friedman put it in 1948 when he offered his policy framework, all ideas were already common knowledge even then, but this chapter can still contribute uniquely to the literature by integrating parts that were not previously connected into a coherent whole, or putting old wine into a new bottle. This study has called that fiscal policy should adopt three countercyclical features: to be designed for countercyclical operation, to be based on time-consistent policy rules, and to accumulate stabilizing power in boom years for release in recessions. This chapter has advocated that federal policy be designed to coordinate vertically federal-state actions and horizontally spending patterns of both the government and the business sectors to render policies the utmost efficacy in mitigating recession impacts. This study extends the Taylor model for infrastructure investment by adding in the Hamilton two-state regime switching component; it proposes a concept of dynamic equity among states in their contribution toward a pool of federal tax revenues and cross-cycle redistribution; combination of these two is new in public finance theory.

Due to space limits and to keep the discussion focused on fiscal aspects of policy design, I have chosen not to elaborate on two aspects: One is the political dynamics in the context of an expanded federal tax and redistribution program; the other is the technical details in designing the new tax and transfer program. This author fully understands the importance of these two, but they are reserved for separate, full-length research. This framework is by no means "watertight"; it has leaks at all places. My hope is to start a new round of "serious discussion about fiscal policy" (Solow 2002).

Appendix: A Model of Countercyclical Infrastructure Investment

Taylor's Model for Multi-period Construction Projects

John Taylor (1982) devised a model for multiple-period construction projects (hereafter "Taylor's model") that well suits my topic. Here I use the Taylor's model to illustrate why and how a countercyclical stabilization program of infrastructure investment may work in theory.

As discussed in Section 4.1, better infrastructure leads to higher productivity. We can take total existing infrastructure as capital and the building of new infrastructure as accumulating capital stock. Infrastructure takes time to build, with construction duration varying from 1 to 3 years (census data on construction projects show that this is a reasonable assumption). Thus, we can establish a *capital accumulation equation*:

$$K_{t+n} = K_{t+n-1} + S_t - hK_{t+n-1}, \tag{11.1}$$

where Kt is capital stock at the beginning of year t, S_t is the level of construction project starts in year t, and h is the rate of deterioration (or depreciation) of existing infrastructure.

Depreciation reduces the value, or capital stock, of infrastructure; deterioration requires either advance resource reserves for replacement or current year outlay for maintenance of existing structure and facilities. Infrastructure is expensive to build, so governments try to minimize the expected cost of building them; thus, we have a *cost equation*:

$$\sum_{t=1}^{\infty} b^{t+n}\left[d/2(vY_{t+n} - K_{t+n})^2 + c_{t+n}I_{t+n}\right], \tag{11.2}$$

where b is a discount factor, Y_t is exogenous demand for infrastructure, I_t is infrastructure investment in year t, v is the desired or optimal infrastructure-GDP ratio, and c_t is cost of investment goods in year t.

Demands for infrastructure (Y_t), capital stock (K_t), investment (I_t), project starts (S_t), and cost (c_t) are all cyclical deviations from their secular growth trend; so their long-run averages are zeroes. If a project is completed within 1 year and thus its value is accounted for in the stock in the same year, then $I_t = S_t$. Demand for infrastructure is exogenously driven and determined by demographic and other factors that are external to the government. The infrastructure-GDP ratio (v) is assumed to be constant since we consider the cyclical (short-term) changes in the relative cost (c_t) of investment into infrastructure. The quadratic term in the cost function implies a U-shaped cost of having too little or too much infrastructure relative to the demand.

In order to minimize the cost, a level of project starts is chosen, as indicated by the *project starts equation*:

$$S_t = vY_{t+n} - (1-h)K_{t+n-1} - (b^{-n}/d)\sum_{i=0}^{n-1} b^i w_{i+1}\left(C_{t+1} - b(1-h)C_{t+i-1}\right), \quad (11.3)$$

where K_{t+n-1} is predetermined at time t and w_i is the fraction of expenditure on projects during the *i*th year of construction.

It is reasonable to assume $I=1, 2, 3$ because most projects are normally completed within 3 years. Project starts in year *t* are determined by the estimated demand *n* years later; estimates are done in the infrastructure improvement (capital budgeting) process and are given in the capital budget. This estimated number of project starts is also the discounted and expenditure-weighted sum of investment costs in the next *n* years. In other words, this equation discounts the expected gap in infrastructure *n* years into the future (which can be seen by multiplying the right-hand side by b^n); the optimal level of starts is a weighted average of the infrastructure gap and the infrastructure outlay to close the gap.

In the process of federal infrastructure improvement planning or state capital budgeting, forecasts are (have to be) made on infrastructure demand nationwide or in each state. These are done with data from the past years; we can assume that it is done with an autoregressive model. The *forecasting equation* is

$$\hat{Y}_{t+n} = \alpha^n Y_t, \quad 0 \le \alpha \le 1 \quad (11.4)$$

Autoregressive forecasts are the best that federal and state governments can do about the unknown future, but such forecasts are not in line with shocks to demand from business cycle fluctuations. (Section 3.2, below, will dwell on this.) To better handle the drastic cyclical shocks, an infrastructure investment stabilization policy can be designed, with the following *policy rule equation* to calculate the expected future cost of infrastructure outlay:

$$\widehat{C}_{t+i} = g\alpha^i Y_t, \quad i = 1,2,.... \quad (11.5)$$

where *g* is a positive policy parameter. As infrastructure demand fluctuates around the long-run trend, the effective price of investment goods moves in the same direction. Substituting Eqs. 11.4 and 11.5 into 11.3, the project starts equation, we obtain

$$S_t = A_n Z_t + hK_{t+n-1}, \quad (11.6)$$

where $A_n = \upsilon\alpha^n - (b^{-n}/d)g\sum_{i=0}^{n-1}\alpha^i b^i w_{i+1}\left(1 - \alpha b(1-h)\right)$ and $z_t = Y_t - Y_{t-1}$.

The first term ($A_n z_t$) is net investment, and the second is replacement of the portion of capital stock that depreciates between years. Net investment materializes through a linear accelerator mechanism. *A* is the accelerator coefficient; it is positively related to the desired infrastructure ratio, *v*, and negatively related to the depreciation rate, *h*. The faster the depreciation, the more expensive it is to maintain a given size of infrastructure stock.

The accelerator (*A*) and its response to the stabilization policy (*g*) both depend on *n*. Thus, the stabilization policy has different total and marginal effects for each value of the length of construction. Infrastructure in year *t* is now a distributed lag of starts over *n* years, with lag weight being weights for new value:

$$I_t = w_1 S_t + w_2 S_{t-1} + \ldots + w_n S_{t-n+1}, \quad w_1 + w_2 + \cdots + w_n = 1. \qquad (11.7)$$

Therefore, the *n-year infrastructure outlay equation* is a *distributed lag accelerator equation*:

$$\begin{aligned} I_t &= A_n (w_1 z_t + w_2 z_{t-1} + \ldots + w_n z_{t-n+1}) + h(w_1 K_{t+n-1} + \ldots + w_n K_t) \\ &= A_n \sum_{i=0}^{n-1} w_{i+1} z_{t-1} \sum_{i=1}^{n} w_i K_{t+n-i} \end{aligned} \qquad (11.8)$$

Two-State Regime Switching

Over 60 years ago the famous study by Burns and Mitchell (1946) told us that the evolution of the business cycle is nonlinear, with regime switching at turning points of the cycle. The Taylor model was devised in the early 1980s. Though the author saw the need for a two-state switching component, it was computationally "very complicated." By the late 1980s advances in time series techniques provided the tools for the breakthrough. In this section I bring in a two-state regime switching component, developed by James Hamilton, to extend the Taylor model.

Incremental forecasts are the best that federal and state governments can do, but they are not in line with shocks to demand from business cycle fluctuations. In the autoregressive forecasting Eq., 11.4, infrastructure demand deviates around (above or below) the secular trend; the deviations are expected to return to the trend gradually over time. That is, assuming demand deviations are due from a simple first-order autoregressive process: $Y_t = a^i Y_{t-1} - u_t$, which is a gradual, continuous process, typical of normal years in a boom but not characteristic of the business cycle.

From the perspective of business cycles, infrastructure demands embed "turning points" that are transition from the expansionary phase (peak) into the contraction phase, and then from contraction (trough) back into expansion (Burns and Mitchell

1946). These turning points are regime switching from boom to bust and back to boom.[8] Hamilton (1993) and Kim and Nelson (1999) provide the algorithm for such a model.

In his seminal paper, Hamilton (1989) proposed a tractable approach to modeling regime changes. He uses the parameters in an autoregression as the outcome of a discrete-state Markov process, which draws probabilistic inferences on the unobservable regime changes with a nonlinear iterative filter that he devised an algorithm for. Research prior to this paper assumed linear stationary process in the first difference of the log of key macroindicator series; Hamilton proposed that these series follow a nonlinear stationary process (Hamilton 1989, 357). The macroeconomy switches between a fast growth phase and a slow (even negative) growth phase of the cycle; the switch is governed by a Markov process (ibid, 362). The Kalman filter is a linear algorithm for continuous unobserved state vectors; the Markov filter that Hamilton devises provides nonlinear inferences which can well handle the phase switches of business cycles.

The *Hamilton's Markov model of trend* is (different from Section 3.1, *s* here indicates *state*)

$$n_t = \alpha_1 s_t + \alpha_0 + n_{t-1}, \quad S_t = 0 \text{ or } 1, \tag{11.9}$$

The transition between states is governed by a stochastic first-order Markov process that is strictly stationary, with the following probability functions:

$$\begin{aligned} Pr[S_t = 1 \mid S_{t-1} = 1] &= p, \\ Pr[S_t = 0 \mid S_{t-1} = 1] &= 1 - p, \\ Pr[S_t = 0 \mid S_{t-1} = 0] &= q, \\ Pr[S_t = 1 \mid S_{t-1} = 0] &= 1 - p. \end{aligned} \tag{11.10}$$

The stochastic stationary process follows an AR(1) representation:

$$S_t = (1 - q) + \lambda S_{t-1} + v_t, \quad \lambda \equiv -1 + p + q, \tag{11.11}$$

where conditional on $S_{t-1}=1$, $V_t=(1-p)$, with probability p and $V_t=-p$, with probability $1-p$; where conditional on $S_{t-1}=0$, $V_t=-(1-q)$, with probability q, $V_t=q$, with probability $1-q$. Equation 11.9 is a special case of a standard ARIMA model

[8] Taylor suggests a higher-order process as an alternative: $Y_t=a_1Y_{t-1}+a_2Y_{t-2}+u_t$. But this second-order autoregressive process still assumes a smooth gradual process. It is not a solution but only more "gradual."

with normally distributed error terms (taken as "innovations"); V_t in Eq. 11.11 is uncorrelated with lagged values of S_t, such that

$$E\left[V_t \mid S_{t-j}=1\right]=E\left[V_t \mid S_{t-j}=0\right]=0, \quad \text{for } j=1,2,\ldots \tag{11.12}$$

Hamilton highlights two differences between Eq. 11.9 and a standard ARIMA. Under the Hamilton's Markov model of trend, the first difference growth rate $(n_t - n_{t-1})$ changes as response to regime switches, but does not necessarily do so in every period. When this model is applied to a linear normal process, it generates a nonlinear process (Hamilton 1989, 362).

Model Integration

To link the two-state Markov regime switching with the identification of actual business cycles, Diebold and Rudebusch (1996) cleverly rewrite Eq. 11.10 as a transition probability matrix:

$$\mathrm{M}=\begin{bmatrix} \mathrm{p}_{00} & 1-\mathrm{p}_{000} \\ 1-\mathrm{p}_{11} & \mathrm{p}_{11} \end{bmatrix}, \tag{11.13}$$

and treat regime switching as different probabilistic objects. We can take $\{y_t\}_{t=1}^{T}$ as the path of the observed time series. In our case, it is the macroeconomic indicator, GDP, or infrastructure investment. $\{y_t\}_{t=1}^{T}$ depends on the state, $\{S_t\}_{t=1}^{T}$. Thus, the density of y_t is conditional on s_t, as in

$$f(y_t \mid_{St};\theta)=\frac{1}{\sqrt{2\pi\sigma}}\exp\left[\frac{-(y_t-\mu s_t)^2}{2\sigma^2}\right]. \tag{11.14}$$

Based on this, they proposed a multivariate dynamic factor model with Markov regime switching:

$$P(f_t \mid h_t;\theta)=\frac{1}{\sqrt{2\pi}\,\sigma}\exp\left[\frac{-\left[(f_t-\mu_{s_t})-\sum_{i=1}^{p}\phi_i(f_{t\text{-}i}-\mu_{s_{t\text{-}i}})\right]^2}{2\backslash\sigma^2}\right], \tag{11.15}$$

where $\{f_t\}_{t=1}^{T}$ is the sample path of our key factor (infrastructure or GDP). The conditional density summarizes the probabilistic dependence of f_t on h_t. The key factor moves around two means: μ_0 is recession and μ_1 is boom. In a regression representation, it is

$$\Delta x_t=\beta+\lambda f_t+\mu_t, \quad D(L)\mu_t=\varepsilon_t. \tag{11.16}$$

The dimension of all elements is $(\mathrm{N}\times 1)$ except $D(L)$ which is $(\mathrm{N}\times\mathrm{N})$ and f which is (1×1). Thus, econometricians have shown that a time-consistent stabilization policy can work in theory on infrastructure investment. My next step is to integrate infrastructure into a federal program and into state capital budgets; see Section 4.4 of the paper "Putting Infrastructure into Federal/State Programs."

References

Albouy D (2009) The unequal geographic burden of federal taxation. J Polit Econ 117(4):635–667

Bergstrom V (1981) Studies in Swedish post-war industrial investments. Ph.D. dissertation. Uppsala University, Sweden

Blinder AS (2006) The case against the case against discretionary fiscal policy. In: Kopche RW, Tootell G, Triest R (eds) The macroeconomics of fiscal policy. The MIT Press, Cambridge, MA

Bradford DF, Oates WE (1971) Towards a predictive theory of intergovernmental grants. Am Econ Rev 61(2):440–448

Buchanan JM (1950) Federalism and fiscal equity. Am Econ Rev 40(4):583–599

Buchanan JM (1952) Federal grants and resource allocation. J Polit Econ 60(3):208–219

Burns A, Mitchell W (1946) Measuring the business cycle. NBER, New York

Diebold FX, Rudebusch GD (1996) Measuring business cycles: a modern perspective. Rev Econ Stat 78(1):67–77

Duncombe WD, Hou Y (2011) Substantiation of transportation infrastructure – patterns of governance and public finance in development: an analytical comparison of the United States and China. Paper presented at the 1st China-India-US symposium on development and governance. Indian Institute of Management-Bangalore (IIMB), 21–23 Jan 2011

Friedman M (1948) A monetary and fiscal framework for economic stability. Am Econ Rev 38(3):245–264

Gordon RJ (2010) Okun's law and productivity innovations. Am Econ Rev 2:11–16

Grady A (2008) Medicaid: the federal medical assistance percentage. Congressional Research Service, Washington, DC

Hamilton J (1989) A new approach to the economic analysis of nonstationary time series and the business cycle. Econometrica 57(2):357–384

Hamilton J (1993) Estimation, inference, and forecasting of time series subject to changes in regime. In: Maddala GS, Rao CR, Vinod HD (eds) Handbook of statistics, vol 11. North-Holland, New York

Jenkins HP (1951) Fiscal equity in the unequal treatment of unequals: a suggested test. J Polit Econ 59:353–357

Kim CJ, Nelson CR (1999) State-space models with regime switching. The MIT Press, Cambridge, MA

Kydland FE, Prescott EC (1977) Rules rather than discretion: the inconsistency of optimal plans. J Polit Econ 85(3):473–491

Lindbeck A (1974) Swedish economic policy. University of California Press, Berkeley

Maguire S (2009) General revenue sharing: background and analysis. Congressional Research Service, RL 31936, 9 Jan 2009. Washington, DC

Office of Legislative and Governmental Affairs, United States Department of Transportation (2007) Financing federal-aid highways. FHWA-PL-07-017

Rich MJ (1989) Distributive politics and the allocation of federal grants. Am Polit Sci Rev 83(1):193–213

Scott AD (1950) A note on grants in federal countries. Economica 17:416–422

Seidman LS (2003) Automatic fiscal policies to combat recessions. M.E. Sharp, Armonk

Solow RM (2002) Is fiscal policy possible? Is it desirable? Presidential address to the XIII World Congress of the International Economic Association, Lisbon

Stein H (1996) The fiscal revolution in America: policy in pursuit of reality. The AEI Press, Washington, DC, 2nd revised edition

Taylor JB (1982) The Swedish investment funds system as a stabilization policy rule. Brook Papers Econ Act 1:57–99

Taylor JB (1993) Discretion versus policy rules in practice, vol 39, Carnegie-Rochester series on public policy. North-Holland, New York, pp 195–214

U.S. Census Bureau. Annual survey of state and local government finances and census of governments, since 1951

Wang W, Hou Y (2009) Pay-go financing and stability of capital spending. Public Budg Finance 29(4):90–107

Weingast BR, Shepsle KA, Johnsen C (1981) The political economy of benefits and costs: a neoclassical approach to distributive politics. J Polit Econ 89(4):642–664

Chapter 12
Prospects for Budget Stabilization by Subnational Governments

Abstract This chapter concludes the book as a nonconclusion. It first briefly summarizes the key points of the whole book, then reviews the performance of countercyclical savings in the Great Recession, thereby touches upon a few issues indirectly related to budget stabilization at the subnational level that this book has not discussed. Finally the chapter offers the caveat that boom-year savings are one of the devices for financial management and budget stabilization in recession years. Savings per se are not enough; whether savings can accumulate in boom years and whether they can be used most efficiently and effectively in bust years is part of fiscal discipline which is the bottom line that we should hold at any time.

12.1 Introduction

In this book I have dissected the theory and practice of budget stabilization at the subnational level by placing it under the public choice perspective and by linking a commonsense intuition in private life to government provision of services. I started with the norm of budget balance and discussed the transition from economic stabilization by central government to budget stabilization by subnational governments; then I reviewed the evolving process of the countercyclical fiscal policy and policy tools. Thereafter, I tested the effects of the saving devices on the accumulation of savings and the effects of savings during bust years. I also discussed implications of adopting and using countercyclical fiscal policy (and capacity) on budgeting, revenue forecasting, and debt use. Further, I explored how federal grants can be better fine-tuned as another policy tool to incentivize state governments toward policy coordination with the federal government for better policy outcome, smoother budgetary operations, and thereby economic stabilization. Till this point, I have drawn a complete circle. This chapter concludes the book as a nonconclusion: Here I look more into the future on what else could be done to achieve the policy goal of better

Y. Hou, *State Government Budget Stabilization: Policy, Tools, and Impacts*, Studies in Public Choice 8, DOI 10.1007/978-1-4614-6061-9_12,

stabilizing the budget operation and implementation of state governments, that is, smoothing public service provision across the boom-bust alterations of the economic cycle.

This chapter is organized as follows: Section 12.2 checks the effects of countercyclical savings during the Great Recession on mid-year program cuts, budgeted revenue increases, and net revenue actions (as I did in Chapter 7 on an earlier sample period), also the effects on full-time equivalent employment and the total payroll of each state. I find that the effects of BSF and GFS are different during the Great Recession than during previous recessions, due from moral hazard of the states in using federal ARRA grants and their own savings. To offer at least a partial explanation of this unsatisfactory performance of CCFP in the past few years, Section 12.3 provides a clearer delineation of countercyclical fiscal capacity (CCFC) and links CCFP to fiscal discipline. It sounds an alarm that whether savings or the broadly defined countercyclical fiscal capacity can accumulate in boom years and how the saved capacity can be fully utilized in a recession is a holistic, strategic issue rather than an isolated, technical issue. Section 12.4 points out potential problems in existing studies in this topical area and other related issues for further research. Section 12.5 concludes the whole book.

12.2 Effects of Boom-Year Savings During the Great Recession

The Great Recession (December 2007–June 2009, with slow recovery till 2012) has been very different from previous, relatively minor recessions covered in this book in terms of its causes, severity, and consequences on the state public sector. Thus, after all the empirical tests on the effects and efficacy of countercyclical fiscal policy (CCFP) and countercyclical fiscal capacity (CCFC) in Parts II and III of this book, a natural question props up – we have to ask ourselves the following: How has been the "performance" of CCFP and CCFC in the Great Recession? Have the boom-year savings helped state governments in stabilizing their budgets in the past few years? If yes, to what extent? Answers to these questions can provide most direct confirmation or negation of the real utility of what I have advocated for in this book. In this section, I extend what I have done in previous chapters to cover the past few years, for further evidence.

12.2.1 Fiscal Landscape of the Great Recession

To test the effects of accumulated savings during the Great Recession, let us start with the fiscal landscape before and during the Great Recession. The average size of state BSF as a ratio of their general fund expenditure (only those states with this fund) was 2% in 1980 and 1990; it was close to 5% in 2000 and 4.5% in 2007. The 50-state average UUB ratio was 4.5% in 1980, fell to negative 2.5% in 1990, and rose to 4.5% in 2000 and further to 5.5% in 2007. Thus, a total of 50-state boom-year savings were about 5% in 1980, negative 2% in 1990; it rose to 7% in 2000 and further to 10% in 2007. In per capita terms, BSF reached $116 and GFS $195 at the end of FY 2007. Prior economic prosperity and widespread adoption among states of CCFP had obviously built up states' countercyclical fiscal capacity for an average recession.

On a different front, however, the understanding about and application of CCFP had seemed to be limited to save some resources; there was almost no evidence that CCFP had been extended to other policy or financial management areas. For example, states on average did not use their debt capacity in a countercyclical way. Long-term debt issuance in FY 2004–2008 was a little above 1% of gross state product each year or about $500 per capita; not much debt was retired so that the total long-term debt outstanding increased from 6.5% to 7%. Procyclical fiscal policy still dominated. For example, in the expansion of the previous economic cycle (FY 2004–2007), most states, after "filling their BSF to the cap level" and stored up their GFS, cut taxes each year for 4 years. That was a golden opportunity lost; they could have done a lot more, had the concept of CCFP been more fully understood and applied.

The Great Recession was deep and long, with co-occurrence of both supply and demand shocks – on the supply-side oil price shot up; on the demand side consumers lost confidence while credit crunch struck both consumers and medium/small businesses; prices of food and oil stayed high. National average unemployment rate doubled from 4.5% in 2007 to 9.5% in 2010. Growth rate of the total real gross state product declined each year from 3.5% in 2004 to about 2% in 2007, with the next 2 years in the negative territory. The growth rate of state tax revenue fell to about 3% in 2008, declined to negative 8% and negative 2% in 2009 and 2010, respectively.

There was not much new in how state governors and legislatures coped with the Great Recession. Revenue estimation remained as a game that fell behind the economic tide. Major strategies in face of revenue decline (2009 and 2010) were program cuts and tax hikes, plus layoffs (or partial layoffs, converting full-time positions into part-time jobs) when outlay cuts and tax raises were not adequate to fill in revenue holes. In the first half of 2008 (second half of Fiscal 2007), states first responded to the downturn with general fund surpluses; so this measure (per capita GFS) fell by $64, from $195 in 2007 to $131 in 2008; meantime some $10 outlays were cut. As a result of using GFS as the first defense line against downturns and some quick belt tightening, (per capita) BSF continued to rise, from $116 in 2007 to $134 in 2008. In the next full 12 months of the deep recession time, states continued to heavily use general fund surplus, which fell further by $87, from $131 in 2008 to $44 in 2009, meantime resorted to huge outlay cuts, $75, with no tax hikes – there was even a tax cut of $1. Surprisingly, only 14% of BSF ($19) were withdrawn. For Fiscal 2010, program cuts (including from personnel) amounted to $65; tax hikes of $39 were installed. Even then, only 21% of available BSF ($24 out of $115) were withdrawn, which was possible only because federal stimulus grants (The American Recovery Reinvestment Act or ARRA) were used. That is, the average financial position of the states at the end of Fiscal 2010 was "better" than in 2002 (close to 2004), let alone the early 1990s. Put in another way, federal ARRA money was used not in the intended countercyclical way; the design purpose of the ARRA stimulus was severely compromised. Even though states already possessed some countercyclical fiscal capacity, they did not fully exploit it at a time of the most urgent need for the most desired purpose.

12.2.2 *Effects of Savings*

Given that states had some countercyclical fiscal capacity and that the federal government provided stimulus grants, to what extent have state CCFC and federal ARRA grants been effective in stabilizing state budgets in 2009 and 2010? A most recent study by Hou et al. (2012) works on these questions. Hou and coauthors extend the Hou-Moynihan (2008) study (see Chapter 7 for details) to test the effects of boom-year savings during the Great Recession. They find BSF was statistically significant on budget cuts, the magnitude of its effect being about 8% elimination of all budget cuts if we use all BSF for this purpose. But BSF was not statistically significant on revenue actions. These two findings are opposite to the 2008 study. BSF effect on net revenue change is significant but its effect is much diluted: For the 1990 and 2001 recessions, it was 21 cents per dollar of BSF; with the Great Recession included, the coefficient falls to a mere 4 cents. These results confirm my descriptive analysis in Subsection 12.2.1: States did not use their BSF to the full extent in the recession, probably due to lack of confidence in their forthcoming revenue streams.

The authors find GFS is statistically significant on all three measures; but its magnitude is smaller once the Great Recession is included in the sample. In the 2008 study, the magnitude of UUB was 6 cents on budget cuts, 12 cents on revenue actions, and 14 cents on net revenue change, respectively. In this study, the coefficient dwindles to 1.2 cents on budget cuts, 7–8 cents on revenue actions, and 6–10 cents on net revenue change, respectively. The smaller effects could have been related (endogenous) to the severity of the Great Recession. This directs us to the issue of whether there is an optimal size of countercyclical savings. I will come back to this issue in the next section.

Even though the amount of reserves increased before the Great Recession, its effect was dampened by the severity of this downturn. The coefficient of reserves (BSF + GFS) on budget cuts was 5 cents per dollar on the 1990 and 2001 recession; it shrank to 1.8 cents with the Great Recession included in the sample period. Each dollar of reserves could dilute tax hike by 14 cents on previous two recessions; its effect fell to about 5 cents with Great Recession included. Its effect on net revenue change was 16 cents per dollar in the 2008 study, but fell by more than half in this study.

One common feature of the two studies is the increasing magnitude of effects of GFS and total reserves on the three measures of recession. One striking difference is BSF seems to have switched role with GFS. In handling the 1990 and 2001 recessions, GFS was the major CCFP tool against unplanned budget cuts; BSF was not. With the Great Recession included, BSF comes to the forefront in fighting budget cuts, though GFS remains as useful. Surprisingly different from the 2008 study, this 2012 study shows that with the Great Recession included, BSF becomes second to

GFS in handling revenue actions planned for the next fiscal year and net revenue changes, the effect of BSF being less than half of the effect of GFS. It seems that faced with a major downturn when state policy makers lost much of their confidence in the economy and their future revenues, they seem to have receded to their old position of relying more on the discretionary, informal CCFP tool of general fund surpluses, not the rule-based, formal CCFP tool, BSF. This fact indicates that state policy makers are still in the muddling-through stage of practicing countercyclical fiscal policy and getting comfortable with their countercyclical fiscal capacity. Of course, it also points to the fact that BSF was not adequate in coping with a major recession; again the issue rests on "optimal size" of boom-year savings.

On another test, Hou et al. (2012) extend Hou (2005) test of own-source expenditure (see Chapter 6 for details). They find that, despite the qualifications discussed above, BSF and GFS as the two major countercyclical savings instruments have survived the harsh test of the Great Recession; they remain reliable policy instruments, as shown in previous studies. To tease out the effects of the federal stimulus grants in 2009 and 2010, Hou et al. (2012) interact the Great Recession dummy with amounts of each state's share from the ARRA program and use this term as an independent variable. They find that effects of BSF and GFS from previous specifications are confirmed. ARRA money in 2009–2010 did not exert the expected negative impact on budget cuts. That is, stimulus grants were not factored into states' current year fiscal responses to the Great Recession. But each ARRA dollar does pose an expected negative effect on revenue action planned for the next year; placing this into the context of the average $19 reduction of own-source revenue, we see that it will need $297 to wipe out the tax hikes, or in conjunction with GFS which carries an effect of 5.8 cents for each dollar of UUB, it takes $166 (a combination of state pre-saved UUB and federal ARRA grants) to avoid tax increases.

Thus, we can conclude that the concepts and practices of countercyclical fiscal policy and related fiscal capacity have withstood the harsh tests of the Great Recession; part of the remaining issue is how to improve our understanding of them and how to implement them in all related, necessary components of public finance.

12.3 Defining CCFC and Fiscal Discipline

To place countercyclical fiscal policy and practice in the context of subnational level public finance, I use two concepts to recapitulate. These two concepts have some overlap, for reinforcement from different aspects.

12.3.1 Defining CCFC

Summing up what I have discussed in previous chapters and in Section 12.2, we are now ready to define the concept of countercyclical fiscal capacity of a subnational level government in a more comprehensive way than before. In this broadened perspective, CCFC includes at least three coherent components – policy orientation, institutional endorsement, and proactive use of fiscal reserves. It starts with the government body, both the executive and the legislative branches, formally adopting the countercyclical policy orientation such that its portfolio of fiscal policies are placed under a multiyear, across-economic-cycle perspective, with the window for budget balancing extended from the current 12-month (annual) span toward a whole economic cycle (5–8 years), thus enabling adequate financial preparedness for downturns.

Besides, financial management and institutions matter. CCFC builds on routine operations in boom years, both on the revenue side and the outlay side of the fiscal equation. Any addition or reduction to the revenue portfolio of the government should pass a cyclical sustainability test: We need to look into not only the short-term variation but also, if not more importantly, the long-term variability or stability. Similarly, any policy initiative to add or increase programs (outlays) and to raise benefit levels of employees ought to pass the same cyclical sustainability test: Even if we can well afford the benefit increases in a boom year, can we finance them without too much difficulty in a bust year? Consideration of both these sides can contribute substantially toward stronger financial preparedness for future downturns, even a deep recession.

To enable countercyclical financial operation on multiple aspects, institutions should be created, as the budget stabilization fund for exclusive countercyclical use, in order to adopt, advocate, and oversee the building of countercyclical fiscal capacity. Policy decisions of any type in any period involve redistribution of benefits among winners and losers, with the focus falling on the current period, short term, or medium term or long term, with very different outcome on electoral politics and financial stability. The current term refers to a time frame of less than 1 year, the short term 1–3 years, the medium term 3–5 years, and the long term 5–10 years. The current and short terms reflect more of a part of the whole, instead of the whole, and serve the interests of a portion of the population instead of the whole population. In contrast, the medium and long terms in most cases reflect the whole and serve the interests of the majority of the population. In cases of recessions, short-term actions come handy and appear easily implementable, but they will only bring short-term relief or benefit less than the majority. Long-term, sustainable policies may look harsh and appear difficult to execute but they are crucial; these cry for institutional support.

A third component is deliberate and timely use of boom-year savings and other facts of reserved fiscal capacity once a recession has been identified. Saving is not for saving's sake or for improving bond rating; savings are a means but not the end; its purpose is for use in downturns. Another side of this issue is that the design of future federal grants must require grantee matching with their own savings, in order to avoid moral hazard issues.

12.3.2 Fiscal Discipline

I have been talking about savings from the beginning of this book; now I should reverse myself a little bit: Savings are not panacea. As true as saving is necessary when harvests are bountiful, belt tightening is also necessary when hard times have set in with us. After all, the logic of financial operation in bust years is different from that in boom years. In a 2011 study, I examine the application of performance-based budgeting (PBB) across three recent periods (the 1990s, the early 2000s, and the 2007–2009 Recession). With a survey of 11 states on their history and experiences with PBB up to 2010, I confirm, among other conclusions, that states use PBB more heavily during strong economic times as opposed to during economic downturns.

Linking the two sides of the fiscal equation and place savings in context of the real world, we should subject ourselves to "fiscal discipline," a term in public finance literature that has been used broadly without strict definition by academia or professional organizations. Richard Musgrave (1959) used this term to mean that a government should cover its current expenditures only with current revenues. Deficits can bring current benefits to residents and win political support for officials but add tax burdens for future taxpayers (Musgrave and Musgrave 1989, 101). The inferences are as follows: First, deficit financing indicates low or even the absence of fiscal discipline. Second, fiscal discipline involves not only elected officials but also voters/taxpayers, both of whom pay more attention to immediately current needs than the future. Third, it is up to professional finance managers (elected or appointed) to correct any erroneous inclination toward deficit in order to maintain proper fiscal discipline.

John Mikesell (1999) upholds Musgrave's point against deficit financing, "restraining expenditures to the limits of available finance," and elaborates on fiscal discipline as part of the budgetary control process, "insuring that enacted budgets are executed, and preserving the legality of agency expenditures" in intent and amount (44–45). Obviously, the "discipline" here is intended for elected as well as appointed officials to abide by the will of the people expressed through their representatives, the legislators. That is, fiscal discipline is exercised if government agencies execute the appropriations bill faithfully by spending approved amounts of money on legislatively intended items or purposes.

The third usage extends the coverage of fiscal discipline to legislators: The legislature should act to "meet its own deadlines…on resolutions, budget and appropriation bills" (Axelrod 1988, 146).[1] Placing the words into context, several inferences can be made. To begin with, legislators are also subject to the restraint of budgetary discipline though as representatives of voters, they may try gaining spending approval for projects in their home districts. Then, cooperation among legislators themselves and with the executive branch is necessary to maintain smooth budgetary processes. If their representation of the voters' interests distorts the normal budgetary procedure, fiscal discipline is discounted.

The interpretations of fiscal discipline from the above three sources are in fact complimentary. Together they form a more complete picture: Fiscal discipline is

[1] The context of the comment by Axelrod is in regard to the United State Congress's delay in coming up with budget resolutions in the early 1980s.

meant for all those involved in governmental finance – legislators, elected officials, civil servants, and citizens as well. If any one group goes astray, finance managers should uphold their professional standards (and ethics) to restore proper discipline. Besides, fiscal discipline is applicable not only to the budgetary process to limit current expenditures within currently available means and to guarantee timely adoption of a reasonable budget to guide governmental operation in the coming fiscal year but also in the implementation of approved budgets so that the fiscal discipline embedded in the budget document can be faithfully executed, and line managers do not go against legislated intents.

The above interpretations, however, focus only on the current (upcoming) fiscal year, which according to more recent research is far from enough. For smooth financial operations, a multiyear perspective on budgeting is necessary (Schick 2000) because any focus on the current year falls short of planning which is an indispensable part of financial management. It is difficult if not impossible to maintain annual structural balance between current revenue and current expenditures without resorting to multiyear financial planning (Hou 2006). In fact multiyear budgeting has become an increasing need even among developing and transitional countries (Boex et al. 2000). The multiyear perspective requires governments to conduct and do well in two more areas: One is revenue and expenditure estimation for the coming years; the other is to gauge the future fiscal impacts of all major management decisions because all decisions carry financial consequences (Brigham 1982, 3).

Furthermore, sound budgetary practices and well-planned budgets must come with mechanisms devised to maintain fiscal health and stability in cases of downturns of the economy and unexpected emergencies which are natural occurrences beyond the control of subnational governments. In the more conventional economic wisdom, the stabilization function belongs only to the national governments (Musgrave 1959; Oats 1972). New theoretical exploration advocates that subnational governments play a role in stabilizing government expenditures during recessions (Gramlich 1987), and recent research has provided evidence that countercyclical fiscal devices have been effective in this regard at the state level in the United States.

Thus defined, fiscal discipline is a broader concept than used in the past. It branches into (1) a multiyear perspective on budgeting and (2) mechanisms to maintain fiscal health and stability over and across the economic cycle. The two branches cover three stages of the governmental finance process: (a) medium- to long-term planning (revenue and expenditure estimation, gauging fiscal impacts of major management decisions, and debt management), (b) budget compilation and adoption (structural balance between current revenues and current expenditures, and adoption of budget prior to start of fiscal year), and (c) budget execution/financial operation (achieving structural balance and maintaining built-in countercyclical devices). This conceptualization of fiscal discipline grasps the core of governmental financial operations. Applied well, it builds up financial management capacity that leads to sound governance at subnational levels. In this sense, the countercyclical fiscal policy and countercyclical fiscal capacity as I have advocated in the book become part of the core of the concept and practice of fiscal discipline.

12.4 Related Issues for Future Research

So far in this book I have discussed only the major aspects as related to state government budget stabilization, mainly the countercyclical fiscal policy and policy tools. There are some related issues that I have not discussed or not discussed thoroughly so far; these are reserved for detailed research in the future. Here I briefly mention two.

The first issue is refinement of the structural features of the stabilization fund. So far, the states have adopted their BSF in various ways. Among the key structural features, should a state set its cap at a medium level or high level? Should the deposit into the fund in boom years and withdrawal from the fund in bust years be formula based (automatic) or leave the (amount of) deposits and withdrawal at the discretion of policy makers? We have obtained some preliminary evidence to show that a high cap is better than a low or medium cap and that formulas perform better than discretionary deposits and withdrawals. We need more time to observe the performance of the funds and generate more solid evidence to convince lawmakers, in the hope that they may then be open to revising their current BSF legislation.

Another important issue, which has been exposed more thoroughly by the Great Recession, is about the "optimal size" of savings: How large should the CCFC be? Is it the normal size designed to handle an average recession? Or should CCFC be equipped with a much larger size of total savings in preparation for (targeting) a deep recession (like the Great Recession) that occurs once every 80 years or so? If we choose the larger size as the policy, then current practices are all under the bar required for a major downturn. Saving to prepare for another Great Recession means stocking up a lot of resources for a relatively less productive purpose; doing so will increase the inherent costs of public finance and also provide ammunition for the political pressure on precautionary savings. If we choose the normal size as the policy, then there will be a huge fiscal capacity gap from what we have done in the past few decades to what we should do in order to prepare for the worst scenario that we are not clear when will occur. Again it is an issue of uncertainty and lack of information. Without clear decisions on this, any discussion of the so-called optimal size of savings as has done in some previous research will seem not meaningful. Empirical analysis of this issue will be the topic of some future studies in both theory and empirical tests.

12.5 Prospects

A sideline from the optimal size of savings is about the political or public acceptability of boom-year savings. Even though we have concluded from a review of the evolution of CCFP at the state level that saving in boom years is derived from private finance, with a solid practical foundation, the overall utility of a large amount of financial resources put aside must be able to pass the utility test. Only then can we be sure that public support for the policy and practice is warranted; and thus, political support will follow in support of the well-intended policy. The Tea Party movement in the past few years has provided some clue as to the public mentality toward a return toward the basic discipline of human life, which is also why this author takes countercyclical fiscal policy and practice as having a natural bearing with the public choice perspective. Out of this view, I am confident that budget stabilization will be more widely accepted by the general public and adopted by more governments in this country and abroad. I also believe that this policy should and will spread to the local level soon. I am an optimist in this regard.

References

Axelrod D (1988) Budgeting for modern government. St. Martin's Press, New York

Boex LFJ, Martinez-Vazquez J, McNab RM (2000) Multi-year budgeting: a review of international practices. Public Budg Financ 20(2):91–112

Brigham EF (1982) Financial management: theory and practice, 3rd edn. CBS College, New York

Gramlich EM (1987) Subnational fiscal policy. In: Quigley JM (ed) Perspectives on local public finance and public policy, vol 3. JAI Press, Greenwich, pp 3–27

Hou Y (2005) Fiscal reserves and state own-source expenditure in downturns. Public Finance Review 33(1):117–144

Hou Y (2006) Budgeting for fiscal stability over the business cycle. Public Adm Rev 66(5):730–741

Hou Y, Wang W, Zhang P (2012) Defining subnational countercyclical fiscal capacity: testing its average effects and performance in the Great Recession. In: Paper presented at the CAAPA-IRSPM-PMRA conference. Fudan University, Shanghai, 26–27 May 2012

Mikesell J (1999) Fiscal administration. Harcourt Brace College, New York

Musgrave RA (1959) The theory of public finance. McGraw-Hill, New York

Musgrave RA, Musgrave PB (1989) Public finance in theory and practice, 5th edn. McGraw-Hill, New York

Oats W (1972) Fiscal federalism. Harcourt Brace Jovanovich, New York

Schick A (2000) The federal budget: politics, policy process, revisedth edn. The Brookings Institution Press, Washington, DC

Appendixes

General Appendixes

Appendix1: Enabling Legislation of Budget Stabilization Funds by State

Panel A: Source of Legislation

State	Source of legislation
Alaska	Alaska Constitution, Article IX, Section 17: Constitutional Budget Reserve Fund
Arizona	Arizona Revised Statutes, 35-144
Arkansas	2002 Arkansas ALS 2; 2002 Ark. Acts 2; 2002 Ark. SB 2
California	California Codes, Government Code, Sec. 16418
Colorado	Colorado Revised Statute 24-75-201.1(d)(III)
Connecticut	Connecticut Statute, Sec 4-30a
Delaware	Delaware Constitution, Art VIII, Sec 6(d)
Florida	Florida Statutes, Title XIV: Taxation and Finance, Ch 215 Financial Matters: General Provisions, Sec 215.32; Ch 216: Planning and Budgeting, Sec 216-222
Georgia	Georgia Code (unannotated) 45-12.93 G
Hawaii	Hawaii Revised Statutes, Sec 328 L-3
Idaho	Idaho Statutes, Title 57: Public Funds in General, Ch 8: Fund Consolidation Act, Sec 14
Illinois	Illinois Compiled Statutes Annotated, Chapter 30. Finance Funds State Finance Act; P.A. 91-703, §10; 92-16, §27
Indiana	Indiana Code 4-10-18
Iowa	Iowa Code 1999 Supplement: Section 8:55; 8:56
Kansas	Kansas Statutes Annotated, Ch 75, Art 67, 02 (b)
Kentucky	Kentucky Revised Statutes, Title VI: Financial Administration, Ch 48: Budget, Section 48-705
Louisiana	Louisiana Constitution, Article VII, 10-3

(continued)

Y. Hou, *State Government Budget Stabilization: Policy, Tools, and Impacts*, Studies in Public Choice 8, DOI 10.1007/978-1-4614-6061-9,

State	Source of legislation
Maine	M.R.S. Title 5: Administrative Procedures and Services, Part 4: Finance, Chapter 141: General Provisions, Section 1513: Maine Rainy Day Fund
Maryland	Annotated Code of Maryland, State Finance and Procurement Article, Section 7-311: Revenue Stabilization Fund
Massachusetts	General Laws of Massachusetts, Part I: Administration of the Government, Title III: Laws Relating to State Offices, Ch 29: State Finance, Sec 2H
Michigan	Act 76 of 1977 (repealed), Act 431 of 1984. Michigan Compiled Laws, Ch 18: Dept. of Mgmt & Budget, Sec. 351-359
Minnesota	Minnesota Statutes 1999, 16A.152: Budget Reserve and Cash Flow Account
Mississippi	Mississippi Code, Section 27-103-203: Working Cash-Stabilization Reserve Fund established; use of funds; notice of transfers
Missouri	Missouri Revised Statutes, Ch 33: State Financial Administration, Section 33.285 BSF created
Nebraska	Nebraska Statutes, Section 84-612: Cash Reserve Fund created; transfers
Nevada	Nevada Revised Statutes, Title 31: Public Financial Administration, Ch 353: State Financial Administration, Sec 353-288
New Hampshire	Revised Statute, Title I, Ch 9:13-e
New Jersey	New Jersey Revised Statutes, Title 52: State Government, Departments and Officers, Ch 44, C.52:9H-14 to 23
New Mexico	NM Laws 1966, Ch 66, Sec 16 (see NMSA 1978 6-4-2.1; 6-4-2.2)
New York	NYS Consolidated Laws, Ch 56 State Finance Law, Article VI: Funds of the State, Sec 92
North Carolina	NC General Statutes, Ch 143 Executive Budget Act, Sec 15.3: Savings Reserve Account
North Dakota	North Dakota Century Code, 54-27.2-03
Ohio	Ohio Revised Code, Title I: State Government, Ch 131: Revenues and Funds, Sec 131.43-44
Oklahoma	OK Constitution, Art. X: Revenue and Taxation, Sec X-23 Balanced Budget – Procedures
Oregon	Oregon Revised Statutes 293.144 Oregon Rainy Day Fund. ORS § 293.144 (2009) History: 2007 c.5 § 1
Pennsylvania	PA Consolidated Statutes, Title 72, Sec 3741.201-05
Rhode Island	RI General Laws, Title 35 Public Finance, Ch 35-3: State Budget, Sec 35-3-20
South Carolina	SC Constitution, Art III, Sec 36 (A); SC Code of Laws, Sec 11-11-310; Sec 36 (B); SC Code of Laws, Sec 11-11-310
South Dakota	SD Statutes, Title IV: Public Fiscal Administration, Ch 7: Preparation and Adoption of State Budget, Sec 4-7-31, 32
Tennessee	TN Code Annotated, 9-4-211
Texas	Texas Constitution, Art 3: Legislative Department, Sec 49-g: Economic Stabilization Fund
Utah	Utah Code Annotated, Sec 63, Ch 38, 63-38-2.5
Vermont	Vermont Statutes, Title 32: Taxation and Finance, Ch 5: Budget, Sec 308
Virginia	Virginia Constitution, Art X, Sec 8: Limit of Tax & Revenue
Washington	Revised Code of Washington, Title 43: State Government – Executive, Ch 43.135 State Expenditures Limitations (formerly: Tax Revenue Limitations), 43.135.045 Emergency Reserve Fund
West Virginia	WV Code, Ch5A: Dept of Adm., Art 2: Finance Division, Sec 20-22
Wisconsin	WI Statute, Ch 20, Sec. 20.003(4) Required General Fund Balance; Sec. 20.875: Budget Stabilization Fund
Wyoming	1982 S.L. Ch 64 – Statute, Title 9, Ch 2, Art 10: Department of Administration and Information, 9-2-1012(e)

Panel B: Purpose and Nature of Fund

State	Fund name	Year of first bal	Purposes of fund	Nature of fund
Alaska	Constitutional Budget Reserve Fund	1992	If amount available for appropriation for a fiscal year is less than the amount appropriated for the previous fiscal year, may be for any public purpose	A separate fund in state treasury; reported as a trust fund in CAFR
Arizona	Budget Stabilization Fund	1994		
Arkansas	Rainy Day Fund	No balance	To make moneys available to assist the state Medicaid program in maintaining its established levels of service in the event that the current revenue forecast is not collected	A special revenue fund
California	Special Fund for Economic Uncertainties	1977	(1) To meet cash needs of general fund. (2) To eliminate any general fund deficit at the end of each fiscal year as of June 30, 1985. (3) Disaster relief	
Colorado	Required Fund Balance	1982		Non-accumulating, within fiscal-year device
Connecticut	Budget Reserve Fund	1981	To fund deficits	A special revenue fund, fund no. 1900
Delaware	Budget Reserve Account	1979	To fund any unanticipated deficit in any given fiscal year or to provide funds required as a result of any revenue reduction enacted by the general assembly	An account within the general fund
Florida	Working Capital Fund	1965	(1) To avoid deficit due to minor fluctuations in revenue or spending. (2) When not 1, as revolving funds for short-term transfers	
	Budget Stabilization Fund	1995	(1) To offset a deficit in the general revenue fund. (2) To provide funding for an emergency. (3) As revolving funds for transfers	
Georgia	Revenue Shortfall Reserve	1976	"In lieu of the working reserve for high-income and low-income periods"	
Hawaii	Emergency and Budget Reserve Fund	2000	As temporary supplemental source of funding during times of emergency, economic downturn, or unforeseen reduction in revenues	Established in state treasury, as a special fund administered by director of finance

(continued)

State	Fund name	Year of first bal	Purposes of fund	Nature of fund
Idaho	Budget Stabilization Fund	1984	To meet GF revenue shortfalls and expenses incurred as the result of a major disaster declared by governor	In state treasury
Illinois	Budget Stabilization Fund	2002	For the purpose of reducing the need for future tax increases, maintaining the highest possible bond rating, reducing the need for short-term borrowing, providing available resources to meet state obligations whenever casual deficits or failures in revenue occur, and providing the means of addressing budgetary shortfalls	
Indiana	Counter-Cyclical Revenue and Economic Stabilization Fund	1985	(1) To assist in stabilizing revenue during periods of economic recession. (2) Loans can be made to local units of government for specific purposes	Is accounted for with the state general fund
Iowa	Cash Reserve Fund	1994	Moneys in the fund may be used for cash flow purposes – nonrecurring emergency expenditures – and be returned to the fund by the end of each fiscal year	A special account, separate from the GF, balance not considered part of GF balance
	Economic Emergency Fund	1993	Be appropriated only for (economic) emergency expenditures	A special account, separate from the GF, balance not considered part of GF balance. Money in the fund shall not revert to GF unless exceeding maximum
Kansas	General Fund Ending Balance	1994	To have an ending balance in the general fund for the ensuing fiscal year	
Kentucky	Budget Reserve Trust Fund Account	1987	Used if actual GF revenue receipts are not sufficient to meet GF appropriation levels authorized by general assembly	
Louisiana	Budget Stabilization Fund	1999	(1) Revenue forecast is smaller than forecast for current FY. (2) Deficit for current FY is projected	(An early Revenue Stabilization and Mineral Trust Fund changed to) expendable trust fund
Maine	Maine Rainy Day Fund	1985	The law lists many uses	
Maryland	Revenue Stabilization Fund	1987	To retain state revenues for future needs and reduce the need for future tax increases by moderating revenue growth	A continuing, non-lapsing fund

Massachusetts	Commonwealth Stabilization Fund	1987	(1) To make up for any difference between actual state revenues and allowable state revenues in any fiscal year in which actual revenues fall below the allowable amount. (2) To replace the state and local loss of federal funds. (3) For any event which threatens the health, safety, or welfare of the people or the fiscal stability of the commonwealth or any of its political subdivisions	A separate fund on the books
Michigan	Counter-Cyclical Budget and Economic Stabilization Fund	1978	To assist in stabilizing revenue and employment during periods of economic recession and high unemployment	
Minnesota	Budget Reserve Account	1996	Used when negative budgetary balance is projected and measures reflect downturns in state economy	Created in the general fund in state treasury
	Cash Flow Account	1987	To meet cash flow deficiencies resulting from uneven distribution of revenue collections and required expenditures during a fiscal year	Created in the general fund in state treasury
Mississippi	Working Cash-Stabilization Reserve Fund	1983	(1) By treasurer for cash flow needs through fiscal year. No borrowing from other special funds when fund balance above 19 million. Treasurer notifies Legislative Budget Office of each transfer. (2) To cover projected deficits that may occur in GF at the end of FY as result of revenue shortfalls. Governor determines deficit may occur; Director of Finance and Administration transfers funds as necessary to GF, not over 50 million in any FY. (3) Provide funds for Disaster Assistance Trust Fund when such funds are immediately needed	
Missouri	Budget Stabilization Fund	1992	For use in meeting program funding requirements of the state	Created in state treasury (may become "[Cash Operating] Budget Reserve Fund" if not rejected in Nov 2000 citizen vote)
Nebraska	Cash Reserve Fund	1984	Among 10 transfer provisions: (1) Revenue shortfall. (2) Cash flow (for delayed receipt of federal funds). (3) Property tax relief	Under direction of State Treasurer

(continued)

State	Fund name	Year of first bal	Purposes of fund	Nature of fund
Nevada	Fund to Stabilize Operation of State Government	1994	Revenue shortfall	Created as a special revenue fund (CAFR – "fiscal emergency trust fund")
New Hampshire	Revenue Stabilization Reserve Account	1987	Deficit reduction	
New Jersey	Surplus Revenue Fund	1993	(1) Revenue shortfall. (2) Emergencies	A restricted reserve fund within general fund
New Mexico	General Fund Operating Reserve	1967	May be expended only in the event GF revenues and balances, including all other transfers to the GF authorized by law, are insufficient to meet the level of appropriations authorized	Created within general fund
	General Fund Tax Stabilization Reserve	Never has any balance	(1) Appropriation is necessary for public peace, health, and safety. (2) When GF revenues, including all transfers to GF authorized by law, are projected to be insufficient	Created within general fund
New York	Tax Stabilization Reserve Fund	1946	(1) For stabilization of revenues of the state derived from taxes, fees, and other sources required by law to be paid into the general fund of the state treasury. (2) Temporary loan to GF as working capital	
North Carolina	Savings Reserve Account	1991	No specification	A restricted reserve in the general fund under state controller
North Dakota	Budget Stabilization Fund	1990	GF revenue is 2.5 % below estimate	A special fund in state treasury
Ohio	Budget Stabilization Fund	1985	(1) Only in cases of economic downturn to prevent tax increases or spending cuts. (2) The balance of the fund may be combined with the balance in the general revenue fund for purposes of cash management	Created in the state treasury
Oklahoma	Constitutional Reserve Fund	1988	(1) Revenue shortfall (up to 1/2 of balance may be appropriated for forthcoming fiscal year, no more than difference between estimate and certification). (2) Emergency	
Oregon	Rainy Day Fund	2007	To assist the State during difficult economic times	An account in the general fund

Pennsylvania	Tax Stabilization Reserve Fund	1986	(1) To minimize future revenue shortfalls and deficits. (2) To provide greater continuity and predictability in the funding of vital government services. (3) To minimize the need to increase taxes to balance the budget. (4) Emergencies	Funds appropriated only in case of emergency or economic downturn that cannot be dealt with through normal budget process. Fund not to begin new programs but only for continuation of vital public programs in danger of being cut off due to financial problems resulting from the economy
Rhode Island	Budget Reserve and Cash Stabilization Account	1985	Solely for providing sums as required to fund unanticipated general revenue deficit caused by general revenue shortfall as identified by controller at close of fiscal year	An account within the general fund, administered by state controller
South Carolina	General Reserve Fund	1978	Only for purpose of covering operating deficits of state government	Capital Reserve Fund must be exhausted before resorting to General Reserve Fund to cover a deficit
	Capital Reserve Fund	1986	To finance in cash previously authorized capital improvement bond projects; to retire interest or principal on bonds previously issued; for capital improvements or other nonrecurring purposes	If revenue forecast is below expenditure appropriations, current year's appropriation into the fund first must be reduced to extent necessary before mandating any reductions in operating appropriations. Any fund not appropriated in whole lapse to GF
South Dakota	Budget Reserve Fund	1992	Only by special appropriation to redress such unforeseen expenditure obligations or such unforeseen revenue shortfalls as may constitute an emergency	Established within state treasury
Tennessee	Reserve for Revenue Fluctuations (to replace Reserve for Working Capital 1956)	1972	To meet unexpected shortfalls of revenue or expenditure requirements in excess of budgeted appropriation levels	On the books and records of state treasury in the general fund. It is legislative intent that to the extent practicable, all revenue shortfalls will be offset by reductions in expenditures before using the reserve
Texas	Economic Stabilization Fund	1990	(1) Deficit after budget adoption. (2) Temporary cash deficiency in general revenue	A special fund in state treasury; transfers by Comptroller

(continued)

State	Fund name	Year of first bal	Purposes of fund	Nature of fund
Utah	Budget Reserve Account	1987	(1) Cover operating deficit. (2) Cover retroactive tax refunds. (3) Fund operating deficits in public education appropriations	A restricted account within general fund
Vermont	General Fund Budget Stabilization Reserve	1987	To reduce the effects of annual variations in state revenues upon the general fund budget of the state	Determined on a budgetary basis and administered by Commissioner of Finance and Management
Virginia	Revenue Stabilization Fund	1993	For use only when GF revenues appropriated exceed revised GF revenue forecast by over 2 % of revenue last FY, up to half of the fund only	
Washington	Emergency Reserve Fund	1989	May be appropriated for any purpose only if approved by 2/3 of each house and by a vote of the people at next general election	"The current budgetary system lacks stability. It encourages crisis budgeting and results in cutbacks during lean years and overspending during surplus years"
West Virginia	Revenue Shortfall Reserve Fund	1995	For revenue shortfalls, emergency revenue needs by natural disaster, or other fiscal needs as determined solely by the legislature. Governor may, with exe order, borrow money from the fund with prior notice of leg. (And cash flow)	
Wisconsin	Required General Fund Balance	1993		
	Budget Stabilization Fund	1985	No	No
Wyoming	Budget Reserve Account	1983	No specification	

Panel C: Sources of Funding

State	Fund name	Funding source	Replenishment
Alaska	Constitutional Budget Reserve Fund	Except for money deposited into the permanent fund, all money after July 1, 1990, involving mineral lease bonuses, rentals, royalties, royalty sale proceeds, federal mineral revenue sharing payments or bonuses, taxes imposed on mineral income, production, or property	If an appropriation is made from the fund, until the amount is repaid, the amount of money in GF available for appropriation at end of each succeeding FY shall be deposited in the fund. Legislature shall implement this subsection by law
Arizona	Budget Stabilization Fund	When annual growth rate exceeds trend rate, excess growth * total GF revenue determines amount to be appropriated into fund	
Arkansas	Rainy Day Fund	Receive moneys only so long as cash is on hand	
California	Special Fund for Economic Uncertainties	Controller transfers to fund at each FY end the lesser of (1) GF unencumbered balance and (2) difference between “appropriations subject to limitation” for FY then ended and its “appropriation limit”	Continuously appropriated
Colorado	Required Fund Balance (non-accumulating)	Following year’s budget must have 4 % reserve requirement accounted for. All from GF revenues	
Connecticut	Budget Reserve Fund	Unappropriated surplus of general fund	
Delaware	Budget Reserve Account	Within 45 days after the end of any fiscal year, the excess of any unencumbered funds remaining shall be paid into the account	
Florida	Working Capital Fund	Moneys in general revenue fund in excess of amount needed to meet GRF appropriations for current fiscal year	
	Budget Stabilization Fund		Five equal transfers from GF beginning first FY after use
Georgia	Revenue Shortfall Reserve	State fund surpluses after the midyear adjustment is fixed. As of June 30 of each fiscal year, state auditor shall reserve from state surplus	

(continued)

State	Fund name	Funding source	Replenishment
Hawaii	Emergency and Budget Reserve Fund	1. 40 % of tobacco settlement received by state 2. Appropriations by legislature	
Idaho	Budget Stabilization Fund	As long as the balance in fund is under 5 % of previous FY's GF receipts, up to 1 % of prev. FY GF receipts are transferred from the GF	
Illinois	Budget Stabilization Fund	By transfer of appropriated funds as passed by the general assembly and approved by governor	
Indiana	Counter-Cyclical Revenue and Economic Stabilization Fund	Moneys are deposited automatically into the fund if growth rate in adjusted personal income exceeds 2 %	
Iowa	Cash Reserve Fund	Appropriated from GF and ending balance of GF in prior FY	
	Economic Emergency Fund		
Kansas	General Fund Ending Balance		
Kentucky	Budget Reserve Trust Fund Account	Direct appropriations, surplus revenue receipts in GF, and certain unexpended appropriations	
Louisiana	Revenue Stabilization and Mineral Trust Fund	All money available for appropriation from GF and dedicated funds in excess of expenditure limit, except…, shall be deposited into fund	
Maine	Maine Rainy Day Fund	1/2 of excess unappropriated surplus of GF rev is transferred by controller at close of each FY	
Maryland	Revenue Stabilization Fund	1. Moneys appropriated in the state budget to the fund (beginning FY 1995, governor shall include in budget bill an appropriation to the fund of 50 million or an amount to make fund balance to exceed 5 % of est. GF revenue) 2. Interest or other income earned from investment of any money in State Reserve Fund	

Massachusetts	Commonwealth Stabilization Fund	(29-5C) 60 % of any remaining amount of consolidated net surplus shall be transferred to the Commonwealth Stabilization Fund from the general fund and 40 % of such net surplus to the Commonwealth Stabilization Fund from the Local Aid Fund	
Michigan	Counter-Cyclical Budget and Economic Stabilization Fund	% of annual growth rate over 2 % shall be multiplied by total state GF revenue of current fiscal year to determine the amount to be transferred to the fund from state GF in next fiscal year	
Minnesota	Budget Reserve Account	Appropriation	Statute prescribes that the budget reserve be restored when economic indicators show that the economic cycle is on an upturn
	Cash Flow Account		
Mississippi	Working Cash-Stabilization Reserve Fund	100 % of unencumbered GF cash balance at close of each FY until fund reaches 40 mil; after that 50 % of such balance	Out of future annual surpluses.
Missouri	Budget Stabilization Fund	In any budget submission, governor may recommend an appropriation to BSF and, when above cap, make new recommendation to fit cap	
Nebraska	Cash Reserve Fund	1. LB59 (1983) Sec 7: Temporary sales tax increase of no more than 9 month yielded $37 million 2. By appropriation when legislature judged necessary 3. Automatic: When there is surplus	Any transfers shall be reversed upon certification by Director of Administrative Services that sufficient funds are available
Nevada	Fund to Stabilize Operation of State Government	Controller shall deposit to the fund two-fifths of general fund revenue in excess of operation appropriations and other statutory reserves	
New Hampshire	Revenue Stabilization Reserve Account	50 % of general fund undesignated fund balance	
New Jersey	Surplus Revenue Fund	1. Appropriations to the fund 2. (Appointed) treasurer credits to the fund 50 % of actual revenue in excess of governor's certification of revenues	

(continued)

State	Fund name	Funding source	Replenishment
New Mexico	General Fund Operating Reserve	Notwithstanding any other provision to the contrary, there shall be deposited to the GF operating reserve cash balances in the fund existing	
	General Fund Tax Stabilization Reserve	Funds directed to it by law and such other funds as the legislature may appropriate from time to time to the reserve	
New York	Tax Stabilization Reserve Fund	Annual fiscal year-end cash surpluses	Repayment in three equal installments from general fund within 6 years. Temporary loans within fiscal year
North Carolina	Savings Reserve Account	Year-end balance	
North Dakota	Budget Stabilization Fund	General fund balance at end of biennium in excess of 65 million	
Ohio	Budget Stabilization Fund	Unobligated, unencumbered balance in excess of 0.5 % of general revenue fund revenues in preceding FY. Director of B&M transfers any amount necessary for BSF to equal 5 % of GRF revenues of preceding fiscal year. Then to income tax reduction fund	
Oklahoma	Constitutional Reserve Fund	Beginning July 1, 1985, all surplus funds shall be placed in a Constitutional Reserve Fund by the State Treasurer (until cap)	
Oregon	Rainy Day Fund	Funded from the general fund's ending balance up to one percent of general fund appropriations for the prior biennium. The legislature may deposit additional funds as it did to create the fund, using surplus corporate income tax revenues from the 2005–2007 biennium. The Rainy Day Fund also earns interest on the moneys in the fund	

Pennsylvania	Tax Stabilization Reserve Fund	1. General assembly may at any time provide additional amounts from any funds available as an appropriation to the fund 2. 15 % of any budgetary basis fiscal year-end surplus of general fund and all proceeds from the disposition of assets not designated for deposit elsewhere	
Rhode Island	Budget Reserve and Cash Stabilization Account	Transfers from GF (spending is limited to 98 % of estimated GF revenues from all sources) at opening of FY, adjustment to be made at FY end	Transferred amount shall be returned in next fiscal year(s)
South Carolina	General Reserve Fund	General assembly shall provide for 3 % of GF revenue of latest completed FY	GA must provide for orderly restoration of funds withdrawn from reserve, within three fiscal years, from future revenues, and out of funds accumulating in excess of annual operating expenditures
	Capital Reserve Fund	Annual general appropriations act	
South Dakota	Budget Reserve Fund	All prior year unobligated cash up to 5 % of GF or 20 million in FY 1992	
Tennessee	Reserve for Revenue Fluctuations	Annual general fund appropriation	
Texas	Economic Stabilization Fund	1. Transfer of 1/2 of unencumbered general revenue fund balance at end of biennium and portions of oil and natural gas production tax collections 2. 75 % of any oil and gas production taxes above the amount received in benchmark year (FY 1987)	
Utah	Budget Reserve Account	Beginning June 30, 1993, 25 % of annual GF surplus be transferred to the account, with priority over other contingency appropriation using surplus funds	
Vermont	General Fund Budget Stabilization Reserve	1. Any budgetary basis undesignated general fund surplus at close of fiscal year 2. Any additional amounts as may be authorized by general assembly	

(continued)

State	Fund name	Funding source	Replenishment
Virginia	Revenue Stabilization Fund	1. Formula: >=0.5[tax revenue last year * (% increase of tax rev last year – average annual % increase last six years)] 2. Additional appropriations at any time if not exceeding cap	
Washington	Emergency Reserve Fund	Treasurer deposits in the fund all general funds in excess of state expenditure limit for that fiscal year, deposits made at end of each fiscal quarter	
West Virginia	Revenue Shortfall Reserve Fund	50 % of all surplus revenues	
Wisconsin	Required General Fund Balance	General fund appropriation by legislature	
	Budget Stabilization Fund	Appropriation	
Wyoming	Budget Reserve Account	1. Proposed budget shall recommend no less than 5 % of estimated general fund receipt for the next biennium be appropriated to the account 2. At end of each biennial budget period, general fund appropriations for the biennium in excess of expenditures, including encumbrances, shall be transferred into the Budget Reserve Account	

Panel D: Cap of Funding Level

State	Fund name	Minimum	Maximum amount allowed
Alaska	Constitutional Budget Reserve Fund	No	No
Arizona	Budget Stabilization Fund	No	5.634 % FY 1998, 6.333 % FY 1999, 7 % FY 2000 and after, of GF revenue for each FY
California	Special Fund for Econ Uncertainties	No	No
Colorado	Required Fund Balance	2 % of general fund budget	4 % of the amount appropriated from general fund be reserved for that fiscal year
Connecticut	Budget Reserve Fund	No	5 % of net GF appropriations for the FY in progress
Delaware	Budget Reserve Account	No	5 % of estimated general fund revenue
Florida	Working Capital Fund	No	10 % of preceding year's net general revenue fund collections
	Budget Stabilization Fund	1 % FY 1995, 2 % 1996, 3 % 1997, 4 % 1998, 5 % 1999 and after of net revenue collections for general revenue fund during the last completed fiscal year	10 % of net revenue collections for general revenue fund during the last completed fiscal year
Georgia	Revenue Shortfall Reserve	3 % of net revenue collections of current fiscal year	4 % of net revenue collections of current fiscal year
Hawaii	Emergency and Budget Reserve Fund	No	No
Idaho	Budget Stabilization Fund	No	5 % of total GF appropriations for FY beginning July 1. Excess shall be transferred to GF by Controller
Illinois	Budget Stabilization Fund	No	5 % of the total of general fund revenues estimated for that fiscal year
Indiana	Counter-Cyclical Revenue and Economic Stabilization Fund	No	7 % of total GF revenues for the same period. Excess is transferred into Property Tax Replacement Fund

(continued)

State	Fund name	Minimum	Maximum amount allowed
Iowa	Cash Reserve Fund	No	Cash reserve goal percentage: 5 % of adjusted revenue estimate
	Economic Emergency Fund	No	5 % of adjusted revenue estimate for fiscal year; excess goes to general fund
Kansas	General Fund Ending Balance	7.5 % or more of total amount authorized to be expendable in current fiscal year	No
Kentucky	Budget Reserve Trust Fund Account	5 % of GF revenue as target	5 % of actual GF revenue receipts collected during the fiscal year just ended
Louisiana	Budget Stabilization Fund	No	4 % of total state revenue receipts for previous fiscal year
Maine	Maine Rainy Day Fund	No	6 % of previous FY's general fund revenue
Maryland	Revenue Stabilization Fund	5 % of estimated GF revenue beginning FY 1995	No appropriations required when fund exceeds 5 % of estimated GF revenues
Massachusetts	Commonwealth Stabilization Fund	No	7.5 % of budgeted revenues and other financial resources preceding year, amounts in excess shall be transferred to the tax reduction fund
Michigan	Counter-Cyclical Budget and Economic Stabilization Fund	No	10 % of combined level of general fund – general purpose and school aid fund revenues. Excess shall be returned to taxpayers on individual income tax returns
Minnesota	Budget Reserve Account	None – but it does appropriate unrestricted GF balance until the balance reaches $622 million	5 % of general fund expenditures have been an administrative practice over past 15 years
	Cash Flow Account		Commissioner of Finance shall transfer amount necessary to bring total of the account to 350 million on July 1, 1995
Mississippi	Working Cash-Stabilization Reserve Fund	Into it shall be deposited 100 % of unencumbered GF cash balance at close of each FY until fund reaches 40 mil	After 40 million, 50 % of unencumbered GF cash balance at close of each FY, not to exceed 7.5 % of GF appropriations for such FY, shall be deposited into fund. Other 50 % remain in GF. After 7.5 %, 50 % go to Education Enhancement Fund, 50 % stay in GF

Missouri	Budget Stabilization Fund	No minimum. A 2.5 % of GRF will be considered in Nov 2000 Constitutional Amendment	5 % of previous FY general revenue fund. At close of FY, excess balance of fund be transferred to GRF by tenth day of succeeding FY
Nebraska	Cash Reserve Fund	No	No
Nevada	Fund to Stabilize Operation of State Government	No	10 % of GF operating appropriations
New Hampshire	Revenue Stabilization Reserve Account	No	10 % of GF last FY's unrestricted revenue
New Jersey	Surplus Revenue Fund	No	5 % of the amount certified by governor as total anticipated revenues in GF and Property Tax Relief Fund
New Mexico	General Fund Operating Reserve	No. 5 % recurring appropriations as executive policy (GPP 2000 survey, not seen in statute)	No
	General Fund Tax Stabilization Reserve	No	No
New York	Tax Stabilization Reserve Fund	No. Cash surplus at close of fiscal year	2 % of general fund disbursements for the fiscal year. Annual transfer capped at 2/10 of 1 % of GF disbursements. (GPP 2000: In 2000 Governor Pataki has proposed increasing the max to 5 % and annual contribution to 5/10 of 1 %)
North Carolina	Savings Reserve Account	1/4 of unreserved credit balance from GF at the end of FY	Max 5 % GF operating budget for preceding FY
North Dakota	Budget Stabilization Fund	No	5 % of current biennial state general fund budget
Ohio	Budget Stabilization Fund	Same as benchmark. No clear provision	It is the intent of the general assembly to maintain an amount approximately 5 % of general revenue fund revenues for preceding fiscal year
Oklahoma	Constitutional Reserve Fund	No	10 % of general revenue fund certification for preceding fiscal year

(continued)

State	Fund name	Minimum	Maximum amount allowed
Oregon	Rainy Day Fund	No	7.5 % of general fund revenues in the prior biennium
Pennsylvania	Tax Stabilization Reserve Fund	No	Intent and goal of general assembly to create a reserve in an eventual amount not to exceed 3 % of estimated GF revenues
Rhode Island	Budget Reserve & Cash Stabilization Account	No	3 % of total fiscal year resources
South Carolina	General Reserve Fund	No	3 % of GF revenue of latest completed fiscal year
	Capital Reserve Fund	No	2 % of GF revenue of latest completed fiscal year
South Dakota	Budget Reserve Fund	No	Cannot be greater than 5 % of GF appropriations for prior FY or 23 million in FY 1992
Tennessee	Reserve for Revenue Fluctuations	Annually at least 10 % of estimated growth in state tax revenues to be allocated to GF and education trust fund or an amount sufficient to maintain the reserve at the 5 % level	5 % of estimated tax revenues to be allocated to GF and education trust fund
Texas	Economic Stabilization Fund	No	10 % of general revenue fund deposits (excluding interest and investment income) in preceding biennium
Utah	Budget Reserve Account	No	8 % of general fund appropriation amount for the fiscal year in which the surplus occurred
Vermont	General Fund Budget Stabilization Reserve	No	5 % of prior year general fund appropriations
Virginia	Revenue Stabilization Fund	No	10 % of average annual tax revenues from income and retail sales as certified by auditor for three immediate preceding fiscal years
Washington	Emergency Reserve Fund	No	5 % of biennial general fund. Amount in excess shall be transferred to education construction fund
West Virginia	Revenue Shortfall Reserve Fund	No	5 % of total appropriations from state fund (general revenue) for the FY just ended
Wisconsin	Required General Fund Balance	No	1 % FY 2000; 1.2 % FY 2001; 1.4 % FY 2002–2003
	Budget Stabilization Fund	No	No
Wyoming	Budget Reserve Account	No	No

Panel E: Use Approval

State	Fund name	Condition and limit on use	Use approval (appropriation)
Alaska	Constitutional Budget Reserve Fund	If amount available for appropriation for a FY is less than the amount appropriated for previous FY. *Limit*: Just enough to make up the difference	By appropriation: upon affirmative vote of three-fourths of each house
Arizona	Budget Stabilization Fund	When annual growth rate is <2 % and < trend rate, difference in rate * total GF revenue determines amount to be appropriated from the fund at FY end. *Limit*: Not to exceed available balance in fund and just enough to make up the difference	Economic Estimates Commission, legislature
California	Special Fund for Economic Uncertainties	Controller may transfer as necessary for cash flow needs, then return the principal as soon as there is sufficient moneys in GF; shall transfer to GF at each FY end an amount necessary to eliminate any GF deficit	Discretion of state controller
Colorado	Required Fund Balance	If revenues fall below estimation, governor must restrict the budget so the GF reserve does not fall below 2 % of appropriations	
Connecticut	Budget Reserve Fund	When in any FY, Comptroller has determined amount of deficit in last FY, to the extent necessary, an amount from the fund shall be deemed to be appropriated for funding the deficit	Comptroller determines amount of deficit, transfer is automatic
Delaware	Budget Reserve Account	To fund any unanticipated deficit in any given fiscal year or to provide funds required as a result of any revenue reduction enacted by the general assembly	3/5 vote of the members elected to each house
Florida	Working Capital Fund		Governor

(continued)

State	Fund name	Condition and limit on use	Use approval (appropriation)
	Budget Stabilization Fund		Statutory provision or appropriation
Georgia	Revenue Shortfall Reserve		Governor
Hawaii	Emergency and Budget Reserve Fund		Legislative appropriations by 2/3 majority vote
Idaho	Budget Stabilization Fund		Appropriation; limited to 50 % in any year after the fund balance has reached 5 %
Illinois	Budget Stabilization Fund		Governor and general assembly
Indiana	Counter-Cyclical Revenue and Economic Stabilization Fund		Moneys are removed automatically from the fund if adjusted personal income declines by more than 2 %
Iowa	Cash Reserve Fund		General assembly and governor
	Economic Emergency Fund		May be appropriated by general assembly
Kansas	General Fund Ending Balance		
Kentucky	Budget Reserve Trust Fund Account		
Louisiana	Revenue Stabilization and Mineral Trust Fund. In 1999 changed to Budget Stabilization Fund as an expendable trust fund		n/a
Maine	Maine Rainy Day Fund		2/3 vote of legislature upon recommendation of governor, only for prepayment of outstanding GF bonds for major construction – any single project with total cost of over $500k
Maryland	Revenue Stabilization Fund		With authorization of general assembly or state budget bill, governor may transfer funds from the fund to general fund. Fund not subject to transfer by budget amendment

Massachusetts	Commonwealth Stabilization Fund	(29-9C) Commissioner of Administration determines deficiency of revenues, notifies governor and legislature, within 15 days shall reduce allotments or shall submit to the general court specific proposals to raise additional revenues equal to the deficiency. Alternatively, governor may recommend an appropriation equal to the deficiency from the fund. (29-2H) General court determines to transfer and appropriate for such purpose
Michigan	Counter-Cyclical Budget and Economic Stabilization Fund	% of annual growth rate under 0 % shall be multiplied by total state GF revenue of current fiscal year to determine the eligible amount to be transferred to state GF from the fund in current fiscal year
Minnesota	Budget Reserve Account	Commissioner of Finance with approval of the governor and notification to the Legislative Advisory Commission
	Cash Flow Account	
Mississippi	Working Cash-Stabilization Reserve Fund	At discretion of the treasurer or governor. Mere notification of Legislative Budget Office is necessary when transfers in and out occur
Missouri	Budget Stabilization Fund	1. General assembly may appropriate annually from BSF 2. In case of reduced expenditure, governor with prior notice to GA may authorize Commissioner of Administration to transfer funds. Authorization is subject to GA disapproval within 30 days of the notice 3. GA shall not appropriate from BSF without authorization from governor
Nebraska	Cash Reserve Fund	Must be authorized by the legislature and may only be used to meet state obligations in the event GF balance is insufficient. "Treasurer transfer funds… upon certification by Director of Administrative Services that current cash balance in GF is inadequate to meet current obligations"

(continued)

State	Fund name	Condition and limit on use	Use approval (appropriation)
Nevada	Fund to Stabilize Operation of State Government		May be appropriated only if total revenue falls by 5 % or more of total anticipated revenue for the biennium or if legislature and governor declare fiscal emergency
New Hampshire	Revenue Stabilization Reserve Account		2/3 approval from each house of legislature and governor
New Jersey	Surplus Revenue Fund		May be appropriated by legislature only
New Mexico	General Fund Operating Reserve		Only upon specific authorization by the legislature in an amount authorized by the legislature
	General Fund Tax Stabilization Reserve		1. May be appropriated only by 2/3 majority vote of both houses of legislature following receipt by legislature of a declaration of governor that such appropriation is necessary for public peace, health, and safety 2. By legislature of amount of projected insufficiency for either or both fiscal years
New York	Tax Stabilization Reserve Fund		The executive (statute does not provide for leg appropriation. Only "transfer" is mentioned)
North Carolina	Savings Reserve Account		Budget director may not use the funds unless the use has been approved by an act of the general assembly
North Dakota	Budget Stabilization Fund		2.5 % revenue short of legislative estimate, governor orders transfer which must be reported to budget section of legislative council, treasurer transfers
Ohio	Budget Stabilization Fund		Legislature and governor
Oklahoma	Constitutional Reserve Fund		1. Legislative action. 2. Governor and 2/3 of legislature or legislature alone with 3/4 vote
Oregon	Rainy Day Fund	Withdrawals from the Rainy Day Fund require one of three triggers, including a decline in employment, a projected budgetary shortfall, or declaration of a state of emergency. Withdrawals are capped at two-thirds of the balance as of the beginning of the biennium in question	Three-fifths of both chambers of the legislature

Pennsylvania	Tax Stabilization Reserve Fund	Governor determines necessity, requests for appropriation, 2/3 vote approval of separate appropriation bill
Rhode Island	Budget Reserve & Cash Stabilization Account	When revenue is below estimate, governor submits proposed appropriation, GA action, controller transfers fund
South Carolina	General Reserve Fund	Only for purpose of covering deficit, per statute
	Capital Reserve Fund	Cap Res, Budget and Control Board who is controlled by governor
South Dakota	Budget Reserve Fund	Legislature
Tennessee	Reserve for Revenue Fluctuations	Chairs of Finance and Ways and Means Committees. Not to exceed 100 million or half of balance in the reserve
Texas	Economic Stabilization Fund	1. 3/5 vote of legislature for a purpose for which an appropriation from general revenue was made by preceding leg; 2. 2/3 vote for any purpose
Utah	Budget Reserve Account	Legislature
Vermont	General Fund Budget Stabilization Reserve	Transfer by Commissioner of Finance and management to the extent necessary to offset a GF deficit
Virginia	Revenue Stabilization Fund	General assembly
Washington	Emergency Reserve Fund	2/3 vote of leg. 2/3 vote and a vote of all people if for any other purpose
West Virginia	Revenue Shortfall Reserve Fund	Governor may, in lieu of imposing reduction in appropriations, request an appropriation by leg from the fund
Wisconsin	Required General Fund Balance	Legislature
	Budget Stabilization Fund	Appropriation
Wyoming	Budget Reserve Account	By legislative appropriation only

Appendix 2: BSF Balance from State CAFRs, in Millions of Current Dollars, FY 1978–FY 2010

State	1978	1979	1980	1981	1982	1983	1984	1985	1986	1987	1988	1989	1990
Alabama	0.000	0.000	0.000	0.000	0.000	0.000	0.000	0.000	0.000	0.000	0.000	0.000	0.000
Alaska	0.000	0.000	0.000	0.000	0.000	0.000	0.000	0.000	0.000	0.000	0.000	0.000	0.000
Arizona	0.000	0.000	0.000	0.000	0.000	0.000	0.000	0.000	0.000	0.000	0.000	0.000	0.000
Arkansas	0.000	0.000	0.000	0.000	0.000	0.000	0.000	0.000	0.000	0.000	0.000	0.000	0.000
California	0.000	0.000	0.000	348.965	0.000	0.000	327.649	1,337.090	443.158	1,046.000	0.000	654.869	0.000
Colorado	0.000	0.000	0.000	0.000	0.000	0.000	0.000	0.000	0.000	0.000	0.000	0.000	0.000
Connecticut	0.000	0.000	0.000	0.213	0.213	0.000	165.177	171.297	198.629	214.824	204.024	102.254	0.000
Delaware	0.000	11.500	29.200	32.250	35.595	38.106	43.900	47.600	50.200	53.300	55.900	62.500	65.400
Florida	0.110	0.110	0.000	0.146	0.000	0.000	0.000	0.000	131.100	102.800	109.279	156.106	161.839
Georgia	66.542	75.225	84.300	93.289	17.439	0.000	65.105	138.234	150.622	162.640	176.727	194.031	0.000
Hawaii	0.000	0.000	0.000	0.000	0.000	0.000	0.000	0.000	0.000	0.000	0.000	0.000	0.000
Idaho	0.000	0.000	0.000	0.000	0.000	0.000	4.267	5.757	0.000	0.000	0.000	12.037	35.184
Illinois	0.000	0.000	0.000	0.000	0.000	0.000	0.000	0.000	0.000	0.000	0.000	0.000	0.000
Indiana	0.000	0.000	0.000	0.000	0.000	0.000	0.000	145.100	153.800	165.400	220.500	265.400	318.000
Iowa	0.000	0.000	0.000	0.000	0.000	0.000	0.000	0.000	0.000	0.000	0.000	0.000	0.000
Kansas	0.000	0.000	0.000	0.000	0.000	0.000	0.000	0.000	0.000	0.000	0.000	0.000	0.000
Kentucky	0.000	0.000	0.000	0.000	0.000	0.000	0.000	0.000	0.000	20.604	26.449	2.000	2.000
Louisiana	0.000	0.000	0.000	0.000	0.000	0.000	0.000	0.000	0.000	0.000	0.000	0.000	0.000
Maine	0.000	0.000	0.000	0.000	0.000	0.000	0.000	1.000	10.000	25.000	25.000	25.000	4.000
Maryland	0.000	0.000	0.000	0.000	0.000	0.000	0.000	0.000	0.000	50.000	68.119	91.989	118.065
Massachusetts	0.000	0.000	0.000	0.000	0.000	0.000	0.000	0.000	0.000	70.330	112.312	0.000	0.000
Michigan	124.329	241.132	9.578	0.000	2.984	0.000	0.000	340.919	385.052	352.043	393.088	419.213	385.074
Minnesota	0.000	0.000	0.000	0.000	0.000	0.000	250.000	375.000	0.000	250.000	265.000	550.000	550.000
Mississippi	0.000	0.000	0.000	0.000	0.000	20.000	5.000	5.500	5.485	5.480	20.305	20.305	17.305

Missouri	0.000	0.000	0.000	0.000	0.000	0.000	0.000	0.000	0.000	0.000	0.000	0.000	0.000
Montana	0.000	0.000	0.000	0.000	0.000	0.000	0.000	0.000	0.000	0.000	0.000	0.000	0.000
Nebraska	0.000	0.000	0.000	0.000	0.000	0.000	37.047	35.574	22.302	23.730	17.685	50.424	40.037
Nevada	0.000	0.000	0.000	0.000	0.000	0.000	0.000	0.000	0.000	0.000	0.000	0.000	0.000
New Hampshire	0.000	0.000	0.000	0.000	0.000	0.000	0.000	0.000	0.000	26.914	27.142	28.543	0.000
New Jersey	0.000	0.000	0.000	0.000	0.000	0.000	0.000	0.000	0.000	0.000	0.000	245.622	0.000
New Mexico	0.000	0.000	0.000	0.000	0.000	0.000	0.000	0.000	0.000	0.000	0.000	0.000	0.000
New York	172.266	152.294	168.496	184.698	48.607	0.000	50.765	101.764	152.627	168.968	52.687	0.000	0.000
North Carolina	0.000	0.000	0.000	0.000	0.000	0.000	0.000	0.000	0.000	0.000	0.000	0.000	0.000
North Dakota	0.000	0.000	0.000	0.000	0.000	0.000	0.000	0.000	0.000	0.000	0.000	0.000	21.902
Ohio	0.000	0.000	0.000	0.000	0.000	0.000	0.000	125.000	140.900	262.400	283.914	340.041	364.363
Oklahoma	0.000	0.000	0.000	0.000	0.000	0.000	0.000	0.000	0.000	0.000	77.994	152.805	151.734
Oregon	0.000	0.000	0.000	0.000	0.000	0.000	0.000	0.000	0.000	0.000	0.000	0.000	0.000
Pennsylvania	0.000	0.000	0.000	0.000	0.000	0.000	0.000	0.000	25.000	51.624	80.720	112.954	128.026
Rhode Island	0.000	0.000	0.000	0.000	0.000	0.000	0.000	3.646	9.963	18.334	27.981	37.375	5.913
South Carolina	0.000	71.342	79.905	76.499	21.129	40.012	98.497	89.128	51.775	75.381	86.092	87.999	87.999
South Dakota	0.000	0.000	0.000	0.000	0.000	0.000	0.000	0.000	0.000	0.000	0.000	0.000	0.000
Tennessee	0.000	32.000	31.000	22.500	29.000	10.000	50.000	75.000	52.100	75.000	96.800	100.000	100.000
Texas	0.000	0.000	0.000	0.000	0.000	0.000	0.000	0.000	0.000	0.000	0.000	0.000	19.294
Utah	0.000	0.000	0.000	0.000	0.000	0.000	0.000	0.000	0.000	20.049	43.914	47.854	52.587
Vermont	0.000	0.000	0.000	0.000	0.000	0.000	0.000	0.000	0.000	8.233	5.000	0.638	0.000
Virginia	0.000	0.000	0.000	0.000	0.000	0.000	0.000	0.000	0.000	0.000	0.000	0.000	0.000
Washington	0.000	0.000	0.000	0.000	0.000	0.000	0.000	0.000	0.000	0.000	0.000	60.000	260.000
West Virginia	0.000	0.000	0.000	0.000	0.000	0.000	0.000	0.000	0.000	0.000	0.000	0.000	0.000
Wisconsin	0.000	0.000	0.000	0.000	0.000	0.000	0.000	0.000	0.000	0.000	0.000	0.000	0.000
Wyoming	0.000	0.000	0.000	0.000	0.000	42.000	110.423	110.356	105.356	117.000	55.302	58.230	2.188

Appendix 2 (cont.): BSF Balance from State CAFRs, in Millions of Current Dollars, FY 1978–FY 2010

State	1991	1992	1993	1994	1995	1996	1997	1998	1999	2000
Alabama	0.000	0.000	0.000	0.000	0.000	0.000	0.000	0.000	0.000	0.000
Alaska	0.000	648.360	679.421	936.881	2,011.870	2,554.630	3,171.740	3,559.140	2,628.330	2,835.960
Arizona	0.000	0.000	0.000	42.126	223.187	233.128	245.811	291.670	386.838	407.821
Arkansas	0.000	0.000	0.000	0.000	0.000	0.000	0.000	0.000	0.000	0.000
California	0.000	0.000	0.000	0.000	0.000	0.000	0.000	74.646	1,260.720	816.081
Colorado	0.000	0.000	0.000	0.000	0.000	0.000	0.000	0.000	0.000	0.000
Connecticut	0.000	0.000	0.000	0.000	0.000	80.503	240.970	336.909	498.604	529.078
Delaware	67.700	68.100	71.700	79.100	87.200	92.900	100.900	114.100	122.100	126.200
Florida	2.584	60.991	161.758	295.314	281.926	410.608	602.938	1,041.930	1,328.220	1,666.120
Georgia	0.000	0.000	85.538	267.195	288.770	313.386	333.942	351.545	380.883	551.278
Hawaii	0.000	0.000	0.000	0.000	0.000	0.000	0.000	0.000	0.000	0.000
Idaho	35.184	29.778	29.678	32.861	32.888	31.888	27.888	36.030	36.030	36.030
Illinois	0.000	0.000	0.000	0.000	0.000	0.000	0.000	0.000	0.000	0.000
Indiana	323.000	328.600	334.800	371.800	420.900	439.500	467.300	493.100	524.700	539.900
Iowa	0.000	0.000	1.947	38.851	92.462	357.771	430.000	439.200	443.800	459.800
Kansas	0.000	0.000	0.000	0.000	0.000	0.000	0.000	0.000	0.000	0.000
Kentucky	20.000	23.500	28.500	90.000	100.000	200.000	200.000	200.000	230.533	239.283
Louisiana	0.000	0.000	0.000	0.000	0.000	0.000	0.000	0.000	23.605	59.000
Maine	0.000	1.000	7.000	17.000	6.422	38.241	45.724	91.691	131.689	143.479
Maryland	0.154	0.332	50.895	161.780	286.115	461.240	490.060	617.913	634.920	697.805
Massachusetts	59.199	230.380	309.512	382.907	425.405	543.303	799.300	1,159.590	1,388.520	1,608.380
Michigan	182.165	20.101	303.433	775.532	987.912	1,153.560	1,152.410	1,000.540	1,222.480	1,264.400
Minnesota	400.000	400.000	360.000	500.000	500.000	570.000	583.500	513.200	622.000	622.000
Mississippi	0.005	0.005	73.260	162.233	203.636	206.190	212.802	225.434	219.369	231.916

Missouri	0.000	17.186	24.760	37.089	23.874	29.186	122.134	128.888	136.084	143.574
Montana	0.000	0.000	0.000	0.000	0.000	0.000	0.000	0.000	0.000	0.000
Nebraska	31.937	26.937	17.437	27.751	20.482	18.190	40.963	132.594	145.700	142.159
Nevada	0.000	0.000	0.000	18.057	100.000	123.392	128.867	128.867	128.867	147.096
New Hampshire	0.000	0.000	19.975	19.975	19.975	19.975	19.975	19.975	19.975	19.975
New Jersey	0.000	0.000	65.328	158.878	263.257	272.316	388.377	534.110	626.867	698.198
New Mexico	0.000	0.000	0.000	0.000	0.000	0.000	0.000	0.000	0.000	0.000
New York	0.000	0.000	67.124	134.248	157.211	236.932	316.652	399.973	472.935	547.235
North Carolina	0.400	41.593	175.926	210.604	423.610	500.952	500.952	522.521	522.521	37.522
North Dakota	22.049	23.053	0.000	0.000	0.000	0.000	17.000	23.000	23.000	23.000
Ohio	300.363	0.000	0.000	281.300	293.093	828.307	828.307	862.707	906.891	953.291
Oklahoma	196.862	135.009	91.141	45.574	45.574	114.301	308.907	298.480	149.887	157.543
Oregon	0.000	0.000	0.000	0.000	0.000	0.000	0.000	0.000	0.000	0.000
Pennsylvania	1.924	2.028	4.884	29.953	66.647	184.413	412.313	657.301	944.031	1,104.950
Rhode Island	0.000	8.429	23.299	43.296	45.081	52.710	55.273	61.208	65.412	71.269
South Carolina	33.427	0.000	66.832	110.178	120.735	127.006	130.380	130.380	137.649	145.371
South Dakota	0.000	20.000	20.919	21.620	11.141	18.167	24.668	29.831	35.152	36.551
Tennessee	7.200	75.800	150.000	101.400	101.400	101.400	101.400	101.400	127.000	165.100
Texas	0.000	163.353	51.696	29.104	8.133	8.042	8.478	58.304	79.997	85.000
Utah	56.748	58.325	31.730	41.692	65.645	71.471	78.941	88.465	94.722	109.724
Vermont	0.000	0.000	0.000	1.000	0.000	0.000	35.121	36.045	40.033	41.240
Virginia	0.000	0.000	79.900	79.897	79.897	151.617	214.963	348.095	555.607	677.979
Washington	260.000	260.000	100.000	125.000	125.000	0.000	0.000	300.278	535.717	754.000
West Virginia	0.000	0.000	0.000	0.000	20.564	54.706	57.370	67.563	64.581	73.219
Wisconsin	0.000	0.000	0.000	0.000	0.000	0.000	0.000	0.000	0.000	0.000
Wyoming	35.256	25.315	41.404	18.508	11.470	2.789	15.944	18.135	9.182	10.013

Appendix 2 (cont.): BSF Balance from State CAFRs, in Millions of Current Dollars, FY 1978–FY 2010

State	2001	2002	2003	2004	2005	2006	2007	2008	2009	2010
Alabama	0.000	0.000	0.000	0.000	0.000	0.000	0.000	0.000	0.000	0.000
Alaska	2,994.721	2,469.253	2,092.417	2,063.937	2,184.137	2,265.578	2,547.186	5,601.126	7,113.736	8,663.509
Arizona	373.351	67.700	13.737	13.545	160.873	651.020	673.531	147.212	2.767	0.000
Arkansas	0.000	0.000	0.000	0.000	0.000	0.000	0.000	0.000	0.000	0.000
California	204.486	0.000	2,524.520	2,216.020	744.541	1,295.007	1,621.516	925.715	500.000	1,300.000
Colorado	0.000	39.622	60.731	207.003	198.751	251.704	267.020	151.721	148.212	0.000
Connecticut	594.698	0.000	0.000	302.155	666.018	1,112.508	1,381.748	1,381.748	1,381.748	103.274
Delaware	128.000	128.930	136.430	148.150	161.100	175.400	182.800	234.800	186.430	186.430
Florida	1,196.240	1,245.540	958.890	966.390	995.805	1,092.081	1,248.490	1,353.690	273.874	274.916
Georgia	734.449	700.274	260.601	51.577	**414.805**	**924.590**	1,700.000	753.000	271.000	268.000
Hawaii	0.000	0.000	0.000	0.000	48.498	48.611	61.451	73.954	60.423	62.493
Idaho	0.000	0.000	0.000	0.000	0.000	147.064	134.172	207.853	196.595	79.935
Illinois	0.000	225.702	225.704	275.704	275.705	275.704	275.704	275.704	275.704	275.704
Indiana	525.100	257.000	248.100	214.500	316.400	328.100	344.200	363.000	365.200	0.000
Iowa	0.000	0.000	0.000	0.000	0.000	0.000	0.000	0.000	0.000	0.000
Kansas	0.000	0.000	0.000	0.000	0.000	0.000	0.000	0.000	0.000	0.000
Kentucky	239.832	0.000	5.087	31.009	50.765	28.765	119.015	231.490	214.775	7.125
Louisiana	0.000	0.000	193.728	232.232	461.724	680.982	681.923	779.581	860.476	643.857
Maine	143.713	32.914	10.579	33.158	47.071	79.903	115.480	128.877	0.195	25.385
Maryland	1,029.970	678.071	513.607	513.026	540.110	805.495	1,589.756	720.298	701.812	614.706
Massachusetts	1,714.990	881.771	641.325	1,137.320	1,729.051	2,155.861	2,335.021	2,119.194	841.344	669.803
Michigan	994.200	145.200	0.000	81.258	1.995	2.017	2.090	2.156	2.179	2.185
Minnesota	972.000	158.148	103.677	403.677	1,003.000	1,112.660	1,112.660	1,004.922	350.000	266.000
Mississippi	179.633	0.000	8.420	8.855	19.802	3.776	58.607	363.250	311.703	230.734

Missouri	0.000	471.048	463.003	444.926	464.405	494.613	539.133	559.206	560.504	527.594
Montana	0.000	0.000	0.000	0.000	0.000	0.000	0.000	0.000	0.000	0.000
Nebraska	110.066	110.066	59.143	87.028	177.168	273.617	516.088	545.546	575.692	467.202
Nevada	136.341	136.341	1.341	86.279	159.709	249.775	280.023	282.757	7.937	–0.081
New Hampshire	55.201	55.201	17.344	17.344	17.344	69.046	89.046	89.046	9.312	9.312
New Jersey	720.000	0.000	0.000	282.416	288.654	559.798	484.565	734.707	0.000	0.000
New Mexico	0.000	0.000	0.000	0.000	0.000	0.000	0.000	0.000	0.000	0.000
New York	627.025	709.935	710.000	794.000	872.000	944.000	1,031.000	1,031.000	1,031.000	1,031.000
North Carolina	157.522	0.000	150.000	267.057	312.641	628.793	786.650	786.650	150.000	150.000
North Dakota	0.000	0.000	0.000	0.000	99.500	99.500	200.000	200.000	325.000	325.000
Ohio	1,002.490	307.028	0.000	74.598	568.377	1,010.000	1,010.000	1,010.000	0.000	0.000
Oklahoma	340.686	72.399	0.136	217.501	461.317	495.690	571.599	596.573	596.573	149.143
Oregon	0.000	0.000	0.000	0.000	0.000	0.000	319.288	330.675	337.545	125.579
Pennsylvania	1,093.210	300.000	0.000	70.303	70.303	171.362	538.764	745.949	745.949	0.000
Rhode Island	79.689	82.024	83.648	84.298	90.887	95.376	78.659	102.869	80.145	112.280
South Carolina	60.523	67.611	0.000	25.155	75.155	153.488	167.732	95.123	0.000	110.883
South Dakota	39.788	39.788	40.681	41.863	42.683	43.000	43.247	43.398	43.398	43.398
Tennessee	178.000	178.000	24.403	217.000	275.400	324.700	542.900	750.000	556.500	453.100
Texas	0.000	0.000	560.487	365.569	6.949	405.190	1,331.393	4,367.915	6,734.165	7,700.000
Utah	120.330	19.453	26.546	53.585	105.613	131.560	170.638	194.280	188.940	105.030
Vermont	43.019	0.000	23.565	44.486	45.771	51.808	55.224	57.839	60.014	57.314
Virginia	715.623	472.376	247.481	340.067	664.195	1,064.665	1,308.944	1,036.191	575.064	295.159
Washington	0.000	0.000	116.000	NA	NA	NA	NA	NA	NA	NA
West Virginia	79.085	56.178	57.751	53.575	79.302	359.051	514.945	581.077	472.626	276.900
Wisconsin	0.000	0.000	0.003	0.032	0.505	0.638	56.395	1.286	1.466	1.684
Wyoming	247.474	211.852	260.938	811.803	506.949	1,249.963	717.251	1,444.338	1,389.947	1,384.218

Note: BSF balances for the State of Washington for 2004–2010 are not reported in CAFR. Inquiries were made to the state, but no data were provided

Appendix 3: General Fund Surplus (Unreserved Undesignated Balance of the General Fund) from State CAFRs, in Millions of Current Dollars, FY 1979–FY 2010

State	1979	1980	1981	1982	1983	1984	1985	1986	1987	1988	1989	1990
Alabama	27.550	14.185	23.201	21.184	12.276	21.666	57.598	8.466	29.893	32.667	22.711	39.989
Alaska	198.994	766.402	450.546	−1,777.400	−520.095	−133.471	−213.941	−196.033	13.694	224.012	162.715	300.133
Arizona	117.144	234.296	133.437	8.787	131.979	55.862	104.741	40.040	55.689	6.107	1.163	−540.102
Arkansas	0.000	0.000	0.000	0.000	0.000	0.000	0.000	0.000	0.000	0.000	0.000	0.000
California	2,680.150	1,997.910	0.000	−154.203	−608.356	0.000	0.000	0.000	528.302	−342.504	0.000	−30.546
Colorado	292.600	259.556	598.000	0.000	0.000	16.027	15.718	4.352	45.141	100.342	134.832	116.563
Connecticut	1.000	3.131	−65.679	−39.838	−47.950	0.000	0.000	0.000	0.000	−149.873	−193.590	−461.777
Delaware	0.000	7.800	6.600	2.500	−2.834	46.734	116.800	70.795	90.390	76.531	110.826	75.625
Florida	601.628	625.926	651.970	404.421	456.498	459.729	112.000	466.349	381.698	553.527	396.069	463.279
Georgia	133.828	158.676	87.254	0.000	0.000	0.000	197.280	34.785	81.456	85.283	78.130	0.000
Hawaii	66.927	179.031	231.692	209.964	129.517	105.063	129.461	136.987	339.096	470.560	629.188	456.317
Idaho	10.137	6.571	1.743	−2.305	0.000	−7.770	−3.380	0.939	0.001	17.118	63.348	49.395
Illinois	56.276	85.127	−310.792	−593.707	−909.203	−661.905	−197.609	−425.355	−757.254	−510.801	−256.038	−614.537
Indiana	345.238	199.922	84.880	−35.540	56.965	96.385	20.630	23.936	45.871	478.525	736.785	649.485
Iowa	91.000	28.000	31.000	22.000	8.000	0.000	0.000	0.000	68.000	62.000	−42.245	−132.577
Kansas	195.900	183.300	152.100	92.400	51.100	95.600	120.400	19.700	73.300	301.200	371.400	272.900
Kentucky	70.291	7.523	11.992	55.705	33.912	121.980	143.521	268.180	154.814	24.427	−9.015	32.779
Louisiana	383.033	549.383	556.329	270.961	180.790	35.249	99.779	−201.611	−445.639	−511.922	655.419	702.311
Maine	17.371	19.158	24.938	18.843	16.421	33.260	41.337	30.903	57.310	114.234	99.250	8.395
Maryland	318.997	293.049	170.915	155.682	33.383	18.190	49.129	52.704	207.820	408.485	390.288	56.984
Massachusetts	219.967	86.016	102.608	178.629	360.517	363.406	92.193	333.302	40.512	41.348	−466.427	−1,296.280
Michigan	29.198	0.000	0.000	−795.804	−586.150	−57.526	139.167	152.615	11.030	21.513	61.073	−310.361
Minnesota	234.486	−16.965	−73.044	−705.268	−32.272	−77.995	−34.852	178.797	61.725	377.134	198.215	106.667

Mississippi	72.000	60.000	77.000	39.000	15.190	10.614	169.125	163.459	176.855	232.527	234.454	112.922
Missouri	343.012	373.464	124.031	115.122	15.714	186.890	109.215	73.031	7.758	109.433	142.600	35.643
Montana	29.000	42.000	61.000	34.000	57.000	39.000	27.545	16.002	10.557	39.472	67.234	89.038
Nebraska	62.389	116.389	57.233	−15.620	16.118	45.904	13.539	−10.867	34.944	143.058	251.931	187.775
Nevada	83.217	66.122	45.117	45.595	50.927	81.337	69.948	86.717	55.517	87.088	56.618	82.831
New Hampshire	22.123	−4.351	−31.000	−60.668	−62.015	−24.443	21.894	32.410	23.200	13.147	5.612	−10.740
New Jersey	217.161	228.688	188.113	78.732	96.194	485.323	716.835	444.502	565.018	491.006	391.540	1.000
New Mexico	100.000	140.000	192.000	209.000	166.000	154.000	112.000	124.000	0.000	0.000	0.000	108.000
New York	348.465	−3,013.360	−2,868.350	−2,321.600	−4,428.850	−4,695.940	−4,965.570	−5,059.510	−4,373.680	−5,480.790	−6,488.650	−6,935.720
North Carolina	187.499	284.969	154.627	116.527	49.491	269.875	394.298	322.211	363.517	368.225	105.020	−13.508
North Dakota	160.000	157.000	176.000	109.000	43.000	110.000	161.000	109.000	19.000	49.000	37.613	68.078
Ohio	357.000	142.000	134.000	226.241	269.906	420.283	849.941	861.191	712.187	269.892	566.277	540.791
Oklahoma	220.086	56.000	544.401	377.000	17.000	6.000	120.778	167.897	90.910	740.307	711.764	147.000
Oregon	289.976	55.774	15.157	−181.391	45.600	134.705	90.369	164.788	1.328	30.137	92.933	145.352
Pennsylvania	28.543	67.956	71.805	7.521	−234.658	76.414	310.468	104.964	347.414	−129.545	−10.228	−701.604
Rhode Island	41.885	63.398	31.032	3.174	26.626	32.018	61.179	52.282	105.760	114.666	13.578	0.000
South Carolina	12.665	6.969	0.000	0.000	0.000	0.000	−11.936	−6.086	−99.396	−62.238	−130.218	−140.568
South Dakota	10.870	16.433	20.458	19.716	18.599	5.000	39.714	31.324	0.000	0.000	0.000	0.000
Tennessee	0.197	0.533	0.634	0.801	0.391	0.559	0.381	0.228	22.154	0.012	0.014	0.081
Texas	620.350	438.664	675.638	1,330.300	1,006.130	741.464	232.530	−231.011	−1,399.840	−1,253.760	−547.132	−525.221
Utah	15.357	20.355	24.448	36.181	11.603	81.728	18.919	1.808	29.207	9.723	35.499	24.657
Vermont	0.000	7.293	−1.245	−0.105	−30.831	−35.822	−20.266	2.951	0.000	0.000	0.000	−2.654
Virginia	97.928	42.152	65.008	40.597	2.404	161.691	47.068	31.572	137.961	121.193	0.000	166.302
Washington	401.927	196.582	7.894	−462.356	−349.227	−323.299	−42.291	9.381	172.932	108.442	455.891	522.123
West Virginia	46.689	50.633	9.203	28.767	12.435	84.903	85.599	50.678	4.421	0.052	24.334	66.716
Wisconsin	280.561	72.627	23.652	26.485	−182.126	360.009	314.084	237.073	232.733	193.981	375.016	−836.436
Wyoming	55.804	104.599	64.467	121.830	23.092	31.013	33.602	43.216	27.667	−14.258	22.147	48.873

Appendix 3 (cont.): UUB from State CAFRs, in Millions of Current Dollars, FY 1979–FY 2010

State	1991	1992	1993	1994	1995	1996	1997	1998	1999	2000
Alabama	17.167	41.020	42.414	19.065	39.038	81.159	74.739	68.653	83.435	80.805
Alaska	696.257	0.000	−56.711	−1,418.770	−1,561.430	−1,875.810	−1,792.460	−2,293.070	−3,359.400	−3,720.420
Arizona	−132.818	−226.491	57.031	295.312	452.338	628.184	759.862	858.141	818.831	952.854
Arkansas	0.000	0.000	0.000	0.000	0.000	0.000	0.000	0.000	0.000	0.000
California	−1,179.360	−3,928.140	−2,807.870	−1,633.120	−2,555.550	−1,109.700	−1,330.410	0.000	0.000	6,263.550
Colorado	16.346	133.299	326.759	320.375	408.927	211.812	208.390	171.826	0.000	−143.910
Connecticut	−1,274.340	−476.502	−503.584	−465.776	−576.879	−639.917	−670.014	−694.308	−602.696	−674.991
Delaware	35.115	34.642	114.169	185.673	349.171	364.543	419.380	616.375	575.543	552.724
Florida	434.497	459.525	879.571	445.581	1,656.490	2,186.090	2,419.010	2,548.770	2,011.540	2,184.210
Georgia	−0.756	−5.260	247.364	107.487	358.775	620.950	776.030	1,165.380	1,161.950	1,142.050
Hawaii	346.505	327.277	207.546	231.146	307.302	367.708	310.842	300.609	331.891	432.169
Idaho	−92.988	6.787	12.003	37.211	180.122	253.650	202.413	243.388	276.219	480.255
Illinois	−1,537.410	−1,825.100	−2,059.800	−1,731.160	−1,404.220	−1,129.680	−604.185	−366.996	−774.700	−494.204
Indiana	398.506	437.550	55.716	1,173.130	1,072.240	1,491.370	1,588.010	597.799	1,748.090	1,357.960
Iowa	−338.281	−408.809	−306.790	105.945	434.701	657.083	815.935	895.926	781.602	711.419
Kansas	162.200	140.500	384.900	454.400	367.000	379.200	527.800	756.300	477.978	337.520
Kentucky	85.382	−113.007	−68.726	81.508	238.239	172.014	96.825	428.178	116.858	206.795
Louisiana	417.983	−83.342	101.138	212.941	145.689	318.039	135.014	94.163	−26.549	80.645
Maine	−88.242	−125.803	−170.271	−64.277	−97.123	−56.707	−13.129	59.288	75.007	250.276
Maryland	0.056	−56.440	10.519	60.016	2.368	−52.760	49.221	339.283	539.293	513.127
Massachusetts	46.229	47.457	49.674	53.077	55.862	54.330	57.981	70.189	71.521	78.511
Michigan	−169.412	0.000	26.000	0.000	0.000	0.000	53.277	55.172	0.000	211.810
Minnesota	−80.280	−301.843	194.976	−44.624	498.022	491.862	642.344	386.795	62.094	451.210
Mississippi	128.413	156.538	352.123	587.604	477.121	417.183	467.747	514.662	589.548	368.612

Missouri	−94.601	76.786	98.830	167.835	426.224	1,103.500	1,214.700	1,168.950	997.162	608.887
Montana	58.700	24.486	41.471	32.593	25.527	30.145	30.315	44.309	109.674	146.000
Nebraska	150.099	87.302	0.000	42.230	77.171	99.292	120.028	265.250	132.661	139.500
Nevada	43.393	0.583	32.732	39.616	−26.809	10.107	−9.360	−89.509	−68.511	46.803
New Hampshire	−24.528	18.617	31.483	11.969	0.000	−44.151	−1.224	41.399	0.000	3.999
New Jersey	1.400	760.845	937.378	925.980	569.209	441.983	280.577	228.264	276.145	187.769
New Mexico	63.000	90.189	194.560	153.034	29.600	−24.653	39.239	230.191	180.085	320.000
New York	−7,841.210	−5,463.000	−3,228.490	−2,565.110	−3,935.930	−3,613.880	−1,695.940	−272.347	433.670	2,400.410
North Carolina	−280.522	−74.307	209.066	433.562	378.337	594.411	417.247	445.029	60.053	64.834
North Dakota	108.677	58.219	27.083	41.939	64.561	85.444	109.262	141.873	86.140	114.609
Ohio	232.356	92.175	199.261	336.294	132.890	301.033	195.450	198.233	322.773	324.312
Oklahoma	782.296	394.339	334.056	435.062	594.048	727.418	763.307	740.339	965.085	1,081.930
Oregon	209.635	301.342	430.249	419.941	283.240	472.687	307.141	25.486	276.878	44.203
Pennsylvania	−1,394.460	−394.091	64.313	79.162	−16.340	−213.005	187.304	497.641	1,055.170	1,700.130
Rhode Island	2.531	0.226	8.712	3.481	5.218	0.193	45.891	132.040	98.300	91.922
South Carolina	−252.482	−252.704	−247.475	−301.808	−202.981	−261.065	−294.233	−109.468	0.000	33.297
South Dakota	69.826	56.963	48.616	39.357	65.507	64.364	66.124	59.952	54.277	54.768
Tennessee	0.078	0.018	0.055	0.206	0.017	0.054	0.071	0.076	0.072	0.163
Texas	−230.647	−632.950	−532.851	−668.920	−204.480	−1,043.750	483.123	745.809	1,388.780	767.792
Utah	29.277	4.852	1.745	12.240	15.246	0.483	2.428	9.408	0.281	25.376
Vermont	−65.388	−65.139	−46.179	0.000	−14.526	−4.814	1.732	24.512	53.861	54.991
Virginia	0.000	52.797	59.712	7.559	0.000	1.077	76.300	33.037	8.256	662.755
Washington	465.749	0.000	234.158	108.082	458.912	422.364	512.857	397.262	461.870	427.631
West Virginia	45.268	4.081	20.566	20.564	43.142	20.339	10.193	4.454	14.638	262.973
Wisconsin	−1,359.420	−1,397.000	−1,418.490	−1,472.150	−1,427.150	−1,211.740	−1,771.730	−1,595.010	−1,229.950	−1,440.050
Wyoming	41.907	53.835	22.565	21.974	24.543	34.357	35.098	128.674	51.012	97.151

Appendix 3 (cont.): UUB from State CAFRs, in Millions of Current Dollars, FY 1979–FY 2010

State	2001	2002	2003	2004	2005	2006	2007	2008	2009	2010
Alabama	103.907	147.941	158.346	232.501	317.879	401.393	399.009	376.391	216.623	77.405
Alaska	−3,717.070	−701.741	−1,850.880	−1,929.660	−1,297.610	−123.785	2,249.070	13,717.700	13,222.879	10,405.256
Arizona	912.423	560.478	343.012	561.029	986.168	1,434.810	1,081.710	108.914	−1,401.381	−825.081
Arkansas	0.000	895.644	973.152	1,384.920	1,532.040	1,988.210	2,272.760	2,309.420	2,256.642	1,814.731
California	4,245.390	−5,987.210	−15,419.600	−3,231.730	−1,410.230	672.862	−4,504.080	−6,282.020	−18,344.400	−20,929.640
Colorado	−457.941	137.595	0.000	0.000	0.000	295.882	95.779	0.000	155.436	−30.822
Connecticut	−781.846	−944.022	−842.318	−900.171	−1,037.650	−1,058.710	−994.314	−1,149.230	−2,303.429	−1,678.971
Delaware	349.987	580.248	643.461	929.157	999.231	1,039.370	956.073	856.479	744.435	843.635
Florida	2,074.180	2,001.520	1,964.500	2,426.500	5,257.270	6,572.190	5,574.680	2,324.590	2,191.735	2,984.775
Georgia	1,425.020	397.279	9.553	17.837	335.828	924.590	2,077.090	1,489.500	−492.520	−41.837
Hawaii	526.354	311.107	267.418	381.740	745.770	1,013.990	881.311	567.474	−87.537	−210.551
Idaho	554.785	324.274	170.935	337.570	497.605	744.413	985.312	1,067.000	631.397	489.697
Illinois	−1,458.470	−3,458.270	−4,490.040	−2,644.500	−3,349.250	−3,020.150	−4,224.670	−4,102.560	−7,722.306	−9,283.283
Indiana	511.059	738.880	871.053	840.956	221.038	740.832	1,046.390	1,306.430	581.892	1,457.683
Iowa	490.902	316.767	180.780	445.627	559.864	897.708	1,052.540	1,118.500	802.767	915.155
Kansas	342.782	60.595	−53.782	115.150	297.059	649.526	791.980	414.713	−201.007	−278.000
Kentucky	−8.870	−36.033	183.922	303.623	593.472	713.339	517.277	−1.937	−49.698	2.533
Louisiana	27.251	33.953	18.330	−10.998	264.185	442.346	1,157.980	793.567	678.662	−201.451
Maine	27.263	−136.169	−81.361	−124.706	−146.328	−355.427	−283.485	−403.874	−390.379	−411.018
Maryland	641.972	265.468	−110.344	0.000	307.525	730.866	690.206	959.412	0.000	0.000
Massachusetts	794.270	1,409.670	619.190	1,014.470	1,730.350	1,861.880	4,899.150	916.197	1,734.822	1,834.783
Michigan	28.072	114.500	173.956	0.000	220.537	2.482	259.080	457.870	177.244	187.220
Minnesota	0.000	56.516	−1,006.870	−448.465	−68.292	0.000	0.000	0.000	−752.490	−973.110
Mississippi	174.332	101.647	868.595	692.120	353.546	436.368	582.385	325.031	244.076	284.081

Missouri	1.522	−1.645	−1,318.000	−1,112.000	326.920	988.240	1,289.030	1,310.240	716.371	645.567
Montana	142.897	78.116	43.065	132.873	289.675	408.580	549.158	433.580	392.526	322.391
Nebraska	89.715	80.612	−17.319	389.447	408.771	691.757	971.205	972.307	855.542	715.530
Nevada	101.012	29.934	−119.908	−6.273	0.000	175.971	0.000	32.398	0.000	0.000
New Hampshire	0.000	−37.869	0.000	15.287	82.202	26.056	61.713	17.184	0.000	65.681
New Jersey	388.698	292.300	373.000	376.500	461.700	1,216.700	1,410.400	469.800	614.200	794.300
New Mexico	384.571	298.084	245.191	427.605	732.395	859.338	681.061	804.311	464.260	355.267
New York	2,410.000	969.499	−4,536.000	−2,063.000	−1,227.000	384.000	373.000	405.000	−5,568.000	−6,663.000
North Carolina	224.922	576.318	−333.127	−393.735	−251.442	1,113.050	1,718.040	819.263	−965.152	−338.526
North Dakota	104.865	114.717	291.090	195.646	280.288	412.886	636.773	785.460	863.093	834.021
Ohio	167.919	0.000	−402.238	0.000	0.000	281.261	556.106	844.713	213.054	−141.212
Oklahoma	1,075.330	863.205	822.047	1,070.580	1,213.950	2,336.020	2,322.290	2,343.510	2,135.167	1,717.486
Oregon	13.623	1,178.320	19.298	−501.913	237.769	736.196	113.579	1.095	−333.796	−542.747
Pennsylvania	1,524.850	1,603.820	1,314.510	1,633.330	927.163	789.958	368.659	9.621	−2,541.099	−1,434.681
Rhode Island	131.182	31.039	42.634	24.451	38.699	38.331	0.000	−42.950	−62.286	17.890
South Carolina	−173.802	−207.562	−204.352	−97.632	0.000	278.298	0.000	−9.977	−125.972	−36.290
South Dakota	72.815	57.029	79.616	76.937	86.098	99.505	99.562	95.485	85.765	90.564
Tennessee	0.125	0.153	0.200	0.203	0.124	0.156	0.199	0.184	0.299	0.357
Texas	1,633.790	−369.352	−2,326.120	−1,561.680	285.756	5,393.160	8,697.980	8,183.980	5,586.375	2,950.253
Utah	11.614	0.000	156.016	16.359	0.000	0.000	64.807	0.000	0.000	0.000
Vermont	86.583	97.898	47.062	61.975	68.610	68.317	68.057	54.458	46.713	72.503
Virginia	405.198	749.102	−220.982	36.941	520.546	973.461	563.367	78.468	−927.977	−1,069.071
Washington	564.928	398.374	404.376	385.436	865.443	569.326	780.510	677.431	189.258	−561.067
West Virginia	294.891	251.520	312.519	293.847	403.294	684.181	137.740	196.483	244.330	270.221
Wisconsin	−1,588.870	−1,877.330	−2,638.150	−2,296.850	−2,459.480	−2,506.930	−2,863.820	−2,852.560	−3,121.381	−3,453.386
Wyoming	78.583	40.730	90.261	9.979	210.391	10.000	528.190	10.000	−195.014	149.392

Author Index

Y. Hou, *State Government Budget Stabilization: Policy, Tools, and Impacts*, Studies in Public Choice 8, DOI 10.1007/978-1-4614-6061-9,

Subject Index

Y. Hou, *State Government Budget Stabilization: Policy, Tools, and Impacts*, Studies in Public Choice 8, DOI 10.1007/978-1-4614-6061-9,

MIX
Papier aus verantwortungsvollen Quellen
Paper from responsible sources
FSC® C105338

If you have any concerns about our products,
you can contact us on
ProductSafety@springernature.com

In case Publisher is established outside the EU,
the EU authorized representative is:
Springer Nature Customer Service Center GmbH
Europaplatz 3, 69115 Heidelberg, Germany

Printed by Libri Plureos GmbH
in Hamburg, Germany